Pilgrims in Place, Pilgrims in Motion

Sacred Travel in the
Ancient Mediterranean

Aarhus Studies in Mediterranean Antiquity (ASMA)

XV

ASMA is a series of monographs and anthologies published by the research programme "Classical Antiquity and its Heritage" in the School of Culture and Society, Aarhus University, Denmark. The programme includes researchers from a wide range of disciplines studying Graeco-Roman Antiquity, such as Classical Archaeology, Classical Philology, Ancient History, the Study of Religion and Theology. The aim of the series of the series is to publish significant new research in Classical Studies and to provide an interdisciplinary platform for the study of the ancient world.

ASMA Editorial Board:
Jakob Engberg, George Hinge, Jens Krasilnikoff, Troels Myrup Kristensen

ASMA Advisory Board:
Rasmus Brandt, Björn Forsén, Lin Foxhall, Tobias Georges, Thomas Heine Nielsen, Cornelia Isler-Kerényi, Inge Nielsen, David Pritchard, Jörg Rüpke

Pilgrims in Place, Pilgrims in Motion

Sacred Travel in the Ancient Mediterranean

Edited by
Anna Collar and
Troels Myrup Kristensen

Aarhus University Press

Pilgrims in Place, Pilgrims in Motion
© The Authors and Aarhus University Press 2024

Cover: The recently discovered Roman altar to Jupiter Dolichenus, a god originating from North Syria, discovered within the fort at Vindolanda on Hadrian's Wall, U.K.
Cover illustration: The Vindolanda Trust / Adam Stanford
Cover design: Jørgen Sparre
Layout and typesetting: Narayana Press
Publishing editor: Sanne Lind Hansen
This book is typeset in Adobe Garamond and LTSyntax and printed on 115 g Arctic Matt
Printed in EU by Scandinavian Book

Printed in Denmark 2024

ISBN 978 87 7184 543 3 (printed book)
ISBN 978 87 7219 324 3 (e-pdf)
ISBN 978 87 7219 893 4 (epub)

ISSN 1399 2686

Aarhus University Press
aarhusuniversitypress.dk

Published with the financial support of:
Aarhus University Research Foundation
Independent Research Fund Denmark

International distributors

Oxbow Books Ltd., oxbowbooks.com
ISD, isdistribution.com

PEER REVIEWED

/ In accordance with requirements of the Danish Ministry of Higher Education and Science, the certification means that a ph.d.-level peer has made a written assessment which justifies this book's scientific quality.

Contents

Preface   7

PART I

Methodological Dialogues on Pilgrimage

1   Place and Motion in the Study of Ancient
    Mediterranean Pilgrimage   11
    Anna Collar and Troels Myrup Kristensen

2   Getting There: Reframing Pilgrimage from Process to Site   35
    David Frankfurter

3   The Uses of Comparison in Pilgrimage Studies   61
    Ian Rutherford

PART II

Pilgrims, Place and Motion: Case Studies

4   Disorderly Pilgrims at the Oracular Sanctuary of Apollo Koropaios   83
    Matthew Dillon

5   The Emperor as a Place of Pilgrimage   107
    Panayiotis Christoforou

6   Virtual Pilgrim? Unchosen Mobility and Religious
    Place-Making in the Roman Army   127
    Anna Collar

7   Thieving Pilgrims between Rome and the Middle Ages   143
    Isabel Köster

8   Failed Connectivities: Paul's Collection and his
    Final Pilgrimage to Jerusalem   159
    Matthew R. Anderson

9 Pilgrims, Piety and Pragmatism:
   Roman Sanctuaries and Late Antique Churches in the Cyclades   179
   Rebecca Sweetman

10 The Rites of the (Late) Ancient Mariners:
   Professional and Casual Sailors as Christian Pilgrims
   in the Late Antique Mediterranean   199
   Amelia R. Brown

11 Jerusalem Mythologies: Pilgrims and the Dome of the Rock:
   Naser-e Khosraw's Reflections on Jerusalem from
   his Book of Travels, the Safarnama   213
   Naomi Koltun-Fromm

12 Jerusalem Agents: Armenian and Georgian
   Pilgrimage to Byzantine Palestine   229
   Yana Tchekhanovets

13 The Stratification of Memory in the Dardanelles:
   From Trojan War to First World War Pilgrimage in the Region   247
   Sarah Midford

PART III
Concluding Responses

14 Pilgrimage:
   An Unruly Method?   271
   Simon Coleman

15 Sacred Travel and Transformation Beyond
   the "Heroic Quest" Paradigm   277
   Elisa Uusimäki

Contributors   283

Index   285

Preface

This volume is one outcome from a collaborative research project entitled "The Emergence of Sacred Travel (EST): Experience, Economy and Connectivity in Ancient Mediterranean Pilgrimage" – sponsored by a generous *Sapere Aude* research excellence grant from the Independent Research Council Denmark (DFF). The project ran from 2013 to 2017 and was directed by Troels Myrup Kristensen of the Department of History and Classical Studies, Aarhus University. The volume publishes revised versions of papers originally presented at the project's third and final symposium held in Aarhus on the 17th–19th May 2017 and entitled "Comparativism and the Study of Ancient Mediterranean Pilgrimage".[1] Although we have opted to change the title of this final publication, we believe that the comparative scope of the conference remains important, as we argue in considerably more detail in the introduction. We would like to thank everyone who participated in or facilitated the symposium and its publication, including a group of external readers who provided invaluable feedback on draft chapters, as well as the two respondents whose contributions conclude the volume. We also thank the speakers and discussants whose papers for different reasons ultimately did not appear in this volume, as well as Signe Barfoed and David Frankfurter for sage advice during the process of finalising it. Thank you also to Andrew Birley and the Vindolanda Trust for use of the cover image.

Both the symposium and the wider project of which it was part aimed to develop a comparative and interdisciplinary platform for the exploration of ancient Mediterranean pilgrimage and its material footprint. Although use of the term "pilgrimage" in the context of the ancient world continues to ruffle some feathers, when understood as a particular method to study ancient religious practices it offers, in our view, a very productive way to investigate connections between the rich religious traditions of the Mediterranean and to develop new theoretical and methodological frameworks for their study. For example, in this volume alone, the umbrella of "sacred travel" (a close cognate of pilgrimage) is able to link up studies of ancient Greek, Roman, Jewish, late antique and Medieval Christian and Islamic traditions, and even modern forms of pilgrimage to battlefields that have developed over the course of the 20th century. The symposium (and not least the response to our original call for papers) furthermore made it clear that the study of pilgrimage (both ancient and modern) is a truly interdisciplinary endeavour. We are therefore pleased that the resulting volume brings together scholars from a wide range of disciplines and both text- and archaeology-based approaches.

AC/TMK, Aarhus and Southampton, September 2023

---

[1] The two previous symposia have been published as T.M. Kristensen and W. Friese (eds.) *Excavating Pilgrimage. Archaeological Approaches to Sacred Travel and Movement in the Ancient World* (Abingdon 2017) and A. Collar and T.M. Kristensen (eds.) *Pilgrimage and Economy in the Ancient Mediterranean* (Leiden 2020).

PART I

Methodological Dialogues on Pilgrimage

1

PLACE AND MOTION IN THE STUDY OF ANCIENT MEDITERRANEAN PILGRIMAGE

ANNA COLLAR AND TROELS MYRUP KRISTENSEN

In the French-Moroccan director Ismaël Ferroukhi's prize-winning film *Le Grand Voyage* (2004), a devout father and his reluctant son set off on a pilgrimage driving by car from France all the way to Mecca. With the son at the steering wheel, the father asks, "Why are you driving so fast?", and at one point even pulls the handbrake on the motorway to force him to slow down. Not long after, he disposes of the son's mobile phone in a garbage can. In a later confrontation between the two, the son angrily asks, "Why didn't you fly to Mecca? It's much simpler!" His father replies, somewhat cryptically, "When the waters of the ocean rise to the heavens, they lose their bitterness to become pure again …" Reda, his son, asks him to explain. His father says, "The ocean waters evaporate as they rise to the clouds. And as they evaporate they become fresh. That's why it's better to go on your pilgrimage on foot than on horseback, better on horseback than by car, better by car than by boat, better by boat than by plane." Slowness encourages reflection, so is cleansing, and results in spiritual purity. It is the journey to Mecca that offers these two men the space to talk, learn about each other's lives, get to know each other better, grow as people. The rejection of the speed of modern life that is implicit in the father's actions and his desire to drive rather than fly resonate with the contemporary appeal of the "slow" movement that responds to the effects of globalisation, capitalism and corporatisation on all aspects of our lives and minds.[1] Did the speed or mode of movement carry the same implications of reflection or spiritual preparedness in the ancient Mediterranean traditions of pilgrimage, such as those related to ancient Greek, Roman, and late antique Christian and Islamic travel? Essentially, if the option had been available to pilgrims in the ancient world, would they too have gone by plane?

In spite of its obviously anachronistic nature, this latter question takes us to the heart of the underlying tension implied by our book's title, specifically that between

---

1 See, amongst the vast literature of all stripes, Berg and Seeber 2013; Servon and Pink 2015.

place and motion in the study of the ancient Mediterranean pilgrimage.[2] "Place" in this context means the shrines, sanctuaries and other sacred places that were visited by ancient pilgrims and that are typically recognised as "sacred" in and of themselves.[3] In this sense, place has been the fundamental scale of research in many studies of ancient Mediterranean religion, not least in classical archaeology where excavations and scholarship since the 19th century have gravitated heavily towards sanctuaries, often those known from classical literature.[4] "Motion", on the other hand, refers to the journeys (regardless of length) that pilgrims undertook and all of the places and landscapes that they passed through on their way to a sacred place, from the pilgrim's home to their final destination and back again. While none of these are "sacred" in the traditional sense, they would all have played a fundamental role in how any pilgrimage was experienced, framed, and structured, not least by individual pilgrims. Pausanias, our "prototypical ancient pilgrim", in fact dedicates substantial parts of his travel account to engagement with the natural features of the landscape (mountains, rivers, trees, animals) that he passed by on his journeys, predominantly by placing them within mythological, aetiological narratives.[5] The sacred is in that sense not only embedded everywhere; it is also in itself mobile. Think only of the sacred snakes that Pausanias tells us slithered across the Epidaurian landscape.[6]

The conversations from *Le Grand Voyage* that we referenced above are emblematic of this "motion" perspective in recognising the experience of travel, even by forcibly attempting to slow it down and prolong the journey. The father's remarks are foreshadowed in interviews that the anthropologist Nancy Louise Frey carried out in Santiago de Compostela in the 1990s.[7] In these, most pilgrims told her that they preferred walking or cycling over any mode form of transportation on their journey. The role of the "road", the means of transportation, and the broader landscape that pilgrims travel through have been highlighted in a range of other studies on pilgrimage, including titles such as *Sacred Journeys, On the Road to Being There* and *Journeying to the Sacred* that all urge us to consider pilgrimage as a process and a practice that extends beyond the final destination.[8] In some conceptions of pilgrimage, the journey even becomes entirely metaphorical, internalised, and thus entirely independent of the climactic arrival at a "shrine". For example, the understanding of pilgrimage as a significant (and sometimes

---

2   "Sacred travel" is a close cognate of pilgrimage, and we use the two terms interchangeably in what follows. On the historiography of pilgrimage studies, see Coleman 2002; Bowie 2006, 237-66; Friese and Kristensen 2017; Bremmer 2017; Elsner 2017a; Graf 2020.

3   That (the meanings and identities of) these places can be also dynamic and even "in motion" is amply shown by Kinnard 2014. For similar contestations of ancient sanctuaries and their spatial politics, see Scott 2010.

4   See, for example, Alcock and Osborne 1994; Pedley 2006.

5   Hutton 2008; Stewart 2013, 236-38. On Pausanias as pilgrim, the classic piece is Elsner 1992.

6   Paus. 2.28.1.

7   Frey 1998.

8   Morinis 1992; Swatos 2006; Maddrell et al. 2015. On travel in the ancient world, see, for example, Adams and Laurence 2001; Niehoff 2017.

difficult or treacherous) journey is embodied in the medieval archetype of the labyrinth as both a physical and a metaphorical space through which to represent the journey of a pilgrim (Fig. 1).[9] According to the World-Wide Labyrinth Locator, more than 6,000 such pilgrims' labyrinths exist today.[10] Walking through a labyrinth (that only in a vague and abstract way represents the journey to a "true" pilgrimage destination, such as Jerusalem or Mecca) is obviously a central part of its appeal, whereas arrival at the "destination" in its centre constitutes little more than the beginning of the return journey. Guides to moving through such labyrinths furthermore emphasise that meeting other pilgrims on the way (either in or out) is an important part of the experience.[11] In a similar fashion, Sara Terreault has approached pilgrimage as constituting a particular state of exile and foreignness that stands in sharp contrast to what she calls "destinational pilgrimage" (*peregrinatio ad loca*).[12] Her work consequently focuses on motion away from (rather than to) a sacred centre. The ascetic practices of late antique Egyptian hermits and Syrian stylite saints can be understood alongside similar lines.[13]

Can (and should) the study of pilgrimage really span this all-encompassing spectrum between "place" and "motion"—and if so, how? Or, alternatively, will it need to focus its attention on one or the other of these two overarching categories? This debate is in fact pivotal to our understanding of ancient Mediterranean pilgrimage to the extent that it even defines the boundaries of the topic itself. For example, one of the objections that the classicist Scott Scullion has raised against the use of "pilgrimage" in the context of the ancient world is the emphasis on travel by many of its proponents.[14] He specifically criticises Matthew Dillon's *Pilgrims and Pilgrimage in Ancient Greece*, one of the first volumes to prominently and consistently use these terms specifically in relation to Delphi, Olympia, and other major Greek ("panhellenic") sanctuaries. Scullion notes, for example, that the reasons to undertake extra-territorial travel were more closely linked to politics and elite behaviour, even curiosity ("wider fame, greater prestige, bigger crowds, and better shows"), than they were religious by nature.[15] Many of his criticisms have usefully been refuted by Ian Rutherford, who notes that "there is every reason to believe that many sanctuaries were regarded as places where divine presence was more immediate",[16] citing, for example, the case of Hellenistic cities launching new

---

9   Beaman 2006.
10 https://labyrinthlocator.com/ (accessed 7 February 2023).
11 https://gracecathedral.org/our-labyrinths/ (accessed 7 February 2023).
12 Terreault 2019.
13 Brown 1971 is a classic study of these practices but makes a rather different argument. Places associated with these holy people could in turn evolve into sacred centres themselves, see Schachner 2010.
14 Scullion 2005, 128-29; discussing Dillon 1997. Another important "early mover" is Coleman and Elsner 1995. See also comments in Elsner and Rutherford 2005b; Rutherford 2013, 13n39.
15 Quote: Scullion 2005, 128.
16 Rutherford 2013, 13.

A pilgrimage labyrinth on the Stanford University campus (photo: Troels Myrup Kristensen).

festivals on the basis of very specific instances of epiphany.[17] Such manifestations of the divine—linked to specific places and moments in time—were thus fundamental to the appeal and ultimate success of any sanctuary (and their ability to attract pilgrims from near and far). In this sense, many cities invested heavily in both a theology and economy of not only "place", but also "motion".

We could go a step further and argue that "slow pilgrimages" (much like those of *Le Grand Voyage* and the walking and cycling crowds at Santiago de Compostela) not only existed in the ancient world, but were the standard mode of travelling to any sanctuary, both in their actual performance and also their conceptualisation. In addition to the previously discussed example of Pausanias, we can point to the two years that Aelius Aristides spent travelling in Asia Minor in search of Asklepios—even if it should be acknowledged, of course, that both works are narrated in a rhetorical and highly literary style that archaeologists in the past approached in too simplistic a fashion.[18] But "slow" extends beyond such individual cases, as evident from the staging of the processional schedule of the Olympic Games that began in the *agora* of Elis, some 60 km from Olympia itself, from where athletes and pilgrims walked in procession.[19] These "slow" elements in the configuration and conceptualisation of ancient pilgrimages were integral to the "total religious experience" that they offered, even if we rarely have the sources to shed light on all of them.[20]

To bridge the tension between "place" and "motion" that we have briefly outlined here in a more systematic fashion, this book (and the broader research project from which it represents one outcome) argues that the study of ancient Mediterranean pilgrimage ultimately needs more critical and more reflective comparative perspectives in order to move forward.[21] Back in 1995, the combined work of anthropologist Simon Coleman and classicist Jaś Elsner resulted in a global, interdisciplinary and long-term history of pilgrimage, from the classical world to contemporary world religions.[22] It follows on from an ambitious comparative history of (non-Christian) pilgrimage from the third millennium BCE onwards compiled by historian Jean Chélini and theologian Henry Branthomme in 1987.[23] Much of the subsequent scholarship on ancient Mediterranean pilgrimage has followed these productive paths of historical comparison, albeit most

---

17   Magnesia-on-the-Meander is an oft-cited case, see Jürgens 2017. On economic aspects of Hellenistic festivals, see Horster 2020.
18   On Aelius Aristides as pilgrim, see Rutherford 1999; Petsalis-Diomidis 2010.
19   On the procession to Olympia, see Paus. 5.16.8 and Sinn 2004, 128-130. On Elis, see Bourke 2018.
20   Quote: Petsalis-Diomidis 2010, 7, noting that "journey, arrival at the sanctuary, activities there, and onward journeys are seen as part of a continuous meaningful process, a total religious experience." The increasing interest in understanding ancient experiences of landscapes is also useful to bridge the gap between "place" and "motion". Important works here include Cole 2004; Spencer 2010; Gilhuly and Worman 2014; Worman 2015; König 2022.
21   See Gagné, Goldhill and Lloyd 2019 on "comparism" as reflexive comparison.
22   Coleman and Elsner 1995.
23   Chélini and Branthomme 1987. On the "long" history of pilgrimage, see also McCorriston 2011; 2017; and Rutherford, this volume.

often on a less ambitious scale, for example by comparing individual elements of contemporary "pilgrimage" to Graceland, the home of Elvis Presley, with Christian experiences of sacred travel during the late antique and Medieval periods.[24] We may simplistically characterise the perspective advanced in these works as "historical comparativism", given that it is typically based on bringing together disparate chronologies and geographies within a single framework of analysis (or, at the very least, within a single frame). This approach has a very long history and recently experienced something of a renaissance in anthropology and art history, amongst other disciplines.[25] Yet what we are pursuing here and in other work is better described as "methodological comparativism". It sets a new form of comparative agenda that sees pilgrimage as a method or unifying theory of religious movement, specifically to bring together different scales of analysis that are typically not discussed alongside each other, such as "place" and "motion", "site" and "landscape", "sanctuary" and "household".[26]

Although we would also encourage the development of other such "methodological comparativisms", one particular framework of comparison that we have found to be useful in studies of ancient Mediterranean pilgrimage is the so-called "New Mobilities Paradigm" or "mobilities turn" formulated by sociologists Mimi Sheller and John Urry, and further developed by a large interdisciplinary group of mobilities scholars.[27] Their work seeks to move beyond what they see as the "static" approaches that dominate the social sciences and encourages the rethinking of movement not only as a "cost", but as important in its own right. The "New Mobilities Paradigm" does not simply *describe* a more mobile world, because mobility is us, mobility is how space is generated. As geographers Tim Cresswell and Peter Merriman remark: "Mobile, embodied practices are central to how we experience the world, from practices of writing and sensing, to walking and driving. Our mobilities create spaces and stories—spatial stories."[28] These "spatial stories" allow us to bring together "place" and "motion" within a single interpretive framework. We contend that perspectives from the "New Mobilities Paradigm" help to take us beyond the discrete destinations of pilgrimage and incorporate the wider landscapes of which sanctuaries were part, their relationship with cities and infrastructural "moorings" that enabled movement (paths, roads, bridges and even the natural environment itself), and the role of the sacred in shaping those infrastructures. Here and elsewhere, we argue that theories, methods and terminologies inspired by the "New Mobilities Paradigm" are helpful in multiple ways to the study of ancient Mediterranean pilgrimage; in turn, such work on the ancient world will expand the

---

24 Vikan 2012, see also contributions to Kristensen and Friese 2017; Luig 2018.
25 Schnegg 2014; Elsner 2017b; Küchler 2017; Candea 2018.
26 For further work that pursues this agenda, see Collar forthcoming; Kristensen forthcoming. For comparable archaeologies of movement, see Connelly 2011; Newsome 2011; Aldred 2021.
27 Sheller and Urry 2006; 2016; Sheller 2014; 2017; Urry 2007. For a recent rebuttal of this "paradigm", see Randell 2020. For a more complete overview of current mobilities scholarship, refer to Adey et al. 2014.
28 Cresswell and Merriman 2011, 5.

temporal and disciplinary scope of this emerging and interdisciplinary paradigm that typically focuses on the modern world.[29] At this stage, it is useful to turn to a specific case of how this can be applied in practice in the interpretation of a specific destination (and landscape) of ancient Mediterranean pilgrimage.

Place and Motion at the Asklepieion of Epidauros

In what follows, a small selection of concepts and methods developed by scholarship associated with the "New Mobilities Paradigm" will be applied to the interpretation of some individual archaeological spaces within the sanctuary of Asklepios in Epidauros, located on the Peloponnese in modern Greece (Fig. 2). The sanctuary's appeal as a "place" was linked to the miraculous narratives of Asklepios' healing abilities, although it is less clear at present how these had become tied to Epidauros, given that many ancient authors located his place of birth in Trikka in Thessaly. In contrast, Epidaurian myth located Asklepios' birth and upbringing within the city's own local landscape.[30] The Asklepieion is a staple in the study of ancient Greek religion and has been intensively investigated since its initial exploration by Panayiotis Kavvadias (1850-1928) and the Archaeological Society of Athens beginning in 1881.[31] Excavations are still ongoing and continue to shed new light on the sanctuary's development, not least its early phases going back to the late seventh century BCE.[32] In the Late Classical period (400-323 BCE), the Asklepieion developed into one of the most important healing sanctuaries in the ancient world and was expanded through a large building programme that has left us with an important suite of temples and other monuments, many features and even costings of which are documented in extraordinary detail in inscriptions.[33]

While closely linked to the seaside town of Epidauros as an extra-urban sanctuary, the Asklepieion attracted pilgrims from many different parts of the Greek world and is as such a very good candidate for the label of an ancient pilgrimage destination.[34] Movement at several different scales was in fact integral to the design of the sanctuary and as such played a fundamental role in the religious experiences that it offered to pilgrims. Firstly, pilgrims travelled on a winding road from Epidauros before reaching their destination at the sanctuary, located in mountainous terrain some 7 km inland. Secondly, within the sanctuary itself, processions and other forms of ritual movement linked up individual parts of the sanctuary in complex ways, depending on the religious

---

29   For an application of methods from this field in the study of ancient Mediterranean pilgrimage, see Kristensen 2018; 2019; 2020; forthcoming; Collar 2020; forthcoming.
30   Dillon forthcoming.
31   Riethmüller 2005, vol. 1, 162-74, 279-95; Melfi 2007, 17-209; Renberg 2017, 126-32.
32   Lambrinoudakis 2018.
33   Wickkiser 2008, 90-94; Prignitz 2014; Lambrinoudakis and Prignitz 2020.
34   On Epidauros as a place of pilgrimage, see Dillon 1997, 74-80. On the *theorodokoi* that hosted Epidaurian *theoroi* (festival announcers) in many Greek cities, see Perlman 2000, 67-98. On Greek extra-urban sanctuaries and their ties to the city-state, see the classic work by Polignac 1995.

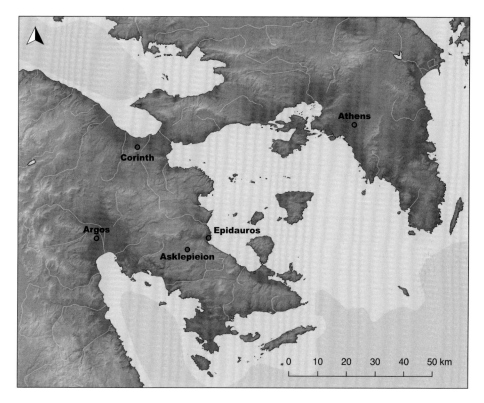

Map showing location of Epidauros and the Asklepeion (courtesy of Niels Bargfeldt). Fig. 2.

schedule of the sanctuary and the occasion of the pilgrims' visits (Fig. 3).[35] Thirdly, the construction of individual buildings in the sanctuary facilitated particular forms of movement through their incorporation of special architectural features, such as ramps and elaborate interior spaces, both over- and underground in the case of the circular, enigmatic Thymele that appears to have been designed with particular acoustic and performative affordances in mind (no. 3 in Fig. 3).[36]

It is clear that the fourth-century monumentalisation of the Asklepieion produced a complex range of immersive spaces and landscapes that cannot be discussed in detail here. Instead, we focus on a monument in the exact location where the perspectives of "place" and "motion" aligned, namely the northern propylon, through which many—if not all—pilgrims would have entered the sanctuary proper, at least from the Hellenistic period onwards (no. 6 in Fig. 3; Fig. 4).[37] The propylon marks a key juncture in the sense that different forms of movement converge in this particular place, addressing

---

35 Kristensen 2018. On similar complexities of movement inside sacred spaces at Olympia, see Hölscher 2018, 29-33.
36 Ramps: Sneed 2020. Thymele: Schultz et al. 2017.
37 Roux 1961, 253-74; Tomlinson 1983, 39-47.

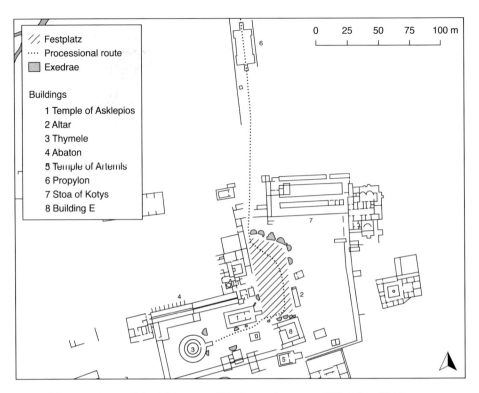

Fig. 3. Map of the central part of the Asklepeion of Epidauros (courtesy of Niels Bargfeldt).

the liminality of the sanctuary's border that Pausanias tells us was clearly defined by *horos*-stones.[38] The building itself is elongated, *c.* 14 × 20 m with its exterior façade originally decorated with six Ionic columns (the remains of which are now reconstructed in the site museum). On the inside, there were Corinthian columns, but no fixtures for any doors or other closing devices have been identified. In this sense, the propylon functioned mainly as an architectural backdrop for pilgrims' movement rather than a barrier that potentially blocked their progress, even if only for a short moment. Sadly, none of the building accounts discovered so far give us details of the construction of the propylon, so we rely on stylistic criteria for the chronology of the propylon. The French architectural historian Georges Roux has proposed a date of construction in the early third century BCE and certainly before 250 BCE, whereas other scholars have preferred an earlier date to place the propylon as part of the larger building programme of the fourth century BCE.[39]

The propylon is located in the northern part of the sanctuary just after the processional way crosses a small stream. Its isolation from other monumental features in the

---

38 Paus. 2.27.1. On passageways as "moments of transition" and a means of constructing sightlines in late antique sanctuaries, see Yasin 2017.
39 Roux 1961, 274; Tomlinson 1983, 47. For the earlier date, see Burford 1969, 69.

The propylon of the Asklepieion of Epidauros, seen from the south (photo: Troels Myrup Kristensen). Fig. 4.

sanctuary may be explained by the presence of a nearby well that appears to date from the fifth century BCE and thus predates the construction of the propylon itself.[40] This suggests that the location already had an established role as a place of purification before the construction of the propylon, constituting a formal and ritually obligatory entry point into the *temenos*.[41] Yet we may also consider what the natural landscape around the propylon offered in terms of its natural, material affordances. Most notably, the small stream that pilgrims crossed immediately before entering the Epidaurian propylon mirrors the location and design of the propylon of Ptolemy II at Samothrace, recently discussed by Bonna Wescoat.[42] The Samothrace propylon actually incorporated a natural stream into its design, making the most of its acoustic and sensory qualities. Wescoat interprets this as part of an effort to enhance the acoustic experience afforded by the natural landscape. The designers of the Epidaurian propylon may have had similar intentions in mind. Furthermore, the propylon is located at the lowest point in the sanctuary, ensuring that, upon exiting, pilgrims entered an open, slightly sloping forecourt from where they climbed further up, not unlike the experience provided by

40 Tomlinson 1983, 46.
41 On purification and the role of water in Greek sanctuaries more broadly, see Ehrenheim, Klingborg and Frejman 2019.
42 Wescoat 2012. Wescoat 2017 covers the onward passage through the sanctuary of the Great Gods. Roux 1961, 274, noting the similarities in the plan of these buildings at Epidauros and Samothrace.

the combination of the Propylaia and the so-called "Periklean entrance court" on the Athenian Acropolis after its fifth-century-BCE building programme (Fig. 5).[43] In this configuration, the Epidaurian propylon presented the sanctuary and its visiting pilgrims with an almost "acropolis-like" pattern and experience of movement.[44]

In previous scholarship, however, the Epidauros propylon has typically been approached as an "island" within the sanctuary of Asklepios that is studied with a particular view towards the reconstruction of its architecture. R.A. Tomlinson even referred to the propylon in a somewhat derogatory way as the Asklepieion's "formal decorative entrance",[45] but it is worthwhile to think more about how the monument affects movement in different ways and explicitly draw on concepts from the "New Mobilities Paradigm." The propylon in fact embodies many key observations made by Sheller and Urry. For example, they argue "that all places are tied into at least thin networks of connections that stretch beyond each such place".[46] They are also narrative connections, whose coming together enables the telling of particular stories at particular places and times: "places are about relationships, about the placing of peoples, materials, images, and the systems of difference that they perform".[47] It follows that the propylon is not an "island", but rather was rather designed to play an important role in the larger network of movement through which pilgrims circulated to and within the sanctuary of Asklepios, located precisely at an important juncture in their pilgrimage to a healing divinity and an important chapter in the "story" that this particular material assemblage constructed for pilgrims.

The "New Mobilities Paradigm" provides us with some further helpful terms and methods to understand the uses of sacred space and its constitution in both "place" and "motion", specifically in the context of the Asklepieion and its propylon. Explicitly drawing on Sheller and Urry, the Danish urban theorist Ole B. Jensen's work on contemporary contexts of mobility is particularly helpful to understand what he terms "mobile situations" within the sanctuary.[48] In Jensen's terms, the open spaces of the sanctuary of Asklepios effectively worked as stages for being "mobile with".[49] Pilgrims moved occasionally as individuals, but more often as members of groups, organised by kin, class or gender. In carefully choreographed processions, groups moved together, sang and watched or performed a range of rituals. While their goal would have been one of the altars in the heart of the sanctuary of Asklepios (and in some cases ultimately the Abaton where incubation took place), they passed through a variety of other locales

---

43   Stevens 1936; more broadly on the Athenian acropolis as "processional architecture", see Rhodes 1995, 28-41; Paga 2017; Valavanis et al. 2022.
44   For a similar interpretation of the Argive Heraion as a man-made acropolis, see Hollinshead 2015, 44-45.
45   Tomlinson 1983, 41.
46   Sheller and Urry 2006, 209.
47   Sheller and Urry 2006, 214.
48   Jensen 2013; 2014.
49   Jensen 2014, 46.

that were given meaning through their actions, including the propylon. Through their movements, the pilgrims thus participated in different mobile situations within well-defined in-groups as well as temporarily staged congregations.[50] The spaces that the pilgrims moved through can be defined as having at least two different effects on them. Jensen defines these as sociofugal; that is, a space that forces people apart and thus to a certain degree dissolves groups or at least separates them spatially. Jensen contrasts this with a sociopetal space that draws people together, such as in cases where a path becomes more narrow and confined.[51] The effect of the propylon was sociopetal, as it required the members of a procession to navigate its architecture and consequently draw together in tight lines that allowed them to pass unhindered through the building's columns. In addition, other studies of movement have noted how the most complex and most meaningful spaces are those in which people stop and where they have to negotiate their role in a new place.[52] Here, it is worth noting some of the other formal qualities of the propylon: for example, its raised base forced anyone approaching to stop and ascend either by means of the steps or the ramps located at both the northern and southern façade of the building. These perspectives offer one set of comparative framework rooted in the "New Mobilities Paradigm" that can be applied in the study of ancient Mediterranean pilgrimage.

Propylaia and other entrances and gateways to sanctuaries are typically interpreted as monuments of spatial control, separating the (profane and ritually polluted) outside from the (sacred and ritually purified) inside.[53] In a recent study, Christina Williamson has also interpreted temple doors as places of epiphany.[54] But in another, more basic fashion their function was to orchestrate and structure movement in a way that was considered to be fit for purpose. In the case of the Epidaurian propylon, while certainly functioning as a monumental demarcation of sacred space (and control thereof), it also represents a considerable contrast to the seemingly unrestricted spaces around it.[55] While the sanctuary certainly had a clearly defined boundary, it is unlikely to have been monumentalised. It is also worth mentioning again that the propylon does not seem to have been furnished with any doorways that effectively restricted access. Yet the propylon profoundly affected the movement of pilgrims as they came to a pivotal point in the procession to the Asklepieion. It raised expectations for what was about to come, both through use of the natural landscape and through the material environment of the propylon itself. We would therefore argue that the purpose of the Epidaurian propylon was primarily to demarcate transition in terms of movement and only secondarily to restrict movement in and out of the sanctuary. In this sense, it can be interpreted through

---

50   Jensen 2014, 81.
51   Jensen 2013, 152; 2014, 46.
52   Laurence 2011, 394-97.
53   See Rhodes 1995, 53ff.
54   Williamson 2018.
55   While Pausanias (2.27.1) tells us that the boundary was marked by *horoi*, no material remains have been identified.

Fig. 5. Looking from the Asklepieion propylon towards the open area to the south, showing the ascent to the main area of the sanctuary (photo: Troels Myrup Kristensen).

the lenses of both "place" (as a monument that pilgrims formally had to pass through and whose materiality they were required to negotiate) and "motion" (as a monument that led pilgrims from one crucial part of the experience of going to "see" Asklepios to another, and in creating a particular moment in the spatial story of their journey from Epidauros town to the sanctuary).

When exiting the propylon, Epidaurian pilgrims arrived at a more open area that would have been an appropriate location for groups to congregate, perhaps in relation to the rituals that took place in the vicinity of the well (Fig. 5). The architects of the sanctuary invested in this area by constructing walls on either side of the pathway, thus restricting movement to a particular direction in a way that is characteristic of sociopetal space. As the pilgrims proceeded to the centre of the sanctuary of Asklepios, spaces and patterns of movement became yet more complicated, as one would expect at a major pilgrimage site.[56] In accounts of these spaces, scholars have placed their emphasis on what Jensen would call "staging from above", that is from the perspective of the architects, priests and benefactors of the sanctuary (from the *polis* in the fifth and fourth centuries BCE to individual patrons in the second century CE). But there remains much work to be done in terms of understanding how pilgrims themselves in turn responded to this staging of the rhythms and structures of movement architecture. For example, it is clear

---

56 On the configuration of this ritual space in the Roman and late antique periods, see Melfi 2010 and Pfaff 2018.

Fig. 6. A sociopetal space where access to the "Festplatz" of Epidauros was restricted by the construction of an exedra, seen to the left (photo: Troels Myrup Kristensen).

that the construction of *exedrae* over several hundred years severely restricted access to the central "Festplatz" in front of the main temples and altars of the sanctuary (Fig. 6).[57] Different tensions between "place" and "motion" thus continued to be fundamental to the experience of visiting the Asklepieion, even after leaving the propylon.

Perspectives on Place and Motion

It is now time to leave Epidauros and return to the contribution of this volume as a whole. The central tension between "place" and "motion" in studies of ancient Mediterranean pilgrimage is explored and challenged in the chapters gathered together in this book. Some offer us clear position pieces, others articulate a new perspective on place or mobility in pilgrimage studies. Other chapters use comparative angles to draw conclusions through time or across geographical space. We view such methodological diversity as a marker of maturity in the study of past pilgrimage, and indeed, bringing ancient, medieval and modern subjects into the same volume means we create something truly interdisciplinary. We hope that the result is a volume that offers the reader the space to recognise both differences and points of connection between approaches, traditions, religions, times and practices, in terms of both their juxtaposition and the ways we categorise and discuss our subjects.

57   Kristensen 2018.

Instead of dichotomising "place" and "motion", we have instead chosen to frame the diverse discussions of this volume through three methodological chapters that make up its first part ("Methodological Dialogues on Pilgrimage"), comprising David Frankfurter's "Getting There: Reframing Pilgrimage from Process to Site", Ian Rutherford's "The Uses of Comparison in Studies of Pilgrimage", and our own present introduction. Each of these chapters has a clear methodological agenda: our own, to ensure the mobility inherent in pilgrimage is tied in with contemporary discussions in theory and is not overlooked in studies of past pilgrimage because it is difficult to access. David Frankfurter has a very different perspective on pilgrimage in the past, instead arguing that recent scholarship on ancient pilgrimage has over-emphasised the significance of the journey. In his view, the "process" of pilgrimage is never, and was never, the meaningful element of pilgrimage in the past, and that we should instead return to the sites that pilgrims visited.

Rutherford's chapter, the third methodological contribution framing the volume, offers another stance, that of comparative work. He highlights three important perspectives that a comparative approach can bring to study of pilgrimage in the ancient world: firstly, the heightening of awareness of pilgrimage traditions across a global framework, both for direct comparison of practices observed and for the theoretical models which are used, and which offer the student of past pilgrimage new ways of thinking about their topic. Secondly, he advocates a closer relationship between study of the "classical" world and that of the contemporary or near-contemporary Near East, meaning Anatolia, the Levant, Egypt and Mesopotamia. Although the barriers between study of these different geographical zones are being surmounted more often, they still represent borders in linguistic knowledge—both ancient and modern—as well in archaeological, historical and cultural spheres. The mobility and exchange of goods and, more importantly, ideas between these different cultural milieux is well known,[58] but perhaps there is scope for greater awareness of the contemporary methods of study and findings across these borders. The final area with which he contends comparativism helps is that of mapping cultural differences in traditions, thinking, for example, of the work of Joy McCorriston on the pastoralist pilgrimages of the Saudi Arabian peninsula and their role as a method of communication across space and time. Although not entirely in agreement with her suggestion that sedentary populations did not therefore engage in pilgrimage practices, he further develops the suggestion that different kinds of pilgrimage might be usefully correlated with different kinds of society—where different kinds of pilgrimage come to symbolise different qualities: elite power, for example, in the Mesopotamian world

---

[58] Study of the so-called "Orientalising" phenomenon in the archaic Greek world comes to mind here, but also more recent work such as that of Rutherford himself on the relationships between the Hittite and Greek worlds in terms of the transfer of myth cycles (*e.g.*, Rutherford 2001; 2020). This has been taken up by Robin Lane Fox in *Travelling Heroes* (Lane Fox 2009), and a recent volume explicitly examining the spread of ideas through social networks, in which some contributions explore the relationships between the Near East and the Greek world (Daniels 2022; Mooring 2022).

of royal pilgrimage, or an imagined community, in situations such as McCorriston's Arabian example, or Greek city-states engaging in *theoria*.

The second part of the volume, "Pilgrims, Place and Motion: Case Studies", brings the reader on a journey through chronological time and different elements of focus. We begin with the chapter by Matthew Dillon, which, although he assumes that motivations for going on pilgrimage were pious, discusses the many differing kinds of misbehaviour of pilgrims on display once in the sanctuary, and their punishments: in this case, at the classical Greek oracular sanctuary of Apollo Koropaios in northern Greece. We then move through chapters that look at different elements of pilgrimage in the Roman world. Panayiotis Christoforou examines the role of the emperor as possessing *numen*, and thus places associated with him, or images of him, having the capacity to become a place of pilgrimage themselves, both in terms of offering sanctuary and as enabling contestation between individuals and authorities. The lens of pilgrimage is extremely valuable here in that it allows us to frame all the different motivations for travel to the place of the emperor together.

Taking an explicitly theoretical standpoint and drawing on ideas expressed in the literature of the "New Mobilities Paradigm" (here referred to as the mobilities turn), Anna Collar explores religious responses to a lack of choice in mobility, through the examples of the enforced, unchosen migration undertaken by Roman soldiers. Through acts of religious place-making—the setting up of communal altars on Hadrian's Wall or on the Euphrates frontier—soldiers made themselves and their identities visible. This took different forms: both proclaiming their belonging to a universal "Roman" identity in places of anxiety (as in the example of Silvanus), and engaging in what is here termed "virtual pilgrimage" to distant, remembered places and homelands (in the case of Jupiter Dolichenus or the Dea Syria). By these acts, these men were able to establish themselves as migrant communities, reclaiming some of the agency that was lost in the act of moving with the army across the Roman world.

The next chapter takes the reader deeper into the pilgrim's experiences: Isabel Köster explores the multiple motivations for visiting sanctuaries, including those which were not fully pious. She examines what happens when pilgrims are also thieves—framing this discussion with examples from the later Roman period and the Middle Ages—and, much as *evocatio* or 'god-napping' conferred divine sanction on the victorious city in the Roman world or in Bronze Age Mesopotamia, considers how the thieving pilgrim can be re-written as pious through the trope of the saint themselves being desirous of a change of scene.

The connections and contestations between established Jewish and emerging Christian communities in an increasingly volatile mid-first century Jerusalem are explored by Matthew Anderson. Towards the end of his life, Paul took a journey there to deliver money to the Temple in exchange for a blessing, a journey he made in the company of a new, weird band of believers: not full proselytes to Judaism, but devotees of the God of Israel through the figure of Christ. The innovation of this journey by a new group of worshippers is underscored by Anderson, emphasising the lack of clarity about whether the offering taken to Jerusalem is the cash collected, or the gentile community itself. The repercussions of it, this first "failed" pilgrimage, are felt in the immediate aftermath and the Jewish rebellion against Rome and the destruction of the place itself, and through later Christian pilgrims' desire to follow in Paul's charismatic but confrontational footprints.

Rebecca Sweetman returns to a question we have explored in earlier work[59] and to which we briefly explore further below, that of the pilgrim's intentionality to go "on pilgrimage" in a world of intermingling rationales for travel. In her discussion of the changing religious emphases of the late antique period in the Cyclades, she considers the topographical settings of sanctuaries on these islands and how these places shift through the transition from polytheism to Christianity—and the role of these places as ways to bridge these two religious traditions, as well as the practical elements involved in sanctifying place within a new religious world order.

Turning from the sanctuaries on land to those at sea, Amelia Brown's chapter looks at the changing ritual practices performed by sailors in this same period of transition, responding to two powerful new factors in the seascapes of the east Mediterranean: the new position of Constantinople at the heart of the world, and the growth of Jerusalem and the Holy Land as a pilgrimage destination. It is the requirements and rituals of sailors themselves, Brown argues, that connected the gods and heroes of the polytheist world and the saints of Late Antiquity, and it is this fundamentally mobile community of seafarers who were responsible for the wide dispersal of these cults across the Mediterranean and Black Sea.

From here, we move on to think specifically about Jerusalem's role as a pilgrimage destination for medieval Muslims as well as Christians of different denominations. Naomi Koltun-Fromm's chapter continues the focus on Jerusalem, but moves beyond the Jewish-Christian contestation into the early Islamic period—and to the deep mythological and theological gravitational pull that the holy city continued to exert. The place itself is what is important for Naser-e Khosraw, a deeply pious Persian Isma'ili Muslim pilgrim, who spent seven years travelling the Muslim world to visit shrines. Despite being sceptical about some of Jerusalem's mythologies, the city is, nonetheless, seen as a place with a profound divine presence. Because of its deep Jewish history and location as the place where David and Solomon first interacted with God, Jerusalem also possessed a latent power to provide personal forgiveness—and this was the central reason for pilgrims to visit.

Where Naser-e Khosraw's visit to the Holy Land is documented in formal written texts (albeit composed after the fact), the only records of pilgrims from the Caucasus are found in much more informal contexts: graffiti. Yana Tchekhanovets examines these personal prayers and messages by Armenian and Georgian visitors to Jerusalem, Nazareth, and the Sinai Peninsula. Dating from the fifth century through to the eleventh, these individual records represent some of the earliest documents in the scripts of Georgia and Armenia, and represent the powerful gravitational pull the Holy Land exerted across different Christian denominations. The power of the Holy City is em-

---

59   Collar and Kristensen 2020a.

phasised by the imitation of Palestinian architectural elements in the construction of churches and monuments in the Caucasus—embodying through these new places and the objects brought back from the Holy Land the relations established through the act of pilgrimage itself.

This central part of the book finishes with a chapter that ties together place through time: Sarah Midford's long-term perspective on pilgrimage traditions in a specific part of western Turkey, in which she considers the emotional timbre and enduring meaning of both ancient and modern pilgrimages to the Dardanelles and the site of two famous battles—the WWI slaughter at Gallipoli, and the plains where the Trojan War was fought.

The final section of the volume encompasses two responses by Simon Coleman and Elisa Uusimäki to the chapters presented here. Coleman places our approach to pilgrimage within anthropological discussions, whereas Uusimäki brings in perspectives from theology.

Where Do We Go From Here?

The dialogue between the perspective on mobility articulated in this opening chapter and that on the site or sanctuary outlined by Frankfurter reminds us of the vagueness that can mark the use of the term "pilgrimage" and the value of comparativism in thinking through the way we categorise elements of the process. In his chapter, Frankfurter scrutinises the concept of pilgrimage as one that is marked by the journey, because as he sees it, the journey is not *the point*. Unlike Reda's father, with whom we opened this introduction, in Frankfurter's view, "when air travel is available, people take airplanes".[60] He notes the common emphasis of the journey undertaken in the definitions of pilgrimage in the ancient world developing since the early 1990s, and the attendant transformation of the pilgrim that is implied or even required in order for an experience to constitute "pilgrimage". He contests this structuralist vision of pilgrimage, drawing as it does on the Turners' conception of the pilgrimage journey as enabling a "rite of passage" and the building of a new *communitas* of spiritually transformed pilgrims,[61] making the point that in today's world, the liminal state of being between identities is more usually occupied by the refugee. He wonders, then, if we fall into the habit of romanticising the pilgrim's journey as the all-important liminal, transformative element of pilgrimage, we do a disservice to the terrifying and open-ended journeys made by refugees today, and also by those subaltern figures of the past: the refugees, the enslaved people, the people without choice.

Choice concerning mobility in the past is a pressing issue and one we return to in this volume (Collar); and we recognise of course that the challenge to the emphasis on the journey is an important one. We have argued elsewhere that pilgrimage in the ancient world was in many instances contingent, drawing on the observation made by

---

60   Frankfurter, this volume.
61   Turner and Turner 1978.

Horden and Purcell that the spiritual or sacred element of a journey may have operated simultaneously alongside a more prosaic economic purpose.[62] Likewise, the emphasis in pilgrimage studies on the transformational quality of pilgrimage may owe too much to a protestant Christian tradition[63]—although "rites of passage" do continue to feature strongly in the way we discuss behaviours and rituals in certain sanctuaries in the ancient world, think, for example of young Athenian girls making the journey to Brauron in rural Attica to engage in the "playing the bear" ritual of puberty at Artemis' sanctuary.[64] But not all pilgrimage was necessarily transformational, and the diversity of experience—on the road, at the site, and on the way home again—is critical to recognising that "pilgrimage" was never just *one thing*, or even many things neatly categorised into a typology.[65] How could it be? Engaging with the mobilities involved in pilgrimage and what the journey or the movements afforded the pilgrim along the way, we see how the rituals and behaviours at the sanctuary destination built a community of pilgrims (or not—see for example the chapters by Dillon and Köster, this volume).

This volume is framed through this ongoing conversation about the twin poles of pilgrimage—"place" and "motion"—that we hope will set up a valuable discussion. Although Frankfurter demands we ditch the term pilgrimage completely, and instead use "shrine visitation", we contend there is no need to see these twin poles of "place" and "motion" in opposition; rather, like the gravitational push and pull between a planet and its moon, or the journey of a swallow between Africa and Britain, both elements are required to make pilgrimage meaningful.[66] As will be obvious from this introduction and our emphasis on the role and importance of mobility in thinking about pilgrimage, we beg to differ with Frankfurter about the modernity of pilgrimage and whether the mode of mobility is insignificant in the past. We leave the debate for the reader to pursue.

Another observation that is apparent from the contributions is that different disciplines have different concerns and aims in relation to the study of ancient Mediterranean pilgrimage. As a historian of religion, Frankfurter wants to get back to the "site" as the main scale of study. For archaeologists—traditionally deeply invested in the study of individual sites and their material assemblages—the term "pilgrimage" has a particular traction as an (almost liberating) method of going beyond the "site" and the individual "monument". This perspective also informs a recent contribution by archaeologist B. Jacob Skousen arguing that "archaeologists are uniquely situated to investigate the connections between non-human phenomena involved in pilgrimage (e.g., landscapes, places, shrines, tokens, deities, myths, memories) and, because of this, archaeologists can and should push pilgrimage studies in new and productive

---

62 Collar and Kristensen 2020a; engaging with Horden and Purcell 2000. See also Whiting 2020; Sweetman, this volume.
63 Cf. Nongbri 2015.
64 See here the important contribution by Sourvinou-Inwood 1990.
65 Cf. Elsner and Rutherford 2005b, 12-30.
66 Cf. Coleman and Eade 2004.

directions".[67] We agree and propose that material culture continues to have an important and often-untapped contribution to make in the comparative history of ancient Mediterranean pilgrimage.

Bibliography

Adams, C. and R. Laurence (eds.) 2001. *Travel and Geography in the Roman Empire*. London: Routledge.
Adey, P. et al. (eds.) 2014. *The Routledge Handbook of Mobilities*. London: Routledge.
Alcock, S. and R. Osborne (eds.) 1994. *Placing the Gods. Sanctuaries and Sacred Space in Ancient Greece*. Oxford: Clarendon Press.
Aldred, O. 2021. *The Archaeology of Movement*. London: Routledge.
Beaman, L.G. 2006. "Labyrinth as Heterotopia: The Pilgrim's Creation of Space," in Swatos 2006, 83-103.
Berg, M. and B. Seeber. 2013. *The Slow Professor: Challenging the Culture of Speed in the Academy*. Toronto: University of Toronto Press.
Bourke, G. 2018. *Elis. Internal Politics and External Policy in Ancient Greece*. London: Routledge.
Bowie, F. 2006. *The Anthropology of Religion. An Introduction*. Second edition. Malden: Blackwell.
Bremmer, J. 2017. "Pilgrimage Progress?," in Kristensen and Friese 2017, 275-84.
Brown, P. 1971. "The Rise and Function of the Holy Man in Late Antiquity." *JRS* 61, 80-101.
Burford, A. 1969. *The Greek Temple Builders of Epidauros*. Liverpool: Liverpool University Press.
Candea, M. 2018. *Comparison in Anthropology. The Impossible Method*. Cambridge: Cambridge University Press.
Chélini, J. and H. Branthomme (eds.) 1987. *Histoire des pèlerinages non chrétiens. Entre magique et sacré: le chemin des dieux*. Paris: Hachette.
Cole, S.G. 2004. *Landscapes, Gender, and Ritual Space. The Ancient Greek Experience*. Berkeley: University of California Press.
Coleman, S. 2002. "Do you believe in pilgrimage? *Communitas*, contestation and beyond." *Anthropological Theory* 2.3, 355-68.
Coleman, S. and J. Eade (eds.) 2004. *Reframing Pilgrimage. Cultures in Motion*. London: Routledge.
Coleman, S. and J. Elsner. 1995. *Pilgrimage. Past and Present in the World Religions*. London: British Museum Press.
Collar, A. 2020. "Movement, Labour and Devotion: A Virtual Walk to the Sanctuary at Mount Kasios," in Collar and Kristensen 2020b, 33-61.
Collar, A. (ed.) 2022. *Networks and the Spread of Ideas in the Past. Strong Ties, Innovation and Knowledge Exchange*. London: Routledge.
Collar, A. Forthcoming. *Mobility / Place. Archaeology and religion in the Roman Mediterranean*. London: Bloomsbury.
Collar, A. and T.M. Kristensen. 2020a. "Embedded Economies of Ancient Mediterranean Pilgrimage," in Collar and Kristensen 2020b, 1-30.
Collar, A. and T.M. Kristensen (eds.) 2020b. *Pilgrimage and Economy in the Ancient Mediterranean*. Leiden: Brill.
Connelly, J.B. 2011. "Ritual Movement through Greek Sacred Space. Towards an Archaeology of Performance," in A. Chaniotis (ed.) *Ritual Dynamics in the Ancient Mediterranean: Agency, Emotion, Gender, Reception*, 313-46. Stuttgart: Franz Steiner.
Cresswell, T. and P. Merriman. 2011. "Introduction: Geographies of Mobilities—Practices, Spaces, Subjects," in T. Cresswell and P. Merriman (eds.) *Geographies of Mobilities: Practices, Spaces, Subjects*, 1-15. Farnham: Ashgate.
Daniels, M. 2022. "'Orientalising' Networks and the Nude Standing Female: Synchronic and Diachronic Dimensions of Ideology Transfer," in Collar 2022, 31-78.
Dillon, M. 1997. *Pilgrims and Pilgrimage in Ancient Greece*. London: Routledge.
Dillon, M. Forthcoming. *Asklepios*. London: Routledge.
Ehrenheim, H. von, P. Klingborg and A. Frejman. 2019. "Water at Ancient Greek Sanctuaries: Medium of Divine Presence or Commodity for Mortal Visitors?" *Journal of Archaeology and Ancient History* 26, 3-31.
Elsner, J. 1992. "Pausanias: A Greek Pilgrim in the Roman World." *Past and Present* 135.1, 3-29.
Elsner, J. 2017a. "Excavating Pilgrimage," in Kristensen and Friese 2017, 265-74.

---

67 Skousen 2018, 262.

Elsner, J. (ed.) 2017b. *Comparativism in Art History.* London: Routledge.

Elsner, J. and I. Rutherford (eds.) 2005a. *Pilgrimage in Graeco-Roman & Early Christian Antiquity. Seeing the Gods.* Oxford: Oxford University Press.

Elsner, J. and I. Rutherford. 2005b. "Introduction," in Elsner and Rutherford 2005a, 1-38.

Frey, N.L. 1998. *Pilgrim Stories. On and Off the Road to Santiago. Journeys along an Ancient Way in Modern Spain.* Berkeley: University of California Press.

Friese, W., S. Handberg and T.M. Kristensen (eds.) 2019. *Ascending and Descending the Acropolis. Movement in Athenian Religion.* Aarhus: Aarhus University Press.

Friese, W. and T.M. Kristensen. 2017. "Introduction: Archaeologies of Pilgrimage," in Kristensen and Friese 2017, 1-10.

Gagné, R., S. Goldhill and G.E.R. Lloyd (eds.) 2019. *Regimes of Comparatism. Frameworks of Comparison in History, Religion and Anthropology.* Leiden: Brill.

Gilhuly, K. and N. Worman (eds.) 2014. *Space, Place and Landscape in Ancient Greek Literature and Culture.* Cambridge: Cambridge University Press.

Graf, F. 2020. "Ritual in Its Space," in Friese, Handberg and Kristensen 2020, 255-66.

Hawes, G. (ed.) 2017. *Myths on the Map. The Storied Landscapes of Ancient Greece.* Oxford: Oxford University Press.

Hollinshead, M.B. 2015. *Shaping Ceremony. Monumental Steps and Greek Architecture.* Madison: University of Wisconsin Press.

Hölscher, T. 2018. *Visual Power in Ancient Greece and Rome. Between Art and Social Reality.* Berkeley: University of California Press.

Horden, P. and N. Purcell. 2000. *The Corrupting Sea. A Study of Mediterranean History.* Malden: Blackwell.

Horster, M. 2020. "Hellenistic Festivals: Aspects of the Economic Impact on Cities and Sanctuaries," in Collar and Kristensen 2020b, 116-39.

Hutton, W. 2008. *Describing Greece. Landscape and Literature in the* Periegesis *of Pausanias.* Cambridge: Cambridge University Press.

Jensen, O.B. 2013. *Staging Mobilities.* London: Routledge.

Jensen, O.B. 2014. *Designing Mobilities.* Aalborg: Aalborg University Press.

Jürgens, K. 2017. "Pilgrimage and Procession in the Panhellenic Festivals: Some Observations on the Hellenistic Leukophryena in Magnesia-on-the-Meander," in Kristensen and Friese 2017, 87-105.

Kinnard, J.N. 2014. *Places in Motion. The Fluid Identities of Temples, Images, and Pilgrims.* Oxford: Oxford University Press.

König, J. 2022. *The Folds of Olympus. Mountains in Ancient Greek and Roman Culture.* Princeton: Princeton University Press.

Kristensen, T.M. 2018. "Mobile Situations: *Exedrae* as Stages of Gathering in Greek Sanctuaries." *World Archaeology* 50.1, 86-99.

Kristensen, T.M. 2019. "New Approaches to Movement in Greek Religion," in Friese, Handberg and Kristensen 2019, 11-19.

Kristensen, T.M. 2020. "Meryemlik, Gathering and the Archaeology of Pilgrimage." *Mitteilungen zur Spätantiken Archäologie und Byzantinischen Kunstgeschichte* 7, 138-56.

Kristensen, T.M. Forthcoming. *Prisms of Pilgrimage. Landscapes, Gatherings and Presence in Ancient Mediterranean Sanctuaries.* London: Routledge.

Kristensen, T.M. and W. Friese (eds.) 2017. *Excavating Pilgrimage. Archaeological Approaches to Sacred Travel and Movement in the Ancient World.* Abingdon: Routledge.

Küchler, S. 2017. "Comparativism in Anthropology. Big Questions and Scaled Comparison—An Illusive Dream?," in Elsner 2017b, 130-44.

Lambrinoudakis, V. 2018. "Anfänge und Entwicklung des Asklepioskultes in Epidauros. Der 'Apollonaltar' und die Tholos," in H. Frielinghaus and T.G. Schattner (eds.) *ad summum templum architecturae. Forschungen zur antiken Architektur im Spannungsfeld der Fragestellungen und Methoden,* 125-38. Möhnesee: Bibliopolis.

Lambrinoudakis, V. and S. Prignitz. 2020. "Neue Bauinschriften aus Epidauros." *ZPE* 213, 117-37.

Lane Fox, R. 2009. *Travelling Heroes. Greeks and their Myths in the Epic Age of Homer.* London: Penguin.

Laurence, R. 2011. "Endpiece: From Movement to Mobility: Future Directions," in Laurence and Newsome 2011, 386-401.

Laurence, R. and D.J. Newsome (eds.) 2011. *Rome, Ostia, Pompeii. Movement and Space.* Oxford: Oxford University Press.

Luig, U. (ed.) 2018. *Approaching the Sacred. Pilgrimage in Historical and Intercultural Perspective.* Berlin: Edition Topoi.

Maddrell, A. et al. 2015. *Christian Pilgrimage, Landscapes and Heritage. Journeying to the Sacred.* London: Routledge.

McCorriston, J. 2011. *Pilgrimage and Household in the Ancient Near East.* Cambridge: Cambridge University Press.

McCorriston, J. 2017. "Inter-Cultural Pilgrimage, Identity, and the Axial Age in the Ancient Near East," in Kristensen and Friese 2017, 11-27.

Melfi, M. 2007. *I santuari di Asclepio in Grecia.* Rome: L'Erma di Bretschneider.

Melfi, M. 2010. "Ritual Spaces and Performances in the Asklepieia of Roman Greece." *BSA* 105, 317-38.

Mooring, J. 2022. "Weak and Strong Ties in the Diffusion of Coinage during the Archaic Period in Greece," in Collar 2022, 79-98.

Morinis, A. (ed.) 1992. *Sacred Journeys. The Anthropology of Pilgrimage.* London: Greenwood Press.

Newsome, D. 2011. "Introduction: Making Movement Meaningful," in Laurence and Newsome 2011, 1-54.

Niehoff, M.R. (ed.) 2017. *Journeys in the Roman East: Imagined and Real.* Tübingen: Mohr Siebeck.

Nongbri, B. 2015. *Before Religion. A History of a Modern Concept.* New Haven: Yale University Press.

Paga, J. 2017. "Contested Space at the Entrance to the Athenian Acropolis." *Journal of the Society of Architectural Historians* 76, 154-74.

Pedley, J. 2006. *Sanctuaries and the Sacred in the Ancient Greek World.* Cambridge: Cambridge University Press.

Perlman, P. 2000. *City and Sanctuary in Ancient Greece. The* Theorodokia *in the Peloponnese.* Göttingen: Vandenhoeck & Ruprecht.

Petsalis-Diomidis, A. 2010. *"Truly Beyond Wonders". Aelius Aristides and the Cult of Asklepios.* Oxford: Oxford University Press.

Pfaff, C.A. 2018. "Late Antique Symbols and Numerals on Altars in the Asklepieion at Epidauros." *Hesperia* 87.2, 387-428.

Polignac, F. de. 1995. *Cults, Territory, and the Origins of the Greek City-State.* Chicago: University of Chicago Press.

Prignitz, S. 2014. *Bauurkunden und Bauprogramm von Epidauros (400-350). Asklepiostempel, Tholos, Kultbild, Brunnenhaus.* Munich: C.H Beck.

Randell, R. 2020. "No Paradigm to Mobilize: The New Mobilities Paradigm is Not a Paradigm." *Applied Mobilities* 2, 206-23.

Renberg, G.H. 2017. *Where Dreams May Come: Incubation Sanctuaries in the Greco-Roman World.* 2 vols. Leiden: Brill.

Rhodes, P.F. 1995. *Architecture and Meaning on the Athenian Acropolis.* Cambridge: Cambridge University Press.

Riethmüller, J.W. 2005. *Asklepios: Heiligtümer und Kulte.* Heidelberg: Verlag Archäologie und Geschichte.

Roux, G. 1961. *L'architecture de l'Argolide aux IVe et IIIe siècles avant J.-C.* 2 vols. Paris: De Boccard.

Rutherford, I. 1999. "'To the Land of Zeus …': Patterns of Pilgrimage in Aelius Aristides." *Aevum Antiquum* 12, 133-48.

Rutherford, I. 2001. "The Song of the Sea (SA A-AB-BA Sir). Thoughts on KUB 45.63", in G. Wilhelm (ed.) *Akten des IV. International Kongresses für Hethlologie, Würzburg, 4.-8. Oktober 1999*, 598-709. Wiesbaden: Harassowitz.

Rutherford, I. 2013. *State Pilgrims and Sacred Observers in Ancient Greece. A Study of Theoria and Theoroi.* Cambridge: Cambridge University Press.

Rutherford, I. 2020. *Hittite Texts and Greek Religion: Contact, Interaction and Comparison.* Oxford: Oxford University Press.

Schachner, L.A. 2010. "The Archaeology of the Stylite," in D. Gwynn and S. Bangert (eds.) *Religious Diversity in Late Antiquity,* 329-97. Leiden: Brill.

Schnegg, M. 2014. "Anthropology and Comparison: Methodological Challenges and Tentative Solutions." *Zeitschrift für Ethnologie / Journal of Social and Cultural Anthropology* 139.1, 55-72.

Scullion, S. 2005. "'Pilgrimage' and Greek Religion: Sacred and Secular in the Pagan *Polis*", in Elsner and Rutherford 2005a, 111-30.

Schultz, P. et al. 2017. *The Thymele at Epidauros. Healing, Space, and Musical Performance in Late Classical Greece.* Fargo: Theran Press.

Scott, M. 2010. *Delphi and Olympia. The Spatial Politics of Panhellenism in the Archaic and Classical Periods.* Cambridge: Cambridge University Press.

Servon, L.J. and S. Pink. 2015. "Cittaslow: Going Global in Spain." *Journal of Urban Affairs* 37.3, 327-40.

Sheller, M. 2014. "The New Mobilities Paradigm for a Live Sociology." *Current Sociology Review* 62.6, 789-811.

Sheller, M. 2017. "From Spatial Turn to Mobilities Turn." *Current Sociology* 65.4, 623-39.

Sheller, M., and J. Urry. 2006. "The New Mobilities Paradigm." *Environment and Planning A: Economy and Space* 38.2, 207-26.

Sheller, M. and J. Urry. 2016. "Mobilizing the New Mobilities Paradigm." *Applied Mobilities* 1.1, 10-25.

Sinn, U. 2004. *Das antike Olympia. Götter, Spiel und Kunst.* Third edition. Munich: C.H. Beck.

Skousen, B.J. 2018. "Rethinking Archaeologies of Pilgrimage." *Journal of Social Archaeology* 18.3, 261-83.

Sneed, D. 2020. "The Architecture of Access: Ramps at Ancient Greek Healing Sanctuaries." *Antiquity* 94 (376), 1015-29.

Sourvinou-Inwood, C. 1990. "Ancient Rites and Modern Constructs: On the Brauronian Bears Again." *Bulletin of the Institute of Classical Studies* 37, 1-14.

Spencer, D. 2010. *Roman Landscape: Culture and Identity.* Cambridge: Cambridge University Press.

Stevens, G.P. 1936. "The Periclean Entrance Court of the Acropolis of Athens." *Hesperia* 5.4, 443-520.

Stewart, D. 2013. "'Most Worth Remembering': Pausanias, Analogy, and Classical Archaeology." *Hesperia* 82.2, 231-61.

Swatos, W.H. Jr. (ed.) 2006. *On the Road to Being There. Studies in Pilgrimage and Tourism in Late Modernity*. Leiden: Brill.

Terrault, S. 2019. "The Eschatological Body: Fleeing the Centre in Pre-Modern Insular Christianity and Post-Modern Secularity." *International Journal of Religious Tourism and Pilgrimage* 7.1, DOI: https://doi.org/10.21427/zb05-sg29.

Tomlinson, R.A. 1983. *Epidauros*. St Albans: Granada Publishing.

Turner, V. and E. Turner. 1978. *Image of Pilgrimage in Christian Culture.* New York: Columbia University Press.

Urry, J. 2007. *Mobilities.* Cambridge: Polity Press.

Valavanis, P. et al. 2022. "Managing the Open-Air Sacred Space on the Athenian Acropolis," in J. Neils and O. Palagia (eds.) *From Kallias to Kritias. Art in Athens in the Second Half of the Fifth Century B.C.,* 11-30. Berlin: Walter De Gruyter.

Vikan, G. 2012. *From the Holy Land to Graceland. Sacred People, Places and Things in Our Lives.* Washington DC: The AAM Press.

Wescoat, B.D. 2012. "Coming and Going in the Sanctuary of the Great Gods, Samothrace," in B.D. Wescoat and R.G. Ousterhout (eds.) *Architecture of the Sacred. Space, Ritual, and Experience from Classical Greece to Byzantium,* 66-113. Cambridge: Cambridge University Press.

Wescoat, B.D. 2017. "The Pilgrim's Passage into the Sanctuary of the Great Gods, Samothrace," in Kristensen and Friese 2017, 67-86.

Whiting, M. 2020. "Braided Networks: Pilgrimage and the Economics of Travel Infrastructure in the Late Antique Holy Land," in Collar and Kristensen 2020a, 33-61.

Wickkiser, B.L. 2008. *Asklepios, Medicine, and the Politics of Healing in Fifth-Century Greece.* Baltimore: The Johns Hopkins University Press.

Williamson, C.G. 2018. "Filters of Light. Greek Temple Doors as Portals of Epiphany," in E.M. van Opstall (ed.) *Sacred Thresholds. The Door to the Sanctuary in Late Antiquity,* 309-40. Leiden: Brill.

Worman, N. 2015. *Landscapes and the Spaces of Metaphor in Ancient Literary Theory and Criticism.* Cambridge: Cambridge University Press.

Yasin, A.M. 2017. "The Pilgrim and the Arch: Paths and Passageways at Qal'at Sem'an, Sinai, Abu Mena, and Tebessa," in Kristensen and Friese 2017, 166-86.

2

GETTING THERE: REFRAMING PILGRIMAGE FROM PROCESS TO SITE

DAVID FRANKFURTER

As this third conference on ancient pilgrimage was conceived to address critically the comparative approach, it is appropriate to begin this chapter with some words on the comparative project itself as it bears on religion.[1] In brief, comparison is not simply the juxtaposition of ancient and modern cases, conjuring similarities across time and space. Comparison, rather, is all about the categories we use—the "etic" terminology—to discuss historical, ethnographic and archaeological cases.[2] For example, what is "sacrifice" that this or that site might provide evidence for it, and what examples substantiate this category? What examples do we call upon to discuss the "votive object"—and what examples seem to be outliers? If a female figurine is left at a shrine, does that make it a votive object? What about if a person brings it home from the shrine? If we designate an image found at a shrine an "idol", what assumptions or biases will inevitably go into its interpretation, and what examples might demand another term?

And so, for the category "pilgrimage": what exactly does this term encompass, and what does it assume about the materials to which we apply it? Is a pilgrimage no more than travel to religious sites, and then how is travel to religious sites different from travel to cities or annual games or, in modernity, museums? Does the term imply something more about that travel? In the past I have tended to use the term in a vague sense to refer to any visit to a shrine of any scope or scale—a kind of ideology of movement that integrates religion and landscape.[3] But since the surge of pilgrimage—especially ancient pilgrimage—studies that began in the early 1990s, a number of scholars have tried to give some definitional substance to the category. For Simon Coleman and Jaś Elsner, pilgrimage amounts to ritualised travel to far-off sacred centres that brought

---

1 For extending my knowledge of spring sanctuaries I am grateful to Fritz Graf and Anna-Katherina Rieger; and for allowing me to reprint images from her series "Pilgrimage" I sincerely thank Mary Frank.
2 Cf. Frankfurter 2012.
3 Frankfurter 1998a; 2015a.

contact with the supernatural and thus reinforced religious identity.[4] For Alan Morinis, it amounts to "a journey undertaken by a person in quest of a place or a state that he or she believes to embody a valued ideal".[5] For Richard Scriven, it is defined by "four interrelated characteristics: movement, place, belief, and transformation. … the pilgrim returns to quotidian life renewed, or even as a new or (spiritually) reborn person."[6] And Jan Bremmer, in his response to the first Aarhus conference on pilgrimage, declared that "to be a meaningful etic category, pilgrimage should comprise the elements of religious motivation, journey, religious site and life-enriching experience".[7]

One sees a pattern emerging here in what scholars *want* to designate when they use "pilgrimage": to wit, the journey. In their foundational 2005 volume *Seeing the Gods*, Elsner and Ian Rutherford, wisely avoiding any strict definitions, commented on "the (probably correct) emphasis on the pilgrim's journey as a rite of passage"; while Troels Myrup Kristensen, in an article on "the representation of pilgrimage," argued for "the importance of representing the sacred journey through a variety of distinct media."[8] The comparative geographer Richard Scriven goes much further, endorsing a "new mobilities paradigm": that is, a focus on "motion and fluidity … that presents a way into the open-ended, ethereal and transitory state of pilgrimage".[9] In some ways this focus on journey is a way of getting at an experiential aspect that "travel" sidelines and "pilgrimage" seems intrinsically to encompass: a distinctive *and transformative* experience.

So what is it that we are really trying to capture when we choose "pilgrimage" as a category over the more prosaic term "travel"? I ask this as a historian of religions, interested in religious stuff, because part of our work and responsibility is to consider seriously the categories we use to compare, to generalize, to frame data for analysis. Consequently, the goal of this chapter is to critique one particular assumption that underlies the category "pilgrimage": that it amounts to a sacred journey in which the subject goes through the equivalent of a rite of passage, gaining existentially a larger understanding of the religion that the shrine represents—even a new identity—and consequently, spiritually, a transformed and elated self. This model, of course, is partly based in the Turners' 1978 book *Image and Pilgrimage*, but in his prior writings Victor Turner framed the topic in a more anthropological sense: the religious difference between the regional or national shrine that is inevitably far off, on the cultural periphery, and the local shrine that belongs to the village landscape. What must happen when a person departs the local domain for the far-off trans-regional shrine, a greater centre, as it were? How does this spatial traverse involve a shift in experience, identity and sense of the world?[10] That was how Turner first presented the topic.

---

4   Coleman and Elsner 1995, 25-26.
5   Morinis 1992, 4.
6   Scriven 2014, 251-52.
7   Bremmer 2017, 278.
8   Elsner and Rutherford 2005, 5; Kristensen 2012, 115.
9   Scriven 2014, 254.
10 Turner 1973; 1974.

But the simplification of Turner's work to focus on the journey—the spiritually transformative process of the liminal phase—has an ethical dimension that we often forget. Today, the most common subjects of such protracted liminality are *not* able spiritual pilgrims but refugees—lost, truly, in no man's lands and open water, in journeys with no end-point. In her arresting sculpture/photography series provocatively entitled *Pilgrimage*, the contemporary artist Mary Frank depicts not some hero's resolute journey to the cosmic Centre but the abject dislocation born of war and trauma that propels so many in our day to flee, *maybe* towards a better (but by no means "ultimate") place (Fig. 1).[11] In one image we see a figure emerging from a demolished cityscape, no "home" to which he might return with blessings from the Centre. What propels this abject "pilgrim" into the journey (which occupies the rest of Frank's series) is, indeed, that there is nowhere else to go. In another image (Fig. 2) we behold the "pilgrims'" vessel, whose passengers do not praise God for arriving in a holy land but, far out on a stormy sea, cry out for aid. Frank's work should alert us to the realities of cultural or existential liminality between (demolished) home and (desperately imagined) goal. Do we, in fact, sideline these realities when we romanticise the pilgrim's journey, when we talk about pilgrimage as an ideal category?

Notably, the medievalist Courtney Luckhardt has called attention to the religious practices and storied divine interventions in the lives of those in ancient and medieval times who travelled in shackles or in desperation (flight, exile)—quite different from those who set out in comfortable conditions to Santiago or Jerusalem. For these refugees and slaves, a "religion of the road" was more a matter of seeking the specific deliverance of local saints and shrines along the way than some personally enlightening quest for the religious centre.[12]

Both the artist Frank and the historian Luckhardt offer strong correctives to the idealisation of the journey as an intentional, unidirectional and transformative passage to the Centre of some sacred geography. This is not to deny that some people engaged in protracted travel to religious sites experienced this sort of idealised journey, but simply to argue that we should be wary of our cultural tendencies to fix a rather romanticised travel experience as defining of the concept of pilgrimage.

The Modernity of Pilgrimage

As a phenomenological discussion of shrines and their concentric catchment areas, Turner's analysis is essential. But there is something quintessentially modern about the special attention to the *journey* in pilgrimage—a post-Reformation, neo-Catholic, post-industrial preoccupation—that seems to impute an awful lot of distinctive experience to a huge range of religiously-motivated travel. The first time I realised this was when I walked the last ten kilometres of the Santiago de Compostela *camino*, which is perhaps *the* paradigmatic pilgrimage for westerners (outside of the Hajj and maybe

---

11 Frank 2017.
12 Luckhardt 2020, esp. chap. 5.

△ ▷ Mary Frank, "Untitled" (2017) [from *Pilgrimage* series]. Clay, stone, wood and pastel, 30 × 40 × 32 inches. Courtesy of Elena Zang Gallery, Woodstock, NY.

Fig. 1.

Jerusalem), and then drove another three hundred kilometres along the route in the opposite direction.

I have visited a lot of holy places over the years, from Jerusalem to Varanasi to Chimayo. In all these pilgrimages the point was really to *get to* the shrine, the basilica, or the holy grounds, to gain the *darshan* of the unique image in its church or temple or of the Kotel in Jerusalem. The shrines of Fatima, Lourdes, Jerusalem, Altagracia and even Mecca have enormous parking lots for buses, from which thousands stream to see the holy sites and engage in desired or requisite devotions. When air travel is available, people take airplanes. If one has to walk the last kilometres, then of course one walks—maybe even on one's knees in order to accentuate the urgency of one's pleas to the saint or the god. I wanted to walk those last ten kilometres to get a sense of entering a great urban shrine from beyond the city gates, as innumerable visitors had done over the centuries.

And yet the Santiago pilgrimage was the first time I have witnessed the shrine as simply the end-point, and the journey itself as the major component of the experience for modern participants. As they wend their ways along the several caminos from France through Spain, participants travel together, meet others *en route*, leave their town routines and identities behind to get out on the road. Many are older women who have clearly had full lives before wanting to take up this physical/spiritual challenge. Arriving in the courtyard of the basilica or before the medieval image of St. James in the basilica is an accomplishment, for sure, but in the sense of the capstone on a lifetime experience: that is, making it to Compostela on foot. In fact, for some people, actually getting there is a letdown after the real experience that they had on the road. Overall, the Santiago pilgrimage very much resembles doing, then finishing, the Appalachian Trail in the eastern United States.[13]

Of course, there is certainly a minority for whom the Camino is simply a utilitarian route to get to the basilica itself and its image, to lay eyes on this image, to hold its shoulders as you can do from behind the altar, although given the accessibility of modern transportation one can get to Santiago de Compostela quite efficiently by plane or bus from all over Europe. But for the pilgrims I saw, and certainly those interviewed by the anthropologist Nancy Frey for her book on the culture of the Camino, that distance and the opportunity it gave them to be "on the road" was the very point of the experience. And in its popularity, especially among fairly secular Europeans, it is also an example of the cultural appeal to modern folk of a quasi-religious (post-Catholic) journey where the vitality, community and deepest personal experiences are cultivated *en route* rather than at some smoky basilica filled with wax ears.[14]

So this is the premise of this chapter: that out of our own modern and romantic notions of the journey—epitomised in the modern Santiago de Compostela pilgrimage—we have lost the focus on the holy site itself (and, as I observed, have sidelined or

---

13 See Frey 1988; with Coleman and Eade 2004, 11.
14 Reader 2007.

appropriated the real plight of the genuinely liminal).[15] Instead, pilgrimage has become for us moderns a metaphor for meaningful movement in the world, a trip towards a place, where even the place becomes merely an abstraction for experiential encounters with religious ideals. Anything but the materiality of the shrine itself! These are the post-Enlightenment, quasi-Protestant sentiments that make the Garden Tomb in Jerusalem or the Saudi version of Mecca intuitively comprehensible, but the Holy Sepulchre (or the now-obliterated Meccan and Medinan sites of Muhammed's life) somehow antiquarian and superstitious.[16] In this way, whenever we apply the category "pilgrimage" to an archaeological site, we tend to draw out a series of assumptions about people's *experiences*: from journey to transcendent encounter to practices of remembering. But at least for antiquity, these assumptions do not seem to fit the evidence. While art historians often project the pilgrimage journey into the iconography of shrine memorabilia, a recent study of graffiti left at southern European shrines in the late antique and early medieval periods found that almost none mentioned the visitor's place of origin.[17] The graffiti reflect commemorations of people's presence *at* the shrine rather than the journey there or the distance from home.

Thus, as a corrective, I recommend we should reemphasise the *local* or *regional* shrine-visit, its practices and materiality, and regard the long-distance or global pilgrimage (like the Hajj) as conceptually and historically anomalous.[18] Pilgrimage, that is, should be about *getting there*, not "heading out there".

But should we still even speak of "pilgrimage" if the journey and what is supposed to take place *en route* is cast as idiosyncratic rather than definitional? Given my concerns about the baggage that the term "pilgrimage" carries, I will use the term "shrine-visitation" for this chapter. The merits of this more specific category are three-fold: first, it construes religious travel as a type of *travel*—that is, purposeful rather than abject movement away or towards; second, it focuses on the places people go and what people do there as the central features; and third, while removing the focus on "the journey", it allows us to refocus on essential forms of movement in the precinct of the shrine. In that sense, I follow Simon Coleman and John Eade in their 2004 volume *Reframing*

---

15   In fact, Turner and Turner 1978 do *not* stress the Santiago pilgrimage as paradigmatic, nor did they ever do the Camino (Rory Turner, personal correspondence, 6 May 2017); rather, they selected more actively traditional shrines like St. Patrick's Purgatory and the new Marian sites. Timothy Larsen, in his analysis of religious sensibilities among anthropologists, notes Victor Turner's adherence to a fairly strict pre-Vatican II Catholic aesthetic (Larsen 2014, 187-88, 194-95). Yet Turner's openness to new social movements of the 1960s and 70s in *Dramas, Fields, and Metaphors* (Turner 1974, 166-230) demonstrates that he was no parochial atavist but a modernist finding new values in traditional Catholic shrine culture. In this sense, Turner's Catholicism and writings anticipated the culture of the contemporary Camino.

16   On the Garden Tomb, see Wharton 2006, 201-6. On the Saudi obliteration of shrines associated with Muhammed in Mecca, see Ahmed 2006; Anonymous 2006; and Ahmed 2016, 532-37.

17   Handley 2017, esp. 575.

18   Note the observations about local visitation in Stafford 2019, 260.

Pilgrimage, who argue that movement—broadly conceived—is essential to pilgrimage.[19] But where they stretch this movement out to the entire journey *to* the shrine, I would concentrate on the shrine precinct itself and movement *in* that space as especially symbolic. That is, at the point that one disembarks from the bus, or car, or one passes into the shrine precinct, there are sequences and circuits to follow, processions to join, dances that move feet and hips, shops to visit, places to deposit votive objects, food to share, and gestures to bring together body and shrine in magical contact. Movement is absolutely constitutive of shrine visitation, but we must look for it especially at the site, not *en route*. And there may well be physical effort involved, whether to climb annually to a local mountain shrine or to engage a vow through walking the last kilometres on one's knees. But such physical effort, whether for vow or even to constitute one's status in a confraternity, can be found in other forms of religious movement, not just getting to shrines. (One thinks of the men bearing heavy *pasos*—processional floats—around Spanish cities during Semana Santa.) Physical effort may contribute to all types of religious experiences, but it is not *typical* of shrine visitation, nor does it imply a particular "pilgrimage" experience.

Overall, a change in terminology from pilgrimage to shrine visitation offers us a different way of framing that central aspect of religion ancient and modern: the desire to *visit* a place and there to *appeal* to, to *dream* of, to *communicate* with, and to make *vows toward* supernatural beings. When we refocus on the place itself, we rediscover the religious creativity, the *syncretism*, that takes place at the shrine. This will constitute the second half of this chapter.

Individual Agency and Collective Experience in Shrine Visitation

Shrine visitation and travel involve *agency*: the commitment on the part of a person to a physical endeavour, the completion of a ritual performance, and presumably some personal religious investment in the process. In the classic historiography on pilgrimage, it is the individual who is motivated to set out to a distant centre sanctioned by her religion and who, over the course of the journey and its ultimate encounter with that centre, experiences a transformation comparable to a rite of passage. In Mircea Eliade's foundational essay on sacred space it was ultimately the individual who sought meaning and union at the cosmic centre. This individual draw and the decision to go are critical to the very category of "pilgrim". But who *are* the agents and what is the nature of individual agency in shrine visitation? The ethnography of shrine visitation discloses an agency that, if personal in many respects, is inevitably subsumed in group endeavours: community delegations, family representatives, private appeals for resolution of social crises, and in the end—at the shrine—*communitas* itself.

In antiquity, the most important context for shrine visitation was the town or regional delegation that must travel to a holy site or temple, perform in activities there, and bring an offering from the homeland, or material blessings back from the shrine visit.

---

19 Coleman and Eade 2004, 3, 16-17.

In their volume *Seeing the Gods*, Rutherford and Elsner return to this model repeatedly in their typology of ancient pilgrimages. Many of these pilgrimages (so-called) involve civic delegations to oracles, images or important civic rituals, where the delegation's goal is *theōria*—beholding or witnessing.[20] In the annals of comparative pilgrimage, this model is also well known from the work of Michael Sallnow on Peruvian village delegations that ascend to shrines high up in the Andes, wearing traditional costumes, playing music and performing special dances.[21] It is difficult to see a unique personal dimension in this delegation experience, although Sallnow proposes there is a shift in the self-definition of the participants in the process, from being residents of particular villages to "Indians".[22] Perhaps there would have arisen in ancient delegations a similar shift in identity.

The new self-definition is reinforced on arrival at the Andean shrine through the delegation's performances as special characters from different parts of Peru. There is differentiation among the various costumed delegations, then, but neither individualistic piety nor transcendent unity; it is a *communitas* of village teams and troupes from all over Peru, there at the Andean shrine to see where Christ appeared and to retrieve blessed ice from the high glaciers.[23]

One need not be a formal member of a traditional delegation to bring to one's shrine visit the responsibility to aid or mediate for family members. At most shrines, visitors come to make personal appeals for healing, conception, safety and blessing. This is the context that has produced the great array of votive objects and the stelae and miracle collections from shrines like Epidauros and Pergamon and, in late antique Egypt, Menouthis and Apa Mena. But the personal appeal does not imply an individuality in the modern sense. Personal efforts to resolve domestic crises, which are certainly more onerous when one is trudging to a regional shrine, bespeak an agency on the part of the individual visitor. But it is an agency that is constructed socially. That is, one heads to the shrine in one's capacity as a socially embedded and responsible person: as mother, as daughter, as father, as breadwinner, as athlete for a town, and so on. And these highly personal appeals are constructed or performed in collective contexts—among other mothers or would-be mothers, sitting in a saint's shrine, watching and advising each other in how to tie a knot in a string or toss a doll, for example.[24] As Fatima Mernissi illustrated with modern Moroccan shrines, there might develop a strong solidarity among mothers at a shrine for childbirth.[25] In these ways, *communitas* comes about at the site, as a function of people together challenged by similar crises, perhaps of the same gender. Again, with shrine visitation we are talking about *social* experience at the most basic level. If

---

20 Rutherford and Elsner 2005, 12-15; see esp. Kowalzig 2005.
21 Sallnow 1987; 1991.
22 Sallnow 1991, 147.
23 See Sallnow 1987.
24 In conceptualising a social model of agency, I am indebted to Rüpke 2015, esp. 348-52, following Emirbayer and Mische 1998.
25 Mernissi 1977; cf. Betteridge 1992; Cuffel 2005; Gemzoë 2005.

someone heads to the Mandulis shrine in Kalabsha, way up the Nile, to gain cosmic wisdom, or Sedona, Arizona, to feel the cosmic vortex, those kinds of personal quests must remain the historical exceptions.[26]

In the end, the shrine itself is a place of rendezvous, of collective activity and participation. It is this (Durkheimian) sense of *communitas*, rather than the interstitial and initiatory – that romantic "on the road" liminality – that most pertains to shrine visitation. Sacred space, as Ann Marie Yasin has insisted, is social space: the space of collective focus and movement; and holiness itself arises from collective concentration.[27] That is what the visitor finds at the shrine. For Turner, *communitas* came especially to mean the collapse of hierarchy and divisions into unity, in which participants are subsumed temporarily: a common identity of *dévoté*.[28] In their 1991 volume *Contesting the Sacred*, Eade and Sallnow warned against romanticising this unity, given the strong competitive and divisive currents that characterise most regional shrines and their cultures. Yet *communitas* does exist in many areas and moments of religious travel and shrine visitation. The question, I think, is whether *communitas* is a principal characteristic of something called pilgrimage or, rather, an epiphenomenon of certain social circumstances to which shrine visitation lends itself. For example, visiting a shrine or temple in its festival period involves enthusiastic immersion in crowds, dances, spectacles and other activities typical of *festivals* but not characteristic of a shrine in its off-hours.[29] *Communitas* can be a function of other social circumstances or conditions in shrine visitation: common dress, for example,[30] shared transportation[31] and even immersion in the lay ranks of liturgical processions. We should conceptualise *communitas* in terms of those particular moments and contexts. (But we should always keep in mind its darker analogue: the shared desperation and fear that refugees carry in a protracted and seldom elevating state of betwixt-and-between).

So although agency in shrine visitation will inevitably include the personally, emotionally, exotically-inspired individual (much like the hiker who sets herself to do the Pacific Coast Trail in the western U.S.),[32] we must think of agency in this area of religious movement in social terms—as traditional, performative, representative, even delegated: endowing the individual with special, yet traditionally configured, responsibility.

---

26 On spiritual tourism to the Mandulis shrine in Roman Egypt, see Nock 1972. On contemporary "new age pilgrimages", see Ivakhiv 2001 and Schaap 2017.
27 Yasin 2009, ch. 1.
28 See Turner 1974, 231-71.
29 Weingrod 1990; Gintsburg 2018. For antiquity see Rutherford 2020.
30 On *communitas* and shared dress on the Hajj, see the classic description by Malcolm X: (Malcolm X and Haley 2015, 318-42). But cf. Abdulai 1984—a distinctly anxious and division-ridden depiction of the Hajj.
31 See, *e.g.*, Gemzoë 2005, 234-37.
32 Cf. Strayed 2013.

Shrine Visitation and Situational Syncretism in Late Antiquity

I now want to turn to several examples of shrine visitation in the late antique Mediterranean world, to demonstrate one particular payoff of focusing on the shrine itself rather than imagining a whole transformative journey for the individual. While we cannot dismiss entirely the notion that the *journeys* to regional shrines had special meaning, the evidence of major regional shrines shows such a diversity of activities there, and such a multifaceted (and often conflictual) effort to define the functions and traditions of the place, that it is difficult and unnecessary to put distinctive religious significance on the journey. As I will discuss, the two late antique Christian shrines show active efforts at *syncretism*—that is, the appropriation of Christian practices in traditional, local terms as well as the revitalisation of local practices in Christian terms. In the third case, the pervasive water sanctuaries of the Roman and late antique world, we see the central "goal" of the spring giving rise to innumerable religious establishments and ritual practices, from healing to the depositing of *defixiones*. Overall, such evidence should draw our—like ancient peoples'—attention away from the journey itself and towards the world where shrine visitation "happens."

Late antique studies have produced some of the richest discussions of pilgrimage culture, and yet it must be said that the notion of late antiquity as an "age of pilgrimage" is a distortion. The institutionalisation of Christianity (and Islam, in its turn) invited a new trans-regional context for the promotion of certain regional shrines as well as a Christian brand of travel literature epitomised in Egeria's travelogue, the Bordeaux itinerary, and the *Historia monachorum in Aegypto*. But it is certainly not evident that more people were heading out on the road, as it were. To be sure, the rise of Christianity did involve the proliferation of regional cults—martyr shrines and holy men—to which people travelled from the cults' immediate environs and *sometimes* from further afield.[33] They headed to regional shrines rather than local shrines because the regional ones seemed to offer greater authority and power—because the shrine offered a prescient oracle, reliability in healing or conception, or vibrant festivals.[34] So much we know from archaeology and ancient literature. But as for the so-called "literature of late antique pilgrimage"—Egeria and the like—these texts are really too idiosyncratic a group of documents to prove a new trend.[35]

So what happens if we take a more ethnographically-informed and comparative approach to the culture of the shrine itself? Setting aside notions of journey, we can begin to see the regional shrine as a crucible, not of individuals engaging materially with scriptural precepts, but of *syncretism*: of the confluence, conflict and juxtaposition of religious traditions brought by supplicants and delegations, by bishops and monastic groups, and invented *ad hoc* by shrine attendants and acolytes.[36] In this process, the Christian religious framework or aegis of so many late antique shrines came under

---

33 See Brown 1971; 1975; Frankfurter 1998b, 179-97.
34 See Montserrat 1998; Rutherford 2005; Petsalis-Diomidis 2005; and Frankfurter 2010.
35 Falcasantos 2017.
36 This rectified sense of "syncretism" is explained in Frankfurter 2017.

constant negotiation, while local traditions of gesture, dance, feasting and so on asserted themselves on the broader culture of the shrine for others to adopt or reject.

The Shrine of Symeon the Stylite
The shrine of Symeon the Stylite in Syria, less than a hundred kilometres from Antioch, was the subject of two papers in the first Aarhus pilgrimage conference.[37] Qal'at Sim'an thrived from the saint's own lifetime in the mid-fifth century until the seventh century. It was a place that you *visited*, not engaged in transformative travel *towards*: as Theodoret notes, the crowds there came to visit Symeon for oracles (19), for blessings (20), for the dispensing of justice (26) and for festivals (24), although it is unclear which festivals were supposed to be best celebrated at the pillar during Simeon's time.[38]

After Symeon's death, Qal'at Sim'an grew to attract visitors from as far afield as Gaul. As an example of a regional cult, it also exemplifies two of my earlier points: (a) the collective nature of visitation,[39] with Arab tribes predominating early on,[40] and (b) the fact that the important dimension of *religious movement* begins already in the town of Telenissos at the base of the small mountain one had to ascend to reach the Symeon shrine (Fig. 2). Archaeologists have pointed to the importance of the processional road that wound up the mountain, through arches and past stores, to the basilica complex on the top of the mountain. The basilica itself was unique in the late antique world for enshrining architecturally not the body but the ascetic device of a saint: the pillar of Symeon, out from whose rotunda extended four large rooms (Fig. 3).[41]

But there were many things distinctive about this cult, and they begin with Symeon himself, who ascended a pillar in full view of a major trade route in the early fifth century. We are accustomed to marvelling at this ascetic strategy as no crazier than what other holy men of the period did; even modern scholars romantically imagine Symeon's motivations as the imitation of Christ on the cross or the desire to ascend or dwell in liminal space.[42] But it is important to take into account the fact that Theodoret of Cyrrhus, his hagiographer, as well as other writers of the period, found it necessary to address ecclesiastical *critics* of Symeon's adoption of the pillar.[43] Clearly church leaders of the time did not see it as a "Christian" act but something else entirely. And that something else—that context in which it must have had particular resonance for people in Syria—involved the various uses of pillars for framing a symbol or act of authority in Roman (and desert) Syria.[44] Three centuries earlier, for example, Lucian discusses a

---

37 Hunter-Crawley 2017; Yasin 2017.
38 Theodoret, *H.E.*, 26.
39 Theodoret, *H.E.*, 26.13-18, 21.
40 See Shahîd 1998; esp. 382, with important details of nomadic Arab religion in Murray 2011.
41 Sodini 2010; 2015; Yasin 2012, esp. 249-53; Yasin 2017; and now Boero 2016; 2021; Hunter-Crawley 2020.
42 Cf. Drijvers 1978; Harvey 1988; Stang 2010; and Hunter-Crawley 2017, 198-99.
43 Theodoret, *H.E.* 26.12, with Theodoret of Cyrrhus 1985, 174n16, and Frankfurter 1990, esp. 188-90.
44 Frankfurter 1990.

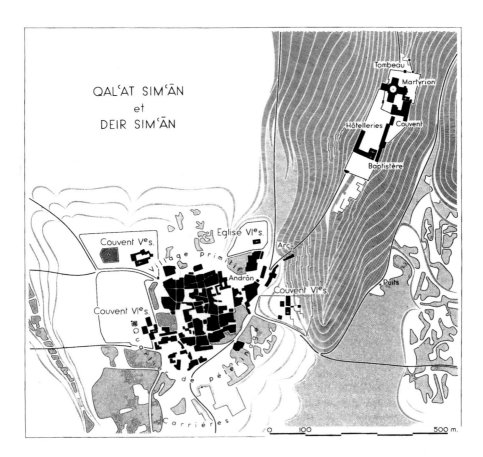

Map of Qal'at Sim'an and village of Telanissos, from Georges Tchalenko, *Villages antiques de la Syrie du Nord*, vol. 2 (Paris, P. Geuthner, 1953-58), pl. cxxxii. By permission of P. Geuthner.

Fig. 2.

popular practice outside the walls of the great Hierapolis temple where local ritual delegates would ascend pillars and imprecate the gods for a week.[45] Pillars lay somewhere between a common religious symbolism and a common ritual *habitus*, not so much linked to a god or goddess as advancing any authoritative symbol or act.[46] Just how fundamental this pillar symbolism was in the region of Qal'at Sim'an is evident in the iconography of stylite saints that developed in the centuries following Symeon himself: that is, from a man atop a pillar to a pillar with two eyes, which came to decorate stelae, lintels and doors in late antique Syria (Fig. 4).[47]

---

45 Lucian, *De Dea Syria* 28-29.
46 Cf. Eastmond 1999. See also Murray 2011, 221-24, on the aniconic *baetyl* tradition among Arab tribes.
47 Frankfurter 1990, 186, following Lassus 1947, 278-79, 286, and Fernandez 1975. See now Schachner 2010, esp. 370-75, and Hunter-Crawley 2020, 268-76.

Fig. 3. Shrine of St. Symeon Stylites, Qalat Siman. Photograph by Troels Myrup Kristensen, by permission.

Thus the allegedly outlandish Symeon became thoroughly assimilated, domesticated, as his images spread everywhere and stylite asceticism itself spread widely—especially in Syria, where there was clearly a cultural predilection for this act.[48] Both Theodoret in his time and, now, archaeology of the facilities at Telanissos and at Qal'at Sim'an suggest that large crowds showed up to make devotions to Symeon. Bishop Evagrius says that, in the mid-fifth century, he "saw, in company with all the people who were there assembled, while the *peasants were performing dances around* [the pillar], a very large and brilliant star, shooting along the whole balustrade …, [which] occurs only at the commemorations of the saint". People expected such a prodigy at Symeon's festival. Indeed, Evagrius reports that people would herd their livestock up to the shrine on these evenings and "repeatedly circumambulate[d] the pillar with their beasts of burden".[49] Dancing and circumambulation with animals are autochthonous traditions, not sanctioned in the hagiography of Symeon but essential to the popular reception of and engagement with this regional shrine.

Thus the cult of Symeon—the man's own performance and then the shrine complex that grew up around his pillar—provided the physical site and material context for the Christianisation of pillar symbolism and the indigenisation of Christian ideas of holy bodies. This twofold process of Christianisation and indigenisation was, of course,

---

48 Iconography: Theodoret, *H.R.*, 26.11. Vikan 2010, 31-33, 54-56.
49 Evagrius, *H.E.*, 1.14.

Fig. 4.

Stela depicting Symeon Stylites merged with his pillar, Syria, 5th–6th centuries CE. 84.5 × 76 × 18.5 cm. Berlin, Byzantine Museum inv. 9/63. Courtesy of Stiftung Preußischer Kulturbesitz, Staatliche Museen zu Berlin—Skulpturensammlung und Museum für Byzantinische Kunst, Berlin (9/63). Photo: Jürgen Liepe.

fundamental to the construction of Christianity in the Roman Empire. Here we see the process taking place within the precinct of Qal'at Sim'an, as farmers processed their animals around the pillar, everybody went up at night to see the prodigy of his image in the sky, and Symeon tokens stamped with his pillar were bought and sold. It was this shrine—and then the many further shrines to stylite holy men—that established the pillar as a place of asceticism, a mount for a holy man, and a symbol that could be efficaciously reproduced in clay, paint or stone.

The evidence of the Symeon shrine and of Stylite cults more broadly points to the shrine as the site of diverse "pilgrims'" activities and experiences, not to the process of travel. Indeed, while elite authors celebrate the visitors who come from far off, the distinctively northern Syrian cultural elements of the cult, from the appeal of the pillar to the material medium of *hnana* (for transferring blessings), reflect a more immediately regional catchment area, whence farmers really could lead their livestock up the mountain.

The Shrine of St. Menas

The famous shrine of Apa Mena, southwest of Alexandria, flourished from the late fourth until the early seventh century. Archaeology affords us comparatively more detail about the life of this site than do the remains of the Symeon shrine: a processional route through a veritable city of hostels, baths and workshops that opened up into a courtyard before an enormous basilica. Visitors to Apa Mena came for healing, for incubation

Fig. 5.

Female figurines found at Abu Mina shrine. Moulded terracotta. 5th–7th centuries CE. From Kaufmann, *Die Menasstadt*, taf. 73. Photo in public domain.

and for festival activities, as we learn especially from the shrine's miracle collection.[50] Ampullae moulded with St. Menas's image between two camels were made here to carry sacred oil home to one's family and community.[51]

One artefact here in particular gives us a sense of the active interaction between local traditions and the Christianity demonstrated at the shrine. A large number of female figurines was discovered at the site, some *in situ* in the baptistery or other places of ritual deposit, others in the workshops, and still others in domestic sites in Alexandria (Fig. 5). Most of the figurines express some form of pregnancy or successful childbirth, while some hold tambourines. Since they bear no identifiers of specific saints (like Thekla or Mary), the figurines presumably served as votive images—left in "active" parts of the basilica complex to express hope for a child—or perhaps to bring home as a kind of blessing on fecundity from St. Menas.[52] Unfortunately there is absolutely no mention of their use in the miracle texts nor in the various polemics against popular religion we find in Coptic literature.

Female figurines are not in any way unique to the Apa Mena shrine, nor to Egyptian Christian saints' shrines in general. Some interesting types were found at the St. Col-

50   See Drescher 1947.
51   Kaufmann 1918, 197-207; Kiss 1989; Cannuyer 1997; Grossmann 1998, 298-300; Bangert 2010.
52   See Frankfurter 2015b.

luthus shrine at Antinoë, and two *nude* variants now in European museums have the name of the saint Phib inscribed on their bellies.[53] However, a great range of types of female figurines have been found in both cemetery and domestic sites all over Egypt from the late Roman period, and museums are full of them. The diversity itself, both in form and manufacture, points to autochthonous traditions: local ways of moulding female forms in order to make them identifiable as a supplicant and efficacious as a material message. We can rightly conclude that, however they were designated or understood or utilized, these figurines were part of the *habitus* of domestic ritual in late antique Egypt.[54]

But then what does it mean that they had come to be manufactured at the Apa Mena shrine, as the commodities of several workshops, moulded alongside the famous Menas ampullae? Simply that the economy and the material repertoire of this shrine had incorporated a common ritual object and now encouraged its use—alongside liturgical performances and the occasional orthoprax sermon. We might say that the forms of the figurines manufactured at Apa Mena cleaved to a more modest type, with long robes, the merest hint of pregnancy and something like haloes by their heads.[55] If this is correct, it would mean that workshops were modelling a Christian self-presentation through the medium of traditional figurines that in other regions might be rendered in the nude. Once again, the site of the saint's shrine becomes the site of negotiation and synthesis between local traditions (with no relationship to "paganism" as commonly understood) and various formations of Christianity. To put it in other terms, all these dynamics take place within the precinct of the shrine, and visitors to Apa Mena bring with them a readiness to engage and construct Christianity *there, in that place*, according to their own needs and gestural traditions.[56]

Water Shrines and the Nature of Supernatural Powers
Both of these examples of syncretism take place at large-scale shrines, in the course of great festivals, various devotional acts, and consequently ecclesiastical efforts to direct behaviour and tradition. The "centres" here become large-scale (if conflict-prone) institutions reflecting and channelling multiple interests and needs on the part of visitors and ecclesiastical authorities. Hagiographical stories depict the potency of shrine materials (oil, *hnana*, dust) and the saints' actual presence at the shrines—occasionally too the trials and obstructions that people encounter *en route*, but not self-transformation in the course of pilgrimage.

The last case, however, involves a smaller, more variable type of shrine that appears in most landscapes of the Roman period: the water shrine or sacred spring. Recent reviews

---

53 See Bayer-Niemeier 1988, 147-48, no. 262.
54 Frankfurter 2014; 2015b.
55 On the idea that figurines from the Christian era show somewhat more modesty, see Teeter 2010, 80n81. It would be a local proclivity, however, given the number of late antique examples stressing the nude form.
56 See in general Frankfurter 2017, ch. 4.

of the data for these shrines in late antiquity by Eberhard Sauer, Maddalena Bassani and Marion Bolder-Boos show that they could grow to be quite developed, with architecture around the water-source, organized attendants, specialties like divination or healing, and established ritual idioms and offerings (from lamps to votive body-parts).[57] Christian authorities often found such shrines a challenge to integrate, even while Christian laity venerated them over many centuries—and still do today. Like other shrines fixed into the natural environment, water shrines invited a variety, or even a constant evolution, of interpretations: is it a god or a *jinn*, a saint or an angel, or in modern times Khidr (Elijah) or the Virgin Mary? Springs in Gaul could become sites of Mithraea, demonstrating the attraction yet mutability of the aquatic site for new shrines. They did not restrict themselves to nymphs or healing gods.[58] An early Roman temple complex on a river in Lebanon bore inscriptions referring to the activities of "the Virgin Hochmaea", a woman who apparently served as an oracle there, inspired by regional gods Hadaranes and Atargatis. Up the same valley lay further shrine structures, probably with other interpretations and customs.[59] Water shrines by nature seem to have entertained multiple devotions and religious orientations at the same site. In his bucolic description of a water shrine in Umbria, Italy, for example, Pliny (late I CE) notes both a "holy temple of great antiquity" with an image of the local god Clitumnus and "a number of small shrines [*sacella*], each containing its god and having its own name and cult, and some of them also their own springs" —evidence of an eclectic concentration of devotions there that would resist theological systematisation.[60] Archaeology of European water-shrines also shows a continuity of coin offerings through late antiquity and the early medieval period, making it unclear how the various shrines fit into the prevailing Christianity of the area.[61]

Despite the eclectic practices of water shrines and their cults, Christian writers were often concerned about making theological sense of them. This is what we find in the Gospel of John (5: 2-13) (late first century CE): "Now in Jerusalem by the Sheep Gate there is a pool, called … Bethzatha, which has five porticoes", where sick people would go for healing. The text bears witness to an architecturally developed water shrine ("five porticoes"). It also relates a legend that to gain healing one had to get into the pool "when the water is stirred up" by some spirit. But which spirit? Some manuscripts include the explanation that "an angel of the Lord went down at certain seasons into the pool and stirred up the water". The story goes that Jesus finds a man too ill to get into the water and cures him on his own. The author presumably knew some tradition about the site from Jerusalem sacred topography—one that continued into the fourth century, when it is one of many water shrines mentioned in the Bordeaux Itinerary

---

57 Rousselle 1990; Sauer 2011; Bassani, Bolder-Boos and Fusco 2019; Graf 2021.
58 Rousselle 1990, 73-75; Walsh 2019, 18-19, 64.
59 Rieger 2020, 359-62.
60 Pliny, *Ep.* 8.8.5, tr. Radice 1969, 2:24-25.
61 Rousselle 1990, 31-75; Sauer 2011.

and is still visited today.⁶² The value of this case is the Christian literary tradition's own ambiguity about what makes the pool sacred: an angel? A spirit? Jesus's visit? Simply the water? It is never settled.

As for practices at water shrines, even these ran the gamut. People came to springs for healing (and to purchase and deposit votive objects), for veneration of a spirit, for oracles and incubation, to leave coins and bowls, and even to deposit *defixiones*—binding tablets and assemblages—which might be addressed to specific local spirits or simply dropped in the water source as the appropriate place.⁶³ Such a range of practices, some oriented towards familiar Roman gods, even more to regional gods, and many inspired simply by the unique features of the spring, again underline the importance of the place itself.

The water-shrine also provides a third example of syncretism at shrines: first, because they constituted a common and vital type of regional holy destination throughout the pre-Roman, Roman, Christian and Muslim worlds, inspiring active and eclectic efforts at interpretation and in the formation of ritual customs; and second, because the ambiguity, the conflicts, the historical shifts and the selective relationship to prevailing religious systems all make the water-shrine a site of perpetual negotiation and claims-making. In this case, it is not syncretism as a process of integration, acculturation or Christianisation but syncretism as ongoing ambiguity and debate. It might "stand for" the resilience of the local landscape and its spirits, perhaps even defining a boundary beyond which the Christian pantheon does not govern; conversely, it might "stand for" the authority of a goddess, or Jesus's footprints, or the Virgin Mary herself. The conversations were never-ending in these respects. And the ritual devotions and offerings that people performed there, with figurines, food or coins, expressed their understanding of religious propriety.

General Conclusions

My emphasis on syncretism in the previous section, as an inevitable cultural effort to assimilate new practices and discourses through creative interpretation, has served to bring out the vital world around shrines—the goals of "pilgrimage". Through performances and conflicts, processions and private devotions, the mediation of specialists and the imitation of others' customs, the shrine becomes a microcosm of interactions between tradition and new religious ideologies, different sorts of authority, and a ritual landscape ever in transformation. It is this world that should be our focus when we discuss pilgrimage—or rather, shrine visitation—not the journey there.

In fact, as I have argued, the focus on the journey comes out of peculiar modern preoccupations and romantic ideals, in which Jerusalem, Mecca and Compostela have become not mythical lodestars, as in earlier times, but places to go to accentuate modern spirituality. This idealisation of the journey as a liminal process of self-transformation

---

62 *Itin. Burd.* 589-90; see Elsner 2000, 192.
63 Rousselle 1990, 77-107; Piranomonte 2010; Sauer 2011; Nutzman 2017; and the rich materials covered in Bassani, Bolder-Boos and Fusco 2019.

has, I have suggested, made liminality so rich a goal that it paradoxically relegates those truly in endless journey, refugees, to another domain entirely. "Journey", I have argued, is not a thing to highlight and romanticise. Too many people are still in passage, without any religious centres at the end nor homes to return to with sacred oil or water.

But to shift the focus to the shrine itself and what happens there does not require the elimination either of *communitas* as a social experience nor of individual agency—the sense of deliberative choice and creativity—in going to the shrine. It is only that we should consider the *communitas* as a function of activities *there*, not solidarity *en route*; and we should consider agency not in terms of quests for individual spirituality but rather as mediating social roles and responsibilities.

The reframing of the devotional self in the world of the shrine brings us back to the microcosm of religious action that the shrine embraces. As I have argued, this is where Christianity (or Buddhism or Islam, and so on) are assembled and tested as ideologies that bear on action, on the body and on the collective.[64] Visitors engage different experiences at festival times and in everyday times, at night or in the daytime, at the central temple or in the peripheral cluster of candles that have recently sprung up by an old tree. This is the life of syncretism: where (in the Symeon cult) the ancient pillar is drawn into Christianity through iconography and performance both, where (at Apa Mena) the ancient habitus of using figurines to communicate with spirits becomes a form of Christian practice, and where (in the water shrines) the topographical power of the spring invites all manner of practices, temples, ritual experts and expectations.

Bibliography

Abdulai, A.I., assisted by J. Chernoff. 1984. "The Pilgrimage to Mecca: An Excerpt from A Drummer's Testament." *The Chicago Review* 34.3, 68-93.

Ahmed, I. 2006. "The Destruction of the Holy Sites in Mecca and Medina." *The Islamic Monthly*, 1 January: https://www.theislamicmonthly.com/the-destruction-of-the-holy-sites-in-mecca-and-medina/ (accessed 1 July 2021).

Ahmed, S. 2016. *What is Islam? The Importance of Being Islamic*. Princeton: Princeton University Press.

Anonymous, 2006. "The House of Sayyida Khadija in Mecca." *Islamica* 15, 71-77.

Bangert, S. 2010. "The Archaeology of Pilgrimage: Abu Mena and Beyond," in D.M. Gwynn, S. Bangert and L. Lavan (eds.) *Religious Diversity in Late Antiquity*, 293-327. Leiden: Brill.

Bassani, M., M. Bolder-Boos, and U. Fusco (eds.) 2019. *Rethinking the Concept of "Healing Settlements": Water, Cults, Constructions and Contexts in the Ancient World*. Oxford: Archaeopress.

Bayer-Niemeier, E. 1988. *Bildwerke der Sammlung Kaufmann I: Griechisch-römische Terrakotten*. Melsungen: Bayer.

Betteridge, A.H. 1992. "Specialists in Miraculous Action: Some Shrines in Shiraz," in A. Morinis (ed.) *Sacred Journeys: The Anthropology of Pilgrimage*, 189-209. Westport, CT: Greenwood Press.

Boero, D. 2016. "Promoting a Cult Site Without Bodily Relics: Sacred Substances and Imagined Topography in The Syriac Life of Symeon the Stylite", in N.P. DesRosiers and L.C. Vuong (eds.) *Religious Competition in the Greco-Roman World*, 233-45. Atlanta: Society of Biblical Literature.

Boero, D. 2021. "Between Gift and Commodity: The Distribution of Tokens and Material Substances at the Pilgrimage Sites of Stylites", in S. Minov and F. Ruani (eds.) *Syriac Hagiography: Texts and Beyond*, 281-339. Leiden: Brill.

Bremmer, J. 2017. "Pilgrimage Process?", in T.M. Kristensen and W. Friese (eds.) *Excavating Pilgrimage: Archaeological Approaches to Sacred Travel and Movement in the Ancient World*, 275-84. London: Routledge.

Brown, P. 1971. "The Rise and Function of the Holy Man in Late Antiquity." *JRS* 61, 80-101.

---

64   Frankfurt 2010; 2017, chap. 4.

Brown, P. 1975. *The Making of Late Antiquity*. Cambridge, MA: Harvard University Press.

Cannuyer, C. 1997. "Saint Mina aux chameaux: autour des origines d'un iconotype copte." *Le Monde Copte* 27/28, 139-54.

Coleman, S. and J. Eade, 2004. "Introduction: Reframing Pilgrimage," in S. Coleman and J. Eade (eds.) *Reframing Pilgrimage: Cultures in Motion*, 1-26. London: Routledge.

Coleman, S. and J. Elsner, 1995. *Pilgrimage: Past and Present in World Religions*. Cambridge, MA: Harvard University Press.

Cuffel, A. 2005. "From Practice to Polemic: Shared Saints and Festivals as 'Women's Religion' in the Medieval Mediterranean." *Bulletin of the School of Oriental and African Studies* 68.3, 401-19.

Drescher, J. 1947. *Apa Mena: A Selection of Coptic Texts Relating to St. Menas*. Cairo: Société d'archéologie copte.

Drijvers, H.J.W. 1978. "Spätantike Parallelen zur altchristlichen Heiligenverehrung unter besonderer Berücksichtigung des syrischen Stylitenkultus." *Göttinger Orientforschungen*, Reihe Syriaca, 17, 77-113.

Eastmond, A. 1999. "Body vs. Column: The Cults of St. Symeon Stylites," in L. James (ed.) *Desire and Denial in Byzantium*, 87-100. Aldershot: Ashgate.

Eliade, M. 1959. *The Sacred and the Profane: The Nature of Religion*. San Diego: HBJ.

Elsner, J. 2000. "The *Itinerarium Burdigalense*: Politics and Salvation in the Geography of Constantine's Empire" *JRS* 90, 181-95.

Elsner, J. and I. Rutherford, 2005. "Introduction," in J. Elsner and I. Rutherford (eds.) *Pilgrimage in Graeco-Roman and Early Christian Antiquity: Seeing the Gods*, 1-38. Oxford: Oxford University Press.

Emirbayer, M. and A. Mische. 1998. "What is Agency?" *American Journal of Sociology* 103, 962-1023.

Falcasantos, R.S. 2017. "Wandering Wombs, Inspired Intellects: Christian Religious Travel in Late Antiquity." *JECS* 25.1: 89-117.

Fernandez, R. 1975. "Le culte et l'iconographie des stylites," in *Les stylites syriens*, 174-203. Milan: Studium Biblicum Franciscanum 16.

Frank, M. 2017. *Pilgrimage: Photographs by Mary Frank*. New York: Eakins Press.

Frankfurter, D. 1990. "Stylites and *Phallobatēs*: Pillar Religions in Late Antique Syria." *Vigiliae Christianae* 44, 168-98.

Frankfurter, D. 1998a. "Introduction: Approaches to Coptic Pilgrimage," in D. Frankfurter (ed.) *Pilgrimage and Holy Space in Late Antique Egypt*, 3-48. Leiden: Brill.

Frankfurter, D. 1998b. *Religion in Roman Egypt: Assimilation and Resistance*. Princeton: Princeton University Press.

Frankfurter, D. 2010. "Where the Spirits Dwell: Possession, Christianization, and Saint-Shrines in Late Antiquity." *HTR* 103.1, 27-46.

Frankfurter, D. 2012. "Comparison and the Study of Religions of Late Antiquity," in C. Calame and B. Lincoln (eds.) *Comparer en histoire des religions antiques: Controverses et propositions*, 83-98. Liège: Presses Universitaires de Liège.

Frankfurter, D. 2014. "Terracotta Figurines and Popular Religion in Late Antique Egypt: Issues of Continuity and 'Survival'," in G. Tallet and C. Zivie-Coche (eds.) *Le Myrte et la rose. Mélanges offerts à Françoise Dunand*, 129-41. Montpellier: Presses Universitaires de Montpellier.

Frankfurter, D. 2015a. "Jewish and Christian Pilgrimage," in C. Fluck *et al.* (eds.) *Egypt: Faith After the Pharaohs*, 132-37. London: British Museum.

Frankfurter, D. 2015b. "Female Figurines in Early Christian Egypt: Reconstructing Lost Practices and Meanings." *Material Religion* 11.2, 190-223.

Frankfurter, D. 2017. *Christianizing Egypt: Syncretism and Local Worlds in Late Antiquity*. Princeton: Princeton University Press.

Frankfurter, D 2010. "Where the Spirits Dwell: Possession, Christianization, and Saints' Shrines in Late Antiquity." *HTR* 103.1, 27-46.

Frankfurter, D. 2017. *Christianizing Egypt: Syncretism and Local Worlds in Late Antiquity*. Princeton: Princeton University Press.

Frey, N.L. 1988. *Pilgrim Stories: On and Off the Road to Santiago*. Berkeley: University of California Press.

Gemzoë, L. 2005. "The Feminization of Healing in Pilgrimage to Fátima," in J. Dubisch and M. Winkelmann (eds.) *Pilgrimage and Healing*, 25-48. Tucson, AZ: University of Arizona Press.

Gintsburg, S. 2018. "Identity, Place, Space, and Rhymes During a Pilgrimage to the Shrine of Moulay Abdessalam, Morocco." *Journal of Religion in Africa* 48, 204-30.

Graf, F. 2021. "Magic and the Baths: A View from Gadara." Unpublished paper, Tel Aviv webinar.

Grossmann, P. 1998. "The Pilgrimage Center of Abu Mina," in D. Frankfurter (ed.) *Pilgrimage and Holy Space in Late Antique Egypt*, 281-302. Leiden: Brill.

Harvey, S. 1988. "The Sense of a Stylite: Perspectives on Simeon the Elder." *VigChr* 42, 376-94.

Hunter-Crawley, H. 2017. "Movement as Sacred Mimesis at Abu Mena and Qal'at Sem'an," in T.M. Kristensen and W. Friese (eds.) *Excavating Pilgrimage: Archaeological Approaches to Sacred Travel and Movement in the Ancient World*, 187-202. London: Routledge.

Hunter-Crawley, H. 2020. "Divinity Refracted: Extended Agency and the Cult of Symeon Stylites the Elder," in V. Gasparini *et al.* (eds.) *Lived Religion in the Ancient Mediterranean World: Approaching Religious Transformations from Archaeology History and Classics*, 261-86. Berlin: De Gruyter.

Handley, M.A. 2017. "Scratching as Devotion: Graffiti, Pilgrimage and Liturgy in the Late Antique and Early Medieval West," in K. Bolle, C. Machado and C. Witschel (eds.) *The Epigraphic Cultures of Late Antiquity* 55-79. Stuttgart: Steiner Verlag.

Ivakhiv, A.J. 2001. *Claiming Sacred Ground: Pilgrims and Politics at Glastonbury and Sedona*. Bloomington: Indiana University Press.

Kaufmann, C.M. 1910. *Die Menasstadt und das Nationalheiligtum der altchristlichen Ägypter in der westalexandrinischen Wüste.* Leipzig: K.W. Hiersemann.

Kaufmann, C.M. 1918. *Die heilige Stadt der Wüste: unsere Entdeckungen Grabungen und Funde in der altchristlichen Menasstadt weiteren Kreisen in Wort und Bild geschildert.* Kempten: J. Kösel.

Kiss, Z. 1989. *Les ampoules de Saint Ménas découvertes à Kôm el-Dikka (1961-1981).* Warsaw: PWN.

Kowalzig, B. 2005. "Mapping out *Communitas*: Performances of *Theōria* in their Sacred and Political Context," in J. Elsner and I. Rutherford (eds.) *Pilgrimage in Graeco-Roman and Early Christian Antiquity*, 41-72. Oxford: Oxford University Press.

Kristensen, T.M. 2012. "Textiles, Tattoos, and the Representation of Pilgrimage in the Roman and Early Christian Periods." *HEROM* 1, 107-34.

Larsen, T. 2014. *The Slain God: Anthropologists and the Christian Faith*. Oxford: Oxford University Press.

Lassus, J. 1947. *Sanctuaires chrétiens de Syrie*. Paris: Guethner.

Luckhardt, C. 2020. *The Charisma of Distant Places Travel and Religion in the Early Middle Ages*. London: Routledge.

Malcolm X and A. Haley. 2015. *The Autobiography of Malcolm X*. New York: Ballantine Books.

Mernissi, F. 1977. "Women, Saints, and Sanctuaries." *Signs* 3.1, 101-12.

Murray, M. 2011. "Religion and the Nomadic Lifestyle: The Nabateans," in P.A. Harland (ed.) *Travel and Religion in Antiquity*, 215-34. Waterloo: Wilfred Laurier University Press.

Montserrat, D. 1998. "Pilgrimage to the Shrine of SS Cyrus and John at Menouthis in Late Antiquity," in D. Frankfurter (ed.) *Pilgrimage and Holy Space in Late Antique Egypt*, 257-80. Leiden: Brill.

Morinis, A. 1992. "Introduction," in A. Morinis (ed.) *Sacred Journeys: The Anthropology of Pilgrimage*, 1-28. Westport, CT: Greenwood.

Nock, A.D. 1972. "A Vision of Mandulis Aion", in Z. Stewart (ed.) *Essays on Religion and the Ancient World*, vol. 1, 356-400. Oxford: Clarendon.

Nutzman, M.S. 2017. "'In This Holy Place': Incubation at Hot Springs in Roman and Late Antique Palestine," in S. Blakely (ed.) *Gods, Objects, and Ritual Practice*, 281-304. Atlanta: Lockwood Press.

Parandowski, P. 1990. "Coptic Terra-Cotta Figurines from Kom El-Dikka," in W. Godlewski (ed.) *Coptic Studies: Acts of the Third International Congress of Coptic Studies, Warsaw, 20-25 August, 1984*, 303-7. Warsaw: PWN.

Petsalis-Diomidis, A. 2005. "The Body in Space: Visual Dynamics in Graeco-Roman Healing Pilgrimage," in J. Elsner and I. Rutherford (eds.) *Pilgrimage in Graeco-Roman and Early Christian Antiquity*, 183-218. Oxford: Oxford University Press.

Piranomonte, M. 2010. "Religion and Magic at Rome: The Fountain of Anna Perenna," in R.L. Gordon and F.M. Simón (eds.) *Magical Practice in the Latin West*, 191-213. Leiden: Brill.

Radice, B., trans. 1969. *Pliny: Letters Bks 8-10; Panegyricus*. Vol. 2. Cambridge: Harvard University Press.

Reader, I. 2007. "Pilgrimage Growth in the Modern World: Meanings and Implications." *Religion* 37.3, 210-29.

Rieger, A.-K. 2020. "'This God Is Your God, This God Is My God: Local Identities at Sacralized Places in Roman Syria," in V. Gasparini *et al.* (eds.) *Lived Religion in the Ancient Mediterranean World: Approaching Religious Transformations from Archaeology, History and Classics*, 351-83. Berlin: De Gruyter.

Rousselle, A. 1990. *Croire et guérir: la foi en Gaule dans l'Antiquité tardive*. Paris: Fayard.

Rutherford, I. 2005. "Down-Stream to the Cat-Goddess: Herodotus on Egyptian Pilgrimage," in J. Elsner and I. Rutherford (eds.) *Pilgrimage in Graeco-Roman and Early Christian Antiquity*, 131-50. Oxford: Oxford University Press.

Rutherford, I. 2020. "The Experince of Pilgrimage in the Roman Empire: Communitas, Paideia, and Piety-Signalling," in V. Gasparini *et al.* (eds.) *Lived Religion in the Ancient Mediterranean World: Approaching Religious Transformations from Archaeology, History and Classics*, 137-56. Berlin: De Gruyter.

Rüpke, J. 2015. "Religious Agency, Identity, and Communication: Reflections on History and Theory of Religion." *Religion* 45, 344-66.

Sallnow, M.J. 1987. *Pilgrims of the Andes: Regional Cults in Cusco*. Washington DC: Smithsonian Institution Press.

Sallnow, M.J. 1991. "Pilgrimage and Cultural Fracture in the Andes," in J. Eade and M.J. Sallnow (eds.) *Contesting the Sacred: The Anthropology of Christian Pilgrimage*, 137-53. London: Routledge.

Sauer, E.W. 2011. "Religious Rituals at Springs in the Late Antique and Early Medieval World," in L. Lavan and M. Mulryan (eds.) *The Archaeology of Late Antique "Paganism"*, 505-50. Leiden: Brill.

Schaap, R. 2017. "The Weird, Mystic Pull of Southwest England." *The New York Times*, 2 July: https://nyti.ms/2ubc03x (accessed 30 June 2021).

Schachner, L.A. 2010. "The Archaeology of the Stylite," in D.M. Gwynn, S. Bangert and L. Lavan (eds.) *Religious Diversity in Late Antiquity*, 329-97. Leiden: Brill.

Scriven, R. 2014. "Geographies of Pilgrimage: Meaningful Movements and Embodied Mobilities." *Geography Compass* 8 (4): 249-61.

Shahîd, I. 1998. "Arab Christian Pilgrimages in the Proto-Byzantine Period (V–VII Centuries)," in D. Frankfurter (ed.) *Pilgrimage and Holy Space in Late Antique Egypt*, 373-89. Leiden: Brill.

Sodini, J.-P. 2010. "Saint-Syméon: L'influence de Saint-Syméon dans le culte et l'économie de l'Antiochène," in J. de la Genière *et al.* (eds.) *Les sanctuaires et leur rayonnement dans le monde méditerranéen, de l'antiquité à l'époque moderne*, 295-322. Paris: Académie des inscriptions et belles lettres.

Sodini, J.-P. 2015. "Les stylites syriens (Ve–VIe siècles): Entre cultes locaux et pèlerinages 'internationaux'," in A. Vauchez (ed.) *Le pèlerinage de l'Antiquité à nos jours*, 1-23. Paris: CTHS.

Stafford, G. 2019. "Early Christian Female Pilgrimage to the Shrines of Saint Menas, Saint Simeon the Elder, and Saint Thecla." *Studies in Late Antiquity* 3.2, 251-93.

Stang, C.M. 2010. "Digging Holes and Building Pillars: Simeon Stylites and the "Geometry" of Ascetic Practice." *HTR* 103, 447-70.

Strayed, C. 2013. *Wild: From Lost to Found on the Pacific Crest Trail*. New York: Vintage.

Teeter, E. 2010. *Baked Clay Figurines and Votive Beds from Medinet Habu*. Chicago: Oriental Institute of the University of Chicago.

Theodoret of Cyrrhus. 1985. *History of the Monks of Syria*. Translated by R. M. Price. Kalamazoo MI: Cistercian Publications.

Theodoret of Cyrrhus. 2013. *History of the Monks of Syria*. Edited by P. Canivet and A. Leroy-Molinghen. Paris: Du Cerf.

Turner, V. 1973. "Center Out There: Pilgrim's Goal." *History of Religions* 12, 191-230.

Turner, V. 1974. *Dramas, Fields, and Metaphors: Symbolic Action in Human Society*. Ithaca: Cornell University Press.

Turner, V. and E. Turner. 1978. *Image and Pilgrimage in Christian Culture*. New York: Columbia.

Vikan, G. 2010. *Early Byzantine Pilgrimage Art*. Revised ed. Washington DC: Dumbarton Oaks.

Walsh, D. 2019. *The Cult of Mithras in Late Antiquity: Development, Decline and Demise, ca. A.D. 270-430*. Leiden: Brill.

Weingrod, A. 1990. *The Saint of Beersheba*. Albany: SUNY Press.

Wharton, A.J. 2006. *Selling Jerusalem: Relics, Replicas, Theme Parks*. Chicago: University of Chicago Press.

Yasin, A.M. 2009. *Saints and Church Spaces in the Late Antique Mediterranean: Architecture, Cult, and Community*. Cambridge: Cambridge University Press.

Yasin, A.M. 2012. "Sight Lines of Sanctity at Late Antique Martyria," in B.D. Wescoat and R.G. Ousterhout (eds.) *Architecture of the Sacred: Space, Ritual, and Experience from Classical Greece to Byzantium*, 248-80. Cambridge: Cambridge University Press.

Yasin, A.M. 2017. "The Pilgrim and the Arch: Paths and Passageways at Qal'at Sem'an, Sinai, Abu Mena, and Tebessa," in T.M. Kristensen and W. Friese (eds.) *Excavating Pilgrimage: Archaeological Approaches to Sacred Travel and Movement in the Ancient World*, 166-186. London: Routledge

3

THE USES OF COMPARISON IN PILGRIMAGE STUDIES*

IAN RUTHERFORD

Introduction

Comparison seems to be in fashion again. It was long rejected because it had been used by European intellectuals to create specious contrasts between Western civilisation and non-Western cultures;[1] or, by appealing to broad similarities between cultures, to support grand hypotheses of cultural and religious evolution.[2] More recently there have been attempts to rehabilitate it. Marcel Detienne and Geoffrey Lloyd have, in different ways, advocated its application in helping us understand cultures;[3] more recently, Lloyd, in collaboration with Renaud Gagné and Simon Goldhill, explored the idea of "comparatism", i.e. the tendency of cultures to show awareness of comparison;[4] Matei Candea has proposed a sophisticated model in which we distinguish "frontal comparison", i.e. comparison between the comparatist's society and another, and "lateral comparison", i.e. comparison of a number of societies.[5]

A useful typology of comparison has been proposed by André Gingrich. He distinguishes five types: binary (which would include Candea's frontal comparison); comparison including a cultural area; temporal comparison; distance comparison; and "time/

---

* *Thanks to participants and in particular to Nicholas Purcell.*

1 See Paden 2000, 182: "While comparativism in the study of religion for many has become associated with the sins of the discipline—colonialism, essentialism, theologism, and anti-contextualism—it simply remains that there is no study of religion without cross-cultural categories, analysis and perspective". See also Lowe and Schnegg 2020, 1; Urban 2000.

2 Thus, James Frazer, one of the great masters of the subject, used it to attribute the origins of Christianity to patterns of dying gods supposedly found in Near Eastern religions, which he interpreted as all being the same.

3 Detienne 2008. See also Lloyd and Sivin 2002, 8: "the chief prize is a way out of parochialism".

4 Lloyd 2019, 448: "while comparing is a first-order activity comparatism is a matter of reflecting on that".

5 So Candea 2019.

space" comparison.⁶ Any of these can be applied to Greco-Roman culture. We can do frontal comparison between our W.E.I.R.D. ("western, educated, industrialised, rich and democratic") culture and theirs; we can compare cultures from a given region (e.g. those of the Mediterranean and those of the ancient Near East); we can do temporal comparison (e.g. Classical Greece and Roman Greece); we can do distance comparison (e.g. warfare in a number of ancient cultures); or time/space or "fluid" comparison (which might involve comparing how a similar nexus of phenomena develops in different cultures at different times, e.g. the link between pilgrimage and tourism).

Another point to consider is that comparison may have different uses.

a. Comparison may enable us to map the occurrence of certain features, and thus to establish distinct cultural regions. It may also allow us to see differences between the phenomena in different cultures.
b. It may enable us to find patterns of correlation, e.g. between aspects of religions and types of underlying social structure. This sort of work could be used as the basis for speculation about cultural evolution.
c. It may be that, in some cases, comparison provides an insight into a phenomenon which is not available if we look at the culture on its own, or at least raises possibilities; and it may help guide our reconstructions. As A. D. Nock observed: "Analogies will not teach us what happens in the past; they may help us to keep our reconstruction within limits consistent with what is known to happen."⁷
d. Similarities between cultures, once established, can be used to argue for the diffusion of patterns ("memes") of religious activity. Such arguments are generally more successful if we have reason to think there is a historical connection between the cultures (so it works if we are studying a region).⁸
e. Finally, an additional benefit of comparing cultures is that learning about them may lead us to become familiar with the methodologies used by scholars who work on

---

6   Gingrich in Gingrich and Thelen 2012, 400. "On the operational level, we now basically are practicing at least five different practical sets of comparative techniques in anthropology. Two of them are more conventional and rather well established, namely binary comparison (contrasting 'this' against 'that' setting, or 'theirs' against 'ours') with its potential of bias and stereotyping, and regional comparison (*e.g.*, political systems in Africa south of the Sahara, or 'cattle for wives' in southern Africa) with its problematic side potential to construct 'cultural areas'. In addition, we also work with temporal comparison in historical anthropology, with 'distant comparison' (as in assessing, say, juvenile rituals in areas X, Y, and Z), and last but not least, with shifting time/space comparison: when Eric Wolf discussed the spread of mercantilism and capitalism out of a few centers throughout the globe, for instance, or when Arjun Appadurai pursues interconnections and connectivity along various transnational dimensions, they employ comparative methods across time and space. In a globalizing world, this is perhaps the 'growth sector' of comparative anthropology's future". This typology is followed by Lowe & Schnegg 2020, 10-12, who call time/space comparison "fluid".
7   From Nock 1944, 101 (reprinted in Nock 1972, 2.603). I cited this in Rutherford 2000, 133n.1.
8   See Malul 1990.

them, which we can then compare with our own, and perhaps apply to our own material. A well-known case of the application of an alien methodological paradigm to ancient Greek culture is that of initiation and rites of passage; in this case, the parallel of other, largely tribal, cultures encouraged scholars of ancient Greece to identify a whole range of initiation rituals hidden in myth.[9] The question remains: did widespread application of a model derived from anthropological investigation of tribal cultures mislead classicists, and make them see things in Greek cultures that were not really there? Or did it at least provide some insight?

On the face of it, pilgrimage seems a good topic for comparative study because it is known to be attested in different forms in so many cultures, both modern and ancient. At the outset we need to recognise that the scope of the term "pilgrimage" and of the implied category has seemed to some problematic. Should it be understood as covering any form of travel connected with religion and the gods, or only certain sorts? Some scholars prefer to see it as a narrow category, found in only a few religions, such as Christianity and Islam, and associated with a specific type of highly ritualised sacred journey undertaken as a religious obligation or as the result of a vow; for other religions, for example most of those of the ancient Mediterranean, they would use other terms such as sacred travel, cultic journeys or perhaps religious tourism. In the end, people have a right to use words however they like, and I am not sure that terminology makes much difference in a situation like this; but I follow the lead of other scholars, many of them historians of religion, who use pilgrimage as a general, global category, of which we gain a richer understanding by studying the forms it takes in different cultures.[10]

Pilgrimage was not much studied from a comparative perspective until recently; it does not seem to have been a topic that interested anthropologists in the 19th and 20th century.[11] The collection in the *Sources Orientales* series (Collectif 1960) provided surveys of a number of cultures, but virtually no synthesis (see pp. 9-10). Two important landmarks were the comprehensive comparative survey by Jean Chélini and Christian Branthomme (1987) and soon afterwards that of E. Alan Morinis in the introduction to his volume (1993). Morinis distinguished six types: devotional, aimed at honouring the divinity (e.g. Buddhist, Christian); instrumental (e.g. for healing); normative (relating to the life cycle or calendrical); obligatory (e.g. the Hajj); wandering (i.e. Basho); and

---

9   There has been a reaction against this: Dodd and Faraone 2004, but see now Bremmer 2021.
10 On the general issue, see Lloyd 2019.
11 See the chapter on pilgrimage in Bowie 2006. The comparative study of pilgrimage may start with Herodotus if, as I suspect, he compares pilgrimage in the Egyptian Delta to Greek pilgrimage. In the early modern period, the Peruvian oracle at Pachacamac was compared to Mecca or Delphi: see Bartoletti 2019, 336; and Mayan pilgrimage to the island of Cozumel was compared to pilgrimage to Jerusalem and Rome: see Patel 2009, 205; Tozzer 1941, 109-10. In the modern period, an early example of an anthropological analysis of pilgrimage is Hertz 1983/1913.

initiatory (which seems to overlap with the normative type).[12] He also distinguishes different types of pilgrimage in terms of formal and informal (p. 15), and sets out five perspectives or "planes": the ego plane, the cultural plane, the social plane, the physical plane and, summing up the rest, the meta plane. This last he sees as a matrix consisting of two conceptual poles that underlie the experience of pilgrimage in any particular culture: the familiar and the other, the known and the mysterious, the imperfect and the perfect (pp. 21-28).

Chélini and Branthomme included surveys of pilgrimage in many cultures, both ancient and modern, though they excluded Christianity. They sum up their views in the epilogue, which includes a weak typology ("the phases of pilgrimage": pp. 453-59), followed by "attempt to classify religious journeying" (pp. 462-66), and a conclusion entitled "a fundamental search for equilibrium and harmony" (pp. 466-68). The "attempt to classify religious journeying" contains the following headings (my numbers).

1. pilgrimage arising from nomadism;
2. pilgrimage arising from first installation in territory;
3. pilgrimage of strong cities and metropolises (covering the pilgrimages of kings);
4. pilgrimage of urban decentralisation;
5. pilgrimage of mythic renewal;
6. pilgrimage of the historical roots.

Not all of this is straightforward, but it is clearly meant to be partly evolutionary, following human development from the nomadic Palaeolithic (1, 2) to human settlements in the Neolithic and later (3, 4).[13] The types described under headings 5 and 6 are focused on the past, ritualising mythical or religious/historical origins. Some recent scholars have followed this approach to some extent, speculating on pilgrimage in the Palaeolithic or the Neolithic.[14]

---

12   Morinis 1993, 10-14. The last of these incorporates Victor Turner's theory that pilgrimage is initiatory, except that Turner had seen it as a defining feature of pilgrimage in general.
13   Their chronological chart on p. 471 goes back 6 million years, to the tertiary era (Pliocene). The volume includes an article on the Palaeolithic by Gabriel Camps (Camps 1987).
14   For pilgrimage and the Middle Palaeolithic, see Shaw et al. 2016, who suggested that a site on what is now the island of Jersey was a "persistent place" frequented by Neanderthals from 240,000 BCE until the point when it became cut off by water. Klaus Schmidt (2005) wondered whether something like pilgrimage or an amphictyony is presupposed by the apparently religious structures of Göbeklitepe dated to the tenth millennium BCE. At Gilat in Israel, evidence for a regional sanctuary has been uncovered from the fifth-fourth millennia BCE: see Aron and Levy 1989. At Tell Brak it has been suggested for the fourth millennium on the basis of eye-idols: see Mallowan.1969. Colin Renfrew (see Renfrew, Boyd and Ramsey 2012) has examined the Aegean island of Keros east of Naxos, where a hoard of broken figurines has been discovered dating from the third millennium BCE, and he has suggested that this be seen as an early Aegean sanctuary, though he is not sure about the word pilgrimage.

Illuminating as it is, this typology is seriously incomplete, above all because it leaves out the role of pilgrimage in community-building, surely one of the most important aspects in its early development. They associate the development of popular pilgrimage in Egypt in the New Kingdom with their heading 4 ("*Le pélerinage populaire était né en Égypte*", p. 464), which implies that they do not see it as significant earlier on.[15] It may be noted that their general bibliography (pp. 495-96) omits Victor and Edith Turner's works, though that may be because their work on pilgrimage was concerned with Christianity, which was excluded from the book.

In this chapter I approach the subject by identifying at three key topics or "perspectives".

Perspective 1: Global Insights

For students of ancient Mediterranean pilgrimage, awareness of pilgrimage traditions in a broad range of world cultures is valuable mainly for two related reasons, listed above. First, because knowledge of other cultures, even very distant ones, may help us understand and identify practices in ones closer to home (point c above); and secondly because the writings of modern scholars, through which we necessarily access unfamiliar evidence, may also provide useful theoretical models (point e above). It should be noted that the historical period of these pilgrimage traditions doesn't make much difference, though most of them will be relatively modern, because those are the ones we have evidence for.

As far as the first of these is concerned, the huge range of pilgrimage traditions in the world is itself a problem. A great variety of practices is attested, and sometimes pointing out parallels seems almost pointless, because some things seem to be bound to happen. For example, in many cultures, prominent natural features are destinations for pilgrims: mountains, rivers, islands, caves. And it is very common for the destination to be a place where there was supposed to have been an epiphany of a deity, or for there to be myths corresponding to the journey. The same could be said for obvious purposes of pilgrimage, such as healing or consulting an oracle. It is no surprise that pilgrims dress in an unusual, ritualised way, or that they sing along the journey, or that the final stretch of the journey is particularly sacred.

But other things are more significant. It is useful to know that the language of pilgrimage is sometimes conceived in terms of vision, because that helps to explain why Greek pilgrims are called "observers";[16] or that a pilgrimage can take people back to a point they believed they had emigrated from;[17] or that pilgrimage can be a "rite of

---

15   Contrast the view of Joy McCorriston (discussed later) that pilgrimage is all about community building; and see Rutherford 2019 on pilgrimage and communication in early societies.
16   For vision in the Greek tradition, see Rutherford 2000; for India, see Eck 1985; for Egypt, see Volokhine 1998, 61, along with van der Plas 1989.
17   In Greece, the pilgrimage made by the Aenianes in Thessaly to Cassope in Epirus, described by Plutarch, *Qu.Gr.*26, who explains it as a re-enactment of the wanderings of the Aenianes, who had started off in the West. On the Huichol Indians of north-central Mexico, who journey a

passage" for young people;[18] or that pilgrimage can be associated with death[19] (all of which are sometimes found in Greece).

Modern pilgrimage traditions, where scholars can observe the movements of people, may also give us clues about the geography of pilgrimage – the "catchment areas" comprising the towns from where the pilgrims come. Hindu pilgrimage in India is a particularly rich resource in this respect.[20] Perhaps the most important single insight is that, in many modern traditions, pilgrimage can be a symbol of national or ethnic identity (Victor and Edith Turner called it "mystical nationalism"), which is one of the main functions of *polis-theoria* to national sanctuaries in the ancient Greek tradition.[21]

As I suggested earlier, comparison of the approaches and theoretical models used by modern scholars working on different traditions may also provide insights. A good example of this comes again from Victor Turner, who proposed that pilgrimage should in some cases be understood as a social process enacting intense and transformational "*communitas*", a model developed on the basis of observing Christian pilgrimage in modern Mexico. This provides a useful perspective for understanding some ancient Mediterranean traditions (e.g. Greek and Judaic), though it is far from being universally applicable.[22] Another recent idea is that pilgrimage is a form of communication: this has been discussed with relation to Western Africa in the context of the Hajj and for India in the period of the British Raj; elsewhere I have argued that it provides helpful insights into how pilgrimage might have been in the ancient world.[23]

Cognitive science, which has been applied to religion with varying degrees of success, may also shed light on pilgrimage.[24] One model that has been widely applied in anthropology and cognitive science is that of "signalling" or "costly signalling", a concept originally from evolutionary biology. The idea here is a simple one: people or animals use signals to impress other people or animals; the signal thus becomes something of supreme importance in which a great deal of energy is invested, and in extreme cases signals can give a misleading impression about the agent's abilities. Scholars have also applied it to religion, seeing it as a system of symbolic actions intended to convince

---

    long distance to reach the high desert called Wirikuta, the abode of their mythical ancestors: see Myerhoff 1978; for background, see Helms 1988, 47.

18   For Greece, see Rutherford 2005c; 2013, 172-73. There is an initiatory pilgrimage at Sabarimala in Kerala in honour of the deity Ayappan, for which see Younger 2002, Osella and Osella 2003.

19   For death and Tibetan pilgrimage, see Nordin 2009; in general, Turner 1977, 25.

20   A good study is Bhardwaj 1973.

21   Ethnic examples: Ireland: Shovlin 1991; Taiwan: Sangren 1987; Mexico, the Virgin of Guadelupe: Turner and Turner 1978; Poland, the Black Madonna of Częstochowa: Turner and Turner 1978. For Greece, see Rutherford 2013, 264-71; India, Benares: Eck 1982, 38-39. Bhardwaj 1973, 43-57. Sax 2000.

22   Turner 1974 (an adapted version of Turner 1972).

23   Thayer 1992, 185: "the hajj in the context of West African Islam can be seen as a vehicle for the diffusion of religious and cultural concepts and practices"; Maclean 2008; Rutherford 2017b.

24   See, for example, Vial 2004, 159, who suggests that Medieval pilgrimage can be seen as an example of Harvey Whitehouse's "imagistic" mode of religiosity.

other people of the signaller's virtues.[25] It is a good fit for pilgrimage as well: John Kantner and Kevin Vaughn have applied this to two sites from the Americas: first, Chaco Canyon in New Mexico, where there is extensive evidence for ceremonial activity in the period 800-1100 AD, indicating that it was a global centre visited by people as far away as Mesoamerica. The other site is in southern Peru, Cahuachi, which belongs to the Nazca culture, a major centre in the first five centuries AD.[26] For Kantner and Vaughn, going on a pilgrimage would have involved costly signalling,[27] but the pilgrimage centres themselves were created as costly signals to the region by the leaders who controlled them. It is easy to see how this could illuminate pilgrimage in ancient Greece, which often involved putting on a grand procession of choral performance at a national sanctuary, such as Delphi or Delos.[28]

Perspective 2: Regional Similarities and the Ancient Near East

The second comparative approach for the student of ancient Mediterranean pilgrimage is to examine other pilgrimage traditions in the general region and in the same general period. To this end I propose to look at pilgrimage in the Ancient Near East (Mesopotamia, Anatolia and Egypt). Plenty of pilgrimage is attested in this region, though it is mostly earlier, some of it dating back as far as the late third millennium BC. It has been little studied, though that is beginning to change.

Ancient Egypt

It is clear that there was pilgrimage in Egypt in the time of Herodotus (2.59), who describes the orgiastic pilgrimage of 700,000 worshippers to the festival of the goddess Bastet at Bubastis in the Eastern Delta. Pilgrimage continued in the Hellenistic and Roman periods; the main source of evidence is the large quantity of graffiti, mostly in Greek, from a number of temples.[29]

In the Pharaonic period we have records of high-ranking individuals (officials, scribes; not members of the royal family) visiting Egyptian temples. We also have records of divine journeys, such as the Festival of the Beautiful Reunion, where the statue of Hathor was carried by boat south to the temple of Horus at Edfu. How much of that

---

25 See Iannacone 1992a and 1992b.
26 Kantner and Vaughn 2012; on Chaco Canyon, however, see Plog and Watson 2012.
27 Kantner and Vaughn 2012, 69: "Pilgrims incur costs in time and resources both in the physical act of traveling from home community to pilgrimage center, while additional costs are often incurred in the ritual and/or service obligations that occur at the center … For example, a pilgrim might be expected to bring gifts to the pilgrimage destination or contribute labor once there; certainly votive deposits are well-known features of most pilgrimage centers."
28 See Rutherford 2013, 239-41.
29 For Egyptian pilgrimage, we have overviews by Jean Yoyotte in the *Sources Orientales* volume (Collectif 1960) and by Youri Volokhine (1998). For Bubastis, see Rutherford 2005b; for the orgiastic side of festivals of Bastet, see Jasnow and Smith 2010/11, 49 with P.Carlsberg 49, for which see Hoffmann and Quack 2018, 342-48.

should be thought of as pilgrimage has been debated; but there is tentative agreement that "pilgrims" may be an appropriate term for visitors to three sites on the West Bank of the Nile (which was associated with the dead):[30] the pyramid of the Old Kingdom pharaoh Sahure at Abusir north of Memphis, which seems to have become a centre for religious activity in the New Kingdom; the Great Sphinx at Giza, probably originally conceived as a representation of the pharaoh Khafre/Chephren (mid-third millennium BCE), which was reinterpreted as a form of the deity Horus in the New Kingdom (later second millennium BCE); and Deir el-Bahari near Thebes in Southern Egypt, where a cult of the goddess Hathor developed on the site of the mortuary temple of a pharaoh; pilgrimage may have been connected to the *Beautiful Festival of the Valley* when images of Amun, Mut and Khonsu were brought from Karnak on the East side of the Nile to visit royal tombs on the West side.

At these sites, the distance travelled was often no more than a few miles, but some visitors probably came from further afield.[31] And while most of the evidence—graffiti and ostraca—concerns individuals, it seems likely that in some cases the context was collective celebration.[32]

The most famous pilgrimage destination in Egypt is probably Abydos, a centre for the cult of Osiris, whose head was said to be buried there. This had a major role in Egyptian beliefs about the afterlife: in Egyptian funerary literature, the dead often express the desire to visit Abydos, and many people were in fact buried there. People visited Abydos while they were still alive as well, and some of these should probably be considered pilgrims.[33]

How does ancient Egyptian pilgrimage compare with Greek? One obvious difference is that Egypt has fewer signs of mass pilgrimage, though there are some (as Chélini and Branthomme correctly observed). There is not much evidence for healing pilgrimage either, though there seems to have been some in the Greco-Roman period.[34] There is also one striking similarity: the most celebrated Egyptian pilgrimage was to honour a god concerned with the afterlife, which bears a general similarity to the Greek pilgrimage to the Mysteries at Eleusis, the aim of which was to secure a blessed existence in the afterlife. We could perhaps approach this as a sort of "time/space" comparison, two complex phenomena that have developed in the same way over time. But are the Abydos-pilgrimage and the Eleusis-pilgrimage wholly independent phenomena, or could there be a connection between them (presumably diffusion from Egypt to Greece, direct or

---

30 For these, see Volokhine 1998, 78-82; Yoyotte 1960, 49-51.
31 See Sabek 2016, 44-45; for a case of someone visiting Deir el-Bahari from beyond Thebes, see p. 104.
32 For Deir-el-Bahari, see the Hieratic graffiti in Sabek 2016, which mention dancing and sex. For Abusir, see Navratilova 2016, 11.
33 Volokhine 1998, 71-76; Rutherford 2003. For pilgrims in the early second millennium BCE, see Lichtheim 1988, 101-28, *e.g.* Ankhu (no. 43). For the idea of visiting Abydos in the afterlife, see the Egyptian *Book of Traversing Eternity*, text 21, in Smith 2009, 407-9.
34 Volokhine 1998, 88-90.

indirect)? It is hard to say. In many cultures, pilgrimage is associated with death. On the other hand, it has been argued since Herodotus that aspects of Greek beliefs about the afterlife may have been influenced by Osirian religion.[35] Another factor worth considering is that the sanctuary at Eleusis underwent expansion in the sixth century BCE, a period of close contact between Greece and Egypt, when Greeks and other Aegean peoples are known to have visited Abydos.[36] If Eleusinian religion owes something to the Egyptian idea of the blessed afterlife, is it possible that the idea of pilgrimage has come from there as well?

The Ancient Near East

In the Ancient Near East, the most commonly attested form of pilgrimage is pilgrimage by kings and members of the royal family (which could be seen as a form of signalling).[37] A second key form is the so-called "divine journey" in which the gods are represented as leaving one temple to visit another. Royal pilgrimage is now attested as early as the mid third-millennium in Ebla and Lagash.[38] In the 18th century BCE, the king of Mari makes cultic journeys of various lengths, including one to the Mediterranean. It has been doubted whether these are pilgrimages, but some of them surely are.[39] Hittite kings make journeys as well, particularly one to the Northern cult centre of Nerik, and they are now known to have stopped at various places on the way.[40] One function of royal pilgrimage is to mark out territory. For example, in Lagash, several multi-day cultic

---

35   Burkert 2004, 88. Egyptian influence on Eleusis was argued by Foucart 1895; against: Cosmopoulos 2015, 155-57.

36   Expansion of Eleusis: Sourvinou-Inwood 1997. Herodotus was so impressed by Egyptian religion that he inferred that the Greeks had borrowed their own religion from there, including "festivals, processions and approaches (*prosagōgai*)" (*Hist.*2.58).

37   See Bottéro 1987; Lebrun 1987; Rutherford 2022. The editors of *Sources Orientales*, p. 8, do not think there was any pilgrimage in the ancient Near East.

38   Ebla: Ristvet 2015, 40-91; Archi 2013. Lagash: Rey 2016. On Ebla, see Ristvet 2015, 36, "The kingdom's coronation ritual ... illustrates the dynamic relationship among pilgrimage, territorial definition, and political power. In order to ascend Ebla's throne, the king, queen and their divine counterparts undertook a pilgrimage around the kingdom, ending with a long ceremony at the royal mausoleum, in which they were remade in the image of their ancestors ..."

39   Pappi 2012, 583 argues against the notion of pilgrimage, using the definition of Hassauer 2007: "A pilgrimage, in a narrow sense, besides a religious destination or a cultic aim, involves a widespread participation of people and is at times determined by occasions within the cultic calendar. Moreover, according to current definitions of pilgrimages, the physical journey should both have a symbolic character and include metaphorical resonance on different levels, such as a rite of passage involving spiritual transformations. Though this is not the place to expand on these points, we can provisionally state that the association of both components with the journeys of Zimrī-Līm has yet to be persuasively argued."

40   Corti 2018 on KBo 23.89. The "Festival of the Road": p. 54: "Taking together all of the information provided by the texts treated here, it is possible to reconstruct the probable stages of the king's pilgrimage to Nerik: Tahurpa → Hanhana → Hattina → Zikmar/Hapatha → [Kaštama/Hakpiš(?) →] Taštarišša → Zinishapa → Nerik."

journeys can be distinguished starting from the town of Girsu, including one that went west to Lagash and Nigin, home of the goddess Nanshe, whereas to the east there was another route that led to the contested area between Girsu and Umma.[41] To a Hellenist, these resemble the religio-political geography of a Greek city state, where visits to sanctuaries in the countryside were a way for cities to assert their claim to their territory.

Divine journeys are attested in literary texts, and also indirectly in economic texts. The destination is usually the sacred cities of Nippur or Eridu. Way-stations are often mentioned, i.e. the journey is ritualised. The texts do not refer to people making the journey with the gods, but they may well have done–in which case we could see the texts as "proxy data" for pilgrimage. Klaus Wagensonner has observed that when the goddess Nin-isina(k) sets out from Isin to Nippur, the celebration in Isin before she leaves resembles a Christian pilgrimage.[42]

Two common forms of pilgrimage seem to be almost unattested (as in the case of Egypt): firstly, there is almost no evidence for healing pilgrimage, although it would not be surprising if pilgrims visited the great goddess of healing Gula at Isin.[43] The second form is communal pilgrimage to a common religious centre. There is no evidence for this in Southern Mesopotamia, although one may suspect it happened to Nippur at least, if people followed the gods as they travelled.[44] Things look different in Northern Mesopotamia and Syria, however. Here there seem to have been two common sanctuaries, Terqa and Tuttul, the "Holy Cities" of the god Dagan– Terqa in the orbit of Mari, Tuttul in that of Emar to the west. Both of these served as common sanctuaries for many kingdoms in the region. Jean-Marie Durand has called these "villes de pèlerinage".[45] In

---

41 Rey 2016.
42 Wagensonner 2005, 159. For divine journeys as pilgrimages, see also Bottéro 1987, 53; Feuerherm 2011; Wagensonner 2007.
43 Healing pilgrimage: the goddess Nin-isina of Isin, identified with Gula/Ninkarrak was an important healing goddess (Bock 2013; Charpin 2017, 31-39). According to one Akkadian text (George 1993, 63-75; Streck 2015; Avalos 1995, 212-16), Ninurta-paqidat of Nippur was bitten by a dog and went to Isin, the city of the Lady of Health, to be healed; Amel-Baba of Isin, the high priest of Gula, saw him, recited an incantation for him and healed him. Spycket 1990 identified votive models of parts at Isin, which are found in the context of pilgrimage in other cultures; see also Charpin 2017, 34-39. Indirect evidence from the 3rd millennium BCE: Tsouparopoulou 2020. On balance, this does suggest the practice of healing pilgrimage, and not just for dog bites. The god Itūr-Mēr is supposed to have performed a healing function at Mari: Nakata 2011; Durand 2008, 193, 631.
44 That Nippur was a centre for mass pilgrimage was suggested by Hilprecht 1904, 40: "Apparently the large mass of pilgrims, having no access to the holy of holies of the temple, was permitted in this court, where at certain times of the year they assembled from all parts of the country, after the fashion of the Mecca pilgrims, in order to lay down their offerings and to perform their prayers at the most renowned sanctuary of Babylonia." See also Gibson 1993, 4: "As is the case with the world's other holy cities, such as Jerusalem, Mecca, and Rome, Nippur was a vibrant economic center. Besides the economic benefits derived from gifts and on-going maintenance presented by kings and rich individuals, there was probably a continuing income from pilgrims."
45 Durand 2008, 370.

the 18th century BCE. Bunama-Addu of Zalmaqum (in the region of Harran) asked permission to sacrifice at Tuttul; he was told he could not do so unless he brought fewer than 20 men.[46] Terqa (a "centre for pilgrimage and a religious reference point for the people of a much wider geographical area"[47]) was visited by Zimri-Lim, king of Mari (18th century BCE), by other Mariote officials,[48] and by other kings and tribal leaders, of whom the authorities are suspicious. One document reveals that a king wanted to visit but was asked to postpone for three days and come at night because of the volume of the sacrifices going on there.[49]

Most interestingly, a letter from an official called Sammetar[50] reports the case of Yagih-Addu who wanted to sacrifice at Terqa but was prevented from doing so; he complains:

> "Before when we resided at Terqa, we declared "Terqa is free (waššur) for Dagan". Before, the Subareans and the people of Hahhum guarded the front of the Great Gate. Now, it's the people of Larsa who do it. What access could I have?"

The expression "is free for Dagan" is worthy of note.[51] It calls to mind religious practice in ancient Greece, where some sanctuaries are owned by one city, others are shared ("common", *koina*), and problems can arise when access to a common sanctuary is blocked to one group. For example, the Macedonian queen Olympias is said to have blocked access to the sanctuary of Zeus and Dione to Athens in 331 BCE.[52] Two "pilgrimage towns" seem unique in the record, but it should be remembered that we know about them only because so much administrative correspondence from Mari and its region has survived. There must have been many more Terqas and Tuttuls.

Perspective 3: Difference and Cultural Mapping

In the introduction I suggested that two uses of comparison were mapping differences and establishing correlations between phenomena and types of underlying conditions. On the basis of what we have seen so far, pilgrimage in ancient Greece has some points of similarity to pilgrimage in ancient Near East and Egypt, but the differences are greater. In particular, in the ancient Near East, the most conspicuous pilgrims are kings, and common sanctuaries seem to be less in evidence. In Greece the focus is on common

---

46 ARM26/1 246:81-82; Feliu 2003, 83.
47 Feliu 2003, 303.
48 Terqa as regional centre discussed by Charpin and Ziegler 2003, 178-79. On pilgrimage there, see Durand 2008, 366-74.
49 See Feliu 2003 102-3; Durand 2008, 2.1, 305ff, 371 (A3019): "Daddi-Hadun wrote to me saying: 'I want to sacrifice to Dagan' and I replied by way of a pretext saying: saying: 'The sacrifices offered by the people of the country are immense; come back in three days and sacrifice at night …'".
50 Durand 2008, 1. 367 (A2552).
51 On the term, see CAD s. *ussuru* 2c, 315.
52 Hyperides 4.24-25; Rutherford 2013, 119. Common sanctuaries: cf. the dispute between Hierapytna and Itanos over the sanctuary of Zeus Diktaios in 140 BCE: Chaniotis 1988, 26-28.

sanctuaries, and the agents we hear most about are city-states sending delegates (*theoroi*) on their behalf. This picture seems to reflect the underlying political structures: in Bronze Age Southern Mesopotamia, monarchy, and in Iron Age Greece, the city-state.

The Greek system of *polis-theoroi* is hard to parallel in other cultures. In Hittite Anatolia, we know that towns sometimes sent delegations to major festivals, and this must have happened elsewhere, even if it was not recorded.[53] In the Assyrian Empire (which influenced Greece in other ways), delegates known as *ṣerani* (from singular *ṣeru*) carried tribute from the provinces; we do not hear of them attending festivals, though they were feasted together.[54] If we consider world pilgrimage traditions, there are certainly parallels, as we have seen, for pilgrimage as a symbol of "mystical nationalism"; there are also many cases where villages and towns send delegations: in previous work I have pointed to an example from the Andes.[55] In Taiwan, towns send delegations to the festival of the goddess Ma Tsu.[56] In India, pilgrimage-delegations ("*dandis*") may comprise people from the same village.[57] A full survey of these would be a desideratum. I do not know any precise parallel to the intricate institutional logistics of Greek *theoria*, though.[58]

On the question of correlation between pilgrimage and political structure, an important recent contribution has been made by Joy McCorriston,[59] who associates pilgrimage with pastoral societies like Southern Arabia, where it is a key mode of communication, and argues that it is absent in the sedentary, urban societies of Mesopotamia.[60] For her, ancient Mesopotamia and Southern Arabia thus constitute alternative "ethnoepochs" with different "meta-structures", the former "Household" and the latter "Pilgrimage". To make this contrast work, she uses a rather narrow definition of pilgrimage, in which the essential feature is the meeting together at a common sacred place of different groups who are not otherwise in contact and who on these occasions sacrifice together.[61]

---

53   Rutherford 2020, 243-44.
54   5000 of them attended the inauguration of a new palace and temple at Kalhu (Nimrud) under Assurnasirpal II in 879 BCE. They had audiences with the king (like *theoroi* to the Alexandrian Ptolemaia); see Postgate 1974, 123-28; Wiseman 1982, 315-16; and now the comprehensive overview of Dubovský 2023.
55   Sallnow 1987; see Rutherford 2004.
56   Sangren 1987, 1993.
57   Stanley 1992, 72-73; cf. also for China: Schipper 1960, 317-18.
58   For thoughts on such groups in China, see Naquin and Yü 1992, 27-28.
59   McCorriston 2017.
60   "Assyrian cultic practices stemmed from a Mesopotamian tradition lacking pilgrimage. Although there were ceremonial journeys by elites and cultic images from one city to the next and from one god's house to the next, these visits referenced hospitality and diplomatic alliances. They did not serve as general gatherings, sacrifices, and feasts to bind wider social identities. Fundamentally Mesopotamian religion was based on the concept of the household, and the house of the god served as a metaphor for social cohesion" (McCorriston 2017, 20; see also McCorriston 2011, 158; and Faist 2006, 158 on Assur).
61   It is interesting that a similar contrast has been made between Mesopotamia and pastoral groups with respect to animal sacrifice, which is seen as something that characterises the former, whereas in Mesopotamian societies animals are used to feed the gods but not for communal sacrifice

McCorriston may well be right to see a certain type of pilgrimage as characterising pastoral Arabia, but I am less convinced by the claim that sedentary societies lack any kind of pilgrimage. For one thing, it would be difficult to reconcile that hypothesis with the modern world, where we have an apparently sedentary society, but apparently rich and multifarious traditions of pilgrimage. In fact, this probably comes down to a matter of definition: if pilgrimage involves different groups meeting at a common sanctuary, there is certainly less of it attested in Mesopotamia, though the common sanctuaries mentioned in the Mari texts might still qualify (I suppose McCorriston might argue that the people mentioned in the Mari texts are Amorite pastoralists, and so close to Arabian nomads). But in fact, there is no reason to limit it in this way.

The idea that different types of pilgrimage can be correlated with different types of society seems worth developing, though. The following types suggest themselves:

i. Societies comprising a number of roughly equal groups or settlements share a common religious centre, where meetings may also serve other purposes, such as politics or trade. The pilgrimage may bring about social integration, establishing an "imagined community".[62] McCorriston's pastoralists belong there, but also Greek city-states sending delegates to Delphi or other panhellenic centres (where they "sacrificed together"), or indeed any amphictyonic structure where a sanctuary is controlled by a number of states. In this type, the centre may be chosen because it is in a central location which isn't particularly identified with any one group (*e.g.* Delphi). It is even possible that a pilgrimage centre served as common ground for pastoralists and a sedentary population, as has been argued for the sanctuary of Baal-Shamin at Si' in southern Syria (ancient North Arabia).[63]

ii. Pilgrimage may be a symbol or *signal* of elite power. Here belong the royal pilgrimages we observed in Mesopotamia and Hittite Anatolia; there are also traces of this in Aegean traditions (e.g. Minos and the Idaean Cave),[64] and in the Hellenistic and Roman periods as well: Alexander the Great's pilgrimage to Ammon, and those made by Roman emperors and members of the imperial family; royal pilgrimage is also known in Chinese tradition.[65] But elite or state control of pilgrimage is a much broader phenomenon than this, and examples are found in many traditions, such as Athenian control of the pilgrimage centre of Delos in the 5th century BCE or

(Abusch 2002). Note also that McCorriston's vision of pilgrimage stands directly opposed to that of Chélini and Branthomme, who, as we saw, seem to neglect the communal element.

62 See Malville and Malville 2001, for a discussion of this à propos of Chaco Canyon in New Mexico. It has even been suggested that states may have arisen from pilgrimage networks: see Yoffee 2014, 91, and Algaze 2008, 115, who attributes the idea to Adams 1966 (cf. 132).

63 See most recently Munt 2016, 24 with references.

64 Plato, *Lg.* 624b, Ps.Plato *Minos* 319b–320b. In fact, Minoan pilgrimage could have been collective: see Watrous 2004, 274.

65 Naquin and Yu 1992, 13-14, 17: *ch'ao sh-shan*; royal-progression (*hsun-hsing*); Schipper 1960, 311-15.

Inca control of the Islands of the Sun and the Moon in Lake Titicaca in the 15th century CE.[66]

iii. Once states are established, there is also the possibility that pilgrimage develops as a form of resistance to it, offering an alternative "counterhegemonic" form of social organisation. This seems to have been what Turner envisaged with his idea of *communitas*. This is hard to prove in the ancient world, but there may be some cases. For example, in the 3rd and 4th centuries CE, part of the Memnonium at Abydos was reconfigured as an oracle of Bes, attracting consultants from throughout the eastern Mediterranean; the imperial authorities seem to have decided that this was a threat, and tried to shut it down.[67]

These three types where the underlying motivation seems to be political surely can't be the whole story, and it seem sensible to posit other forms in which the religious prestige of the pilgrimage centre is the critical factor. Examples here from the Greek world might be pilgrimage to the Eleusinian Mysteries or to regional healing sanctuaries of Asclepius, or to transnational centres known for their magical or oracular power—such as Ephesian Artemis and Apollo of Claros. However, we cannot exclude the possibility that politics was a factor for some of these as well: pilgrimage to Eleusis, for example, took place under the patronage of the Athenian state, which retained considerable cultural power even after it lost its empire. And more generally, any occasion when people from different geographical regions regularly meet together to perform rituals is bound to trigger questions about who belongs to the group and who is considered outside it. In the end, it may be that politics-free pilgrimage was surprisingly rare.

Bibliography

Abusch, T. 2002. "Sacrifice in Mesopotamia," in Baumgarten 2002, 39-48.
Adams, R.M. *The Evolution of Urban Society. Early Mesopotamia and Prehispanic Mexico*. Chicago: Aldine.
Alcock, S.E. 1997. *The Early Roman Empire in the East*. Oxford: Oxbow.
Algaze, G. *Ancient Mesopotamia at the Dawn of Civilisation. The Evolution of an Urban Landscape*. Chicago: University of Chicago Press.
Alon, D. and T.E. Levy. 1989. "The Archaeology of Cult and Chalcolithic Sanctuary at Gilat." *Journal of Mediterranean Archaeology* 2, 163-221.
Archi, A. 2002. "Šeš-II-ib: A Religious Confraternity." *Eblaitica* IV, 23-55.
Archi, A. 2013. "Ritualization at Ebla." *Journal of Ancient Near Eastern Religion* 13, 212-37.
Avalos, H. 1995. *Illness and Health Care in the Ancient Near East: The Role of the Temple in Mesopotamia, Greece and Israel*. Atlanta: Scholars Press.
Babcock, B. A. (ed.) 1978. *The Reversible World*. Ithaca, NY: Cornell University Press.
Bartoletti, T. 2019. "Greek Divination from an Amerindian Perspective. Reconsidering 'Nature' in Mantike." *HAU: Journal of Ethnographic Theory* 9, 334-58.

---

66 Bauer and Stanish 2001, 18-19; see Eade and Sallnow 1991, 3-4.
67 Abydos: Effland 2014. Other cases: Lightfoot 2005, 348; Elsner 1997; see Eade and Sallnow 1991, 4-5; Bauer and Stanish 2001, 20-21. For a similar interpretation of a Mayan pilgrimage to the island of Cozumel, see Patel 2009.

Bauer, B.S. and C. Stanish. 2001. *Ritual and Pilgrimage in the Ancient Andres. The Islands of the Sun and the Moon.* Austin. University of Texas Press.

Baumgarten, A.I. (ed.) 2002. *Sacrifice in Religious Experience.* Leiden: Brill.

Bhardwaj, S.M. 1973. *Hindu Places of Pilgrimage in India (A Study in Cultural Geography).* Berkeley, CA: University of California Press.

Bottéro, J. 1987. "Processions et pèlerinages en Mésopotamie ancienne," in Chélini and Branthomme 1987, 45-53.

Bowie, F. 2006. *The Anthropology of Religion: An Introduction.* Second edition. Oxford: Blackwell.

Bremmer, J.N. 2021. *Becoming a Man in Ancient Greece and Rome: Essays on Myths and Rituals of Initiation.* Tübingen.

Bumbaugh, S. 2011. "Meroitic Worship of Isis at Philae," in Exell 2011, 66-69.

Burkert, W. 2004. *Babylon, Memphis, Persepolis: Eastern Contexts of Greek Culture.* Cambridge, MA: Harvard University Press

Camps, G. 1987. "La naissance du sentiment religieux durant les temps préhistoriques et les premiers pèlerinages," in Chélini and Branthomme 1987, 25-34.

Candea, M. 2019. *Comparison in Anthropology: The Impossible Method.* Cambridge: Cambridge University Press.

Cecil, L.H. and T.W. Pugh. (eds) 2009. *Maya Worldviews at Conquest.* Boulder: University Press of Colorado.

Chaniotis, A. 1988. "Habgierige Götter, habgierige Stadte. Heiligtumbesitz und Gebietsanspruch in den kretischen Staatsverträgen." *Ktema* 13, 21-39.

Charpin, D. 2017. *La vie méconnue des temples mésopotamiens.* Paris: Les Belles Lettres.

Charpin, D. and N. Ziegler. 2003. *Mari et le Proche-Orient à l'époque amorrite: essai d'histoire politique.* Paris: SEPOA.

Chélini, J. and J. Branthomme. 1987. *Histoire des pèlerinages non chrétiens. Entre magique et sacré: le chemin des dieux.* Paris: Hachette.

Collectif 1960. *Les Pèlerinages: Égypte Ancienne, Israël, Islam, Perse, Inde, Tibet, Indonésie, Madagascar, Chine, Japon.* Paris: Éditions du Seuil.

Corti, C. 2018. "Along the Road to Nerik. Local Panthea of Hittite Northern Anatolia." *Die Welt des Orients* 48, 24-70.

Cosmopoulos, M.B. 2015. *Bronze Age Eleusis and the Origins of the Eleusinian Mysteries.* Cambridge: Cambridge University Press.

Da Riva, R., M. Lang and S. Fink (eds.) 2019. *Literary Change in Mesopotamia and Beyond and Routes and Travellers between East and West. Proceedings of the 2nd and 3rd Melammu Workshops.* Münster: Zaphon.

Del Olmo Lete, C. 2008. *Mythologie et religion des sémites Occidentaux.* 2 vols. Leuven: Peeters.

Detienne, M. 2008. *Comparing the Incomparable.* Stanford: Stanford University Press.

Dodd, D.B. and C.A. Faraone (eds.). 2003. *Initiation in Ancient Greek Rituals and Narratives: New Critical Perspectives.* London: Routledge.

Dubovský P. 2023. "The Role of Emissaries (ṣīrāni) in the Assyrian Administrative Machinery: What should an Emissary Learn about Assyria?" in R. Rollinger, I. Madreiter, M. Lang and C. Pappi (eds), *The Intellectual Heritage of the Ancient Near East.* Vienna: Austrian Academy of Sciences Press, 751-82.

Durand, J.-M. 2008. "La religion Amorrite en Syrie à l'époque des archives de Mari," in Del Olmo Lete 2008, vol. 1, 163-703.

Eade, J. and M.J. Sallnow. 1991a. "Introduction" in Eade and Sallnow 1991b, 1-29.

Eade, J. and M.J. Sallnow. (eds) 1991b. *Contesting the Sacred: The Anthropology of Christian Pilgrimage.* London: Routledge.

Eck, D.L. 1982. *Banaras. City of Light.* Princeton. Princeton University Press.

Eck, D.L. 1985. *Darsan. Seeing the Divine Image in India.* Second edition. Chambersburg, PA: Anima Books.

Effland, A. 2014. "'You will open up the ways in the underworld of the god': Aspects of Roman and Late Antique Abydos," in O'Connell 2014, 193-205.

Elsner, J. 1997. "The Origins of the Icon: Pilgrimage, Religion and Visual Culture in the Roman East as 'Resistance' to the Centre," in Alcock 1997, 178-99.

Elsner, J. and I.C. Rutherford (eds.) 2005. *Pilgrimage in Graeco-Roman and Early Christian Antiquity. Seeing the Gods.* Oxford: Oxford University Press.

Exell, K. (ed.). 2011. *Egypt in its African Context: Proceedings of the conference held at The Manchester Museum, University of Manchester, 2-4 October 2009.* Oxford: Archaeopress.

Faist, B. 2006. "Itineraries and Travellers in the Middle Assyrian Period." *State Archives of Assyria Bulletin* XV, 147-60.

Feliu, L. 2003. *The god Dagan in Bronze Age Syria.* Leiden: Brill.

Feuerherm, K.G. 2011. "Have Horn, Will Travel: The Journeys of Mesopotamian Deities," in Harland 2011, 83-97.

Foertmeyer, V. 1989. *Tourism in Graeco-Roman Egypt.* ProQuest Dissertations Publishing. http://search.proquest.com/docview/303802536/?pq-origsite=primo.

Frankfurter, D. (ed.) 1997. *Pilgrimage and Holy Space in Late Antique Egypt.* Leiden: Brill.

Frayne, S. 1983. "Šulgi, the Runner." *Journal of the American Oriental Society* 103, 739-48.

Foucart, P.F. 1895. *Recherches sur l'origine et la nature des mystères d'Éleusis.* Paris: Imprimerie nationale.

Gagné, R., S. Goldhill and G. Lloyd (eds.) 2019. *Regimes of Comparatism. Frameworks of Comparison in History, Religion and Anthropology.* Leiden: Brill.

George, A.R. 1993. "Ninurta-paqidat's Dog Bite, and Notes on Other Comic Tales." *Iraq* 55, 63-75.

Gibson, M. 1993. "Nippur-Sacred city of Enlil." *Al-Rāfidān* 14, 1-18. https://oi.uchicago.edu/research/projects/nippur-sacred-city-enlil-0

Gingrich, A. and T. Thelen. 2012. "Comparative Anthropology: Achievements, Failures and Future." *Ethnologie française* 42, 395-401.

Golden, M. and P. Toohey (eds.) 1997. *Inventing Ancient Culture.* London: Routledge.

Harland, P. 2011. *Travel and Religion in Antiquity.* Waterloo: Wilfrid Laurier University Press.

Hassauer, F. 2007. "Pilgrimage," in *The Brill Dictionary of Religion* III, 1452-56. Leiden: Brill.

Helms, M.W. 1988. *Ulysses' Sail. An Ethnographic Odyssey of Power, Knowledge and Geographical Distance.* Princeton: Princeton University Press.

Hertz, R. 1983 (orig. 1913). "St. Besse: A Study of an Alpine Cult," in Wilson 1983, 55-100.

Hilprecht, H.V. 1904. *In the temple of Bêl at Nippur. A lecture delivered before German court and university circles.* Philadelphia: University of Pennsylvania.

Hoffmann, F. and J. Quack (eds.) 2018. *Anthologie der demotischen Literatur.* Second edition. Münster: LIT.

Iannaccone, L. 1992a. "Religious markets and the economics of religion". *Social Compass* 39, 123-31.

Iannaccone, L. 1992b. "Sacrifice and Stigma: Reducing free-riding in cults, communes, and other collectives." *Journal of Political Economy* 100.2, 271-91.

Jasnow, R. and M. Smith. 2010/11. "'As for those who have Called me Evil, Mut will Call them Evil': Orgiastic cultic behavior and its critics in Ancient Egypt (PSI Inv. [provv.] D 114a+PSI Inv. 3056 verso)." *Enchoria* 32, 9-53.

Kantner, J. and K.J. Vaughn. 2012. "Pilgrimage as Costly Signal: Religiously Motivated Cooperation in Chaco and Nasca." *Journal of Anthropological Archaeology* 31, 66-82.

Kristensen, T.M. and W. Friese (eds.) 2017. *Excavating Pilgrimage: Archaeological Approaches to Sacred Travel and Movement in the Ancient World.* Abingdon: Routledge.

Lebrun, R. 1987. "Pèlerinages royaux chez les Hittites," in Chélini and Branthomme 1987, 83-94.

Lichtheim, M. 1988. *Ancient Egyptian Autobiographies Chiefly of the Middle Kingdom. A Study and an Anthology.* Göttingen: Vandenhoeck & Ruprecht.

Lightfoot, J. 2005. "Pilgrims and Ethnographers: In Search of the Syrian Goddess," in Elsner and Rutherford 2005, 333-52.

Llop, J. and D. Shibata. 2016. "The Royal Journey in the Middle Assyrian Period." *Journal of Cuneiform Studies* 68, 67-98.

Lloyd, G.E.R. 2019. "The Fortunes of Comparatism: History, Anthropology, Philosophy," in Gagné, Goldhill and Llyod 2019, 447-58.

Lloyd, G.E.R. & N. Sivin. 2002. *The Way and the Word: Science and Medicine in Early China and Greece.* New Haven, CT: Yale University Press.

Lowe, E.D. and M. Schnegg. 2020. "Introduction – Comparative Ethnography; its promise, process and successful implementations," in Schnegg and Lowe 2020, 1-20.

Maclean, K. 2008. *Pilgrimage and Power: The Kumbh Mela in Allahabad, 1765-1954.* New York: Oxford University Press.

Mallowan, M.E.L. 1969 "Alabaster Eye-Idols from Tell Brak, North Syria," in *Les Mélanges de l'Université Saint-Joseph* 45, 393-96.

Malul, M. 1990. *The Comparative Method in Ancient Near Eastern and Biblical Legal Studies.* Neukirchen-Vluyn: Neukirchener Verlag.

Matthews, R. and C. Roemer. 2003. *Ancient Perspectives on Egypt.* London: UCL Press.

McCorriston, J. 2011. *Pilgrimage and Household in the Ancient Near East.* Cambridge: Cambridge University Press.

McCorriston, J. 2013. "Pastoralism and Pilgrimage: Ibn Khaldūn's *Bayt*-State Model and the Rise of Arabian Kingdoms." *Current Anthropology* 54, 607-41.

McCorriston, J. 2017. "Inter-cultural Pilgrimage, Identity, and the Axial Age in the Ancient Near East," in Kristensen and Friese 2017, 11-27.

Morinis, E.A. (ed.) 1992. *Sacred Journeys: The Anthropology of Pilgrimage*. Westport, CT: Greenwood Press.

Munt, H. 2016. "Pilgrimage in Pre-Islamic Arabia and Late Antiquity," in Tagliacozzo and Toorawa 2016, 13-30.

Murray, M.J. and L. Moore. 2009. "Costly Signaling and the Origin of Religion." *Journal of Cognition and Culture* 9, 225-45.

Myerhoff, B.G. 1978. "Return to Wirikuta: Ritual Reversal and Symbolic Continuity on the Peyote Hunt of the Huichol Indians," in Babcock 1978, 225-35.

Nakata, I. 2011. "The god Itūr-Mēr in the middle Euphrates region during the Old Babylonian period." *Revue d'assyriologique* 105, 129-36.

Naquin, S. and C.-F. Yu. 1992a. "Introduction," in Naquin and Yu 1992b, 1-38.

Naquin, S. and C.-F. Yu (eds.) 1992b. *Pilgrims and Sacred Sites in China*. Berkeley, CA: University of California Press.

Navratilova, H. 2015. *Visitors' Graffiti of Dynasties 18 and 19 in Abusir and Northern Saqqara: With a Survey of the Graffiti at Giza, Southern Saqqara, Dahshur and Maidum*. Second, revised edition. Wallasey: Abercromby Press.

Niehoff, M.R. (ed.) 2017. *Journeys in the Roman East. Imagined and Real*. Tübingen: Mohr Siebeck.

Nock, A.D. 1944. Review of H. Wagenvoort, *Imperium, Studiën over het 'mana'-begrip in zede en taal der Romeinen* (Amsterdam, 1941). *American Journal of Philology* 65, 99-105.

Nock. A.D. 1972. *Essays on Religion and the Ancient World*. 2 vols. Oxford: Oxford University Press.

Nordin, A. 2009. "Good-death Beliefs and Cognition in Himalayan Pilgrimage." *Method and Theory in the Study of Religion* 21, 402-36.

Norman, A. and C.M. Cusack (eds.) 2015. *Religion, Pilgrimage, and Tourism*. London: Routledge.

O'Connell, E.R. (ed.) 2014. *Egypt in the First Millennium AD. Perspectives from new Fieldwork*. Leuven: Peeters.

Osella, F. and C. Osella. 2003. "'Ayyappan Saranam': Masculinity and the Sabarimala Pilgrimage in Kerala." *The Journal of the Royal Anthropological Institute* 9, 729-54.

Paden, W.E. 2000. "Elements of a New Comparativism," in Patton and Ray 2000, 182-92.

Pappi, C. 2012. "Religion and Politics at the Divine Table: The Cultic Travels of Zimrī-Līm," in Wilhelm 2012, 579-90.

Patel, S. 2009. "Religious Resistance and Persistence on Cozumel Island," in Cecil and Pugh 2009, 205-18.

Patton, K.C. and B.C. Ray (eds.) 2000. *A Magic Still Dwells: Comparative Religion in the Postmodern Age*. Berkeley: University of California Press.

Plog, S. and A.S. Watson. 2012. "The Chaco Pilgrimage Model: Evaluating the Evidence from Pueblo." *American Antiquity* 77, 449-77.

Postgate, J.N. 1974. *Taxation and Conscription in the Assyrian Empire*. Rome: Biblical Institute Press.

Regulski, I. (ed.) 2019. *Abydos: The Sacred Land at the Western Horizon*. Leuven: Peeters.

Renfrew, C., M. Boyd and C.B. Ramsey. 2012. "The Oldest Maritime Sanctuary? Dating the Sanctuary at Keros and the Cycladic Early Bronze Age." *Antiquity* 86, 144-60.

Rey, S. 2016. *For the Gods of Girsu: City-state Formation in Ancient Sumer*. Oxford: Archaeopress.

Reynolds, F. 1977. *Religious Encounters with Death: Insights from the History and Anthropology of Religions*. University Park: Pennsylvania State University Press.

Ristvet, L. 2015. *Ritual, Performance, and Politics in the Ancient Near East*. Cambridge: Cambridge University Press.

Roscoe, P. 2009. "Social Signaling and the Organization of Small-Scale Society: The Case of Contact-Era New Guinea." *Journal of Archaeological Method and Theory* 16, 69-116.

Rutherford, I.C. 2002. "Theoria and Darshan: Pilgrimage as Gaze in Greece and India." *Classical Quarterly* 50, 133-46.

Rutherford, I.C. 2003. "Pilgrimage in Greco-Roman Egypt: New Perspectives on Graffiti from the Memnonion at Abydos," in Matthews and Roemer 2003, 171-89.

Rutherford, I.C. 2005a. "The Dance of the Wolf-men of Ankuwa. Networks, Amphictionies and Pilgrimage in Hittite Religion," in Süel 2005, 623-40.

Rutherford, I.C. 2005b. "Down-Stream to the Cat-Goddess: Herodotus on Egyptian Pilgrimage," in Elsner and Rutherford 2005, 131-50.

Rutherford, I.C. 2005c. "In a Virtual Wild Space. Pilgrimage and Rite de Passage from Delphi from Sabarimalai," in Yatromanolakis and Roilos 2005, 323-38.

Rutherford, I.C. 2013. *State-Pilgrims and Sacred Observers in Ancient Greece: A Study of Theoria and Theoroi*. Cambridge: Cambridge University Press.

Rutherford, I.C. 2017a. "Concord and Communitas: Themes in Philo's Account of Jewish Pilgrimage," in Niehoff 2017, 257-72.

Rutherford, I.C. 2017b. "Pilgrimage and Communication," in Talbert and Naiden 2017, 192-207.

Rutherford, I.C. 2019. "Religious Networks and Cultural Exchange: Some Possible Cases from the Eastern Mediterranean," in Da Riva, Lang and Fink 2019, 229-40.

Rutherford, I.C. 2020. *Hittite Texts and Greek Religion. Contact, Interaction, Comparison.* Oxford: Oxford University Press.

Rutherford, I.C. 2022. "Religious Travel and Pilgrimage in Mesopotamia and the Anatolia: Problems of Evidence and Typology," in R. Da Riva, A. Arroyo and C. Debourse (eds.) *Ceremonies, Feasts and Festivities in Ancient Mesopotamia and the Mediterranean World: Performance and Participation. Proceedings of the 11th Melammu Workshop*, 241-54. Münster: Zaphon Verlag.

Sabek, Y. 2016. *Die hieratischen Besucher-Graffiti dsr-3h.t in Deir el-Bahari.* London: Golden House Publications.

Sallaberger, W. 2008. "Rechtsbrüche in Handel, Diplomatie und Kult. Ein Memorandum aus Ebla über Verfehlungen Maris (ARET 13, 15)." *Kaskal* 5, 93-110.

Sangren, P.S. 1987. *History and Magical Power in a Chinese Community.* Stanford: Stanford University Press.

Sangren, P.S. 1993. "Power and Transcendence in the Ma Tsu pilgrimages of Taiwan." *American Ethnologist* 20, 564-82.

Sauren, H. 1969. "Besuchsfahrten der Götter in Sumer." *Orientalia* 38, 214-36.

Sax, W.S. 2000. "Conquering the quarters: Religion and politics in Hinduism." *International Journal of Hindu Studies* 4, 39-60.

Schipper, K. 1960. "Les pèlerinages en Chine. Montagnes et Pistes," in Collectif 1960, 305-42.

Schnegg, M. and E.D. Lowe (eds.) 2020. *Comparing Cultures: Innovations in Comparative Ethnography.* Cambridge: Cambridge University Press.

Schott, S. 1953. *Das schöne Fest vom Wüstentale.* Mainz: Steiner.

Schmidt, K. 2005. "Ritual Centers and the Neolithisation of Upper Mesopotamia." *Neo-Lithics* 2/05, 13-21.

Shaw, A. et al. 2016. "The Archaeology of Persistent Places: The Palaeolithic Case of La Cotte de St Brelade, Jersey." *Antiquity* 90/354, 1437-53.

Shovlin, J. 1991. "Pilgrimage and the Construction of Irish National Identity." *Proceedings of the Harvard Celtic Colloquium* 11, 59-76.

Sjöberg, A.W. 1957-71. "Götterreisen". *Reallexikon der Assyriologie* 3, 480-83. Berlin: De Gruyter.

Smith, M. 2009. *Traversing Eternity: Texts for the Afterlife from Ptolemaic and Roman Egypt.* Oxford: Oxford University Press.

Snape, S.R. 2019. "Memorial Monuments at Abydos and the 'Terrace of the Great God'," in Regulski 2019, 255-72.

Sourvinou-Inwood, C. 1997. "Reconstructing Change: Ideology and the Eleusinian Mysteries," in Golden and Toohey 1997, 132-63.

Spycket, A. 1990. "Ex-voto Mésopotamiens du IIe millénaire av. J.-C.," in Tunca 1990, 79-86.

Stanley, J.M. 1992. "The Great Maharashtrian Pilgrimage: Pandharpur and Alandi," in Morinis 1992, 65-87.

Streck, M. P. 2015. "Ein Arzt ohne Sumerisch-Kenntnisse ist ein Idiot". *Akademie aktuell* 2/2015, 21-23.

Süel, A. (ed.) 2005. *V. Uluslararası Hititoloji Kongresi bildirileri/Acts of the Vth International Congress of Hittitology.* Ankara: Nokta Ofset.

Tagliacozzo, E. and S. Toorawa. 2016. *The Hajj. Pilgrimage in Islam.* New York: Cambridge University Press.

Talbert, R.J.A. and F. Naiden (eds.) 2017. *Mercury's Wings. Exploring Modes of Communication in the Ancient World.* Oxford: Oxford University Press.

Thayer, J.S. 1992. "Pilgrimage and its Influence on West African Islam," in Morinis 1992, 169-87.

Tozzer, A.M. 1941. *Landa's Relación de las Cosas de Yucatan.* Cambridge, MA: Tozzer Museum.

Tsouparopoulou, C. 2020. "The Healing Goddess, her Dogs and Physicians in Late Third Millennium BC Mesopotamia." *Zeitschrift für Assyriologie* 110, 14-24.

Tunca, Ö. 1990. *De la Babylonie à la Syrie en passant par Mari. Mélanges offerts à Monsieur J.-R. Kupper à l'occasion de son 70ᵉ anniversaire.* Liège: Université de Liège.

Turner, V. 1972. "The Center Out There: Pilgrim's Goal." *History of Religions* 12, 191-230.

Turner, V. 1974a. "Pilgrimages as Social Processes," in Turner 1974b, 166-230.

Turner, V. 1974b. *Dramas, Fields and Metaphors. Symbolic Action in Human Society.* Ithaca: Cornell University Press.

Turner, V. 1975. "Death and the Dead in the Pilgrimage Process," in Whisson 1975, 107-27.

Turner, V. and E. Turner. 1978. *Image and Pilgrimage in Christian Culture.* Chichester: Columbia University Press.

Urban, H.B. 2000. "Making a Place to Take a Stand: Jonathan Z. Smith and the Politics and Poetics of Comparison." *Method and Theory in the Study of Religion* 12, 339-78.

Van der Plas, D. 1989. "'Voir' Dieux. Quelques observations au sujet de la fonction des sens dans le culte et la devotion de l'Égypte ancienne." *Bulletin de la société française d'égyptologie* 115, 4-35.

Vial, T. 2004. "Modes of Religiosity and Changes in Popular Religous Practices at the Time of the Reformation," in Whitehouse and Martin 2004, 143-56.

Volokhine, Y. 1998. "Les Déplacements Pieux En Égypte Pharaonique: Sites et Pratiques Culturelles," in Frankfurter 1998, 51-97.

Wagensonner, K. 2005. *"Wenn Götter Reisen..." Götterreisen, -prozessionen und Besuchsfahrten in den sumerischen literarischen Texten.* MA thesis, Vienna.

Wagensonner, K. 2007. "Götterreise oder Herrscherreise oder vielleicht beides?" *Wiener Zeitschrift für die Kunde des Morgenlandes* 97, 541-59.

Watrous, L.V. 2004. "State Formation (Middle Minoan IA)," in Watrous, Hadzi-Vallianou and Blitzer 2004, 253-76.

Watrous, L.V., D. Hadzi-Vallianou and H. Blitzer (eds.) 2004. *The Plain of Phaistos. Cycles of Social Complexity in the Mesara Region of Crete.* Los Angeles: Cotsen Institute of Archaeology.

Whisson, M. (ed.) 1975. *Religion and Social Change in Southern Africa. Anthropological Essays in Honour of Monica Wilson.* Cape Town: David Philip.

Whitehouse, H. and L.-H. Martin (eds.) 2004. *Theorising Religions Past. Archaeology, History and Cognition.* Walnut Creek: Altamira Press.

Wilhelm, G. (ed.) 2012. *Organization, Representation, and Symbols of Power in the Ancient Near East. Proceedings of the 54th Rencontre Assyriologique International at Würzburg 20-25 July 2008.* Winona Lake: Eisenbrauns.

Wilson, S. (ed.) 1983. *Saints and their Cults: Studies in Religious Sociology, Folklore and History.* Cambridge: Cambridge University Press.

Wiseman, D.J. 1982. "'Is It Peace?': Covenant and Diplomacy." *Vetus Testamentum* 32, 311-26.

Yatromanolakis, D. and P. Roilos. 2004. *Greek Ritual Poetics.* Cambridge, MA: Harvard University Press.

Yoffee, N. 2004. *Myths of the Archaic State: Evolution of the Earliest Cities, States, and Civilizations.* Cambridge: Cambridge University Press.

Younger, P. 2002. *Playing Host to Deity: Festival Religion in the South Indian Tradition.* Oxford: Oxford University Press.

Yoyotte, J. 1960. "Les Pèlerinages dans l'Égypte Ancienne," in Collectif 1960, 17-74.

PART II

Pilgrims, Place and Motion: Case Studies

4

DISORDERLY PILGRIMS AT THE ORACULAR SANCTUARY OF APOLLO KOROPAIOS

MATTHEW DILLON

When an individual pilgrim in ancient Greece made his or her way to a pilgrimage sanctuary, presumably their primary, and perhaps their only, motivation will have been to express their personal piety towards the deity or deities of that sacred place, and to gain some specific benefit for themselves. In the case of those pilgrims participating in a state-sponsored delegation, a *theoria*, they too will have been motivated by considerations of personal piety. More importantly, the members of a *theoria*, the *theoroi*, will have been affected by a sense that they were meeting and fulfilling the pious concerns of the city which they were representing. This sense of piety felt by individual pilgrims and *theoroi*, however, did not guarantee that pilgrims would engage only in pious behaviour while at pilgrimage sites, and their religious sensitivities did not necessarily preclude what could be termed non-pious, disorderly conduct. Inscribed regulations from pilgrimage sites, many of which were panhellenic, indicate that the behaviour of pilgrims was not always as religious as it could have been.

Misbehaviour and disorderly conduct of pilgrims at sacred sites fell into two main categories.[1] Some misbehaviour might be of a fairly innocuous kind, such as wearing the wrong type of clothing to a religious ceremony, and might not have represented a gross infraction. Such misdemeanours which were not of an excessively serious nature could result in a pilgrim being fined a sum of money, or in this case, at Andania, in having the clothes confiscated. Other pilgrim misbehaviour, however, could be quite blatant, such as acting in a disorderly manner during the conduct of ritual procedures. The presence of official staff-bearers, *rhabdouchoi* and *rhabdophoroi*, at some sacred pilgrimage sites indicates that sanctuary authorities anticipated active misbehaviour, presumably because they had had some experience of it from pilgrims in the past.

---

1   For a range of regulations from several pilgrimage sites, designed to ensure the good behaviour of pilgrims, and to prevent damage to the shrines and their grounds, see Dillon 1997a, 149-82; Dillon 1997b.

Korope and Keeping Order at Apollo's Oracular Sanctuary

The oracular centre of Apollo at Korope in Magnesia in northern Greece provides an interesting case study in regard to a discussion of the disorderly pilgrim in ancient Greece.[2] A lengthy inscribed decree (*psephisma*) of the city of Demetrias provides a unique and very detailed insight into how pilgrimage centres employed law-enforcers to act in policing roles at pilgrimage sites, and a further decree regulates some aspects of the sanctuary area itself.[3] Yet this inscription concerning this pilgrimage centre is generally neglected by modern scholarship, and its measures concerning pilgrims do not appear in standard treatments of ancient Greek pilgrims, or in discussions of sacred laws.[4]

The civic authorities of the city of Demetrias, which controlled the oracular sanctuary of Apollo Koropaios at Korope (in north-eastern Greece, in the territory of Magnesia, near modern Volos), published two decrees inscribed on one stone, which have been dated to anywhere between 100 BCE and 100 CE.[5] Demetrias was founded by Demetrios Poliorketes in 294/3 BCE,[6] and became the main urban centre of a political entity which had several constituent demes, or towns, several of which are referred to in this inscription. These had undergone a *synoikismos*, a political unification with the new foundation, but not in this case involving the movement of the populations of the towns into Demetrias.[7] This city was an important one in a strategic sense: so much so that it was named by the ancient sources as one of the 'fetters' of Greece in connection with controlling the whole country.[8] Demetrias was also the chief city (along with its demes) of the league (*koinon*) of the Magnesians.[9] Various cults of the area were organised at the

---

2   For the oracular shrine of Apollo Koropaios, see Robert 1948; Parke 1967, 104-08; Rosenberger 2001, 29-32; Mili 2014, 330-31; Dillon 2017, 349-51.

3   The inscription was discovered in 1881, and is now in the museum of Volos (E714).

4   Editions of the text: *IG* IX2 1109; *LGS* 80 (Ziehen); *LSCG* 83-84; Michel *Recueil* 842 A; Robert 1948, 16-28; *SEG* 17.302, 24.404, 25.686, 54.498 (specifically mentioning the *rhabdouchoi*); *SIG3* 1157 (which is the text employed here as the most accurate). The only English translation of this inscription of which the author is aware is that of Grant 1953, 34-37, but with some errors, and with decree II, lines II.70-95 not translated. Other inscriptions concerning the sanctuary are: *IG* IX2 1109-10, 1202, 1203-6.

5   The name Alexandros son of Meniskos (without the deme name Spalauthra), as a nomophylax in the Korope inscription (*SIG3* 1157, decree I, lines 6-7), also appears in Pouilloux & Verdélis 1950, 33-39 no 1, lines 8-9 as a strategos; another individual, [Lysi]as son of Zoilos in the same inscription at lines 7-8 appears in yet another inscription which is dated to around 130 CE (see Pouilloux & Verdélis 1950, 37). If the Alexandros son of Meniskos in *SIG3* 1157 and the one in Pouilloux & Verdélis 1950, 33-39 no 1 are the same, this gives a possible date of early in the second century CE for *SIG3* 1157. But, of course, the practice of naming sons for their grandfathers means that there could have been more than one Alexandros son of Meniskos.

6   For the epigraphic and archaeological evidence for a ruler-founding cult at Demetrias, see Martzavou & Papazarkadas 2008, 255-75.

7   For the *synoikismos*, see Strabo 9.5.15 (note Livy 39.23.12 on the city's importance).

8   Polyb. 18.11.5, 18.45.5-6; Strabo 9.4.15, 9.5.15; Livy 32.37.3; Paus 7.7.6; App. *Maced.* 8.

9   For Demetrias and its demes (towns, and cities in their own right), see Stillwell 1976, 463-64; Cohen 2004, 111-14 (with references to earlier scholarship at 112); Hansen & Nielsen 2004, 689,

time of the *synoikismos* as extra-polis entities.[10] The first decree, referred to in modern editions as (I), is a lengthy one concerning procedures at the oracular shrine (*manteion*) of Apollo Koropaios at Korope; the second decree (II) concerns the maintenance of the grounds at his sanctuary. In the rescript indicating the officials in power when the decree was passed, Dionysodoros son of Euphraios of Aiolis is named as general (*strategos*) of the Magnesians, as Demetrias was a member of the Magnesian league.[11]

While Korope had been incorporated into the territory of Demetrias,[12] it was only sometime in the first century BCE to the first century CE (depending on the dating of the inscription) that the oracular centre there, for whatever reason, began to be quite popular, necessitating regulations about the behaviour of those visiting the site with their oracular enquiries.[13] Specific regulations were laid down as to the procedures by which pilgrims and local individuals were to consult the oracle. In essence, the decree specifies provisions about consulting the oracle, provisions that clearly represent changes in the previous oracular cultic ritual. Because of this, the rescript that prefaces the decree is particularly detailed as to the proposers of the motion, who held office at the time the decree came into effect:

> **I (1)** *When Krinon son of Parmenion was priest, on the tenth of the month Areios, Krinon son of Parmenion, of Homolion, priest of Zeus Akraios, and Dionysodoros son of Euphraios of Aiolis general of the Magnesians, and the* **(5)** *generals (strategoi) Aitolion son of Demetrios of Pagasai, Kleogenes son of Amyntas of Halai, Menes son of Hippios of Aiolis, and the guardians of the laws (nomophylakes) Menelaos son of Philippos of Iolkos, Ainias son of Nikasiboulos and Alexandros son of Meniskos of Spalauthra, and Menander son of Nikios of Korope proposed the motion.*

The full force of the civic authority of the city of Demetrias and its parts (here city-office holders from the constituent demes of Homoloion, Aiolis, Pagasai, Halai, Spalauthra and Korope are mentioned) is called into play here. The decree is preceded by a listing of a solid consortium of citizens from throughout the constituent demes who held religious or civic office when the decree was passed, and who proposed it; none of the generals or nomophylakes named, in fact, is from Demetrias itself, but one of the nomophylakes is from Korope. Moreover, Dionysodoros son of Euphraios of Aiolis, while from one of the demes of the city, was general of the Magnesians (i.e. the *koinon* (league) of the Magnesians) and is listed as one of the proposers. The decree itself is not one of the

---

699, 721; Kravaritou 2011, 114-16; Mili 2014, 198. The demes are listed by Cohen 2004, 112 and Mili 2014, 198.

10 See Kravaritou 2011 (Korope briefly at 118, 120).

11 For a map of the cities of Magnesia and the location of the sanctuary of Apollo Koropaios, see Boehm 2019, 79. Demetrias is about 30 kilometres from Korope.

12 For the cults of Demetrias, see Mili 2014, 197-212; Boehm 2019, 151-61, with 157 briefly on Apollo Koropaios.

13 For the physical structure of the sanctuary, see Mili 2014, 330 with bibliography.

koinon of Magnesia but of the city of Demetrias, indicating that it was this city that had ultimate jurisdiction over the sanctuary. These four generals came from demes of Demetrias, namely Pagasai, Halai and Aiolis (two). Similarly, the four nomophylakes who are named came from Iolkos, Spalauthra (two) and Korope. These officials might well, at a previous meeting of the assembly of Demetrias, have been given the task of formulating provisions when the increased popularity of the shrine was discussed. The priest of Zeus Akraios, four generals and, appropriately, four nomophylakes ('guardians of the law') are named. (Zeus Akraios, along with Apollo Koropaios, and Artemis Iolkos,[14] were the chief deities of Demetrias and its territory, and the priesthood of Zeus Akraios was the most prestigious of Demetrias.[15]) These individuals were the agents for ritual reform in the cult of Apollo Koropaios; their combined religious and civic authority is clearly important, being set out at the beginning of the decree. Their proposal was approved by the city (otherwise the decree would not exist), sanctioning the religious changes and authorising a new direction for the cult.

Justifying Ritual Change at Korope's Oracular Shrine

> **(8)** *Since our city is piously disposed both towards the other gods and not least towards Apollo Koropaios,* **(10)** *and since it honours him with the most conspicuous honours because of the benefactions (euergesiai) of the god, as he prophesies through his oracular shrine (manteion) both for the community (koinon) and for each person individually (idia) concerning matters pertaining to health (hygieia) and safe-keeping (soteria)....*

Piety is the reason presented for the changes: not only in respect of the other gods besides Apollo Koropaios, but towards him especially. The proposers of the decree thereby ensure that the gods know they are all piously venerated. They remind Apollo Koropaios in particular that they have honoured him most conspicuously: in this way they are jogging his memory concerning their religious services in his honour, and so seeking his approval for their changes. They honour him because of his prophetic services, through which he assists both the community (*koinon*) of Demetrias and its demes, and individuals. Prophetic centres throughout the Greek world, such as Delphi most famously, served both the state and individual enquirers.[16] Apollo Koropaios is stated to prophesy concerning health (*hygieia*) and safe-keeping (*soteria*). The mention of *hygieia* sounds very much as if this could have been a healing oracular sanctuary, but it is probably more the case that Apollo Koropaios was consulted in matters of public health (widespread illnesses and the like), as at Delphi. *Soteria* is so broad a term it cannot be narrowed down to anything more specific than what is good both for the city and those people who consult Apollo Koropaios.

---

14 These three deities are listed in lines I.54-59 as the deities to whom those officials in charge of the days of oracular consultation are to swear that they have carried out the provisions of the decree.
15 Boehm 2018, 210-11.
16 See Dillon 1997a, 80-98; Dillon 2017, 353-78.

The inscription then moves on to provide the reason for the decree:

(13) *It is right and proper, since the oracle is ancient and has been held in the highest esteem by our forefathers,* **(15)** *and increasing numbers of strangers (xenoi) are coming here to consult the oracle, that the city should take more diligent care regarding appropriate maintenance of good order (eukosmia) in the oracular shrine (to manteion)…*

An authentic history is thus claimed for the oracular sanctuary: it might at present be more popular than ever before, and visited by ever-increasing numbers of those seeking prophetic guidance from the god, but this is the only change that has taken place. The forefathers (*progonoi*) had always held the oracular shrine in the 'highest esteem'—nothing has changed *except* that the shrine is attracting more visitors from outside: *xenoi* are now coming to the shrine in significant numbers. Moreover, the proposers are not claiming that they would like to make changes in order for the shrine to become more popular but rather that it has become so already, and it is these circumstances that have led to a necessity for ritual change. In this context of increased visitation of the shrine, the maintenance of good order (*eukosmia*) has become a principal concern. *Eukosmia* also appears later in the decree,[17] and the preoccupation with ensuring this is given here (in the introduction to the actual new arrangements for consultation) as one of the primary reasons why changes are being made to the oracular procedure.

Some of those consulting the shrine are referred to as *xenoi*, strangers—that is pilgrims, as they are visiting a shrine not in their locality—and the decree spells out and states as its motivation that it has been passed because more *xenoi* than ever before were coming to the shrine, seeking oracular advice. Several officials from the deme cities close to Demetrias are named—the generals and the nomophylakes come from the towns constituting the state of Demetrias, namely Pagasai, Halai, Aiolis, Iolkos, Spalauthra and Korope itself. The inhabitants of these towns, as members of the *synoikismos* of Demetrias, would not have been referred to as *xenoi*. Rather the *xenoi* are 'strangers' visiting from outside the territory of the *koinon*. But, of course, it is the city Demetrias itself which passes the decree, as Korope is one of the demes within its territory:

(16-17) *it has been resolved by the Council and People that…*

This is a typical decree of a city—its boule and demos are responsible. The proposal would first have been made in the city's boule, which would then have organised its introduction to the assembly of the demos. After this long preamble, the inscription moves on to the crux of the matter:

(18) *… whenever consultation of the oracle takes place, both the priest of Apollo appointed by the city,* **(20)** *and a general and a guardian of the laws, one from each magistracy, and one prytanis and the treasurer and the secretary of the god and the*

---

17 See the discussion of *eukosmia* at line 30 below.

prophet shall present themselves; and if any of the aforementioned should be sick or away, he is to send someone (to replace him), …

What follows will clearly lay down how the city will in future enact what the prescript envisages, managing the shrine with more 'diligent care' (line 16). As for consultation dates, the decree does not indicate when the oracle could be visited (e.g. once a month or once a year). Surprisingly, the priest of Apollo appointed by the city lacks an epithet (*epiklesis*): one could expect the 'priest of Apollo Koropaios', but presumably it was sufficient in the decree to indicate Apollo, as it is after all his shrine that is being discussed. At this point, the personnel involved do not quite match the proposers of the decree: there is to be one general and one law-giver. These will 'present themselves', obviously at the *manteion*, when the two-day oracular consultation took place. Presumably the general would come fully armed and dressed in hoplite gear, in order to impress on the consultants the serious nature of the oracular procedure. The nomophylax ('guardian of the law') would also be present. Clearly the presence of these two individuals at the shrine was important in order for them to have a say on whether regulations in the decree had been observed or broken.

To the one general and one nomophylax is added a *prytanis*, referring, as at Athens, to a member of the subcommittee of the boule that was on duty at any one time and in charge of day-to-day administration. Also included is the treasurer (*tamias*) of the cult, as the decree moves on to financial matters, with which he needed to deal. While the decree does not include a reference to a payment for consultation, there may well have been one, as the *rhabdouchoi* are to be paid from the monies collected over the two days of the oracular consultation (lines 26-27; see below).

The god's secretary (*grammateus*) had to be present at the shrine for he had an important role to play in the new arrangements for consulting the oracle. Possibly he possessed a copy of the decree that regulated the behaviour of the *xenoi* and other consultants, but in addition, as will be seen, he was responsible for organising and publicising the order in which consultations would take place.

A natural inclusion amongst the officials is the prophet of the shrine, the *prophetes*, but his (or perhaps her) actual involvement is not made clear, and this is in fact the first and only mention of the *prophetes* in the decree. Clearly his or her role has not changed from previous arrangements, which the city did not feel the need to codify— it is only changes to ritual which are being enumerated. The importance of the presence of the officials is indicated by the fact that if they cannot attend for one of two specific reasons (ill health or absence), they must ensure that they send a replacement, for they are needed for the oracular consultations. A martial tone of discipline and order would be added by the presence of the general; moreover, generals were important personages in the city, and lent the weight of their authority to the proceedings. The presence of these officials was clearly intended to impress upon the many pilgrims the importance of the occasion, and that this oracular process was part and parcel of the civic and ritual ceremonial of the city, being an expression of its piety towards the god Apollo Koropaios.

Staff-bearers to Keep Order at the Oracular Shrine

Taking even more diligent care of the shrine than in the past required organising a small body of men who would act as a type of police-force when the shrine was being visited by the locals and the ever-increasing numbers of pilgrims:

> **(23)** ... *the generals and guardians of the laws are also to enrol staff-bearers (rhabdouchoi) from the citizens,* **(25)** *three men under 30 years of age, who are to have the authority to stop anyone behaving in a disorderly fashion. The staff-bearer is to be paid wages out of the monies collected over two days, a drachma per day. If any of those enrolled is absent intentionally, he is to pay a fine to the city of fifty drachmas, with the generals and guardians of the laws having recorded him [as absent].*

Later in the decree there is more information on the staff bearers (*rhabdouchoi*) maintaining orderly behaviour (lines 50-51), just as here in these lines the *rhabdouchoi* are given the authority 'to stop anyone behaving in a disorderly fashion'. These three citizens would each bear a rod or staff (*rhabdos*) to employ against the misbehaving pilgrims if and when the need arose. Some of the *xenoi*, and locals, coming as oracular consultants might well have been engaging in disorderly behaviour, perhaps because there were now apparently large crowds attending the shrine.

Slaves were not chosen as *rhabdouchoi* to prevent misbehaviour, for that would involve the rods of the *rhabdouchoi* being wielded by slaves against free men; instead, three citizens are chosen. Their age is to be under 30 —presumably because the city wanted to engage the services of young, energetic men who could ply their rods effectively in cases of misconduct.[18]

These three *rhabdouchoi* are given full authority to maintain order at the sanctuary; that is, they did not need to wait for permission from one of the officials, such as the general or a nomophylax who were present, before proceeding to employ their rods against the disorderly. Why employ rod-bearers unless it was conceivable to the authorities that the rod-bearers would need to employ their weapons? Clearly there had recently been an occasion or occasions in which some crowd control would have been useful, but no crowd control had been available—until this decree was passed.

Details of these *rhabdouchoi* also provide some information about the finances of the cult: each *rhabdouchos* was to be paid one drachma a day, a standard per diem rate in the Greek world. This payment would come from the monies collected over the two days required for the oracular procedure. As the decree later indicates, the oracular procedure took two days, and clearly payment was required from the consultants. Whenever the oracular sanctuary was open to pilgrims, the *rhabdouchoi* were to be present, and if they were deliberately absent (i.e. not sick or away as mentioned for the general and nomophylax above), they would be fined. The amount is actually a modern restoration

---

18   Ziehen, followed by Dittenberger in *SIG*3 1157, at line 25 inserted a 'not' here, to mean that the *rhabdouchoi* were to be not younger than 30 years of age, but this is not necessary; the negation is rejected by Daux 1959, 287.

in the decree—a rarity as, in the 30 lines so far, each letter is preserved, until there is some damage to the stone at line 50, when about 25 letters are missing (and again at line 80, for which see below). This erasure is restored as fifty drachmas, which is comparable with the fines levied against free persons for infractions at another sacred site, and this amount must have been meant as a deterrent.[19] But it could equally be any amount that would conceivably fit into one space: ten or even five. The erasure is deliberate: was the penalty being increased or decreased? Moreover, there is precisely the same erasure of an amount at line 83, where fifty drachmas is restored as the penalty for someone who cuts down or lops trees, or pastures or stables animals in the sanctuary grounds (see decree II, discussed below).

Having taken all these precautions, the authorities did not want to be in a position in which there were no *rhabdouchoi*, or not enough, to enforce order, and wished to prevent consultations of the oracle occurring without the reassuring presence of the rod-bearers. In cases of deliberate absence, not only would the absent *rhabdouchos* be fined, but their name would be recorded, presumably to shame him and so to act as a precaution against dereliction of duty via absenteeism: the general and guardian of the laws would no doubt have noted their absence.

Rhabdouchoi and *rhabdophoroi* in the Greek World

It is in fact their age that underlines the importance of the *rhabdouchoi*—they were to be under 30 years old. This is the only age stipulation for rod-bearers at pilgrimage sites or even elsewhere. Appointing *rhabdouchoi*—and this stress on their being able (and willing) to repress bad behaviour through thrashing those responsible—must indicate that problems had recently arisen at the *manteion*. The overall purport of the decree, to ensure good order during the consultation process, must point to specific recent problems and disturbances.

Similarly, rod-bearers or similar officials are found at other pilgrimage sites. At the Andanian Mysteries in the Peloponnese,[20] the first-century BCE to first-century CE inscription regulating the cult has a section[21] entitled 'Concerning the Disorderly Ones', instructing the sacred men to scourge (literally, 'to whip', but here meaning to thrash with rods) anyone being disobedient or acting in an indecent way when the sacrifices were being performed and the Mysteries conducted: all onlookers are to be obedient

---

19 The sanctuary of Apollo Erithaseos at Athens: *LSCG* 37 (*SIG*3 984; *IG* II2 1362); cf. a 50-drachma fine at Pergamon for an offence regarding the public fountain: *OGIS* 483.

20 See two recent excellent commentaries, with texts and translations: Deshout 2006 (French) and Gawlinski 2012 (English). There is an Italian translation (with text) of the Andanian decree in Zunino 1997, 304-15. Gawlinski 2012, 65 gives references to numerous principal discussions; see *SEG* 57.364 for *SEG* citations.

21 There are 26 distinct sections in the inscription, each governing a particular subject, given at the beginning of each section, of pilgrims' behaviour.

and silent at these times.²² This reference to scourging leads to a separate section on *rhabdophoroi*, the equivalent of the *rhabdouchoi* at Korope.

In the long and complex rules for the Mysteries at Andania, the importance of the *rhabdophoroi* is indicated by their having their own section, the tenth (of 26 sections). Twenty (see below) Andanian *rhabdophoroi*, as opposed to three *rhabdouchoi* at Korope, might reflect the greater number of pilgrims at Andania. Or it might perhaps simply be that Andania had so many regulations, more than are known for any other sacred site, and hence the potential for infractions by pilgrims was greater, and so a larger number of law enforcers was required.

Important, too, is that at Andania (unlike at Korope) there were also controls imposed on the rod-bearers. Rod-bearers themselves would be punished if they misbehaved. If accused of wrong-doing, a rod-bearer would be tried by the Andanian Sacred Men of the Mysteries, and if guilty he would be debarred from participating in the sacred rites. This of course was a very serious punishment. The wrong-doing of the rod-bearers might relate to punishing pilgrims actually innocent of any infraction. So, the authorities were keen to discourage and punish inappropriate behaviour on the part of the rod-bearers and avoid acquiring a reputation for arbitrary and unjustified punishment.

Further, towards the end of the Andanian inscription, there are two rather miscellaneous references to the *rhabdophoroi*, apparently added as something as an afterthought. Firstly, *rhabdophoroi* were to be chosen by the officials known as the Ten, choosing them from those 'most capable' of the task,²³ from amongst the mystery officials known as the 'sacred men'. This reference to those 'most capable' calls to mind the reference to the *rhabdouchoi* at Korope being under 30 years of age. The second reference indicates who had authority and jurisdiction over the *rhabdophoroi*: 'The *rhabdophoroi* are to scourge anyone the Ten order them to scourge.'²⁴ But lest it seem as if whipping and fining were the order of the day, the rules for the Andanian Mysteries also stress preventative measures. By setting out various regulations, the authorities alerted the pilgrim to what behaviour was, and was not, acceptable.

At Diokaisareia (Uzuncaburç in Turkey), an inscription lists both priests and *rhabdouchoi*, indicating that the latter role was seen as an important one and, along with the priesthood, a valuable way of serving the gods. It was also a public record of those who would be responsible for bearing staffs or rods and carrying out punishments.²⁵ There were also *rhabdophoroi* at Lebadeia in Boeotia, as known from an inscription of the first century BCE; it is along the lines of the inscription of Diokaisareia and lists

---

22 *LSCG* 65, lines 39-41; for the *rhabdophoroi* at Andania, see the commentary of Deshours 2006, 81; Gawlinski 2012, 151-53; as well as Harter-Uibopuu 2002, 139, 142-45.
23 *LSCG* 65, lines 145-48; see Harter-Uibopuu 2002, 147-48; Gawlinksi 2012, 235.
24 *LSCG* 65, lines 165-67; for the Andanian *rhabdophoroi*, see Deshout 2006, 80; Gawlinksi 2012, 239.
25 *SEG* 37.1294, CI, from line 6 on: perhaps 15 rhabdouchoi were listed. The inscription dates broadly from the first century BCE to the second century CE. The god or gods of the cult is/are unknown.

several *rhabdophoroi*.[26] This seems to have been a position held with honour, namely, to bear a rod to ensure good behaviour towards the gods. This is the intent of a third-century BCE inscription from Larissa: 'Damakos, son of Artemidoros, *rhabdouchos*,'[27] which honours Damakos for his role in this capacity.

Rhabdophoroi and *rhabdouchoi* were not limited to sacred contexts (nor of course were *mastigophoroi*, whip-bearers) as will be seen below. Plato refers to a *rhabdouchos* alongside an *epistates* ('supervisor') and *prytanis* ('chairman') as one who could keep order.[28] A scholiast reports that *rhabdouchoi* kept order in the Athenian theatre.[29] One can also note the *rhabdouchoi* as prison guards at Philippi (more like police officers generally answering to the *strategoi*) in the Acts of the Apostles.[30] Oenanthe, mother of Agathocles (the grandson of the Agathokles, tyrant of Sicily), had female *rhabdouchoi* at Alexandria, presumably for her protection.[31] Polybius's and other Greek authors' use of this term to translate the title of the bearer of the fasces (the lictor) that were carried in front of Roman officials—the rods surrounding an axe—makes clear the nature of the *rhabdouchoi* as bearers of rods.[32]

Rhabdouchoi could thrash free pilgrims at Korope, Andania and Olympia. Rods are employed because there was a tacit agreement amongst the Greeks that free men were not to be flogged with whips. The overall principle is in fact articulated by pseudo-Dionysius of Halicarnassus, who writes that slaves were flogged, but that it was hubris to flog free men.[33] So in the Andanian inscription, free men and women are fined for various infractions of the rules, and could be thrashed, but slaves were to be flogged.

Divinatory Sacrifice Prior to Consultation

Moving on from the *rhabdouchoi*, the Korope decree then seems to come to the crux of the matter and the issue that appears to have resulted from so many *xenoi* coming to consult the oracle: who would be the first to present their enquiry. This in fact seems to have been what had caused recent inappropriate behaviour.

> (30) ... when the aforementioned have come to the oracle and have completed the sacrifice in accordance with ancestral custom and obtained good omens, ...

---

26 *IG* vii 3078, lines 13-15, 20-22, 25-26, 30-31, 35-37 (in pairs, or singly).
27 *IG* ix.2 735.
28 Plat. *Prot.* 338a 8: in this case, in a discussion.
29 Ar. *Peace* 734-35, with schol.
30 Acts of the Apostles 16.35.
31 Polybius 15.29.13.
32 Polybius 5.26.10.
33 Pseudo-Dionysius of Halicarnassus *Art of Rhetoric* 7.6. See also, at Athens: Dem. 22.54-55, 24.166-67.

Such a divinatory sacrifice performed by the city controlling the oracular sanctuary before any consultants were called into the temple is not known from other oracular sanctuaries. A preliminary sacrifice took place at Delphi, in which the consultant provided a victim. In Plutarch's day, on one occasion prior to the consultation, the sacrificial beast refused to nod its head to acquiesce in its sacrifice, which was an ill omen. The consultation went ahead but ended in disaster with the Pythia running screaming from the shrine and dying a few days later.[34] Presumably, if good omens were not received in this sacrifice at Korope, another sacrificial victim would be offered. It is unlikely that the oracular procedure would have been cancelled, with so many *xenoi* in the city wishing to consult Apollo Koropaios.[35]

Those Who Wish to Consult the Oracle

As soon as this divinatory procedure was performed, the secretary of the god would receive the declarations (*anagraphai*) of the local and pilgrim consultants, take the names of those there to consult the oracle, and write their names 'straightaway' on a whitened board in the sanctuary.

> **(32)** … *the secretary of the god is after this to receive the declarations (anagraphai) of those who wish to consult the oracle,* **(35)** *write all the names on a whiteboard, set up the whiteboard straightaway in front of the sanctuary and introduce them, summoning them in accordance with each declaration in succession, unless any of them have been given permission to enter first. And if the one summoned is not present, he is to admit the next one, until the one who has been summoned arrives.*

As soon as the names of the consultants had been received and written up, the order of consultation was publicly posted by the secretary of Apollo, who then summoned each consultant one by one, according to the order in which their names were recorded. Each consultant had an *anagraphe*, and had written their name on it—clearly and in full, one imagines, in order to avoid confusion over identity. This *anagraphe* could be a piece of broken pottery (as in the ostraka of Athens) or a small wooden board. The secretary would put the names on the board, reading and writing them from each of the *anagraphai*, in the order in which he had received them.

How the secretary initially worked out the order in which to write up the names is not at all clear. This is something the decree does not deal with, but which could have been a matter for potential trouble: as with all crowds, having one's turn as early as possible would have been an issue. Clearly the order in which the *anagraphai* are taken up became the order in which the names were recorded, and thus the order of consultation. Nothing in the decree deals with this issue; for example, there is no mention of putting

---

34 Plut. *Mor.* 438a-c.
35 The sale of the hides of animals sacrificed at Korope were used to fund the cult of Zeus Akraios: *IG* ix.2 1110 (*LSCG* 85).

names in a container and pulling them out, or the use of a slot machine such as was used in Athens, with juror's names put into such a machine (the *kleroterion*).[36] This in effect was a crucial part of the proceedings, as one can imagine that it may have been the jostling to consult the oracle first that had caused problems in the past. Presumably those who were the first to arrive had precedence in the order of consultation.

As the secretary called out each name, he would lead that person into the temple, unless that person was not present, in which case he would continue the process with the next named individual. This strongly suggests that there might have been disagreements in the recent past, perhaps even physical fights, about the order in which consultants went into the shrine.

'Unless some are allowed to enter first' also raises the possibility of some form of preferential treatment. At Delphi, this took the form of *promanteia*—the right of consulting the oracle before anyone else.[37] Even there, if there was more than one person representing a state that had *promanteia*, nothing is known about how this was decided, though of course the lot, regarded by the Greeks as ascertaining the will of the gods, could have been employed in the decision.

Clothing Misbehaviour at Pilgrimage Sites

The general, nomophylax and other officials were each to sit in the sanctuary, observing good behaviour, dressed in radiantly white clothes, ritually pure, sober, and wearing wreaths of laurel. This emphasis on sobriety and good behaviour points to a desire on the part of the proposers of the decree to add a certain majesty to the oracular proceedings, as well as ensuring that the officials behaved. It can be assumed that these requirements pertaining to them would also, although not specified, apply to the actual consultants:

> *The aforementioned persons [the officials] are to be seated in the sanctuary in an orderly fashion (kosmiōs) dressed in white garments,* **(40)** *crowned with crowns of laurel, purified and sober . . .*

'In an orderly fashion—*kosmiōs*', the adverb of *eukosmia*, good order, is of course the entire theme of the new arrangements.[38] The Andanian decree, with its numerous sections regulating the pilgrims' behaviour, is almost wholly concerned with *eukosmia*. A decree of the Iobacchoi from Athens demonstrates similar concerns, ordering those at a meeting to behave: no-one was to be on the couch, there was to be no singing, no making a loud noise, no clapping; everything was to be done with *eukosmia*, with participants keeping quiet during the meeting, and when speaking and carrying out their

---

36 Boegehold 1995, 230-33, 33 fig. 3.
37 *Promanteia* at Delphi: Sokolowski 1954; Dillon 2017, 371, 397.
38 See briefly Stavrianopoulou 2006, 122, no. 17.

role they were to do so with *eukosmia*.³⁹ The writers of the Korope decree presumably similarly envisaged a state of dignified silence (or relative quiet) while the enquirers waited their turn.

Drinking is, perhaps surprisingly, not a matter for regulation in sacred laws dealing with issues such as clothing and behaviour. Apparently, the authorities at sacred sites assumed that worshippers would arrive at their ritual activities sober. This is a surprising omission, for if anything is conducive to misbehaviour, it is alcohol, and the drafters of the Korope inscription clearly realised this. Yet this principle is applied to the office-bearers of the city themselves, rather than to the consulting pilgrims. Similarly at Andania, there are, somewhat surprisingly, no laws governing drunkenness. A hint of a similar regulation is provided by a fourth-century BCE decree of Knidos: men and women were to be forbidden from sleeping in the sanctuary of Bakchos: the reason was that nocturnal damage had occurred in the shrine, perhaps caused by drunken behaviour.⁴⁰

The authorities at Knidos wished to establish the principle of *eukosmia* in the shrine. Both the decrees concerning Korope and other sacred decrees were also keen to ensure this, as a means of respect for the gods of course, but also because disorderly behaviour is difficult to control, and detracts from the piety and solemnity of the occasion.⁴¹ Yet at Korope it is the officials who are enjoined to sobriety, suggesting that their own behaviour had not been above reproach in the past.

Several inscribed laws deal with clothing, and these are often extremely precise. At Korope, the law is a simple one, and in fact does not even apply to the pilgrims, compared with some of the clothing regulations from sanctuaries which were clearly para-local, such as at Andania and Lykosoura. Officials at Korope were to wear white garments and a wreath. Unlike the detailed Andanian prescriptions, this one is ungendered.

The mystery celebrations of Andania provide the Greek world's most expansive and detailed document concerning how people were to behave at the celebration of the Mysteries. The behaviour of both officials and those being initiated (the *mystai*) is regulated. Turning to the *mystai*, most of whom would have been pilgrims who had made their way to Andania for the Mysteries, the inscription lays down clothing provisions largely relating to the women pilgrims; male pilgrims seeking initiation had to follow a simple prescription: to be barefoot and wear a white tunic.⁴²

At Andania, the regulations are to prevent women from making ostentatious displays of their dress. While the female cult officials had prescribed clothing, it is the restrictions on the dress of the female pilgrims which is of interest here. The value of any clothing for women initiates was to be limited to 100 drachmas, and for female slaves

---

39 *LSCG* 51 (*SIG*³ 1109; AD 164/5 BC), lines 63-66. See Kloppenborg and Ascough 2011, 241-57 no. 51 for a translation and commentary; see 256 for the behaviour of cult members.

40 Knidos: *LSAM* 55.

41 See Deshours 100-1 for *eukosmia* in Greek sanctuaries; the entire Andanian inscription is in fact an exercise in ensuring the *eukosmia* of pilgrims: see esp. lines 39-45.

42 Andania: *LSCG* 65, section 3, lines 15-26; Dillon 1997a, 197-98; Gawlinski 2012, 113-33. There were also regulations on what the sacred officials had to wear: see lines 15-26.

fifty drachmas; clothing was not to be diaphanous, and any stripes were only to be half a finger wide or less (hence not 'showy' and attracting attention). Jewellery, rouge and white cosmetics were prohibited, as indeed were braided hair and hair bands. Shoes were allowed, of felt or leather from sacrificed beasts. At Lykosoura in Arcadia, the cult of Despoina allowed no gold to be worn into the temple unless the intention was to dedicate the items, and similarly, rings could not be worn; purple or black clothing was prohibited, as was any bright clothing; women had to be barefoot.[43] At both of these pilgrimage centres, clothing was therefore regulated—in particular, women's clothing.[44] At Lykosoura, chthonic overtones are detected in the prohibition of black and purple, while at Andania the regulations seem mainly to have been sumptuary in nature.[45]

The Oracular *Pinakia* of the Pilgrims at Korope

Returning to the Korope decree, the officials then received the tablets—*pinakia*—from those consulting the oracle. This is the first mention of the *pinakia*, and it must be assumed that each consultant had brought a *pinakion* (a small tablet on which a consultant would have written, presumably, the question they wished to put to the oracle) with them into the temple when they were called by the secretary. When this process was completed, the *pinakia* were to be placed in an urn, to be sealed with the seals of the generals, the nomophylakes and the priest, and placed in the temple. At dawn the next day, the secretary of the god (not the *prophetes*) was to take out the urn, and show the seals on it to officials, clearly to indicate that the seals had not been broken. Each *pinakion* was then returned to its respective consultant in the order of the list on the whiteboard. These persons (the general, nomophylax and priest) would then deal with the next stage of the procedure:

> *They are to receive the tablets (pinakia) from those who are consulting the oracle: when the consultation takes place, they are to throw them into a vessel, and seal it with the seal of the generals and guardians of the laws,* **(45)** *and similarly with that of the priest, and allow them to remain in the sanctuary; at dawn the secretary of the god is to bring in the vessel, show the seals to the aforementioned and open them, and call them up from the record and hand over to each their tablets (pinakia) ….* [About 25 letters are missing here, then there is a reference to *oracular responses: chresmoi.*]

These regulations all appear very straightforward, but the decree reveals little of the actual process of consultation and response because apparently the oracular mechanism itself did not need to be given. What form this response took is completely unknown

---

43 Lykosoura: *LSCG* 68; Dillon 1997a, 198-99.
44 For the issue of women's clothing in Greek cults, see Mills 1984; Culham 1986; Dillon 1997a, 196-99.
45 Other inscribed clothing laws, beside Andania and Lykosoura: *LSCG* 28, 32; *LSCG Suppl.* 32, 91; *LSAM* 6, 16, 14, 35, 77, 84.

(as at Dodona, in which consultants made use of lead tablets).[46] Yet as the decree indicates, the oracle was more popular than ever before with outsiders, so its reputation was obviously a good one, and it satisfied the enquirers with its prophetic responses.[47]

'Maintaining Orderly Behaviour'

Next, the decree after this missing section briefly mentions the *rhabdouchoi* again:

> **(50)** *The staff-bearers are to give thought to maintaining orderly behaviour…*

The *rhabdouchoi* are being requested to maintain order during the oracular procedure, and are to use their initiative to think of means by which they could maintain good behaviour, implying a need to think about how to *prevent* disorderly behaviour.

The Oath to Enforce the Decree

There is then a section on ensuring that the office-bearers have carried out their assigned tasks correctly. Interestingly, the oath to be sworn is applied after the actual oracular proceedings, whereas, in the Andanian inscription, cult personnel take oaths prior to the proceedings.[48] The oath is therefore an examination of conduct during office, a *euthyna*, to ensure that the officials have obeyed the decree's instructions. Whereas Zeus Akraios and Apollo Koropaios have been previously mentioned, this is the first reference to Artemis Iolkia (Artemis of Iolkos), one of the deities of Demetrias named in the prescript, with Iolkos being one of the towns within the *synoikismos* of Demetrias; the nomophylax Menelaos son of Philippos came from that city. She was clearly an important local goddess to be mentioned alongside these two other prominent deities.

> *When the official assembly meets in the month Aphrodision, first of all the examiners (exegetai) in the presence of the people are to administer to the aforementioned persons the following oath: 'I swear by Zeus Akraios and* **(55)** *Apollo Koropaios and Artemis Iolkia and all the other gods and goddesses that I have performed everything as clearly stated in the decree regarding the oracle ratified during the priesthood of Krinon son of Parmenion.'* **(60)** *And when they have sworn, they will be blameless, but if anyone does not take the oath he is to be liable to prosecution by the examiners and anyone of the citizens who wishes on account of this dereliction, and if the examiners fail to carry out any of the duties aforesaid, they are to be answerable to the examiners who succeed them and to anyone else who wishes.*

---

46 For *pinakes* at Dodona, see Parke 1967, 1-163; Dillon 1997a, 80-81, 94-97; Dillon 2017, 324-32, with examples of two tablets: 328-29 figs 8.2 & 8.3.
47 For the *pinakes* at Korope, see esp. Robert 1948, 25-26.
48 Oath of the Sacred Men and Sacred Women, *LSCG* 65 lines 1-11, 132-37; oath of the *gynaikonomos*, lines 26-28.

'And a copy of the decree is to be inscribed on a stone stele'

As with such decrees, they were inscribed and the *stelai* set up where they could advertise their provisions: in this case, in the sanctuary of Apollo Koropaios, next to the building that the *neokoros* made use of, the *neokorion*, where in fact this inscription was discovered. This is the first mention of a *neokoros*, found in many Greek sanctuaries, who was responsible for the overall care and maintenance of a sanctuary.

> *In order that the decree may be in force for all time,* **(65)** *the generals and guardians of the laws elected each year are to hand over this decree to the officials who have been appointed in due course. And a copy of the decree is to be inscribed on a stone stele after a contract has been put out by the officials in charge of repairing the city walls (teichopoioi), and then erected in the sanctuary of Apollo Koropaios.*

Preserving the Sanctuary Grounds from the Pilgrims

A second decree, now numbered as II, follows. An increase in the number of pilgrims brought with it a process of sanctuary embellishment and expansion. The decree in fact points to this at Korope: 'to make the grandeur of the place more apparent,' the *temenos*, the area around the temple itself, had been expanded and extended. But this desire for the grandeur of the setting had in turn raised concerns about what was always a significant part of a sanctuary: its trees. Many sacred laws, in fact, have provisions to protect a sanctuary's trees against visitors.[49]

> **II (70)** *When Krinon son of Parmenion was priest, on the tenth of the month Areios, Krinon son of Parmenion of Homolion priest of Zeus Akraios, and Dionysodoros son of Euphraios of Aiolis general of the league (koinon), and the generals and guardians of the laws proposed the motion:*
>
> *Since the existing trees in the sanctuary of Apollo Koropaios have been destroyed,* **(75)** *we consider it to be necessary and advantageous that some attention be paid to this, so that when the precinct (temenos) has been increased in size, the large extent of the area becomes more noticeable. Therefore it has been resolved by the Council and the People that the person appointed to be the neokoros (supervisor) is to make clear to all those who are present at the sanctuary at any time that no-one, whether citizens, others living here, or visitors staying here,*[50] **(80)** *is permitted to cut down or lop trees*

---

49 For other regulations prohibiting the cutting of wood from sanctuary trees for firewood, and even collecting fallen branches, see: *LSCG* 36, 37, 47, 57, 65, 84, 91, 111, 148, 150a–b; *LSCG Suppl.* 36, 81, 115a; *IG* XIV.645.I.128-38; *BCH* 1920 p. 78, no. 11; *SIG*³ 685, cf. 1097; Paus. 2.28.7. See the lists at *LSCG Suppl.* 81, p. 143; Dillon 1997b, 115; Kloppenborg and Ascough 2011, 51 (partial).

50 Thirteen letters are missing here. This translation is based on the restoration of *SIG*³ 1157. *IG* IX2 1109 restores the missing letters to give the term '*metics*' (resident foreigners); this would take up too many letter spaces but the sense of 'others living here' is the same: i.e. *metics*, foreigners

in the designated area, and likewise that they are not to bring in animals for the sake of pasture or stabling. If not, he is to pay a fine of [50] drachmas to the city, and **(85)** *half of the fine exacted shall be immediately given by the treasurers to the informant. If he is a slave, he is to be whipped with a hundred lashes in the agora by the generals and guardians of the laws and pay a fine of one obol per animal. The information about such acts is to be laid with the designated magistrates.*

It would, as is often the case, be the responsibility of the *neokoros* to inform those visiting the shrine that no damage was to be done to its trees. This in fact seems to have been what had actually happened at the sanctuary. In a culture in which the main form of fuel was wood, there was a temptation for those visiting the shrine—either locals or the *xenoi*—to take an axe to the most readily accessible fuel. Moreover, once again similarly to other sacred sites, there was a provision against grazing animals within the newly extended *temenos*.[51] Some of the *xenoi* might well have brought their own sacrificial animals with them for worshipping the gods and as a source of sustenance, as well as beasts of transport such as horses and mules. The emphasis in these lines is on making the sanctuary more attractive to the greater number of consultants who are now coming to the shrine.

The fine of fifty drachmas for free men transgressing and committing an infraction would have been substantial: this figure is, however, restored. The decree provides that the person who successfully denounced someone for harming the trees, that is an eyewitness, would receive half of this substantial amount. As soon as the fine was paid the informant received his half: an inducement to inform.

Slaves, however, would be flogged and not fined: as always, given that they would usually have been committing this felony because of their master's orders, they bear the punishment, but a flogging would also mean that the slave would be unable to work for some time, and hence be a punishment for his master. One hundred strokes of the lash would be delivered in the agora—a very public place, and presumably before the flogging commenced, the name of the owner of the slave would be publicly announced.

The provision at Andania was similar: no wood could be cut from with the sanctuary grounds. A slave would be flogged and a free man fined, but no details of the amount of the penalty are given in either case.[52]

---

residing in the country. The visitors are the *xenoi* who are staying there for the consultation of the oracle. All categories of free persons 'who are present at the sanctuary at any time' are thus dealt with by the decree.

51 For inscriptions concerning the grazing of beasts and the presence of beasts in general within sanctuary grounds, see *SIG3* 685.80-82; 826 G.21; 963.35-37; *IG* I3 4.14-15; *IG* II2 295; IG II2 310; *LSCG* 57.3-4; 67.13-26; 79.25-31; 84.13-14; 91.11-12; 104.2-8; 105; 116.2-14; 136.21-33; *Hesperia* 10, 1941, p. 67, no. 31.39; *BCH* 44, 1920, 78 no. 11d.5-8. Compare the references given at: *LSCG* 116, p. 211; *LSCG* 104 p. 199; Dillon 1997a, 120 n.68.

52 *LSCG* 65, lines 78-80.

Publicising the Regulations

Prominent positioning of inscribed regulations was of course quite typical for sacred sites. But the existence of inscribed compilations of rules does raise the usual question of the extent of ancient literacy.

> *A copy of the decree is to be recorded on a whiteboard by Philon, which is to be set up in front of the entrance of the neokorion,* **(90)** *after a contract has been put out by the officials in charge of repairing the city walls, so that all those present shall comply with what has been decided. This decree is also to be handed over as possessing the authority of legislation to the generals and guardians of the laws who have been elected in due course. This was resolved by the Council and the Assembly.*

One could perhaps assume that the rules might be read out in public prior to the actual celebration of pilgrimage events, for the Greeks, of course, were accustomed to public readings. In the case of the Andanian Mysteries, however, the regulations are very detailed and long: some 116 lines, each of some length, in the Greek.

So how did pilgrims hear about the rules at places to which they would travel, which might be several days' journey or more away? One role of *spondophoroi*, 'peace-bearers', might have been not merely to announce sacred truces for pilgrimage festivals but also to proclaim the rules governing them.[53] In addition, to what extent did the sacred officials rely on word of mouth, the rules 'doing the rounds,' and so becoming established in the folklore? Oral transmission can be assumed in some cases. The woman pilgrim who turned up at Andania with a chestful of clothes all with stripes bigger than half a finger wide and diaphanous, or only garments each worth more than one hundred drachmas, would have been in serious trouble. She would either have to flout the laws and risk the punishment (confiscation of the offending garments), or would need to make new wardrobe arrangements as quickly as possible. Clothes that did not fit the rules were confiscated, dedicated to the gods of the Mysteries. Perhaps the markets referred to in the Andanian inscription would sell appropriate clothing for initiates participating in the Mysteries.

Several inscriptions for pilgrimage sites regulate what clothing and jewellery could be worn, with prohibitions concerning hair styles and cosmetic make up. Andania, Korope, Lykosoura and others had specific sacred discourses about clothing. Specific punishments were applied when the rules were not obeyed: confiscation was usually the penalty for the offending item. In looking at the behaviour of pilgrims at Greek sacred sites, an abundance of epigraphic testimonia provide relevant information. There are several inscriptions dealing with the behaviour of worshippers at panhellenic and regional pilgrimage centres. There are methodological problems as always. Do inscribed rules about behaviour reflect that problems of behaviour had occurred in the past? Or, on the other hand, are the authorities anticipating potential trouble, based on their

---

53   For *spondophoroi*, see Dillon 1997a, 1-10; Rutherford 2013: 42, 72, 88, 92, 186.

experiences at other sacred sites, reports of misbehaving pilgrims elsewhere, or their knowledge of the human psyche?

Who Wrote the Rules?

A distinction between sacred and civic authority is not generally discernible for ancient Greek sanctuaries. The larger sanctuaries were not owned by a cult group: temples, lands and sanctuaries were not the property of the devotees of a particular god but rather the state in which the sanctuary was situated. It was the smaller shrines that were owned—and managed–by what could be called 'private' cult groups, such as that of the Iobacchoi discussed above. The state generally administered the finances, lands and festivals of the god, and regulated the behaviour of worshippers, and at Andania this entailed everything from their collecting of firewood to their use of bathing water. Even when a small shrine was owned by a group of private citizens, it adopted the same civic procedure, with the male members meeting together and passing decrees about the cult they controlled.

Often the circumstances behind the passing of sacred laws are not given. The civic authorities do not generally indicate what had prompted them to pass the regulations, although one can presume several possibilities. Some infringement of a customary but not legislated provision may have occurred (as seems to have been the case at Knidos, see above). For the Mysteries of Despoina at Lykosoura, it may well have been traditional that women not wear gold ornaments or purple, black or bright clothes, nor shoes, nor braided hair. Perhaps some infringement of these customary practices then led to these being written up as sacred regulations, and inscribed on stone. Or it might simply have been the epigraphic habit of the Greeks—as the centuries rolled by, the Greeks became more and more proficient at inscribing matters of importance, and this could be part of that process. Sacred matters mattered—it was important to worship the gods appropriately.

Fining and Thrashing Pilgrims

So far, these have all been rules made by sanctuary authorities to govern behaviour and indicate their expectations. To ensure that these rules were adhered to, *rhabdouchoi* were present not only at Korope, but also at the Andanian Mysteries and Olympia. But managing a few pilgrims would have been quite different from controlling an unruly crowd. Three *rhabdouchoi* at Korope were thought sufficient to control the proceedings, but actual 'crowd-control' would have been difficult. Sanctuaries do not seem to have employed a police force as such.

According to Diodoros, 20,000 Greeks attended the Olympics in 324 BCE to hear the official pronouncement of Alexander the Great's 'Exiles Decree.'[54] This is a immense number of people. And yet there were no police as such at Olympia, except for a handful

---

54   Diod. Sic. 18.8.2-8; 18.8.5.

of whip-bearers. Contrast this with the three hundred Scythian archers the Athenians employed to keep order in the Athenian assembly place, where there was probably room for 6,000 Athenian citizens to assemble.[55] Ancient sources, particularly Epictetus and Lucian, describe the dust, thirst and heat at Olympia, as well as the flies.[56] One would have thought that tempers would flare more often than they did. Perhaps if they did, the *hellanodikai* would call upon the *mastigophoroi* to restore order: but clearly when there was a riot, they would have been powerless. When a crowd of pilgrims rioted at the Olympic festival in 388/7 BCE, nothing is said by the sources of any attempt to subdue the rioters or to punish them:[57] this would have been beyond the ability of the Olympic *rhabdouchoi*.

There were two main methods by which the civic authorities in charge of sanctuaries punished those who did not obey the inscribed regulations. These were, firstly, fining those who disobeyed the rules, or, secondly, by having them thrashed with rods. Exclusion from the cult activity itself was also utilised as a punishment in the case of the Andanian Mysteries. While fines could be heavy, they did not involve public humiliation as such, except when these fines were accompanied by a public record of the offence, as at Olympia. Thrashing by the *rhabdouchoi* and *rhabdophoroi* to maintain control will have been a public exercise, and therefore humiliation was part of the punishment.

Fining was common for offences at pilgrimage centres. There are no fines in the first decree concerning pilgrims at the shrine at Korope, simply the threat of blows for consultants. The proposers of the decree regarding the oracle at Korope, and those who voted for it, envisaged that the use of rods to inflict blows would be the main means of keeping order. Pushing and shoving was perhaps the main issue, not the breaking of regulations as such. This is in marked contrast with other pilgrimage centres, which routinely resorted to fines. For example, athletes at Olympia who broke their sacred oath, sworn on the flesh of a boar sacrificed to Zeus, were fined. From the proceeds of the fines, statues of Zeus—called Zanes—were commissioned. Pausanias describes these and how cheating could occur. In fact, he devotes an entire chapter to the Zanes and the reasons why specific statues were erected. That is, it was a significant theme and he dwelt on it at length.[58]

To pursue the example of Olympia a little further, fines could be levied when an athlete bribed the other competitors to 'throw' the match. This happened on several occasions. In one case, the fathers of two of the boy competitors came to an agreement. One was desperate that his son should win, while the other was more interested in the money. Pausanias specifically states that the *hellanodikai* fined[59] not the two boys, but

---

55 Andokides 3.5.
56 Epictetus *Discourses* 1.6.23-29, also 1.18.22; Luc. *Anacharsis* 17; Hdt. 8. Cf. for Olympia's flies: Ael. *Nat. An.* 5.17; Paus. 5.14.1.
57 Diod. 14.109.1-3; Dion. Hal. *Lysias* 29-30.
58 Paus. 5.21, esp. 5.21.2 for his definition of the Zanes.
59 For the *hellanodikai*, see Dillon 2020.

their fathers.⁶⁰ Herodotos knows of beatings at Olympia, for he refers to those starting before the signal as being 'struck'.⁶¹ Athletes in the gymnasium at Beroia who were guilty of misdemeanours were struck with rods.⁶²

The case of Lichas the Spartan at Olympia is also relevant for pilgrims: the Spartans had been banned from the Olympic festival of 420 BCE by the authorities of Elis who controlled the festival. Lichas nevertheless decided to enter a two-horse chariot team in that event. When it was victorious, the victory was proclaimed by the *hellanodikai* not as one for Sparta (as it had been excluded) but for Boeotia: but Lichas then came into the stadium and crowned the charioteer, to indicate that he, a Spartan, owned the horses. For this, Thucydides points out, he was thrashed by the *rhabdouchoi*.⁶³ One assumes that this was on the orders of the *hellanodikai*: Pausanias states that the *hellanodikai* whipped Lichas (rather than that he received blows from the *rhabdouchoi*), but Thucydides is more accurate.⁶⁴ Clearly there were no socio-economic distinctions about receiving blows,⁶⁵ and this will also have applied at Korope. Lichas was, after all, wealthy enough to have entered a two-horse chariot team in the races and to have made the pilgrimage to Olympia with it; moreover the sources indicate that he was elderly.⁶⁶

With whipping, particularly as prescribed for slaves for various offences in the Andanian decree, there would have been some formal judicial procedure, and then the convicted slave would have been placed in a whipping frame, and flogged. On the other hand, beating with rods required no formal binding of the offender's limbs: in the incident involving Lichas, it seems as if the *rhabdouchoi* came into the stadium and rained blows on him where he stood. This might very well have been like the beatings the athletes in training are seen receiving on Athenian vases. Lichas's case also seems to indicate that there were no interstate sensitivities: the *rhabdouchoi* beat him despite his being a Spartan—Sparta being a powerful state. But the Eleians and Spartans were on unfriendly terms at this stage, which could account for this, and he may have been being punished specifically because he was a Spartan. Questions of authority and jurisdiction also come into play. Once a pilgrim entered a sacred site, they became subject to the regulations that the relevant civic and religious authorities had decided upon for that site: the regulations were often, as at Andania and Korope, made clear through inscribed decrees.

---

60 Paus. 5.21.17. Pausanias records other instances of fines for competitors: e.g. Paus. 6.6.6.
61 Hdt. 8.59.
62 *SEG* 27.261b, lines 8-10, 21-23, 69-70.
63 Thuc. 5.49-50; Xen. *Hell.* 3.2.21-22; Paus. 6.2.2-4; cf. Diod. 14.17.4 (on the ban).
64 Paus. 6.2.2; cf. Xen. *Hell.* 3.2.22.
65 There is no Greek word for receiving blows that is equivalent for flogging (*LSJ⁹* 1417 col. ii; Thuc. 6.50.4 writes 'Lichas received blows').
66 For this incident see, Forbes 1952, 170; Crowther and Frass 1998, 67; Dillon 1997a, 46-47, 54, 114; esp. Hornblower 2000, 212-25. On punishment in Greek athletics, see Forbes; Crowther and Frass 1998. After the Peloponnesian War, Lichas had some revenge by erecting a victory-statue of himself at Olympia (Paus. 6.2.4).

The number of blows given to unruly consultants is not recorded in the Korope inscription and possibly there was no set prescription. Similarly, the otherwise meticulous rules of the Andanian Mysteries are vague in recording the number of blows to be delivered against those misbehaving when the sacrifices were being performed or the Mystery rites took place. In prescribing a whipping for slaves for various offences, there is simply a vague reference to a 'lashing'. There might have been some standard number for when a slave was flogged as a punishment, though the severity of the offence would also have been considered by the relevant authorities. At Korope, in cases of disturbances, the *rhabdouchoi* might well simply have struck blows or used their staffs to threaten consultants until order was restored.

Given the large numbers of pilgrims that attended some of the panhellenic festivals, it is a wonder that more is not heard about difficulties of policing them. For example, the *telesterion* (initiation hall) for the Eleusinian Mysteries had a seating capacity of about three thousand people.[67] And yet they all processed in and out, and viewed the revelation of the Mysteries, without any particular problems ever being recorded. Presumably the pilgrim *mystai* were in a state of awe as they entered and left, subdued and pious, filled with reverence.

The Behaviour of Pilgrims from Andros at Delphi

It is perhaps this material about fining and thrashing at pilgrimage sites, resulting from pilgrim misbehaviour, that helps to explain and contextualise a well-known decree of Andros.[68] This involves the self-regulation of its official state contingent (*theoria*) of pilgrims to Delphi. Concerns for the nature of the behaviour of the official participants are made clear. Five members of the *theoria*, chosen by the Andrian boule, were to fine disorderly *theoroi*—up to five drachmas each day, presumably for the duration of their bad behaviour. Misbehaviour is not defined by the decree: the decision was presumably made, perhaps jointly, by the five as to what constituted this. Upon their return to the island of Andros, the *theoroi* were to report to the boule the names of their fellow *theoroi* whom they had so punished. So, there was a fine, as well as public humiliation when the *theoroi* returned home. Such a stipulation is not otherwise known for other *theoroi* visiting Delphi or other sacred sites, but it is possible that it existed elsewhere. On the other hand, a specific incident that occurred during a previous Andrian *theoria* might well have prompted this legislation, or it might simply have been a contingency arrangement, just in case. Other states might well have assumed that their *theoroi* would behave, or that the authorities at the panhellenic site would deal with this (as indeed the *rhabdouchoi* at Korope and Andania would have done).

---

67 Dillon 1997a, 64; see Clinton 1974, 13 for estimates of how many were initiated at Eleusis each year.
68 *LSCG Suppl.* 38 a & b; Rougemont 1977, 37-47 is still essential; see esp. Rutherford 2013, 369-72 B3.

Conclusion

Pilgrims of ancient Greece making their way to panhellenic and other sacred sites will presumably have been motivated by piety, and in the case of the state-financed pilgrims (*theoroi*) also by a sense of duty to their state. This piety, and the desire to worship the gods at their main sanctuaries did not, however, preclude acts of misbehaviour by pilgrims at all levels. In fact, at Korope, the very anxiousness on the part of worshippers to participate and to derive the maximum benefit from their religious experience might itself have led to misbehaviour, with pilgrims possibly jostling to be amongst the first to consult the oracle or receive their response. A primary motivation of the changes to the oracular procedure at Korope was to ensure *eukosmia*, good order, throughout the oracular proceedings, which took place over two days, during which there would have been many consultants within the sanctuary. New procedures were embodied in decrees of the sovereign assembly of Demetrias, which had jurisdiction over the sanctuary, and were publicly displayed so that worshippers would be aware of them. At Korope, city officials and law-enforcers (*rhabdouchoi*) were empowered to act to ensure *eukosmia*. Ritual change was brought about through the agency of the state's appointed officials, who were ritual agents only because the demos empowered them to be so. The deity, Apollo Koropaios, had bestowed many benefactions (*euergesiai*), and orderly behaviour throughout the sanctuary, for the two days set apart for consultation, was a mark of piety on the part of the community. Authorities at pilgrimage sites such as Korope punished transgressions with blows, whippings, fines and exclusion from their rites. Yet the final conclusion must be that while piety, and the desire to worship the gods at their main sanctuaries, did not preclude acts of misbehaviour by pilgrims, most worshippers abided by the rules and were not disorderly.

Abbreviations

IG	*Inscriptiones Graecae*
LGS	Prott, J. de & Ziehen, L. 1896-1906. *Leges Graecorum sacrae e titulis collectae*, Leipzig.
LSCG	Sokolowski, F. 1969. *Lois sacrées des cités grecques*, Paris.
Michel *Recueil*	Michel, C. 1900. *Recueil d'inscriptions grecques*, Paris.
SEG	*Supplementum Epigraphicum Graecum*
SIG3	Dittenberger, W. (ed.) 1915-24. *Sylloge Inscriptionum Graecarum*, vols 1-4, Leipzig.

Bibliography

Boehm, R. 2019. *City and Empire in the Age of the Successors: Urbanization and Social Response in the Making of the Hellenistic Kingdoms*. Cambridge: Cambridge University Press.

Budin, S. 2016. *Artemis*. London: Routledge.

Clinton, K. 1974. "The Sacred Officials of the Eleusinian Mysteries." *TAPhA* 64, 1-143.

Cohen, G.M. 2004. *The Hellenistic Settlements in Europe, the Islands, and Asia Minor*. Berkeley: University of California Press.

Crowther, N.B. and M. Frass. 1998. "Flogging as a Punishment in the Ancient Games." *Nikephoros. Zeitschrift für Sport und Kultur im Altertum* 11, 51-82.

Culham, P. 1986. "Again, What Meaning Lies in Colour!" *ZPE* 64, 235-45.

Daux, G. 1959. "Sur les décrets de Démétrias relatifs au sanctuaire d'Apollon Coropaios." *BCH* 83.1, 285-87.

Deshours, N. 2006. *Les mystères d'Andania: étude d'épigraphie et d'histoire religieuse*. Paris: Ausonius Éditions.

Dillon, M.P.J. 1997a. *Pilgrims and Pilgrimage in Ancient Greece*. London: Routledge.

Dillon, M.P.J. 1997b. "The Ecology of the Greek Sanctuary." *ZPE* 118, 113-27.

Dillon, M.P.J. 2017. *Omens and Oracles. Divination in Ancient Greece*. London: Routledge.

Dillon, M.P.J. 2020. "Hellanodikai," in C. Baron (ed.) *The Herodotus Encyclopedia*, 663-64. London: Wiley-Blackwell.

Forbes, C.A. 1952. "Crime and Punishment in Greek Athletics." *The Classical Journal* 47.5, 169-73, 202-3.

Gawlinski, L. 2012. *The Sacred Law of Andania: A New Text with Commentary*. Berlin: De Gruyter.

Grant, F.C. 1953. *Hellenistic Religions*. New York: Liberal Arts Press.

Harter-Uibopuu, K. 2002. "Strafklauseln und gerichtliche Kontrolle in der Mysterieninschrift von Andania." *Dike. Rivista di Storia del Diritto Greco ed Ellenistico* 5, 135-60.

Hornblower, S. 2000. "Thucydides, Xenophon, and Lichas: were the Spartans excluded from the Olympic Games from 420 to 400 BC?" *The Phoenix* 54, 212-25.

Kloppenborg, J.S. and R.S. Ascough. 2011. *Greco-Roman Associations: Texts, Translations, and Commentary. I. Attica, Central Greece, Macedonia, Thrace*, Berlin: De Gruyter.

Kravaritou, S. 2011. "Synoecism and Religious Interface in Demetrias (Thessaly)." *Kernos* 24, 111-35.

Kennell, N.M. 2013. "Boys, Girls, Family, and the State at Sparta," in J. Evans Grubbs, T. Parkin and R. Bell (eds.) *The Oxford Handbook of Childhood and Education in the Classical World*, 381-95. Oxford: Oxford University Press.

Martzavou, P. and N. Papazarkadas. 2008. *Epigraphical Approaches to the Post-Classical Polis: Fourth Century BC to Second Century AD*. Oxford: Oxford University Press.

Meyer, M.W. 1987. *The Ancient Mysteries. A Sourcebook*. Philadelphia: University of Pennsylvania Press.

Hansen, M.H. and T.H. Nielsen (eds.) 2004. *An Inventory of Archaic and Classical Poleis*. Oxford: Oxford University Press.

Mili, M. 2014. *Religion and Society in Ancient Thessaly*. Oxford: Oxford University Press.

Mills, H. 1984. "Greek Clothing Regulations: Sacred or Profane?" *ZPE* 55, 255-65.

Parke, H.W. 1967. *The Oracles of Zeus*. Cambridge, MA: Harvard University Press.

Pouilloux, J. and N.M. Verdélis. 1950. "Deux inscriptions de Démétrias." *BCH* 74, 33-47.

Robert, L. 1948. *Hellenica: Recueil d'épigraphie, de numismatique et d'antiquités grecques,* vol. 6. Paris: Librairie d'Amerique et d'Orient Adrien-Maisonneuve.

Rosenberger, V. 2001. *Griechische Orakel*. Darmstadt: Theiss.

Rougemont, G. 1977. "Les théores d'Andros à Delphes." *BCH* Suppl. 4, 37-47.

Rutherford, I. 2013. *State Pilgrims and Sacred Observers in Ancient Greece*. Cambridge: Cambridge University Press.

Sokolowski, F. 1954. "On Prothysia and Promanteia in Greek Cults." *HTR* 47.3, 165-71.

Stavrianopoulou, E. 2006. *Ritual and Communication in the Graeco-Roman World*. Liège: Kernos.

Stillwell, R. (ed.) 1976. *Princeton Encyclopedia of Classical Site*. Princeton: Princeton University Press.

Zunino, M.L. 1997. *Hiera Messeniaka. La storia religiosa della Messenia dall'età micenea all'età ellenistica*, Udine: Forum.

5

THE EMPEROR AS A PLACE OF PILGRIMAGE

PANAYIOTIS CHRISTOFOROU

Introduction: Spontaneous Religiosity at the Ox-Heads

Natus est Augustus M. Tullio Cicerone C. Antonio conss. VIIII. Kal. Octob. paulo ante solis exortum, regione Palati ad Capita Bubula, ubi nunc sacrarium habet, aliquanto post quam excessit constitutum. Nam ut senatus actis continetur, cum C. Laetorius, adulescens patricii generis, in deprecanda graviore adulterii poena praeter aetatem atque natales hoc quoque patribus conscriptis allegaret, esse possessorem ac velut aedituum soli, quod primum Divus Augustus nascens attigisset, peteretque donari quasi proprio suo ac peculiari deo, decretum est ut ea pars domus consecraretur.

> "Augustus was born just before sunrise on the ninth day before the Kalends of October in the consulship of Marcus Tullius Cicero and Gaius Antonius, at the Ox-Heads in the Palatine quarter, where he now has a shrine, built shortly after his death. For it is recorded in the proceedings of the senate, that when Gaius Laetorius, a young man of patrician family, was pleading for a milder punishment for adultery because of his youth and position, he further urged upon the senators that he was the possessor and as it were the warden of the spot which the deified Augustus first touched at his birth, and begged that he be pardoned for the sake of what might be called his own special god. Whereupon it was decreed that that part of his house should be consecrated."[1]

The setting is Rome, projecting backwards into the fateful year of the infamous Catilinarian Conspiracy: the boy who would grow up to be Augustus is born, *regione Palati ad Capita Bubula*.[2] The place itself reportedly becomes a shrine shortly after Augustus's death, whereupon there emerged a curious story. A certain Gaius Laetorius argues in the

---

1 Suet. *Aug.* 5; all translations are from the Loeb Library editions, unless otherwise stated.
2 On the birthplace of Augustus, and a different interpretation of *Ad Capita Bubula*, see King 2010, 450-69 who argues that it in fact refers to the centre of the new geometric design that split Rome up into *vici*, with Augustus being topographically and ideologically the centre of that system,

face of adultery charges that he was in possession of the spot that Augustus had touched at birth – and accordingly requested a pardon for his crimes, citing him as a protector and personal deity. It seems to be an apocryphal story, but it suggests an interesting aspect of interactivity between a place associated with an emperor and political, cultural, religious and legal issues that can precipitate from such a situation. Importantly, it indicates that a place associated with an emperor held a numinous quality, and that it became the focus of contestation between individuals and the authorities.

There are several points of note in the passage, which largely correspond to the organisation of this chapter. The first relates to the sacred nature of the space associated with and pertaining to the emperor. In this context, sacredness is associated with a shrine dedicated at the place of Augustus's birth. As a comparison, there is a similar story connected with a space related to Augustus, which was in fact a competing place of sacredness associated with his birth.[3]

> Nutrimentorum eius ostenditur adhuc locus in avito suburbano iuxta Velitras permodicus et cellae penuariae instar, tenetque vicinitatem opinio tamquam et natus ibi sit. Huc introire nisi necessario et caste religio est, concepta opinione veteri, quasi temere adeuntibus horror quidam et metus obiciatur, sed et mox confirmata. Nam cum possessor villae novus seu forte seu temptandi causa cubitum se eo contulisset, evenit ut post paucissimas noctis horas exturbatus inde subita vi et incerta paene semianimis cum strato simul ante fores inveniretur.

> "A small room like a pantry is shown to this day as the emperor's nursery in his grandfather's country-house near Velitrae, and the opinion prevails in the neighbourhood that he was actually born there. No one ventures to enter this room except of necessity and after purification, since there is a conviction of long standing that those who approach it without ceremony are seized with shuddering and terror; and what is more, this has recently been shown to be true. For when a new owner, either by chance or to test the matter, went to bed in that room, it came to pass that, after a very few hours of the night, he was thrown out by a sudden mysterious force, and was found bedclothes and all half-dead before the door."

This time it is a small room at his grandfather's house at Velitrae to the south-east of Rome, shown to visitors (*ostenditur adhuc locus*) with a warning as to the presence of a mysterious force to anyone who enters there, with the reported conviction that it was indeed there that he was born, rather than *ad Capita Bubula*. This betrays a fascination with such places (with a concomitant competitiveness and contestation), the power associated with them, and the important notion that one would go to see and experience them.[4]

---

    the empire and the world. For more on the godly and the emperor Augustus in Suetonius, see Wardle 2012.
3   Suet. *Aug* 6.
4   Wardle 2012, 323-25 for more analysis on the religious nature of this description in Suetonius.

This interactive aspect brings us to a second point: that there is a social and legal aspect to these interactions. Gaius Laetorius cites his ownership of that bit of land which Augustus had touched at birth to help avoid legal trouble. Indeed, this is an essential theme in our evidence, that people would go and use places associated with the emperor and his image to get protection, suggesting that they were highly contested. What this entailed will be elaborated on further below, but a preliminary analytical point should be made here: there is a certain spontaneous religiosity at play in new modes of interaction that happen in a landscape that is ever-changing with the existence of an emperor and places associated with him; and indeed, modes that are not necessarily started or evoked from the top-down, but rather ones that are instigated by choices and journeys people make in this world.[5]

The purpose of this chapter is to map out the contours of the political, legal and religious with respect to examples of places associated with the Roman emperor and how they affected interactions between people. The context of this volume is a perfect situation for such an exercise, since a comparison with the ideas of pilgrimage helps illuminate fascinating aspects about how people experienced the emperor, particularly with an attention to the aspects of religiosity associated with the term. In other words, does couching the evidence of this interaction in terms of sacred travel or pilgrimage help bring out an interesting dynamic in contemporary society that involves the discourse about the emperor's divinity? Does the act of purposeful movement towards a place to seek asylum or the intercessory power of the emperor make sense solely in legal and political terms, or do the ideas of pilgrimage add to the complexity of these modes of interaction? Other discussions that have dealt with the material that will be outlined below have sought to understand the emperor in diplomatic, legal and political terms.[6] However, there is a numinous quality as well, which deserves attention. This chapter will argue that this quality is fundamental to understanding this phenomenon, which will be discussed through the examples below.[7]

The first theme involves the seeking of asylum at the statue or image of an emperor and the legal implications of this problem; problems that seemingly emerged due to the sacredness of such images, an aspect that should be duly appreciated. The second theme involves the constant phenomenon of embassies to the emperor, not only concerning the issues of mutual benefaction and *euergesia*, but also the expectation of an intercessory power that the emperor could provide, with the potential that he could solve conflicts and problems brought to him. One particularly rich text will be explored here: Philo of Alexandria's *Legatio ad Gaium* or *Embassy to the Emperor Gaius*. Before commencing, a caveat should be stated. With this chapter, I am attempting to suggest the interesting different perspectives that the lens of pilgrimage can bring to the subject

---

5   Compare with the impact of the emperor on the landscape of Rome in the form of the *Lares Augusti*: Flower 2017, Part IV, 255ff.
6   See Bauman 1974; Millar 1977, 507ff.
7   Though this cannot provide an exhaustive treatment, this chapter is the start of a wider enquiry on numinous spaces associated with the emperor and evidence of pilgrimage to those sites.

of the Roman emperor. This should not diminish the importance of other aspects that have been studied before, particularly with respect to the political, social and cultural interactivity of the Roman empire that have done so much to further our understanding of how Roman society worked.⁸ That said, it is through an appreciation of those different strands that this novel application can commence, which we turn to now.

Scholarly Inspiration and Problems

First, some brief context is necessary, both in terms of the inspiration for this chapter, and some pertinent historiography. The purpose of this chapter is to highlight a set of evidence that has not been analysed in this manner before, namely exploring the phenomenon of imperial statues being places of pilgrimage and asylum and explaining how that came to be, looking at the intersection of politics, law, religion and the act of pilgrimage or sacred travel. This is due in no small part to the nature of the evidence and the different concerns of the disparate strands of scholarship that form the germ of this particular historical experiment, insofar as they cover vastly different topics and historical questions. The focus of this section, therefore, is to recount the scholarly underpinning of this chapter and briefly to describe the historiography of four different topics of enquiry in the ancient world, which all contribute to how the evidence in this paper can be viewed. In short, through the appreciation of the questions and breakthroughs posed by these historiographical strands, we can get closer to the thought-world that gave spaces associated with the Roman emperor a numinous quality that prompted spontaneous pilgrimage for intercession and safety.

The four strands of historiography are as follows, and will be treated in this order: first, I will discuss the scholarship on the position of the Roman emperor, and how Roman historians have come to understand this enigmatic and ideologically complex monarchical position. Second, I will outline the historiography of the equally enigmatic topic of the emperor's divinity, exploring scholarly consensus and disagreement on how to understand the widespread phenomenon of the 'imperial cult' or emperor worship. Third, I will summarise scholarship on imperial statuary, particularly the important work of Jas Elsner and Peter Stewart on the encountering of images and statues in the Roman world, and how this can touch upon interacting with images of the emperor. Fourth, and not least, is the work on pilgrimage in the ancient world, exploring the definition of sacred travel and pilgrimage, how different activities of movement with a religious aspect can be described as 'pilgrimage', and the problems of defining this notoriously woolly and potentially anachronistic phenomenon. As Horden and Purcell stated, "The salient point about pilgrimage is that it need not always be a journey undertaken exclusively or even principally for religious reasons."⁹ The point here, then, is to stress the *polyvalency* of pilgrimage as an activity, and to explore how this hermeneutical tool

---

8 In particular, the place of benefaction and *euergesia* in our understanding of the Roman world: Veyne 1976; Price 1984a; Ando 2000; Zuiderhoek 2009; Noreña 2011, 107-77.
9 Horden and Purcell 2000, 445

maps onto the ritual phenomenon of taking refuge at imperial statues. All these strands of scholarship converge at this point: the place of pilgrimage in helping us understand imperial images being used as places of safety, which incorporate these overlapping themes in the study of the ancient world.

First, on the position of the Roman Emperor. The problem is a perennial one, even when posed simply: what is an 'emperor', and what in fact is the 'Roman Emperor'? This seemingly simple shorthand belies a rather complex aetiology, particularly given that this term is a neologism. Briefly, there were many titles, names and honorifics that described the imperial position, not least Augustus and Caesar: respectively, an honorific title bestowed on Octavian in 27 BCE[10] and the cognomen of the *Iulii Caesares*, of which Julius Caesar was the most famous. *Imperator*, from which our 'emperor' comes, had a more circumscribed meaning in Latin, given to a victorious general as an honorific from his troops, famously taken by the young Octavian as his *praenomen*. In other words, *imperator* does not quite cover the full sematic meaning of its modern descendant.[11] Rather, it was a combination of various titles that appear variously in imperial formulae across the empire, all of which add to the complexity of describing the position. Even the title *princeps* (whence we get the convenient descriptor of the era, 'principate') cannot necessarily be used as a shorthand *in toto*, though it preserves both the idea of primacy (being the most prominent in the state) and an adherence to republican antecedents and political formulations.[12] As Cooley has recently restated, for Augustus and Tiberius, the term *statio* was used to describe their position, which designated a guard post or a watch, thus implying aspects of protection and service as part of their remit.[13] All this to say that the position of the Roman emperor was both complex in its function and roles, and similarly challenging to delineate.

This is, moreover, reflected in the historiography of the Roman emperor. A full discussion of the vast bibliography on the Roman emperor would be impossible, but the most important matter to note about these interpretations is variety. From wider studies of the position as a whole, such as Mommsen's 'constitutional' interpretation of the emperor as nothing more than a magistrate, through to Millar's 'Emperor at Work', where he was a reactive administrator responding to petitions, towards Ando and Noreña's work on the emperor as a unifying symbol, and more concentrated works on the constitutional and charismatic aspects of the position as formulated by Augustus, and particular studies on emperors, such as Osgood's important contribution to understanding the position

---

10 *RG* 34.2: Cooley 2009, 262: "'Augustus' was pregnant with potent polyvalent implications: sanctity, heroization; divine election; mediation between gods and the Roman people …"
11 cf. Drinkwater 2019, 1 for the problems of the moniker 'emperor'.
12 This tension between accentuating primacy and showing deference and adherence to older political structures was a feature of the emperor being embedded into imperial society; cf. Dench 2018, 136.
13 Cooley 2019, 73-79 for a comprehensive treatment of the use of *statio* in Augustan and Tiberian terminology. See, for example, the *senatus consultum de Pisone Patre* (Eck 1996) in particular, ll. 129-30: '*omnem spem futuram paternae pro r(e) p(ublica) stationis in uno repos[i]ta<m>*' cf. Vell. Pat. 2.124, 131.

through his study of Claudius[14]—what is fundamental here is to underline the variety of scholarly interpretation on the position, suggesting the vast potential for different impressions of the Roman emperor.

Indeed, the view from Ando and Noreña that concentrated on the organisation of opinion through ideology and official media is fundamental, as it pointed towards appreciating perceptions of the Roman emperor, and how they matter in understanding how the emperor *seemed* to his subjects. This particular historiographical impetus can be seen in the recent work of Olivier Hekster on the imperial succession, which explores how Rome and other communities across the empire understood the imperial family,[15] and Kaius Tuori's work on the emperor's position with respect to the law, which reflects perceptions of the emperor's legal and judicial role.[16] Furthermore, the impact of Flaig's groundbreaking work on the legitimation of the imperial position is still being felt and realised, particularly in his idea of an *Akzeptanzsystem*, which meant that the emperor had to be 'accepted' by important constituents across the empire or he could risk removal, suggesting a more subjective understanding of how political legitimation worked in the early empire.[17] In all, we are in a scholarly moment that is attempting to take the 'popular' role of the Roman emperorship more seriously. This strives to access and chart the thought-world concerning the Roman emperor from the perspective of inhabitants across the Roman empire. This chapter, in many ways, builds on this work.

Second is the closely related world of the 'imperial cult', or in particular the question of the emperor's divinity. Similarly, the bibliography on this topic is immense, with the potential for studying the phenomenon more widely being steadily improved, with further evidence published and made available for analysis.[18] Not only is the material plentiful, but the nature of the phenomenon is similarly extensive. As Beard, North and Price stated in their *Religions of Rome*, "there is no such thing as *the* Imperial Cult,"[19] which is to say that the rituals and practices associated with honouring the emperor and his family with cannot be easily categorized and defined, on numerous aspects such as religious feeling, agency, whether 'local' or 'state-mandated', and the similarities and differences of those practices empire-wide. Thus any comprehensive treatment of the historiography of the imperial cult in its various forms is impossible here, though a couple of points should be made.[20]

---

14 Mommsen 1887/8; Millar 1977; Hopkins 1978; Ando 2000; Noreña 2011; Osgood 2011, 25-26. cf. Levick 2010.

15 Hekster 2015, esp. 1, where the importance of appearance and perception is underlined.

16 Tuori 2016.

17 Flaig 2010, 275-80; cf. Flaig 1992.

18 For overviews on the bibliography, see Herz 2007, 316; Naylor 2010, 208-15 and McIntyre 2018. Important studies include: Price 1984a; Fishwick 1987; Friesen 1993; Harland 2003; Burrell 2004; Fujii 2014.

19 Beard *et al.* 1998, 348. This is provocatively placed at the head of the introduction to McIntyre 2018, 1.

20 A more comprehensive explanation of the historiography of the 'imperial cult' appears in the literature review articles by Naylor 2010, which is a good summary of work on the imperial cult

Before Price's *Rituals and Power*, the question of emperor worship was treated under the category of political life, thus describing a phenomenon of building political favour, which was poorly clothed as a religious practice.[21] Price problematised this distinction, and concentrated on ritual practice and what it means for defining the emperor's position, thus helping bridge the gap between religious practice and political and diplomatic engagement in the Greek east during the imperial period. Though this book remains influential, consensus is hardly secure, not least due to the fact that a comprehensive treatment of the whole phenomenon eludes us, with many studies focusing on certain time periods, regions or cities in order to make the analysis of the material more manageable.[22] What is fundamental to stress, however, about this particular moment in the study of the imperial cult is the appreciation of its polyvalency. To paraphrase Herz, the imperial cult is both a religious and a social phenomenon, changing in time and space, found across the empire, and cannot be reduced to a dichotomy of ritual practice and belief (or lack thereof).[23]

Furthermore, this recent work has pushed closer to appreciating the 'godly' aspects of emperor worship.[24] Though staying clear from calling the emperor a 'god' in a theological sense, this work has fleshed out aspects of the divine around the imperial position, including honours received in the Greek east, and the meaning of the Latin terms *genius* and *numen*, which appear in contexts of worship.[25] One particular tension that has been scrutinised is the place of the imperial centre and provincial communities in patronising and expanding the imperial cult, with a concentration on what that means for peer-polity interaction across the Mediterranean, questions of engendering loyalty, and the cultivation of favour.[26] This work does much to explain the function and results of the imperial cult, yet it skirts around a perennial issue in the study of this phenomenon; namely, how to explain the variety of activities that fall under the rubric of 'emperor worship' that may seem to fall outside state or civic religion, and what they could suggest about the people who undertook those activities.

To return to Herz's paradigm, the 'imperial cult' was a polyvalent phenomenon, and thus not a single set of practices. This brings us to the question of perception, thinking about emperor worship from the bottom up, and how people interacted with the emperor's divine status. The evidence discussed in this paper, namely slaves and women going to imperial statues for protection, brings us very close to real-world interactions

---

in Roman history and early Christian studies, and McIntyre 2018, which explores different aspects of the phenomenon.
21 Nock 1930; cf. Naylor 2010, 209-10.
22 See Herz 2007, 307-16 for a good survey of different potential avenues of inquiry into the 'imperial cult'.
23 Herz 2005, 638, summarised and analysed in McIntyre 2018, 2.
24 Veyne 2002: "Il n'était pas dieu en vertu de son mérite personnel, il était dieu parce qu'il était empereur."
25 Price 1980; Price 1984b; Scheid 2003, 159-65: "It was power that could be understood and thought of as the epiphany of a divine power in the hands of a mortal"; Gradel 2002.
26 cf. Harland 2003, 88-89.

between people and representations of the Roman emperor.[27] It suggests that this activity not only had a political/legal dimension, but also a fundamentally religious one, thus bringing it into line with established scholarship that problematised strict demarcations between politics and religion in the Roman world, though viewing that haziness through a different lens. As Gradel showed in his influential work on emperor worship in Italy, the semantic range of divine honorifics to the emperor was ambiguous enough to problematise distinctions between human and divine honours, which suggests an ambiguity in how people understood and interacted with imperial representations.[28] In other words, it should not be surprising that statues and images of emperors were regarded numinously, which has very important implications for how we understand the acts of movement towards those representations.

Building on this idea of ambiguous understandings of the emperor and the imperial cult is a third strand of scholarship on imperial statuary. This chapter is underpinned by certain assumptions and findings of the work of Jas Elsner and Peter Stewart. First, in an article on ancient responses to art, Elsner points out that responses to statues, images and representations need not only be philosophical or literary, but also allow for a range of responses, including ritual practices, the sacred, numinous and miraculous.[29] This opens up the scope of potential responses to imperial representations that build from questions of the emperor's divine status. In his monograph *Statues in Roman Society*, Stewart describes the proliferation and ubiquity of statues in Roman society, both at Rome and across the empire.[30] Similar to Elsner, Stewart outlines the various potential responses and understandings of statuary, both in the taxonomies of terms used to describe statues and images in both Greek and Latin, and the impact of these statues on different aspects of life. Through his careful description of the terminology of statues,[31] Stewart argues that though there were distinctions in the usage of terms, particularly between statues that depict gods and those that depict humans, there was some degree of flexibility, suggesting a haziness:[32]

> "But these were expectations rather than clear-cut and consistent religious beliefs or compelling normative values. The language of the cult image arose from social practice rather than conceptual distinctions. Even among the painstakingly precise taxonomies of Roman law, the religious status of a statue was not always clear, or at least, the terms were sufficiently vague as to elude modern scholarship."

---

27 Herz 2007, 311 on the place of statues in those interactions.
28 Gradel 2002, esp. 234-50.
29 Elsner 1996, 526. Cf. Chaniotis 2017, esp. 11 and Chaniotis 2014, esp. 268; cf. Osborne 2012 67, 72 on the power of images.
30 Stewart 2003, 125-28; cf. Tac. *Ann.* 2.53.
31 Stewart 2003, 20-28, and esp. 186-87.
32 Stewart 2003, 190: "Language often appears to challenge norms as well as reinforce them."

This problem is particularly important for the emperor and his images, which operates in this world of vagueness. The key, then, is to explore the perception of these images and interactions with them, accentuating the ambiguities, viewing this from the bottom up, rather than purely exploring the power dynamics of imperial images across the empire and their role in Roman dominance.[33] Again, polyvalence is the essence here.

This brings us to the final strand of scholarship and the inspiration for this chapter, namely pilgrimage in the ancient world. Pilgrimage is a challenging concept to engage with because of the looseness of the terminology, and the fact that it has closely been associated with the practices of Christianity. This background presents a formidable problem, as those who study ancient religions have tried to move away from importing Christianising assumptions into the rituals and practices of antiquity.[34] Yet, forms of travel with a religious component are indeed a feature of ancient societies that require explanation outside the concerns and prejudices that we as scholars may import on those activities. As Elsner and Rutherford have articulated:

> "The problem of all this is that it denies the cult-centres of antiquity their rightful place at the centre of a vital network of religious activity whose meanings were not solely about politics or economics but also about subjectivity, culture, and individual as well as collective identity."[35]

This statement informs the purpose of this chapter, particularly in looking at evidence of asylum-seeking at imperial statues and religious spaces associated with the emperor within a framework of pilgrimage. In other words, I seek to view such activity from different angles that do not only have to do with the politics and economics of the emperor in the Roman world. My particular interest in pilgrimage is to accentuate a certain spontaneity and agency to those who sought out imperial intercession, particularly at images of the Roman emperor. For me, pilgrimage helped focus a couple of common characteristics to the examples I will discuss: the existence of numinous spaces, *purposeful* travel towards them, and the expectation of help and protection when there. The focus is then, from a wider perspective, to explore how people in the Roman empire interacted with spaces associated with the Roman emperor. Building off Elsner and Rutherford's 'typology of ancient pilgrimage', this chapter, seeks to add

---

33 Ando 2000, 237: "The ability of portraits to demand veneration, as it were, made them active forces within local affairs. They were instruments of power, they became powerful and animate in their own right"; Stewart 2003, 170: "Perhaps most importantly the cult of the emperors with their temples and sanctuaries, altars and statues was, like some of the other statuary dedications considered above, a centripetal cult, serving to reinforce long-distance relationships with the absent emperor or the imperial house and thereby also emphasizing the distance and the difference."
34 Elsner and Rutherford 2006, 6-7.
35 Elsner and Rutherford 2006, 8.

a wrinkle to their typology,[36] which will hopefully form the basis of a larger study on travel towards and concerning the Roman emperor with a religious component.

The Problem with Statues and the Case of Annia Rufilla

The first theme involves the legal problems to do with the image of the emperor, which speaks to the ambiguities of perception and interaction that have been outlined in the various historiography trends above. Particularly in the *Digest,* which was a compilation of Roman legal texts made in the sixth century, the chapter on *maiestas*, most often translated as 'treason' committed against the emperor in the early principate, has several entries on legal issues arising from imperial images and statues.[37] Examples include damage inflicted on the emperor's statue, leading to different provisions in law where people were not thought to be liable, such as melting 'rejected' statues (i.e. those that had not been consecrated), or throwing a stone that inadvertently hit a statue.[38] The specificity of these provisions almost seems absurd, yet they do highlight the status of imperial images and their sacredness, and the difficulty it must have presented to jurors.[39] There is open subjectivity to these examples, as the believability of the stone being thrown indeterminately and just happening to strike a statue of the emperor is at least questionable, meaning that it could be completely discretionary whether or not such cases were tried.

Nonetheless, it does show the array of potential problems that could abound from improper conduct with imperial images, which is reflected in further evidence. It should be stated that the nature of the evidence does not seem to make clear whether or not such instances resulted in trial and capital punishment, but it is not the purpose here to discuss the remit and validity of *maiestas* trials, but rather highlight the interesting notion that images of the Roman emperor could be problematic nodes of contention in society, thus highlighting their sacredness. As such, it is interesting to note that earlier in the *Tiberius*, it is said that the citizens of Nemausus in Transalpine Gaul threw

---

36   Elsner and Rutherford 2006, 12-27 for their typology on Greco-Roman pilgrimage, which involves many examples with public sanction, such as the *theoria*; cf. Elsner and Rutherford 2006, 29 for Christian activities with respect to icons and images.
37   *OCD3* sc. *Maiestas* for a short introduction on the origins of the term.
38   *Dig.* 48.4.4.1 = Scaevola *Reg.* 4.: "*Hoc crimine liberatus est a senatu, qui statuas imperatoris reprobatas conflaverit.*" *Dig* 48.4.6 = Venuleius Saturninus *de iudic. publ.* 2: "*Qui statuas aut imagines imperatoris iam consecratas conflaverint aliudve quid simile admiserint, lege iulia maiestatis tenentur.*" For a discussion of the origins of this particular problem, see Bauman 1974, 82-83, referring to a passage in Tacitus where Tiberius vetoes a case concerning a L. Ennius, who had been charged with *maiestas* for melting a silver statue of Tiberius (Tac. *Ann.* 3.70).
39   cf. Bauman 1974, 84 and Plin. *Ep.* 10.81.2, concerning the charges against the orator Dio Chrysostom for placing a statue of Trajan near the sepulchre of his wife and son. Trajan (10.82) rejects the suit. The implication is that such a case could have been taken up, if it were not for Trajan's intervention. Thus, there were many potential permutations from such cases. *Dig* 48.4.5.1 = Marcianus *Reg.* 5.

down Tiberius's images and busts during his exilic years before he became emperor.[40] In Suetonius's *Nero*, the emperor's statues were being decorated with props and verses in criticism of his proclivities and waning acceptability.[41] In Suetonius's *Galba*, one of the reported *omina* that predicted the fall of the Julio-Claudians saw the heads of statues of the Caesars struck off.[42] In Plutarch's *Galba*, scenes of vigilante justice occur in proximity to fallen statues of Nero, where Spiculus the Gladiator gets destroyed.[43] In Dio, there is a case that is comparable to the list Suetonius provides above, where a woman gets sentenced to death for undressing in front of an image of Domitian.[44] In the *Historia Augusta*, the author describes the fall of Commodus's regime as the 'casting down' of his statues.[45] Under Caracalla are further stories of instances that correspond to Suetonius's list above, which includes a young knight who took a coin with the emperor's image into a brothel,[46] and an example of men being condemned for urinating near the statues and images of the *princeps*.[47] Despite the nuances and differences in these stories, they all contain the focal point of the Roman emperor's image at its core, with the correlation that these ubiquitous images created situations of potential social cohesion and conflict, used in a myriad of ways to express opinion, allegiance and disparagement towards the emperor. Such activity, then, makes them interesting objects to think with due to their suggestive sacred status, especially in light of Stewart's stress on flexibility as discussed above.

This context brings us to the use of these statues as refuges or asylums.[48] Similar to the issues of *maiestas*, Justinian's *Digest* contains many different excerpts concerning the status of statues and images of the emperor, particularly pertaining to use of these as sources of protection or places of refuge.[49] The opinions of the jurists included can be split into two groups, which take different stances on the validity of taking refuge at an imperial statue. First is Ulpian, who describes the duties of governors in cases of maltreatment of slaves at the hands of their masters. It is in this context that Ulpian

---

40 Suet. *Tib.* 13.1.
41 Suet. *Ner.* 45.2. cf. Suet. *Dom.* 13.2, for another example of a quip placed on an imperial monument.
42 Suet. *Galb.* 1.
43 Plut. *Galb.* 8.7; cf. 22.4 and 26.7, where statues of Galba are overthrown by soldiers. cf. *Dig.* 48.4.7.4 = Modestinus, *Pand.* 12., which states that any violations of images or statues are more serious when perpetrated by soldiers.
44 Dio 67.12.2. Cf. Dio 68.1.1.
45 SHA, *Pert.* 6.3. cf. Gleason 2011, 49 for a discussion of Commodus's fall, and Dio 74(73).2.1 in particular; cf. Barry 2008, 222-46 for the evidence of collective violence and the mutilation of bodies during the ritual executions at the *Scalae Gemoniae* at Rome.
46 Dio. 78(77).16.5.
47 SHA, *M. Ant.* 5.7.
48 Bauman 1974, 85-92.
49 *Dig.* 1.6.2 = Ulp. *de off. procons.* 8; *Dig.* 1.12.1.1 = Ulp. *de off. praef. urb.* 1; *Dig.* 21.1.17.12 = Ulp. *ad ed. aedil. curul.* 1; *Dig.* 47.10.38 = Scaevola *Reg.* 4.; *Dig.* 48.19.28.7 = Callistratus *de cogni.* 6

provides an example from a rescript of the Emperor Antoninus Pius which involved the fleeing of slaves to an imperial statue due to alleged brutal treatment, which is as follows:

> Dominorum quidem potestatem in suos servos illibatam esse oportet nec cuiquam hominum ius suum detrahi: sed dominorum interest, ne auxilium contra saevitiam vel famem vel intolerabilem iniuriam denegetur his qui iuste deprecantur. ideoque cognosce de querellis eorum, qui ex familia Iulii Sabini *ad statuam confugerunt*, et si vel durius habitos quam aequum est vel infami iniuria affectos cognoveris, veniri iube ita, ut in potestate domini non revertantur. qui si meae constitutioni fraudem fecerit, sciet me admissum severius exsecuturum.

> "It is proper that the power of masters over their slaves should remain unimpaired, and that no man should be deprived of his right; but it is to the interest of the masters themselves that relief from cruelty, hunger, or intolerable injury, should not be denied to those who justly implore it. Therefore, take cognizance of the complaints of those slaves of Julius Sabinus who fled for refuge to the Imperial statue; and if you find that they have been treated with greater severity than was proper, or subjected to disgraceful outrage, order them to be sold, under such conditions that they may not be restored to the power of their master; and if he violates this my Constitutions, let him know that he will be more severely punished."[50]

Accordingly, those at the bottom of society were here seen to have used images and statues of the emperor for protection against their masters, and even if the rights of the master were protected, nonetheless there was this sense that one could thus appeal to Caesar for protection.[51] It seems the ability to take refuge at imperial statues is directly connected to their sacred status, which then prompts the legal response. In this case, then, this is a response to spontaneous and purposeful pilgrimage to imperial statues for imperial intercession, and one that had to be regulated by imperial authorities. Along these lines, Hopkins rightly pointed out that in this rescript Antoninus Pius had to walk a fine line between protecting the rights of the masters and saving the slaves from cruelty.[52] Indeed, this can also be observed in the next passage, which goes against the use of these images to injure anybody else, including the mobile use of an emperor's image to provoke someone else:

---

50 *Dig.* 1.6.2 = Ulp. *de off. procons.* 8; cf. *Dig.* 1.12.1.1 = Ulp. *de off. praef. urb.* 1. on the similar duties of the prefect at Rome. Compare with an early statement from Seneca in his *De Clementia*, on the ability of slaves to take refuge at the emperor's statue: Sen. *Clem.* 1.18.2: *servis ad statuam licet confugere*: "It is allowed for slaves to seek refuge at a statue" cf. *Dig.* 21.1.17.12 = Ulp. *ad ed. aedil. curul.* 1, which includes the opinion that slaves who flee to statues should not be seen as fugitives; cf. Hopkins 1978, 222.

51 Hopkins 1978, 222-24.

52 Hopkins 1978, 222.

Ad statuas confugere vel imagines principum in iniuriam alterius prohibitum est. cum enim leges omnibus hominibus aequaliter securitatem tribuant, merito visum est in iniuriam potius alterius quam sui defensionis gratia ad statuas vel imagines principum confugere

"It is forbidden to seek sanctuary at the statues or portraits of the Emperor, in order to cause another injury; for as the laws afford equal security to all men, it seems reasonable that he who takes refuge at the statues or the portraits of the Emperor does so rather in order to injure another than to provide for his own safety …"[53]

Thus, steering a delicate course could actually be the perception of support for one group over another, leaving a polarised impression of the emperor's conduct in terms of law and justice.[54] Moreover, it brings into relief the several different potential actors: not only masters and the slaves, but also governors, urban prefects and curule aediles, who had to navigate the intricacies and ambiguities of these cases that revolved around the contested space that an imperial image or statue created due to the nature of who it represented, which was a novel and abundant locus of interaction between different members of society. This meant that the emperor was not only the mediator that had to solve disputes, in that he had the power to enact and override statutes, with expectations of fairness and civility being placed on him in order to find solutions to social and legal problems, but he was also the reason such interactions could occur in the first place. This is complicated further due to perceptions of the sacredness of the image, which prompted asylum-seeking and travel to those spaces. The intercessory aspect of this phenomenon should not be underestimated, and suggests that there was a certain religiosity surrounding the interaction with these images, based on being able to escape and go to these images for protection.

A striking example of such an interaction is the case of Annia Rufilla in 21 CE, as written by Tacitus:

Exim promptum quod multorum intimis questibus tegebatur. incedebat enim deterrimo cuique licentia impune probra et invidiam in bonos excitandi arrepta imagine Caesaris: libertique etiam ac servi, patrono vel domino cum voces, cum manus intentarent, ultro metuebantur. igitur C. Cestius senator disseruit principes quidem instar deorum esse, sed neque a diis nisi iustas supplicum preces audiri neque quemquam in Capitolium aliave urbis templa perfugere ut eo subsidio ad flagitia utatur. abolitas leges et funditus versas, ubi in foro, in limine curiae ab Annia Rufilla, quam fraudis sub iudice damnavisset, probra sibi et minae inten-

---

53   *Dig.* 48.19.28.7 = Callistratus *de cogni.* 6; The multivalency of potential legal cases that were brought to the attention of the emperor is staggering as shown in Millar 1977, 507-49, which provides a comprehensive look at the various cases. The brandishing of effigies evokes what Matthew Dillon has described in his contribution to this volume on the rules of engagement in Greek religion.
54   cf. above Chapter 1.2, for the similar problem of the emperor's relationship to the law.

dantur, neque ipse audeat ius experiri ob effigiem imperatoris oppositam. haud dissimilia alii et quidam atrociora circumstrepebant, precabanturque Drusum daret ultionis exemplum, donec accitam convictamque attineri publica custodia iussit.

"Next there came into the open a matter which, given the secrecy of their complaints, many had been covering up. All the basest individuals had been overcome by a form of licence whereby their stirring up abuse and resentment against good people was accomplished with impunity, since at the same time they were grasping an image of Caesar; and even freedmen and slaves were dreaded spontaneously when they raised their voices and hands against patron or master. Therefore C. Cestius, a senator, said that, *though principes were of course like gods,* the gods did not listen unless the pleas of their suppliants were just, and no one escaped to the Capitol or the City's other temples to use them as a refuge for outrageous purposes; the laws were inoperative or turned upside down when in the forum, at the threshold of the curia, abuse and threats were levelled at him by Annia Rufilla, whom he had convicted of fraud before a judge, and he for his part dared not risk a trial because of her brandishing against him the Commander's likeness. Drusus was enveloped by similar cries from others (and by ones of a more frightful nature from some), and they kept pleading that he should set an example of retribution, until finally he ordered that, once summoned and convicted, she should be held in public custody."

Her actions were described as part of a growing tendency for those of lower station in society provoking the *boni* in society by grasping an *imago Caesaris*. The result was a seeming change in the power dynamics between opposed groups.[55] Against this general background was the more specific case of Gaius Cestius and Annia Rufilla, with the latter abusing the former in public and then seeking protection from an *effigies imperatoris*.[56] In light of such occurrences, Cestius himself sought refuge in appealing to Drusus the Younger for aid, since he argued the laws effectively had been overturned and become useless.[57] The result was that Drusus set an example by convicting and imprisoning Annia Rufilla.[58] It is interesting that both chose a recourse that involved the emperor or the imperial family. The imperial image, and by proxy the emperor, would be seen as a protector of her opinions and thoughts, shielding her from potential reprimand and litigation from others in society. Accordingly, the emperor and his image were a pressure valve, adding to the idea that they were locations of social cohesion and conflict, where problems of justice could be negotiated. Not only do these episodes highlight the expectations of success and fear of failure with respect to justice and legal matters, they also show the potential for religious interpretation of such matters. From all this

---

55 Tac. *Ann.* 3.36.1; translation is from Woodman.
56 Tac. *Ann.* 3.36.3:
57 Tac. *Ann.* 3.36.2-4
58 Tac. *Ann.* 3.36.4.

evidence, then, we can tentatively reconstruct a history of 'pilgrimage' to such images of the Roman emperor, considering the polyvalent considerations behind this phenomenon, including the nature of the Roman emperor, his political and divine status, and the place of statues in society. Fleeing to images of the emperors, then, seems to be a purposeful act that acknowledges the sacredness of his position and that his representations reflect this status, with all the problematic ambiguities that entailed. Note too how, in the passage above, the emperors are described by Cestius as *instar deorum*, and then he proceeds to use a religious context to argue why Rufilla's actions were impious: based on interpretations that the pleas of the suppliants were in fact just, and that asylum was used at sanctuaries for proper reasons only. Therefore, this conceptually acknowledges the similarity of the emperor's image to religious locations and places, which is of course corroborated by Rufilla's actions of using them as a place for protection against others, and thus that sacred travel and pilgrimage was a potential activity.

The Case of Philo's *Legatio Ad Gaium*

The second example involves a discussion of an account of an embassy in the first century CE. It should be stated here that there is a theme of similarity to the evidence of the statues just discussed, namely the expectation of intercession or justice in the presence of the Roman emperor. Indeed, in Millar's *Emperor in the Roman World*, prime place is also given to the story in Philostratus of Marcus Aurelius at Sirmium hearing an embassy on an accusation against Herodes Atticus at Athens for tyranny.[59] The full context falls out of scope here, but it does elucidate the great array of possibilities of location for such interactivity, made all the more complex by the itinerant nature of emperor. In this section, the discussion will be restricted to a couple of examples from Philo's *Legatio ad Gaium*, or the Embassy to the Emperor Gaius.

Philo was an Alexandrian Jew who was a member of a prominent family in the city and his community.[60] Of particular note are two treatises that discuss the intercommunal turmoil occurring at the beginning of the first century CE at Alexandria, notably the *In Flaccum* (Against Flaccus), directed at the governor of Egypt and his incompetence, and the *Legatio*, which is a long treatise detailing the account of that strife, as well as that of the embassies that went to Caligula to settle their dispute. Of course, its length allows Philo to explore several different topics of interest, revealing fascinating perspectives on the position of the Roman emperor in the world, including descriptions of the frenzied revelry surrounding the accession celebrations of Gaius, continual examples of subsequent misconduct by Gaius, a long digression on how he did not in fact resemble gods that he attempted to emulate, the virtues of conduct of both Augustus and Tiberius as emperors, and also the escalation of concern in the run-up to the embassy, namely the attempt to build a statue of Gaius in the Temple

---

59 Millar 1977, 4-5.
60 For more on this context, see Smallwood 1970. On a new biography of Philo and particularly his intellectual thought, see Niehoff 2018.

at Jerusalem.⁶¹ There are several potential vignettes on which one could focus, but a couple will have to suffice.

The first comes in the part of the narrative that discusses the virtues of Augustus, and involves the description of the Sebasteion facing the harbours at Alexandria, the jewel amongst other edifices dedicated to the divine Augustus, but here especially showing an interesting comparison to the religious activity associated with maritime travel for the safety of their voyage:

> οὐδὲν γὰρ τοιοῦτόν ἐστι τέμενος, οἷον τὸ λεγόμενον Σεβαστεῖον, ἐπιβατηρίου Καίσαρος νεώς, <ὃς> ἀντικρὺ τῶν εὐορμοτάτων λιμένων μετέωρος ἵδρυται μέγιστος καὶ ἐπιφανέστατος καὶ | οἷος οὐχ ἑτέρωθι κατάπλεως ἀναθημάτων, [ἐν] γραφαῖς καὶ ἀνδριάσι καὶ ἀργύρῳ καὶ χρυσῷ περιβεβλημένος ἐν κύκλῳ, τέμενος εὐρύτατον στοαῖς, βιβλιοθήκαις, ἀνδρῶσιν, ἄλσεσι, προπυλαίοις, εὐρυχωρίαις, ὑπαίθροις, ἅπασι τοῖς εἰς πολυτελέστατον κόσμον ἠσκημένοις, ἐλπὶς καὶ ἀναγομένοις καὶ καταπλέουσι σωτήριος.

> "For there is elsewhere no precinct like that which is called the Sebasteion a temple to Caesar on shipboard, situated on an eminence facing the harbours famed for their excellent moorage, huge and conspicuous, fitted on a scale not found elsewhere with dedicated offerings, around it a girdle of pictures and statues in silver and gold, forming a precinct of vast breadth, embellished with porticoes, libraries, chambers, groves, gateways and wide open courts and everything which lavish expenditure could produce to beautify it—the whole a hope of safety to the voyager either going into or out of the harbour."⁶²

The description of the offerings on display at this *temenos* is astounding, and it gives us a tiny glimpse into the activity associated with the emperor concerning an important aspect of his rule: the maintenance of the peace and prosperity of the empire. Moreover, the mention of a temple with a specific epithet, which can perhaps be rendered as 'Caesar the Disembarker',⁶³ suggests a direct connection between the seafaring traffic of the harbour, the religious activity of the area and the place of the emperor within that context of movement. This means that there was a cognitive connection between religious ideas and expressions of safety in movement, and the place of the emperor in those ideas as the figure who ensures of the safety of the empire as a whole. This vignette also suggests that this precinct was a place to visit in and of itself, and with its connections to safety, it can be compared with the expectations of safety at imperial statues.

---

61   Philo *Leg.* 188.
62   Philo *Leg.* 151, cf. Fishwick 1984 for a study on the Sebasteion.
63   cf. Paus. 2.32.2: "τούτου δὲ ἐντὸς τοῦ περιβόλου ναός ἐστιν Ἀπόλλωνος Ἐπιβατηρίου", which refers to a temple at Troezen with the same epithet, in the context of thanksgiving after a sea-voyage. This suggests allusions to both Augustus's connection with Apollo more generally seen in his iconography, and an association with safety with respect to seafaring.

To move onto the embassy itself, there is a vignette of both of the Alexandrian delegations attempting to follow and catch the attention of Gaius, leaving Rome to go to Campania. Philo describes the despair of the Jewish delegation in the wake of the news concerning the proposed image of Jupiter to be set up in the Temple, and their anxieties about not being able to gain an audience with him after such trials and tribulations of the journey getting to Italy.⁶⁴ After many frustrated attempts, they gain an audience at the Gardens of Maecenas in Rome itself:

ἡμεῖς δὲ ὡς αὐτὸν εἰσαχθέντες ἅμα τῷ θεάσασθαι μετ' αἰδοῦς καὶ εὐλαβείας τῆς ἁπάσης νεύοντες εἰς τοὔδαφος ἐδεξιούμεθα, Σεβαστὸν Αὐτοκράτορα προσειπόντες· ὁ δὲ οὕτως ἐπιεικῶς καὶ φιλανθρώπως ἀντιπροσηγόρευσεν, ὡς μὴ μόνον τὴν ὑπόθεσιν ἀλλὰ καὶ τὸ ζῆν ἀπογνῶναι. σαρκάζων γὰρ ἅμα καὶ σεσηρώς, "ὑμεῖς," εἶπεν, "ἐστὲ οἱ θεομισεῖς, οἱ θεὸν μὴ νομίζοντες εἶναί με, τὸν ἤδη παρὰ πᾶσι τοῖς ἄλλοις ἀνωμολογημένον, ἀλλὰ τὸν ἀκατονόμαστον ὑμῖν;" καὶ ἀνατείνας τὰς χεῖρας εἰς τὸν οὐρανὸν ἐπεφήμιζε πρόσρησιν, ἣν οὐδὲ ἀκούειν θεμιτόν, οὐχ ὅτι διερμηνεύειν αὐτολεξεί. πόσης εὐθὺς ἀνεπλήσθησαν ἡδονῆς οἱ τῆς ἐναντίας μερίδος πρέσβεις, ἤδη κατωρθωκέναι διὰ τῆς πρώτης ἀναφθέγξεως Γαΐου τὴν πρεσβείαν νομίζοντες· ἐπεχειρονόμουν, ἀνωρχοῦντο, | τὰς θεῶν ἁπάντων ἐπωνυμίας ἐπεφήμιζον αὐτῷ.

"When we were brought into his presence, the moment we saw him we bowed our heads to the ground with all respect and timidity and saluted him, addressing him as Emperor Augustus. The mildness and kindness with which he replied to our greeting was such that we gave up not only our case but our lives for lost! In a sneering, snarling way he said, "Are you the god-haters who do not believe me to be a god, a god acknowledged among all the other nations but not to be named by you?" And stretching out his hands towards heaven he gave utterance to an invocatory address which it was a sin even to listen to, much more to reproduce in the actual words. How vast was the delight which at once filled the envoys on the other side! They thought that Gaius's first utterance had secured the success of their mission. They gesticulated, they danced about and invoked blessings on him under the names of all the gods."⁶⁵

Much like the case of Annia Rufilla, there is a contestation in the presence of the emperor concerning the appropriate conduct towards him, which also includes aspects of a religious encounter. There seems to be an ever-changing set of rules of engagement here, made problematic with the question of the divinity of Gaius in this context. This problem was brought to the forefront by the accusation of Gaius that they do not consider him a god. However, it should be noted that the Jewish delegation is described as paying due reverence to the emperor; and it should be remembered that the Alexandrian

---

64 Philo *Leg.* 185-92.
65 Philo *Leg.* 352-55.

Jews are there to gain favour with Caligula in order to secure their rights and safeguard the Temple. An important comparison should be drawn with the Alexandrian Greeks, who had made a similar trip in order to gain audience and favour with the emperor as well, and seem to be on the opposite end of the spectrum to the Jews with respect to treating emperors as godly.[66] This scene is made all the richer by the theme of religiosity in the topics of conversation, involving the sacrifices offered by the Jewish community for Gaius's recovery from his sickness, which should blur the lines between the political and the religious. Essentially, this evidence elucidates the aspect of going to the emperor with a purpose for favour, made complex by his status between the human and the divine, and the conflicts that arose from all the ambiguities that status elicited.

Conclusion

Whilst the examples here were not meant to be exhaustive, they should be suggestive of a thought-world that allowed for the intertwining of the political, cultural, religious and legal aspects with respect to the emperor. Images and places of importance related to the emperor became nodes of contestation for the inhabitants of the empire, which created opportunities for pilgrimage, whether it was to visit a place associated with an emperor, seek refuge at a statue for asylum and hope for his intercession, seek protection for travel itself, or go to the emperor personally to solve disputes. All of these activities have aspects of sacred travel embedded in them, and taking inspiration from the idea of pilgrimage allows us to treat them together. Travel concerning the emperor had a sacred component to it, in that the power of an emperor could create spaces into which people could go for protection, which conjures up comparative images of asylum-seeking at temples in the ancient world or seeking sanctuary at churches in later history. Importantly, the ambivalence of this evidence rather suggests the complex place of the emperor in his world, in which he had to fulfil several roles simultaneously. Thinking about how people would travel to an image of the emperor, or even to the emperor himself, in this manner adds to the complexity of this world, in which aspects of the divine and human affairs could be inextricably mixed, evading simple delineation into different categories. Thus, pilgrimage becomes an essential concept with which to think about encounters with the emperor and his image in the Roman world.

---

66   Cf. Wardle 2012, 320-21 for a 'religious' encounter with the emperor Augustus in Suet. *Aug.* 98.2, with allusions to cult practices. The scenes of joy and exultation are similar in both Philo and Suetonius, as is the idea of the emperor being a focus of cult: "The sailors had probably prayed or Augustus Epibaterios for a safe voyage in the Caesareum at Alexandria as they left."

Bibliography

Ando, C. 2000. *Imperial Ideology and Provincial Loyalty in the Roman Empire.* Berkeley: University of California Press.

Barry, W.D. 2008. "Exposure, Mutilation, and Riot: Violence at the *Scalae Gemoniae* in Early Imperial Rome." *Greece and Rome* 55, 222-46.

Bauman, R.A. 1974. *Impietas in Principem: A Study of Treason against the Roman Emperor with Special Reference to the First Century A.D.* Munich: C.H. Beck.

Beard, M., J. North, J. and S.R.F. Price, 1998. *Religions of Rome.* Cambridge: Cambridge University Press.

Béranger, J. 1953. *Recherches sur l'aspect idéologique du principat.* Basel: F. Reinhardt.

Burrell, B. 2004. *Neokoroi: Greek Cities and Roman Emperors.* Leiden: Brill.

Champlin, E. 2008. "Tiberius the Wise." *Historia* 74, 408-25.

Chaniotis, A. 2014. "Ἡ Ζωὴ τῶν ἀγαλμάτων." *Proceedings of the Academy of Athens* 89, 246-97.

Chaniotis, A. 2017. "The Life of Statues of Gods in the Greek World." *Kernos* 30, 91-112.

Christoforou, P. 2023. *Imagining the Roman Emperor: Perceptions of Rulers in the High Empire.* Cambridge: Cambridge University Press.

de Coulanges, F. 1891. *Histoire des Institutions Politiques de l'ancienne France: La Gaule Romaine, part 2, vol. 1.* Paris: Hachette.

Dench, E. 2018. *Empire and Political Cultures in the Roman World.* Cambridge: Cambridge University Press.

Drinkwater, J.F. 2019. *Nero: Emperor and Court.* Cambridge: Cambridge University Press.

Eck, W., A. Caballos and F. Fernández (eds) 1996. *Das senatus consultum de Cn. Pisone patre.* Munich: C.H. Beck.

Elsner, J. 1996. "Image and Ritual: Reflections on the Religious Appreciation of Classical Art." *The Classical Quarterly* 46, 515-31.

Elsner, J. and I. Rutherford (eds.) 2005. *Pilgrimage in Graeco-Roman & Early Christian Antiquity: Seeing the Gods.* Oxford: Oxford University Press.

Ewald, B.C. and C.F. Noreña (eds.) 2010. *The Emperor and Rome: Space, Representation, and Ritual.* Cambridge: Cambridge University Press.

Fishwick, D. 1984. "The Temple of Caesar at Alexandria." *American Journal of Ancient History* 9, 131-34.

Fishwick, D. 1987. *The Imperial Cult in the Latin West: studies in the ruler cult of the western provinces of the Roman Empire.* Leiden: Brill.

Fishwick, D. 2007. "*Numinibus domus divinae.*" *Zeitschrift für Papyrologie und Epigraphik* 159, 293-96.

Flaig, E. 1992. *Den Kaiser herausfordern: Die Usurpation im Römischen Reich.* Frankfurt: Campus.

Flaig, E. 2010. "How the Emperor Nero Lost Acceptance in Rome", in Ewald and Noreña 2010, 275-88.

Flower, H. 2017. *The Dancing Lares and the Serpent in the Garden: Religion at the Roman Street Corner.* Princeton: Princeton University Press.

Friesen, S.J. 1993. *Twice Neokoros: Ephesus, Asia, and the cult of the Flavian Imperial Family.* Leiden: Brill.

Fujii, T. 2013. *Imperial Cult and Imperial Representation in Roman Cyprus.* Stuttgart: Franz Steiner Verlag.

Gleason, M. 2011. "Identity Theft: Doubles and Masquerades in Cassius Dio's Contemporary History." *Classical Antiquity* 30, 33-86.

Gradel, I. 2002. *Emperor Worship and Roman Religion.* Oxford: Clarendon Press.

Harland, P.A. 2003. "Imperial Cults within local cultural life: Associations in Roman Asia." *Ancient History Bulletin* 17, 85-107.

Hekster, O. 2015. *Emperors and Ancestors: Roman Rulers and the Constraints of Tradition.* Oxford: Oxford University Press.

Herz, P. 2005. "Caesar and God: Recent Publications on Roman Imperial Cult." *Journal of Roman Archaeology* 18, 638-48.

Herz, P. 2007. "Emperors: Caring for the Empire and Their Successors," in Rüpke 2007, 304-16.

Horden, P. and N. Purcell, 2000. *The Corrupting Sea: A Study of Mediterranean History.* Oxford: Blackwell.

Hopkins, K. 1978. *Conquerors and Slaves.* Cambridge: Cambridge University Press.

King, R.J. 2010. "*Ad Capita Bubula*: The Birth of Augustus and Rome's Imperial Centre." *Classical Quarterly* 60, 450-69.

Levick, B. 2010. *Augustus: Image and Substance.* Harlow: Longman.

McIntyre, G. 2019. "Imperial cult." *Brill Research Perspectives in Ancient History* 2, 1-88.

Millar, F. 1977. *The Emperor in the Roman World: 31 BC–AD 337.* London: Duckworth.

Mommsen, T. 1887/8. *Römisches Straatsrecht.* Third edition, 3 vols. Leipzig: S. Herzel.
Naylor, M. 2010. "The Roman Imperial Cult and Revelation." *Currents in Research* 8, 207-39.
Niehoff, M. 2018. *Philo of Alexandria: An Intellectual Biography.* New Haven: Yale University Press.
Nock, A.D. 1930. "Σύνναος θεός." *Harvard Studies in Classical Philology* 41, 1-62.
Noreña, C.F. 2011 *Imperial Ideals in the Roman West: Representation, Circulation, Power.* Cambridge: Cambridge University Press.
Osborne, R. 2010. "Relics and Remains in an Ancient Greek World Full of Anthropomorphic Gods." *Past and Present* 206, 56-72.
Osgood, J. 2011. *Claudius Caesar: Image and Power in the Early Roman Empire.* Cambridge: Cambridge University Press.
Peppard, M. 2011. *The Son of God in the Roman World: Divine Sonship in its Social and Political Context.* Oxford: Oxford University Press.
Price, S.R.F. 1980. "Between Man and God: Sacrifice in the Roman Imperial Cult." *Journal of Roman Studies* 70, 28-43.
Price, S.R.F. 1984a. *Rituals and Power: The Roman Imperial Cult in Asia Minor* Cambridge: Cambridge University Press.
Price, S.R.F. 1984b. "Gods and Emperor: The Greek language of the Roman Imperial Cult." *Journal of Hellenic Studies* 104, 79-95.
Rüpke, J. ed. 2007. *A Companion to Roman Religion.* Oxford: Blackwell.
Saller, R.P. 1980. "Anecdotes as Historical Evidence for the Principate." *Greece and Rome* 27.1, 69-84.
Sartre, M. 2009. *Histoires Grecques: Snapshots from Antiquity*, trans. C. Porter. Cambridge, Mass.: Belknap Press of Harvard University Press.
Smallwood, E. 1970. *Philonis Alexandrini Legatio ad Gaium.* Leiden: Brill.
Stewart, P. 2003. *Statues in Roman Society: Representation and Response.* Oxford: Oxford University Press.
Tuori, K. 2016. *The Emperor of Law: The Emergence of Roman Imperial Adjudication.* Oxford: Oxford University Press.
Veyne, P. 1976. *Le Pain et Le Cirque: sociologie historique d'un pluralisme politique.* Paris: Seuil.
Veyne, P. 2002. "Qu'était-ce qu'un empereur romain? Dieu parce qu'empereur." *Diogène* 199, 3-25.
Wallace-Hadrill, A. 1981. "The Emperor and His Virtues." *Historia* 30, 298-323.
Wardle, D. 2012. "Suetonius on Augustus as God and Man." *The Classical Quarterly* 62, 307-26.
Zuiderhoek, A. 2009. *The Politics of Munificence in the Roman Empire: Citizens, Elites, and Benefactors in Asia Minor.* Cambridge: Cambridge University Press.

6

VIRTUAL PILGRIM? UNCHOSEN MOBILITY AND RELIGIOUS PLACE-MAKING IN THE ROMAN ARMY

ANNA COLLAR

Introduction

Movement naturally forms an intrinsic part of the study of pilgrimage, whether this is the movement to and from the shrine in question, movements within a sacred location, or mobile performances such as dancing or other kinetic rituals and their role in the construction of sacred places.[1] In this chapter, however, I want to invert the notion that pilgrimage is something that requires a physical journey to a particular place. Here, I want to consider how the term 'pilgrimage' can also be used to frame the mental processes of reconnection with a distant place when people are removed from it, as part of a narrative that extends into different times and places. I want to suggest that it might be possible to see migrant people engaged in what can be termed 'virtual pilgrimage' to a special place they have left behind.

One of the key issues raised in scholarship of the 'mobilities turn'[2] in the social sciences is that mobility is not always chosen, or something one has control over.[3] In this unchosen situation, the rebuilding of and reconnecting with religious practices and memories from 'home' has been shown to be an important strategy of migrant place-making within a new context. I wonder if such acts of religious place-making by people who have been removed from their home can also be included under the umbrella term of 'pilgrimage': as Rutherford and Elsner suggest, part of the "usefulness of pilgrimage" is in its capacity to "enliven the surviving data with that extraordinary

---

1 Coleman and Eade 2004; Kristensen 2018; Collar and Kristensen, this volume; for an alternative perspective, see Frankfurter, this volume.
2 See discussion in the introduction to this volume.
3 Sheller and Urry 2006.

range of possibilities present in the lived and living practices of pilgrimage".[4] With this expressly comparative approach and the agenda of this volume in mind, in this chapter I will consider the religious place-making strategies of those who have undergone unchosen mobility as 'virtual pilgrimage'. I will look at soldiers serving in the Roman army: men who followed orders from above as to the enacting of their mobility. By looking at their lives from the perspectives of mobility and pilgrimage, it is possible to examine their religious behaviours from a different angle—in other words, to see their actions as enabling them to create meaning and reclaim power and a sense of place in their world of motion over which they otherwise had little control.

Choice, Migration, and Religious Place-Making

I will start by considering the fact that migration and mobility is not always chosen. To me, one of the most interesting elements in the mobilities turn is the stated attempt to account for "zones of connectivity, centrality and empowerment in some cases, and of disconnection, social exclusion, and inaudibility in other cases".[5] In other words, mobility is a resource to which people have unequal access, and which is framed by the ways in which materials and institutions operate that can exert economic and political coercions on movement. There are subaltern voices that are inextricably bound into mobility—the "idealisation of movement, or transformation of movement into a fetish, depends upon the exclusion of others who are already positioned as not free in the same way".[6] People who have less control over mobility—whether this means their ability to be mobile, or their ability to *refuse* to be mobile—are those who have usually formed the subaltern: women, children, the poor, the enslaved and, to some extent, ordinary soldiers.

Sociological work with modern migrant women, for example, has shown that although these women have left their families to work abroad for economic reasons, they do not phrase this mobility as a choice. These are women from developing countries who have been 'fortunate' enough to be able to leave their homes to find work in first-world countries, from which they send their earnings home in order to give their children a better life. However, although they couch their mobility in terms of 'fortune' or 'luck', they also demonstrate continuing anxiety over their situation. This anxiety is centred on the lack of finality to their migration: they want to be with their families, but do not have the financial means to bring them over to where they now live, or else are locked into patterns of repeated and emotionally painful travel in order to visit 'home'. Riven as they are from their loved ones, they cannot be settled, even two decades in to their migrant lives.[7] In fact, their mobility—although it technically is 'chosen'—serves to demonstrate the unevenness of mobility itself: "this may take the form of uneven quali-

---

4   Rutherford and Elsner 2005, 7.
5   Sheller and Urry 2006, 210.
6   Ahmed 2004, 152.
7   Lee and Pratt 2013.

ties of experience, uneven access to infrastructure, uneven materialities, uneven subjects of mobility, and uneven events of stopping, going, passing, pausing and waiting".[8] This inequality inherent in mobility—whether this is the power to go or the power to stay, is emphasised as a crucial aspect of mobility research.

Part of the way that migrants—whether they are willing or unwilling—respond psychologically to their migration is through the reconstitution of agency, meaning and power in their lives and the creation of a sense of belonging. This is done in many ways—in particular through material culture, which I will explore further below—but it is also expressed through religious practices. I have found it fruitful to look to scholarship in the sociology of religion that has explored how many migrant diaspora groups respond to their new situations through processes described as religious 'place-making'. Such groups, whether they are willing or unwilling migrants, use religion to "carve out spaces of livelihood".[9] In his important new theory of religion, Thomas Tweed argues powerfully that religion is a major anchoring feature for people: it situates us in our bodies, our homes, our homelands and the universe. Tweed further elucidates the ways migrant groups make their new space their own: through "overlapping processes of mapping, building, and inhabiting […] it is homemaking. In other words, as clusters of dwelling practices, religions orient individuals and groups in time and space, transform the natural environment, and allow devotees to inhabit the world they construct."[10] Religion is therefore a 'key medium' that migrants use to negotiate, transform and to inhabit their new spaces.

Sociologists of religion and leading figures in theorising religion and religious practices Manuel Vásquez and Kim Knott have done important work in thinking about religious practice and religious place. They drew on three modern case studies to explore interconnected aspects of religious place-making among migrant groups. I will outline these in detail because they present potentially very useful ways of thinking about mobility and religious behaviours in the past. Their case studies were drawn from different migrant communities with different faiths in Johannesburg, London and Kuala Lumpur. The first examined the use of the individual migrant body to embody performance; the second looked at how religious community belonging was embedded at multiple different social and spatial levels from the local to the international; and the third explored the context of creating migrant visibility through the spatial management of difference and belonging.[11]

In their first case study, Vásquez and Knott showed how Christian migrants from Nigeria oriented themselves in their new context in Johannesburg through the enactment of their religious devotion. Their embodied performances of prayer and fasting were acts of bodily endurance and physical suffering. These acts built up what Peña has termed 'devotional capital', which is demonstrated through their tired and suffering

---

8   Sheller 2016, 17.
9   Vásquez and Knott 2014, 326.
10 Tweed 2006, 82.
11 Vásquez and Knott 2014, 327.

bodies.[12] This was done specifically within the contexts of what was seen by them as the 'sinful' city of Johannesburg and, in so doing, generated new and spiritually pure spaces for the migrants.[13] Beyond the individual migrant's body, religious place making can also be enacted across different scales. In their London case study, Vásquez and Knott explored how a Muslim group conducted such scalar place making—from the micro-scale of the born-again body of the convert engaged in new religious habits and a new set of gestures that connected them to others, through the meso-scale operation of missionary activities in the local region that served to connect groups and individuals into a broader social network, and beyond that to the engagement of the group with other Muslims at a macro national and international level—so providing a sense of common religious purpose at all these levels.[14]

Vásquez and Knott's final case study is perhaps the most immediately relevant to archaeological research: here, they explored the significance of spatial placement of shrines in a community and the embedding of migrant religion in Kuala Lumpur as a process of homemaking, contestation and full inhabitation.[15] A small Indian Hindu shrine was established around 1900 in the middle of a plantation, to serve the Hindu labourers who worked there. Over time, the shrine became surrounded and overshadowed by Muslim Malay suburbs of the growing city. When a particular Indian family became more involved in the shrine and increased the levels of religious activity and so the visibility of the shrine and its worshippers, the local Muslim community complained to the authorities, who decided to move or demolish the shrine in response. The patriarch of the Indian family, who was also temple president, used the case to demonstrate the inherent racism of the council. The implication was that, even though the Hindu temple was a hundred years old and the surrounding suburbs were new, it was the Hindu community who were seen as not 'belonging', who were being forced out and moved on, so segregating and dividing the community along lines of race and religion, and the perceived sense of their place—both geographical, and social. The legal battle over the temple formed an essential part of the politics of recognition for the Indian Hindu migrant community: by refusing to allow their temple to be destroyed, they became visible to, and so began to be accepted by their Malay neighbours.

This work demonstrates that establishing presence within the new setting is at the heart of migrant religious experiences. Diasporic religion is also often strongly connected with memory and intentional evocation of a missing place: "the recognition of a present absence of a place that must be recalled, if not in physical then in symbolic forms […] diasporic religions are in this sense memory performances".[16] Furthermore,

---

12 Peña 2011.
13 Vásquez and Knott 2014, 332-36.
14 Vásquez and Knott 2014, 340-43.
15 Vásquez and Knott 2014, 336-40.
16 Johnson 2007, 11.

sacralisation of person and spaces often involves some level of contestation with others in the community, and this is particularly the case with migrant groups. As Tweed has argued in an earlier work which looks in depth at the religious rituals of modern diaspora communities, this is because "the significance of religious mapping, as well as the precarious character of both spiritual cartography and identity formation, seems clearest when people become out of place".[17] The act of carving out of new religious spaces by migrants—whether this is demonstrated through the construction of physical buildings, acts of embodied religious performance, or linking with other, non-local religious communities to gain a sense of common purpose—is political. Creating (and re-creating) place is significant, and precarious, because it establishes the migrant's presence.

Archaeology and Material Culture within the Frame of Mobility

However, finding migrants in the archaeological record is hard, and finding information about migrants' reasons or explanations for their mobility is even harder. But the upsurge of interest in mobility expressed in geography and the social sciences offers some potential ways forward, especially where the framework of mobility explicitly connects with material culture. The connections between material culture and the diffusion of people were major areas of interest in archaeology in the nascent years of the discipline, where the differences in material culture and practices as witnessed on the ground were seen as the end results of large-scale movements of ethnically distinct populations. As part of a response to the increasing interconnectivity of the modern world, geography in the second half of the 20th century focused on movement as rational and chosen, fitting the movements of humans into 'transport geography',[18] that is, into science, and it came too with the supposition that movement would always involve as little effort as possible—relying as it did on the functionalist tenets of Rational Choice Theory—something that still plagues GIS in archaeology through the tendency to analyse a landscape for the 'least cost' paths of movement through it.[19] 'Irrational' movements were "beyond the scope of spatial science",[20] and movement itself was always considered secondary to the endpoints, the places and locations people hurried to move between.

What the mobilities turn offers in terms of new directions forward for thinking about mobility in the past is the appreciation of the apparently 'irrational' movements, the rethinking of movement not as a 'cost', but as important in its own right, in order to generate "a different kind of social science: more open, more wide-ranging, more

---

17 Tweed 1997, 93.
18 See discussion in Cresswell and Merriman 2011, chapter 1.
19 See discussions in Conolly and Lake 2006, chapter 11; and more recently, Gillings, Hacıgüzeller and Lock 2020, especially chapter 18.
20 Cresswell and Merriman 2011, 3.

attuned, more speculative".[21] Overturning the assumption that sedentarism and stasis was the 'norm' in the social sciences has allowed emphasis instead to be placed on the normalcy of motion, distance, change and placelessness in human existence.[22] Some even go so far as to suggest that the mobilities turn has flipped the primacy of sedentarism over mobility and of the settled over the nomadic.[23]

Given the continued—increasing—hostilities towards mobile people, whether they are permanent nomads, refugees or economic migrants, it seems there is still some way to go before an equilibrium between settled and mobile is reached. But the ideas expressed in the mobilities turn have begun to attract the attention of archaeologists, interesting because archaeology is a discipline made up of sites and places. As a result of this traditional focus, "site formation and the archaeological record end up being represented as static, or worse still, thought of as static entities".[24] Taking up the challenges outlined by a focus on mobility as the norm will help archaeology to re-envision the past beyond such 'static entities'. However, 'mobility' must be used 'in a way that works for us' as archaeologists: it will not do to simply apply themes from other disciplines.[25] Sheller and Urry outline methods for the social sciences—including observation of people's movements, mobile ethnography or participation in patterns of movement, asking participants to record their movements in time-space diaries, looking at the imagined 'virtual' mobilities of people through their Internet use, imaginative travel using poetry and literature to think about what atmosphere or feeling might have been contained in movement, interrogating the links between memory and movement through affective material—photographs, letters, images, souvenirs and objects, and finally, the investigation of 'transfer points', such as airports or waiting rooms, which are involved in mobility but are themselves fixed.[26]

Many of these methods are incompatible with archaeological research—it is not possible to observe the movements of subjects, only the end traces (although these too are difficult to find: indications of migrant status in literary or epigraphic documents, for example, are laden with biases)[27] and although it is possible to discover individual migrant people through osteoarchaeological analysis and isotopic research using skeletal and dental remains,[28] these are still rather uncommon, and there is not always a body to analyse. However, some of the methods outlined in the mobilities turn do offer fruitful avenues to think through for archaeology. Participation in past movement patterns—especially if aided by using the remnants of the 'transfer points' or 'moorings' that mobility requires, for example bridges, road systems, ports, paths, etc., in combination

---

21   Sheller 2016, 319; see also Collar and Kristensen, this volume.
22   Sheller and Urry 2006, 208.
23   See discussion of Zygmunt Bauman's *Liquid Modernity* in Coleman and Eade 2004.
24   Aldred 2013, 21.
25   Aldred 2013, 21.
26   Sheller and Urry 2006, 217-19.
27   Eckardt et al. 2014, 535.
28   For example, Eckardt et al. 2015; Müldner et al. 2011.

with landscape phenomenology, is one of the ways it might be possible to really engage with past mobility contextually, from the bottom up. By using the phenomenological experience of modern archaeologists to examine "past movement in the present through the shared interface of the material itself",[29] it is possible to get closer to understanding the immaterial—the movements—that have been materialised in the archaeological landscape.[30] Where this is possible, I agree: there is much to be learned and achieved in the study of past landscapes and human experience through the enactment of moving through landscapes with our own bodies, with mobility in the forefront of our interpretations.[31] However, this is not always possible, for any number of reasons. If it is not possible to engage with the archaeological landscape phenomenologically, then the links between memory and movement—and their location in affective material—is another potentially fruitful route.

Material culture theorists have demonstrated the interfaces between memory, emotion and material culture, and the connections that memory and emotion have with movement. Ahmed has argued that as objects pass between people, they can become imbued with memories and emotions, "sticky, or saturated with affect"[32] in a way that renders them laden with meaning. A problem for modern social scientists is that these objects and memories are private, and are therefore difficult to access—and this is a problem amplified for the archaeologist: this private world is almost always permanently lost. However, although it is not possible to verify the precise memories or emotions connected with material, as sociologists can, archaeologists can nevertheless recognise the affective dimensions or qualities of material culture, and consider emotion as part of the past landscapes they encounter and interpret. Although the development of an archaeology of emotion is somewhat difficult, it is progressing.[33]

The archaeology of emotion and the archaeology of mobility truly intersect, especially because long-distance movements such as migration carry with them heavy burdens of emotion—nostalgia and homesickness, fear, excitement and hope. For archaeologists, the material culture of migrants can be studied for these sticky, affective meanings: the signs of emotional ties to a homeland, and a recent volume collects papers that explore these emotions through the lens of migration in many different contexts.[34] Instead of seeing migrants' objects in the archaeological record as "adaptations to new worlds or conservative retentions of 'identity'", Shannon Dawdy argues that these assemblages can instead be read as "efforts to restore some part of what was lost".[35] Cultural geographers have shown how the things people take with them when mobile can be used to explore

---

29 Aldred 2013, 31.
30 Aldred 2013, 38.
31 See for example Kristensen 2018.
32 Ahmed 2004, 11.
33 See, for example Tarlow 1999; 2000; Harris 2010; Harris and Sørensen 2010; Chaniotis 2012; 2013; Collar 2018.
34 Baudry and Parno 2013.
35 Dawdy 2013, 258.

how such materials are used by migrants to transform their new surroundings, how such material is used as a way to 'home-make', to "reassemble memories, practices and even landscapes" of places that they have left.[36]

Bringing together these elements of phenomenological engagement with place, emotion and material culture theory offers a particularly useful way forward for beginning to approach the lived experiences of migrants in the past, and the ways in which places were produced through the intertwining of memory, action and emotion.[37] In order to go deeper into understanding the experiences of past migrants, scholarship needs to recognise and address the present absences in the material culture of migrants. To begin to access peoples' religious responses to mobility in the past, their objects or buildings need to be seen as physically manifest memory performances between past and present, and crucially, also between places.

Creating Stasis, Establishing Presence: Roman Soldiers on Hadrian's Wall

Difficult though it is to find mobile people in the archaeological record, there is one group of people who are categorically mobile, and that is soldiers. To some degree, their mobility is unchosen, disengaged: even if they join the army freely, with the opportunities for travel, adventure, status, comradeship (or citizenship, in the Roman world) as a motivating factor, their mobility is nevertheless directed by someone else, the state. They are not free to go where they like. This lack of control over their own mobility is suggestively described thus: "Bodies are forced along at a given pace and are to some extent unresponsive to the environment they move through. Interaction on a march like this is minimal—head up, eyes forward, deaf to the world, as they move along roads from one marching camp to the next."[38]

Evidence of religious behaviour within the military makes a good case study in which to explore the question of if and how these forcibly mobile people may have engaged in religious place-making in the past. In this case, I will look at soldiers in the Roman army stationed on Hadrian's Wall in the north of England. These men who found themselves stationed at the far northern frontier of the Roman Empire were drawn from diverse communities across Europe and the Near East. There are a number of non-native and non-'Roman' deities worshipped at the Wall, reflecting the ethnic origins of these migrant communities and their religious heritages, and which have long been used to demonstrate the multiculturalism of Britain and the Roman army. But I would argue that they can also be viewed as examples of migrant place-making, or even as signifiers of 'virtual pilgrimage' back to longed-for home communities.

To try to understand the past landscape of Hadrian's Wall as one marked by migrant place-making, I here adopt the three elements outlined in Vásquez and Knott's discussion of modern migrant religious place-making to think through three case studies

---

36 Tolia-Kelly 2006, 344.
37 See Collar 2018.
38 Vergunst and Ingold 2008, 9.

from Roman military contexts. The first explores the presence of altars as records of embodied performance at Carvoran. The second considers the cult of Silvanus as part of the soldiers of the Roman army's spatial response to difference and belonging. The third considers how the construction of the Vindolanda sanctuary of Jupiter Dolichenus within the boundaries of the fort there indicates a level of religious ownership and visibility in the community, and connects this group beyond Vindolanda into a broader understanding of this religious group across the Roman army.

Carvoran: Embodied Performance

Carvoran, or Magna, is an unexcavated Roman fort just to the south of Hadrian's Wall. We know from inscriptions that Carvoran was home to, among others, the first cohort of Hamians, archers originally from Hama, the city on the banks of the Orontes in Syria. Hama, as part of Syria, had been annexed by Pompey in 64 BCE, but the politics of the region remained volatile for some time, in part due to Rome's civil war and the Parthian invasion,[39] and only became more permanently stable after the integration of the neighbouring kingdoms of Cappadocia and Commagene into the Roman Empire in the first century. The Hamian cohort first appear in Britain in 122 CE, when they were engaged in helping to build the fort at Carvoran,[40] but it now seems probable that they had been used in Trajan's wars in Dacia and were brought to Britain by 118 CE.[41] The cohort was then moved to Bar Hill on the Antonine Wall in the 140s CE, probably supplemented here by additional members from Gaul, as an inscription by soldiers from the cohort was dedicated to the Deo Mars Camulus,[42] with the additional suggestion by Birley that they called themselves 'Gallic citizens'.[43] The cohort returned to Carvoran around 163 CE. The percentage of Syrian/Hamian natives still present in the unit by this date is uncertain, although while at Bar Hill the cohort was led by Caristanius Justianus, whose aristocratic heritage was eastern, from Antioch in Pisidia.[44]

Altars from Carvoran demonstrate that a wide variety of deities were present there, including Mars Blatucairus, Epona, Jupiter Dolichenus, Hercules and Veteris.[45] There is also evidence of deities from Syria: the presence of cult dedications to Jupiter Heliopolitanus, the god of Heliopolis-Baalbek,[46] and Hammia,[47] apparently a local goddess of the city of Hama itself. These dedications seem to indicate the worship of localised Syrian divinities, presumably by Syrians in the cohort, although Kennedy rightly points

---

39   Butcher 2001, 36-38.
40   Kennedy 1980: 112; *Roman Inscriptions of Britain (RIB)* 1778, *RIB* 1818.
41   Birley 2012.
42   *RIB* 2166.
43   Birley 2012, 8.
44   Birley 1980, 64.
45   *RIB* 1784; *RIB* 1777; *RIB* 1782; *RIB* 1781; *RIB* 1795.
46   *RIB* 1783.
47   *RIB* 1780.

out that Heliopolitanus was not exclusively worshipped by Syrians.[48] Alternatively, Hammia may be a deity specifically of the unit itself. The inscription is undated: if it is early, there is a stronger case for the former, if it is later, for the latter. But even after a two-decade sojourn on the Antonine Wall and the inclusion of Gallic recruits to the unit, there is still an explicit religious connection being made to Syria by the Hamian cohort in the form of dedications to the Dea Syria. Licinius Clemens, prefect of the cohort, dedicated to the Dea Syria between 163-166 CE,[49] and she is also named as the recipient (in part) of another dedication given by a later prefect of the cohort, Marcus Caecilius Donatianus, to Virgo Cælestis and the Dea Syria,[50] which is dated to the reign of either Marcus Aurelius (169-176) or Commodus (180-192).

The Dea Syria is the Roman interpretation of Atargatis: an ancient Aramaean deity whose central sanctuary in the Roman period was at Hierapolis in Syria, famous from Lucian of Samosata's description of the temple and extraordinary rites. The first inscription for the Dea Syria was in fact found some miles from Carvoran, at Melkridge, which is closer to Vindolanda; it may have been brought *post hoc* from the fort at Carvoran,[51] or else it may represent a shrine beyond the fort. The second dedication to the Dea Syria was found in the north-east corner of the fort at Carvoran itself, perhaps indicating the presence of a shrine there. Although excavation would certainly help to ascertain details of religious place-making by troops stationed here—for example, through the identification of shrines, sacred spaces or ritual practices—the inscriptions allow the exploration of the concept of embodied performance. In the modern case study, this was enacted through fasting and the suffering of the physical body through prolonged periods of prayer and deprivation. Here, it is necessary to imagine the altar in use, as the site of action, in order to access its role in embodied performance. Altars were both offerings in themselves and sites for other more ephemeral offerings: specific foods, flowers, libations, sacrifice, and as a focus for prayer, song, dance, festival. Altars are emotional, powerful, sticky objects: both memory performances and memory generators.

I suggest that these altars to Syrian deities can be read as a demonstration of the men of the Hamian unit retaining and continuing to express their devotion to the deities of their Syrian homeland long after they had been moved to the British Isles. They were surely proud of their status as members of the Roman army, but did it subsume all others? The dedication of these small stone altars—some of which do not mention any Roman or military status—demonstrate an active decision to worship deities from far away, possibly even from their place of origin. In so doing, these men were creating religious place in their new context, and making themselves, their origins and their beliefs visible to the wider community. This can also be seen as a kind of 'virtual' or 'imagined' pilgrimage on the part of these men, with the objects dedicated acting perhaps as a 'stand-in' for

---

48   Kennedy 1980, 113.
49   *RIB* 1792.
50   *RIB* 1791.
51   Haverfield 1911, 368.

a remembered place in their former homes.[52] By engaging with epigraphy as material artefacts as well as texts, it is possible to rethink them as objects enmeshed in networks of narratives:[53] objects given and used at specific events, which prompted memories and emotions among participants, and which served to focus worshippers' embodied religious performance and to enable them to journey 'home', even for a short while.

Silvanus: The Spatial Management of Difference and Belonging
Participation of soldiers in a Roman military identity is clearly also important: and in this case, the concept of 'imperial diaspora' is useful. I mean this in the sense of the diaspora produced by colonisers who move in the service of the army and administration, and the ways in which their identities were defined and developed.[54] What I should like to consider here is the presence of the Roman deity Silvanus on the frontiers of the Roman Empire as a form of religious place-making related to the migrant identity of the Roman imperial diaspora. Silvanus was a protector of forests and of fields, especially field boundaries; and of cattle against wolves. There are over 1100 known dedications to Silvanus, and they are found from Scotland to Syria.[55] Here, I take just two examples of his worship, from the Antonine Wall and from the Euphrates.

It is easy to overlook the fact that the world was once different from how it is now, and the landscapes of the Roman frontiers across the Empire were, in places, extremely wild, although very different in different areas of Europe. For example, the closed-canopy Hercynian forest, along the Danube, was so large that, according to Julius Caesar at least, it would take nine days to march across it, and sixty to march its full length.[56] In Britannia, the wild uplands of Northumbria and Scotland where Hadrian's Wall and the Antonine Wall run are today mostly turned over to agriculture and pasture, although there are areas of upland blanket bog that suggest there were once trees here. Archaeoscientific methods are making it clear that the process of clearing the primary oak woodland or wood-pasture had begun prior to the Roman period.[57] At the time of the Roman occupation, however, the environment was varied, with some pasture and agriculture, some patches of denser oak woods, and some secondary woodland regrowth of birch and alder, perhaps indicating a decaying agricultural landscape undergoing rewilding.[58] The landscape of northern Roman Britain was relatively extreme—there are cliffs and scarps, bogs and mountains, and it is very often cold, windy and wet. Caristanius Iustianus, the prefect of the cohort of Hamian archers, when they moved to the Antonine Wall Bar Hill fort from Carvoran, saw fit to dedicate to Silvanus.[59]

---

52 On virtual travel and pilgrimage see Urry 2000; Coleman and Eade 2004; Beebe 2014.
53 Eidinow 2011; White 2006.
54 Eckardt et al. 2014, 536; Cohen 2008, 69.
55 See Dorcey 1987.
56 Caesar, *De Bello Gallico* 6.25.
57 Manning *et al.* 1997.
58 Tipping and Tisdall 2005.
59 *RIB* 2167.

On the Syrian frontiers, the landscape was wild in different ways—the heat in summer is stupefying, the thunderstorms immense, and the river Euphrates cuts a great swathe through the Syrian deserts. Soldiers serving with the Legio IV Scythica, stationed at Zeugma, quarried stone from the cliffs of the river at modern Ehneş. In the process of quarrying the stones, these men also carved a number of altars into the rock face, all dedicated to Silvanus—some alongside Jupiter Optimus Maximus.[60] Perhaps these dedications should also hint to us of a lost forested landscape, as discussed by McCarty with regard to the forests of North Africa.[61]

But from the perspective of the mobility of the people who were stationed there, both these locations can be viewed as 'hostile': the landscapes themselves may have been unfamiliar, the weather similarly so, and soldiers were often face to face with enemies just over the border. Dedications to Silvanus, protector of the frontiers between wild and civilised, make sense in structuralist terms in both these locations, different though they are. However, these dedications can also be viewed in a different way, from the perspective of migrant religious place-making. By calling upon Silvanus, the mobile men dedicating in these locations were demonstrating their belonging, across huge tracts of space, to the core reference point of their imperial diaspora identity: the Roman army, the Roman gods of wildness but also of Rome itself, the core of the civilised, ordered world.

Vindolanda: Embedding across Networked Spaces, or Migrant Place-making without Ethnicity
The final case study to explore from the perspective of religious place-making is that of the recently discovered Dolichenus temple situated within the Roman fort at Vindolanda also situated on Hadrian's Wall. Jupiter Dolichenus is a deity of eastern origin, from Doliche in Commagene in eastern Turkey, but one who was adopted through the military social networks of the Roman army and whose worship was spread with them, beyond ethnic groups as time wore on, to become a deity closely associated with the military as a social group.[62]

The temple at Vindolanda was only discovered in 2009.[63] It is dated from the first half of the third century and had three building phases, in the third of which the temple contained two rooms, including one that was luxuriously heated. Animal bones, knives and whetstones were discovered during the excavations, which seems to indicate that sacrifice and ritual meals were taking place here, but this was apparently not solely a religious space: the westernmost room of phases 2 and 3 has been interpreted as a barn or stable.[64] Nevertheless, three altars were found *in situ*, which clearly demonstrate the active worship of Jupiter Dolichenus in this place—surprising, perhaps, because Jupiter Dolichenus was not an official deity of the Roman state or the Roman military.

---

60 Sinclair 1990; Stoll 2001.
61 McCarty 2022.
62 See discussion in Collar 2013, 79-145.
63 Birley and Birley 2012.
64 Birley and Birley 2012, 31.

The worshippers of Dolichenus have here carved out a physical space for themselves within the structure and community of the Roman army; they have made themselves official. In so doing, they are indicating a level of religious ownership and visibility in the community, and connecting the cult of Dolichenus to other communities beyond Vindolanda, as part of a broader understanding of the importance of the religious group across the Roman army in this period. Although it is not possible to claim that the worshippers here were aware of their engagement in multiple scales of religious place-making, they were possibly aware of the cult in other locations—many of the men who dedicated to this deity were highly mobile.[65] By constructing a temple to Dolichenus within the boundaries of the fort, it is possible to suggest that the worshippers were engaged in a different form of migrant place-making—this was no longer to do with ethnicity and remembering an absent place;[66] here, this was the religious place-making of a religion that had mobilised, and come to stand for, mobile people.

Soldiers in the Roman Army are usually referred to in passive terms: pawns in the broader game of legionary movements and long-term successes or failures, moved at will and redeposited in new places. But these soldiers were real, complex and active people, whose lives were marked by their participation in unchosen mobility, men whose homes and families were left far behind when their orders were to march great distances across Europe and North Africa. These mobilities had profound emotional as well as physical impacts on their lives. By engaging with contemporary accounts of how humans perceive the world as textured with memory and emotion, and how meaningful senses of place and senses of belonging are generated by migrants in new surroundings and among new communities, new interpretive tools for the ancient world become apparent, with which it is possible to start to learn something of these migrant soldiers' lives and experiences in the past.

Return to Pilgrimage—A Pilgrimage of Return?

In this chapter, I have outlined three ways of re-approaching the epigraphic record of the soldiers of the Roman army, which allow us to engage with the cult beliefs and ritual behaviours represented on these stones from new angles. Drawing on the observations of migrant religious place-making behaviours by contemporary sociologists of religion, I have proposed that it is possible to see these behaviours in the past too: at Carvoran, the Syrian archers from Hama gave altars to Syrian deities, which demonstrates their continued devotion to the deities of their Syrian homeland, the altars acting both to prompt and to embody their ritual performance and establishing their presence among the diverse communities on the northern frontier of the Roman Empire. By contrast, the presence of the cult of Silvanus on the frontiers represents something different, the creation of a dispersed empire-wide community of belonging that brought together the diversity of soldiers under the aegis of a common protector of liminal spaces. Finally,

---

65 Collar 2013.
66 As I have argued the cult of Dolichenus was elsewhere—see Collar 2018.

at Vindolanda, I have argued that the construction of a temple to Jupiter Dolichenus within the boundaries of an official Roman military fort suggests that the worshippers here were both making their community officially visible but also participating in international-level scales of religious place-making, both of which signified the adoption of Dolichenus into the sphere of the military more formally.

But how do these soldiers' acts of devotion relate to pilgrimage? Where the dedications are made in places far removed from the homeland, to home deities or recalling home sanctuaries, then perhaps it is possible to see something akin to an 'inverse' or 'virtual pilgrimage'. Distribution of the 'Miraculous Medal' associated with the visions of the Virgin Mary at the chapel at Rue de Bac in Paris to non-pilgrims has been argued to represent 'inverse pilgrimage': where the sacred medal has left the chapel and travels to and with the non-mobile wearer.[67] In this case, the object itself has physical and emotive links to the holy place of origin. The dedications from Carvoran examined in this chapter do not possess physical ties to the places that might be recollected, so cannot be described as 'inverse' in quite this way; however, the physical presence of the altars acts to focus ritual behaviours among the soldiers, which may well have involved the use of items, the consumption of foodstuffs or drinks, or the performance of movements that did possess stronger physical ties to the places recollected.

However, the term 'virtual pilgrimage' might work better as a description of these soldiers' behaviours: it implies a journey to a shrine or sacred place made through the act of remembrance, which may well have been prompted by their acts of dedication. Sociologists have used the term 'virtual pilgrimage' to describe imagined journeys made only in the mind—in contemporary situations, through internet usage and virtual travel,[68] but the term has also been used by historians to describe the 'imagined' pilgrimages of written accounts of real pilgrimages of the Medieval period.[69] Beyond the imagined travels contained in written accounts, 'virtual pilgrimage' has also been used to discuss the participation of real pilgrims in small, localised acts of worship and ritual at a nearby religious centre, which were transformed into something greater, as proxies for trips to major pilgrimage centres. Towards the end of the nineteenth century, new forms of spiritual engagement with pilgrim shrines began: "In return for a modest, sometimes optional enrolment fee, virtual pilgrims were invited to travel to a specific local chapel or church and engage in a short retreat or series of guided prayers. They would receive all the blessings and indulgences of a physical trip to Rome or elsewhere."[70] The migrant soldiers of the Roman Empire engaged in localised acts of worship that recalled deities and shrines from their homelands might also be said to be 'virtual pilgrims': men gathering collectively to commune with each other and to receive blessings from a divinity from some blue remembered hills.

---

67   Venbrux 2012, 89.
68   Urry 2000.
69   Beebe 2014.
70   Greenia 2017.

Bibliography

Ahmed, S. 2004. *The Cultural Politics of Emotion*. Edinburgh: Edinburgh University Press.

Aldred, O. 2014. "Past Movements, Tomorrow's Anchors. On the Relational Entanglements Between Archaeological Mobilities," in J. Leary (ed.) *Past Mobilities* 21-47. Aldershot: Ashgate.

Beaudry, M. and T.G. Parno (eds.) 2013. *Archaeologies of Mobility and Movement*. New York: Springer.

Beebe, K. 2014. *Pilgrim and Preacher. The Audiences and Observant Spirituality of Friar Felix Fabri (1437/8-1502)*. Oxford: Oxford University Press.

Birley, A. and Birley, A.R. 2012. "A new Dolichenum, inside the Third-century Fort at Vindolanda," in M. Blömer and E. Winter (eds), *Juppiter Dolichenus*, Orientalische Religionen in der Antike 8. Tübingen: Mohr Siebeck, 231-57.

Birley, A.R. 1980. *The People of Roman Britain*. Berkeley and Los Angeles: University of California Press.

Birley, A.R. 2012. "The Cohors I Hamiorum in Britain." *Acta Classica* 55, 1-16.

Chaniotis, A. (ed.) 2012. *Unveiling Emotions I: Sources and Methods for the Studies of Emotions in the Greek World*. Stuttgart: Franz Steiner.

Chaniotis, A. and P. Ducrey (eds.) 2013. *Unveiling Emotions II: Emotions in Greece and Rome: Texts, Images and Material Culture*. Stuttgart: Franz Steiner.

Coleman, S. and J. Eade (eds.) 2004. *Reframing Pilgrimage: Cultures in Motion*. London: Routledge.

Collar, A.C.F. 2013. *Religious Networks in the Roman Empire: The Spread of New Ideas*. Cambridge: Cambridge University Press.

Collar, A.C.F. 2018. "A Long Way from Home: Meshworks of Migration, Memory and Emotion in the Roman Empire," in J. Yoo and A. Zerbini (eds.) *Migration and Migrant Identities in the Near East from Antiquity to the Middle Ages*, 173-96. Aldershot: Ashgate.

Cresswell, T. and P. Merriman (eds.) 2011. *Geographies of Mobilities: Practices, Spaces, Subjects*. Aldershot: Ashgate.

Dawdy, S.L. 2013. "Afterword: Archaeologies of Movement," in M. Beaudry and T. G. Parno (eds.) *Archaeologies of Mobility and Movement*, 257-262. New York: Springer.

Dorcey, P.F. 1987. *The Cult of Silvanus in the Roman World*. Columbia University.

Eckardt, H., G. Müldner and M. Lewis. 2014. "People on the Move in Roman Britain." *World Archaeology* 46.4, 534-50.

Eckardt, H., Müldner, G. and Speed, G. 2015. "The Late Roman Field Army in Northern Britain? Mobility, Material Culture and Multi-Isotope Analysis at Scorton (N Yorks.)." *Britannia* 46, 191-223.

Eidinow, E. 2011. "Networks and Narratives: A Model for Ancient Greek Religion." *Kernos* 24, 9-38.

Eidinow, E. 2020. "What will you give me? Narratives of Religious Exchange," in A.C.F. Collar and T.M. Kristensen (eds.) *Pilgrimage and Economy in the Ancient Mediterranean*, 187-203. Leiden: Brill.

Gillings, M., Hacıgüzeller, P. and Lock, G. 2020. *Archaeological Spatial Analysis. A Methodological Guide*. London: Routledge.

Greenia, G. 2017. "Pilgrimage and the Economy of Salvation," blog post for *Pilgrim Libraries: Books and Reading on the Medieval routes to Rome and Jerusalem*. A Leverhulme International Research Network, PI: Professor Anthony Bale: http://www.bbk.ac.uk/pilgrimlibraries/2017/07/24/greenia-3/

Harris, O. 2010. "Emotional and Mnemonic Geographies at Hambledon Hill: Texturing Neolithic Places with Bodies and Bones." *Cambridge Archaeological Journal* 20:3, 357-71.

Harris, O. and T.F. Sørensen. 2010. "Rethinking Emotion and Material Culture." *Archaeological Dialogues* 17:2, 145-63.

Haverfield, F.J. 1911. "Cotton Iulius F. VI. Notes on Reginald Bainbrigg of Appleby, on William Camden and on Some Roman Inscriptions." *Transactions of Cumberland and Westmorland Antiquarian and Archaeological Society*, 2nd Ser. 11, 343-78.

Leary, J. (ed.) 2014. *Past Mobilities*. Farnham: Ashgate.

Lee, E. and Pratt, G. 2011. "Migrant Worker: Migrant Stories," in T. Cresswell and P. Merriman (eds.) *Geographies of Mobilities: Practices, Spaces, Subjects*, 225-237. Farnham: Ashgate.

Lury, C. 1997. "The Objects of Travel," in C. Rojek and J. Urry (eds.) *Touring Cultures: Transformations of Travel and Theory*, 75-95. London: Routledge.

Johnson, P. 2007. *Diaspora Conversions: Black Carib Religion and the Recovery of Africa*. Berkeley: University of California Press.

Kristensen, T.M. 2018. "Mobile Situations: *Exedrae* as Stages of Gathering in Greek Sanctuaries." *World Archaeology* 50.1, 86-99.

Manning, A., R. Birley and R. Tipping. 1997. "Roman Impact on the Environment at Hadrian's Wall: Precisely dated Pollen Analysis from Vindolanda, northern England." *The Holocene* 7.2: 175-86.

McCarty, M. 2022. "Reforesting Roman Africa: Woodland Resources, Worship and Colonial Erasures." *Journal of Roman Studies* 112, 105-41.

Müldner, G., C. Chenery and H. Eckardt. 2011. "The 'Headless Romans': multi-isotope investigations of an unusual burial ground from Roman Britain." *Journal of Archaeological Science* 38.2: 280-90.

Peña, E. 2011. *Performing Piety: Making Space with the Virgin of Guadalupe,* Berkeley: University of California Press.

Price, S. 2012. "Religious Mobility in the Roman Empire." *The Journal of Roman Studies* 102, 1-19.

Sheller, M. 2016. "Uneven Mobility Futures: A Foucauldian Approach." *Mobilities* 11.1, 15-31.

Sheller, M. and J. Urry. 2006. "The New Mobilities Paradigm." *Environment and Planning A* 38, 207-26.

Sinclair, T.A. 1990. *Eastern Turkey: An Architectural and Archaeological Survey, Volume IV.* London: The Pindar Press.

Stoll, O. 2001. "'Silvanus im Steinbruch'. Kulttransfer durch Soldaten der *legio III Scythica* in Syrien?," in O. Stoll *Römisches Heer und Gesellschaft: Gesammelte Beiträge 1991-1999*, 99-146. Stuttgart: Franz Steiner Verlag.

Tarlow, S. 1999. *Bereavement and Commemoration. An Archaeology of Mortality.* Oxford: Blackwell.

Tarlow, S. 2000. "Emotion in Archaeology." *Current Anthropology* 41 (5), 713-46.

Tipping, R. and E. Tisdall. 2005. "The Landscape Context of the Antonine Wall: a review of the literature." *Proceedings of the Society of Antiquaries of Scotland* 135, 443-69.

Tolia-Kelly, D. 2006. "Mobility/stability: British Asian Cultures of 'Landscape and Englishness.'" *Environment and Planning A* 38, 341-58.

Tweed, T. 1997. *Our Lady of the Exile: Diasporic Religion at a Cuban Catholic Shrine in Miami.* New York and Oxford: Oxford University Press.

Tweed, T. 2006. *Crossing and Dwelling: A Theory of Religion.* Cambridge: Harvard.

Unwin, T. 2000. "A Waste of Space? Towards a Critique of the Social Production of Space …." *Transactions of the Institute of British Geographers* 25.1, 11-29.

Urry, J. 2000. *Sociology beyond Societies: Mobilities for the Twenty-first Century.* London and New York: Routledge.

Vásquez, M. and K. Knott. 2014. "Three Dimensions of Religious Place Making in Diaspora." *Global Networks* 14.3, 326-47.

Venbrux, E. 2012. "The Miraculous Medal: Linking People Together Like the Beads of the Rosary," in W. Jansen and C. Notermans (eds.) *Gender, Nation and Religion in European Pilgrimage*, 89-104. London: Routledge.

White, H.C. 2008. *Identity and Control. How Social Formations Emerge* (2nd ed). Princeton University Press.

7

THIEVING PILGRIMS BETWEEN ROME AND THE MIDDLE AGES

ISABEL KÖSTER

In this chapter, I explore a by-product of pilgrimage: the theft of sacred objects.[1] While most journeys to sacred sites are motivated by pious intentions, some visitors turn into thieves. On occasion, they are motivated by greed and look to acquire precious objects of high material value. In other cases, thefts are acts of devotion through which the miscreants hope to gain ownership of a piece of the sacred either for themselves or for their communities.[2] Regardless of what drives the thief, this kind of mobility of sacred objects is always undesirable for a pilgrimage site.[3] In extreme cases, it can even disrupt worship at the site if the objects that disappear were central to ritual practice. The thieving pilgrim can therefore be an existential threat.

I investigate thefts from sacred sites in the Roman period and the Middle Ages through the lens of Patrick Geary's *Furta Sacra: Thefts of Relics in the Central Middle Ages*. Geary shows that despite legislation against stealing from pilgrimage sites, successful thefts were also regularly celebrated as manifestations of a saint's desire to move to a new communi-

---

1   I would like to thank the organisers and participants of EST3 ("Comparativism and the Study of Ancient Mediterranean Pilgrimage") for a stimulating symposium and the anonymous referee for the comments on an earlier version of this chapter. Abbreviations of ancient sources follow the *Oxford Classical Dictionary*. For the medieval sources, *AASS* =*Acta Sanctorum* 3rd edition (Paris and Brussels, 1863-1925). Translations throughout are my own.
2   The idea of theft as devotion has been particularly well studied for cults of saints where the thief is seen as looking for a personal relationship with the saint. See e.g. Geary 1990, esp. 14-15 and 25-28 and Wycherley 2015, 7 for medieval Christianity, and Trainor 1992 for Buddhism. For the personal relationship between Christian saints and their followers more broadly, see Brown 1981, 50-68.
3   Thefts are therefore different from the intentional mobility represented, for example, by travelling icons. These also destabilise notions of sacred space, but more in the sense that sacred space becomes intentionally mobile than in the sense that the sacred permanently moves elsewhere; see the discussion in della Dora 2009. Thefts are also different from the various other methods for circulating sacred objects, especially relics: sale and gift giving. For an overview of these practices and wider issues surrounding the commodification of relics, see Geary 1986.

ty.⁴ The thief is therefore not a criminal, but a pious instrument. By extension, the theft, while still undesirable to the saint's original host community, should only be condemned if it was motivated by personal greed, in which case the act is usually unsuccessful.

Geary's book provides a rewarding basis for comparing ancient Roman and medieval views on thieving pilgrims. In the Roman world, too, there are two ways in which sacred objects can leave a site: they can be the targets of a criminal act or they can be transferred elsewhere to start new communities of worship. Unlike in the Middle Ages, thefts and cult transfers were treated as entirely separate categories.⁵ One act was considered a serious offence, the other a community-sanctioned religious ritual. Geary's work challenges us to bridge the conceptual gap between thefts and pious acts and to look for common threads in how Roman and medieval authors write about the disappearance of sacred objects. In order to do so, this chapter is divided into two parts, the first dealing with thefts that are treated as contemptible, the second with cult transfers. I argue that for the first category, there is a remarkable continuity between the two religious traditions, which casts the divine powers as active agents of moral judgement and crime prevention. Stories of cult transfers, on the other hand, highlight profound differences in religious outlook, although they share some narrative similarities.

Unacceptable Thefts

My sources for investigating thieving visitors to sacred spaces are accounts drawn from rhetoric and historiography on the Roman side and hagiography for the medieval material. These narratives are united by a concern with using stories of thefts as a framework for exploring the character of the thief and the nature of divine power. Descriptions of thefts therefore hinge on the relationship between the human actor and the supernatural: gods and saints regularly take an active role in determining whether the attempt to steal will be successful. They are seen to assess the potential thief's motives and act

---

4   See especially Geary 1990, 132-34, in which he argues that "[a] real conviction that the relic was the saint, that the relic was a person and not a thing, undoubtedly helped mitigate the more blatantly immoral aspects of stealing ... [T]he theft of relics was at once a kidnapping and a seduction; overcome by the force of the thief's ardor and devotion, the saint allowed himself to be swept away to a new life in a new family" (132-33). Geary generally casts the saint as a rather passive element in the theft who can be persuaded to leave or can just be taken. By contrast, I see a much larger element of divine agency at play in these accounts. I am not the first reader of Geary to do so: the importance of divine will in accounts of thefts also emerges prominently in Trainor 1992, which uses Geary's work as a framework for examining Buddhist relic thefts.

5   Thefts from ancient sites have received little scholarly attention. For inscriptions concerning the protection of sacred possessions in the Greek world, see Lupu 2005, 21-30 with further references. Dillon 1997, 204-6 briefly discusses thefts within the context of Greek pilgrimages. For the Roman world, Scheid 1981, 137-42 offers a useful general overview of concerns with temple robbery in the late Republic. For temple robbery in Greek and Roman invective, see, for example, Frazel 2009, 71-123. The literature on cult transfers is far richer; see, for example, Ando 2008 (primarily for the western part of the Roman world) and Chaniotis 2009 (primarily for the eastern part).

accordingly. When a theft is unsuccessful, this is often cast in the following narrative pattern: an exceptionally greedy individual wants to steal sacred objects for his or her own gain, but is foiled by divine intervention.

The single richest collection of temple robbery narratives from antiquity is contained in Cicero's prosecution in 70 BCE of Gaius Verres, a former governor of Sicily, for abusing his official powers to enrich himself.[6] The thefts are an essential element in the orator's efforts to portray the defendant as a contemptible human being: he is so greedy that he even attempts to steal from the gods. The regular norms of human conduct mean nothing to him. From the beginning of his career in service to the Roman government, so Cicero, Verres is interested in his personal profit. While he is serving on the staff of Gnaeus Cornelius Dolabella, the defendant sets his sights on one of the most famous ancient sanctuaries:

Delum venit. Ibi ex fano Apollinis religiosissimo noctu clam sustulit signa pulcherrima atque antiquissima, eaque in onerariam navem. suam conicienda curavit. Postridie … subito tempestates coortae sunt maximae, iudices, ut non modo proficisci cum cuperet Dolabella non posset sed vix in oppido consisteret: ita magni fluctus eiciebantur. Hic navis illa praedonis istius, onusta signis religiosis, expulsa atque eiecta fluctu frangitur; in litore signa illa Apollinis reperiuntur; iussu Dolabellae reponuntur. Tempestas sedatur …

He came to Delos. There from the most sacred shrine of Apollo he secretly removed at night the most beautiful and ancient statues and took care to have them piled into his transport ship. On the next day … suddenly, judges, very great storms arose, so that Dolabella was not only unable to set out when he wanted, but also hardly managed to stay put in the town: they were tossed by such large waves. At this time, the ship of that robber, weighed down with religious statuary, was broken up, expelled and tossed out by a wave. Those statues of Apollo were found on the shore; they were put back by order of Dolabella. The storm subsided …[7]

Verres is seen as being engaged in a perverted pilgrimage: he undertakes the difficult journey to a site of major religious significance, but not to worship, but to enrich himself on the treasures that the island has amassed because of its sacred status.[8] The storms that damage Verres's ship and return the stolen statues to the island also reveal his crime to the entire community and force Dolabella to intervene.

---

6 For an introduction to the speeches and their legacy in later discussions about art ownership, see Miles 2008. Frazel 2009, especially 187–221, discusses what the temple robbery accounts contribute to Cicero's overall rhetorical goals.

7 Cic. *Verr.* 2.1.46.

8 The Delos narrative is not the only one that follows this narrative template. So, for example, at *Verr.* 2.4.106-12, Verres ventures to the temple of Ceres at Henna. Cicero's detailed description of the landscape leaves no doubt that it is an arduous journey, but the governor is driven to undertake it anyway because of the riches that the site is said to contain.

The Delos episode in the *Verrines*, furthermore, is intertextually marked as a divine intervention. In the *Odyssey*, Odysseus's decision to allow his men to eat the Cattle of the Sun results in a storm and a fatal shipwreck.[9] For temple robbery in particular, the fate of Pyrrhus of Epirus, who invaded Italy in 280 BCE, is an instructive example. During his campaigns, the king comes to Locri Epizephyri, a remote town famous only for its sanctuary of Proserpina. He immediately turns to plundering it. Then, as Diodorus Siculus tells it:

κατὰ τὸν ἔκπλουν ἐπιγενηθῆναι πνεύματά φασιν, ὥστε στόλῳ παντὶ ναυαγῆσαι τοῦτον. τὸν δὲ Πύρρον δεισιδαιμονήσαντα τὴν θεὸν ἐξιλάσασθαι καὶ μὴ πρότερον ἀπελθεῖν ἕως ἀπεκατέστησε τὰ χρήματα.

It is said that such storms arose when they sailed out that he suffered shipwreck with his whole army. Then Pyrrhus, struck with religious fear, propitiated the goddess and did not depart until he had returned the treasures [to the temple].[10]

Pyrrhus therefore immediately associates his shipwreck with divine punishment and knows that he has to make restitution to the goddess before resuming his military campaign. In this case, therefore, the theft narrative becomes a conversion story: the king has learned that this particular site is protected by powerful forces.[11]

With his emphasis on the persuasive power of divine punishment, Diodorus foreshadows a common narrative pattern in the medieval texts. An account concerning the 11,000 Virgins of Cologne, a group said to have been martyred by the Huns in the third century, offers a veritable catalogue of saints stopping the theft of relics.[12] It is set in the early 12th century, shortly after the rediscovery of the relics during the construction of new city walls. We are told that the fame of the relics had spread far and wide and hence they attracted potential thieves. Not all of them are successful, and so the narrative tells of three foiled thefts: in the first, a woman steals some relics in the hope of curing her illness. A girl appears to her in a dream telling her that she will only become healthy again if she returns what she has taken. In the second, a man who has stolen some relics finds himself walking in circles around the church and is only able to escape after he has made restitution. In a third account, an angel threatens a merchant with a punishment already familiar from antiquity: shipwreck. Once more the thief decides to return the relics.

---

9   Hom. *Od.* 12.260-419.
10 Diod. Sic. 27.4.3 cf. Livy 29.8.9, Livy 29.18.7-8 and Val. Max. 1.1.20-1.
11 For Pyrrhus's fate as a warning to other potential thieves, see Köster 2014, 326-30.
12 *AASS* October IX, 239. The legends surrounding the 11,000 Virgins, including this text, have received attention in recent years, especially for the evidence that they contain of Cologne's efforts to create a story that gives the city primacy in the cult. See Montgomery 2009 and, for tensions between the written and archaeological records about the cult, Militzer 2016.

The three potential criminals come from different parts of Europe: the woman appears to be local, the wanderer is from Swabia, and the merchant English. This geographical diversity underscores the widespread fame of the cult and the desire for relics. It also reflects what Scott Montgomery has identified as a consistent theme in the cult of the Virgins: a tension between the notion that all the bones of all of the saints are located in Cologne and the widespread circulation of relics of the Virgins in central Europe, which suggests a more decentralised mode of worship.[13] The three stories of thefts, in effect, have it both ways. They stress the unity of the whole group of martyrs because each thief is punished for attempting to take just a few bones, not relocate the entire cult. At the same time, the active role taken by the supernatural leaves open the possibility that the saints may occasionally identify someone as worthy of taking some of the remains. Therefore, this narrative does not entirely contradict the reality that part of the relics travelled far and wide. It does, however, highlight the connection of the Virgins to Cologne while also attesting to their popularity on a wider geographic scale.

In the case of the 11,000 Virgins, the emphasis does not fall on stopping thefts, but on getting the thieves to return what they took. A narrative set at the church of Reginswind in the German town of Lauffen am Neckar in the ninth century CE, by contrast, emphasises prevention. St. Reginswind was killed and thrown into the river by her nurse when she was only seven years old. Her body was recovered in a completely preserved state, and her relics were discovered to have healing properties. She was quickly declared a saint, and her cult became regionally popular. This prompted the city of Würzburg, some 100 km away, to want to steal the relics of Reginswind for itself:

At custos aedis suae omniscius Christus, non sinens locum, quem tanto sublimavit honore, impio violare latrocinio, prohibuit eos tali modo: cum attentius illi male maturis inservirent excubiis, nocte quadam opportunum tempus existimantes, quo mente coepta opere tenus peragerent, orationem enixius simulantes, clanculo irruperunt atque thesaurum Domini, loco illo caelitus et ante secula praedestinatum, unca manu rapere, patriamque ... moliuntur repedare. Sed ecce repente de caelo super eos nimius timor ac tremor irruit, adeo ut fundamentum ecclesiae minaci terrae motu quateretur et ipsi fulminum ac tonitruorum ictibus graviter semiustulati terratenus pene exanimes corruerent pallidulu. Postquam vero, divino cessante terrore ... magna precum instantia divinitati supplicantes, emendationis inducias perobstinate flagitarunt.

But the guardian of his church, the omniscient Christ, did not allow the place, which soared with such great honour, to be violated by impious theft and stopped [the thieves] in the following way: since they guarded the church less carefully late into the watch, the thieves decided that the time was right during a certain night to finish what they had begun in their minds. Feigning rather earnest prayer, they secretly broke in and set to plunder with a crooked hand the treasure of the Lord, which had been divinely assigned to that place earlier, and to return to their

---

13   Montgomery 2009, especially 1-8 and 19-46.

land rather quickly. But behold! Suddenly very great fear and trembling broke forth from the sky above them, so that the foundation of the church shook with a menacing earthquake and they themselves, having been quite seriously burnt by strikes of thunder and lightning, tumbled on the ground pale and almost dead. And afterwards, indeed, when the divine terror had stopped, they supplicated the divine power with the great urgency of prayers and vigorously begged for a period of grace for betterment.[14]

An earthquake, thunder and lightning affirm that Reginswind is to stay in Lauffen. These phenomena are marked as divinely inspired: while a thunderstorm would be a normal occurrence, this one is particularly large and hence unusual. An earthquake—especially a major one—is not normal for this region of the world, and hence sends a strong sign that something is happening against divine wishes. The thieves are seized by terror and end up praying for their lives. They have been convinced of the divine power protecting the place and will presumably now go off and tell their story, which in turn will confirm the divine favour shown to Reginswind's church and increase the appeal that Lauffen has to pilgrims. A foiled robbery, after all, is good advertisement for a sanctuary: it shows that there is something worth stealing there, but at the same time confirms the special status of the site by highlighting its supernatural protection mechanisms. The event authenticates the sacred nature of the objects that the thief tried to take.

Furta Sacra

Just as divine powers can keep objects in a certain place, they can also prompt their move (*translatio*) to a new location. *Furta sacra*, sacred thefts, are, in effect, divinely sanctioned crimes: they still involve a furtive element since the sacred objects have to be stolen from a community that would object to their removal, but there is no threat of divine punishment. In medieval hagiography, most accounts follow a narrative template that Patrick Geary describes as follows:

> "A monk or other cleric goes on pilgrimage; he stops in a town or village where rests the body of a saint. Impressed with what he has heard of the saint's life, virtue, and miracles, he determines to steal the body for his own community. The thief waits until the dead of night, then enters the church and exhorts the saint to come with him. He then breaks open the tomb, takes the relics, and hurries home where the new saint is greeted by a joyful throng of the faithful."[15]

This summary shows that a *furtum sacrum* works on a fundamentally different premise from the acts discussed in the first part of this chapter. In the case of a sacred theft, the thief is a person of manifest piety who is concerned with the saint's wishes. The primary

---

14   *AASS* July IV, 95.
15   Geary 1990, xi–xii.

motivations for the theft, therefore, are the interests of the saint and the enrichment of a new faith community. It is a cult transfer, not a temple robbery. In this guise, *furta sacra* narratives also exist in pre-Christian antiquity, although the theme is less pronounced than in the Middle Ages. Furthermore, unlike the medieval narratives, the ancient ones generally avoid celebrating thefts and employ a variety of techniques to persuade readers that the act was in no way criminal in nature.[16]

The tale of the bones of Orestes offers an especially rich basis of comparison with medieval material.[17] The Roman narratives concerning the hero and what happened with his remains are based on local Italian myths and are only poorly preserved. It is therefore helpful to look to the Greek tradition in order to explore the power of the bones and why a community might be keen to possess them. As the story goes, Orestes arrives in Greece after his escape from the Tauris and establishes a new cult of Artemis at Brauron where his sister becomes the presiding priestess. The hero eventually dies in Arkadia and is buried at Tegea. Then, as Herodotus tells us, the burial is forgotten until the Spartans consult the oracle at Delphi regarding what they should do about their inability to defeat the Tegeans in war.[18] The Pythia tells them that they must obtain the bones of Orestes. The Spartans eventually manage to locate the remains at Tegea.[19] Once they have been taken to Sparta and reburied, there is a reversal of military fortunes. The bones thereby become the foundation of Sparta's success.

Herodotus does not go into the Tegean side of the story. For this, we need to turn to Pausanias. In his description of Sparta he mentions the transfer of the bones, but without much detail.[20] More interesting is a brief reference to the episode in the narrative concerning Tegea:

Ἡ δὲ εὐθεῖα ἐπὶ Θυρέαν τε καὶ κώμας τὰς ἐν τῇ Θυρεάτιδι ἐκ Τεγέας παρείχετο ἐς συγγραφὴν Ὀρέστου τοῦ Ἀγαμέμνονος μνῆμα, καὶ ὑφελέσθαι Σπαρτιάτην τὰ ὀστᾶ αὐτόθεν οἱ Τεγεᾶται λέγουσι· καθ' ἡμᾶς δὲ οὐκέτι πυλῶν ἐντὸς ἐγίνετο ὁ τάφος.

---

16 Lexical searches of the Packard Humanities Institute's database of Latin texts (latin.packhum.org) show that the phrase *furtum sacrum* is not found in extant classical literature. The phrase therefore postdates the Roman period.

17 Greek and Roman hero cults and the medieval cult of saints are regularly cast as related religious phenomena (see Jones 2010, 84-92, for a summary of the discussion, which goes back to early Christian authors). Deborah Boedeker's discussion of moving the bones of heroes in ancient Greece identifies such acts as 'translations' in direct correspondence to medieval terminology (Boedeker 1993). Such scholarship invites the comparisons I make here.

18 Hdt. 1.67-8.

19 As Carolyn Higbie has shown, it is a trope in Greek narratives that the bones of heroes are accidentally discovered after some hints from an oracle, especially that of Apollo at Delphi (Higbie 1997, 299-303).

20 Paus. 3.3.5-6 and 3.11.10.

> The straight road from Tegea to Tyrea and the surrounding villages features the remarkable monument of Orestes the son of Agamemnon, and it is from here that the Tegeans say the bones were stolen away to Sparta. In our time the tomb is no longer within the walls.[21]

This version implicitly casts doubt on Herodotus's assertion that the Spartans rescued the bones from a forgotten grave.[22] In fact, the Tegeans have turned the empty tomb into a prompt for talking about the perfidy of their enemies—the verb used to describe the theft, ὑφαιρέω, carries connotations of secrecy and underhanded dealings. This version of the story is not one of Spartan cunning and piety, but instead shows them as common thieves. Even a plundered grave can therefore be a rhetorically useful monument.

For Pausanias, the story of the bones of Orestes stops in Sparta. There is, however, a second tradition involving the hero's remains, which is incompatible with the versions found in Herodotus and Pausanias. In this version, instead of settling in Greece after rescuing Iphigenia, he travels to Italy and settles in Aricia near Lake Nemi where he founds a cult of Diana.[23] When he dies, he is buried there. Eventually his bones are transferred from Aricia to Rome and placed in front of the temple of Saturn in the Forum. A mid-first century CE relief found in Rome is likely a reference to the event: it shows Diana and Apollo standing in front of the temple of Saturn in the Forum where Orestes's remains had been reburied.[24]

Diana's appearance on the relief is curious in light of the richest surviving textual evidence for the transfer. It comes from Servius's commentary on Virgil's *Aeneid*. While Servius is a problematic source on Roman religion, his discussions of why the bones of Orestes were moved to Rome nevertheless offer insights into the reasons that could be given for such a cult transfer even if we cannot confidently assume that these reflect the actual decision-making process.[25] In the first instance, a reference to the sacrifice of Iphigenia at Verg. *Aen.* 2.116 prompts Servius to explain how the girl was saved, became a priestess of Diana and was eventually rescued by her brother. The siblings brought the

---

21 Paus. 8.54.4.
22 Maria Pretzler, in contrast, sees Pausanias's narrative as based on Herodotus's and does not note any differences in outlook (Pretzler 1999, 96).
23 On the sanctuary, see especially Green 2007, which persuasively argues that Nemi is a healing sanctuary with deep Latin roots and that the fusion with the Greek Artemis represented by the Orestes story is a much later tradition. When and how Orestes becomes associated with Nemi is an open question; evidence for cults of Orestes in southern Italy and Sicily date back to the archaic period (see Cingano 1993, 356-68, and Fischer-Hansen 2009, especially 224-26 for evidence from Rhegium), but the link with Nemi is more tenuous. I thank Ian Rutherford for drawing my attention to this debate and Cingano's article.
24 *LIMC* s.v. Artemis/Diana number 276 (E. Simon).
25 See the negative assessment of Servius's reliability as a source on Roman religion in the Age of Augustus in Cameron 2011, 567-626.

cult image of Diana to Aricia.[26] There, a strange cult involving human sacrifice developed under Orestes's guidance, which was eventually found to be unsuitable for Romans.[27] The cult of Diana is exported to Sparta, where such ritual behaviour is acceptable, and "the bones of Orestes were transferred from Aricia to Rome and buried in front of the temple of Saturn, which is before the Capitoline Hill next to the temple of Concord".[28] On such a reading, the move sanitises the cult of Orestes. He becomes disassociated with Aricia and its bloody rituals, and the transfer marks not just a physical change in location, but a fundamental reinterpretation of the hero's nature.

The second reference is just a phrase, but combines with other evidence to yield another explanation for why the bones are moved. In his commentary on Verg. *Aen.* 7.188, Servius famously supplies a list of seven objects that he believes guarantee the security of Rome's empire.[29] These include the ashes of Orestes (*cineres Orestis*). Here, then, we have a second reason why the remains were moved to Rome: it makes sense to keep things of such enormous significance in the city. The bones therefore perform a similar function to their role in Sparta: they are there to ensure the state's success.

Missing from Servius's discussions is a reference to the aspect of the transfer of the bones that has most fascinated modern scholars: the connection between Orestes and the emperor Augustus.[30] Augustus was most likely the one who initiated the move.[31] Especially at the beginning of his career, he associated himself closely with the hero, and the transfer helped strengthen the connection.[32] Once more the move from the supposed periphery of Aricia to the capital is important: Orestes, as in Herodotus, literally becomes a central figure.

Integrating the Greek and Roman material therefore yields three major explanations for the transfer of the bones: they are moved because the Romans desire to put a stop to the foreign rituals at Aricia, they need to be in a central location because of their importance for the safety of the empire, and their transfer symbolises the strong per-

---

26   Servius is not internally consistent on this point: *ad* Verg. *Aen.* 3.331 he has Orestes and Iphigenia bring the cult to Attica.
27   As Servius puts it, it happened "when the cruelty of the rites displeased the Romans" (*cum… Romanis sacrorum crudelitas displiceret*). Particularly at issue is the rite of the *rex Nemorensis*, a priest who has to kill his predecessor to take office. He gives an explanation of the ritual and Orestes's connection to it *ad* Verg. *Aen.* 6.135. A famously fanciful description of the *rex Nemorensis* opens the first chapter of James George Frazer's *The Golden Bough*. For Orestes as the prototype of the *rex Nemorensis* and the evidence provided by Servius, see further Green 2007, 203-5.
28   *Orestis … ossa Aricia Romam translata sunt et condita ante templum Saturni, quod est ante clivum Capitolinum iuxta Concordiae templum* (Serv. *ad* Verg. *Aen.* 2.116).
29   Servius calls them *pignora*. For the difficulties of rendering this term into English, see Ando 2008, 182. This is the only extant reference to the bones of Orestes performing this role and may be Servius's invention (on this point see Cameron 2011, 618).
30   See especially Hölscher 1990 and Champlin 2003.
31   For Augustus's role and why alternatives are unlikely, see Green 2007, 41-48.
32   So Pausanias famously tells of a statue of Orestes on the Peloponnese that comes with an inscription identifying it as actually being a statue of Augustus (Paus. 2.17.3).

sonal connection that Augustus felt he had with the hero. All these factors—changing the nature of religious practice, ensuring the prosperity of a community and stressing a personal relationship—also play a role in other accounts of cult transfers.

The transfer of the bones of Orestes, furthermore, is a variation on the occasional practice of bringing foreign gods to Rome in order to worship them there. The most famous example is that of the goddess Cybele whose cult is brought to the city during the Second Punic War. Ovid's account of these events in the *Fasti* brings into focus the typical elements found in the narrative of such a move.[33] First, there is usually some kind of crisis that prompts authorities to consult an oracle about how to address the situation. The oracle will then demand the introduction of a god. Although there is still need for individual initiative—someone has to go and obtain the statue of the deity—the activity is sanctioned by both political and religious authorities.

In Ovid's Cybele narrative, there is a deliberate ambiguity about whether the arrival of the goddess marks a new development in Roman religion or a homecoming. In Latin the instructions of the oracle are as follows: *Mater abest: Matrem iubeo, Romane, requiras*.[34] The line could mean either "your mother is absent: I order you, Roman, to seek your mother" or "The mother (i.e., the Great Mother, a cult title of Cybele) is absent …". Depending on the interpretation, therefore, Cybele is just a long-lost part of Rome's pantheon.[35] Next, the Romans travel to Phrygia to obtain the statue of the goddess that is said to represent the cult; the leader of the expedition is an exceptionally pious person. The cult's original host community denies the Roman request, but an earthquake and a miraculous speaking statue indicate that the goddess is in favour of a move. The journey back to Italy then proceeds without incident. Although the transfer presumably destroys Cybele's Phrygian cult site and happens against the wishes of the foreign community, there is divine approval at every turn. This is just one of many Roman narratives showing that the gods have their own wishes and priorities that they will communicate in no uncertain terms.

The Romans do not claim to have invented the practice of moving cults in response to divine wishes. An illustrative episode is the arrival of the god Serapis in Egypt, which Tacitus discusses as part of his description of the emperor Vespasian's visit to Alexandria shortly after coming to power in the civil war of 68-9 CE. In the Roman world, Serapis was understood to be a quintessentially Egyptian god with strong ties to the Ptolemaic rulers.[36] He was therefore a legacy of the province's Greco-Egyptian identity. Tacitus, however, writes that the god himself was imported to Egypt by Ptolemy I for a specific purpose:

---

33   Ov. *Fast.* 4.255-349. See also Livy 29.10-14.
34   Ov. *Fast.* 4.259.
35   The ambiguity is further enhanced by the fact that the goddess is to be taken from Phrygia, the mythical home of the Romans (who, after all, derived their origins from the Trojans). On the importance of Rome's Trojan origins in Ovid's telling of the episode and their wider context in Augustan literature, see Fantham 1998 *ad Fast.* 4.271-2, and Orlin 2010, 79-82.
36   See, for example, Pfeiffer 2008.

> *Origo dei nondum nostris auctoribus celebrata: Aegyptiorum antistites sic memorant, Ptolemaeo regi, qui Macedonum primus Aegypti opes firmavit, cum Alexandriae recens conditae moenia templaque et religiones adderet, oblatum per quietem decore eximio et maiore quam humana specie iuvenem, qui moneret ut fidissimis amicorum in Pontum missis effigiem suam acciret; laetum id regno magnamque et inclutam sedem fore quae excepisset: simul visum eundem iuvenem in caelum igne plurimo attolli.*

The origin of the god has not yet been talked about by our authors. The Egyptian priests recall that, in a dream, a youth of remarkable beauty and greater than human size appeared to King Ptolemy, the first to establish Macedonian power in Egypt, when he had just founded Alexandria and given the city walls and temples and religious cults. The youth instructed him that he should send his most trustworthy friends to Pontus and obtain his statue. It would be a happy thing for the kingdom and the place that would receive his statue would become great and famous. Immediately the same young man seemed to be taken to the heavens in a fiery blaze.[37]

The dream setting, the unusual size of the youth, and his supernatural disappearance all mark the account as clearly epiphanic. As he continues his narration, Tacitus further mentions that the priests say that in response to Ptolemy's dream, they consulted people knowledgeable about Pontic religion to determine exactly which god wished to be brought to Alexandria.[38] When, after a period of several years, the king finally sends his men to Pontus, the god provides aid once more by threatening the local ruler if he does not release the statue. He even gives him a taste of divine punishment when he does not cooperate.[39] These aspects remove any connotations of theft from the narrative: while the transfer happens against the wishes of the people of Pontus, the manifest divine approval puts them in the wrong. Serapis wants to move to Egypt and become the guarantor of Alexandria's success as a city. Hence the temple is so appealing to Vespasian: like Ptolemy I, he is trying to establish his authority and needs a sign that the gods are on his side. At least in the province of Egypt, there is no better symbol of divine favour for a new ruler.[40] That he is able to miraculously

---

37 Tac. *Hist.* 4.83.1-9. The version of Serapis's origins given here is similar to that in Plut. *De Is. et Os.* 28 and the chronological relationship between these two accounts is disputed (see Hicks 2013). It is also not the only story told of Serapis's origins; see the summary in Tac. *Hist.* 4.84.18-26. It is worth noting that Serapis does not have foreign origins in all versions—sometimes he is simply an adaptation of the Egyptian Osiris.

38 Tac. *Hist.* 4.83.11-18. At 4.83.23-7, the Oracle at Delphi acts as a third confirmation of which god is to be brought to the city. It seems that Ptolemy is availing himself of every possible source of religious pronouncements before moving the statue.

39 Tac. *Hist.* 4.84.7-9.

40 As Albert Henrichs has argued, the narrative of Vespasian's time in Egypt not only establishes a connection between him and Ptolemy I, but also between him and Alexander (Henrichs 1968, 55-56). Egyptian religious sites are apparently where foreign rulers go to legitimise their rule.

heal two sick people who approach him at the temple further shows that Serapis has now chosen to support the new Flavian dynasty.[41] The continued performance of divine miracles, after all, is a confirmation that the god approves of what has happened. The kind of cult transfer represented by Serapis is therefore a legitimate way of creating new centres of worship.

For Cybele and especially for Serapis, the cult transfer also marks a transition out of obscurity. They had been worshipped in remote locations and had only been of regional significance. Now, however, they become the guarantors of the safety of the empire. In Serapis's case, Vespasian's visit indicates that his new temple is, in anachronistic terms, a site of international significance. In the Middle Ages, too, a divinely approved theft usually leads to a significant increase in a saint's popularity. The medieval accounts show many structural similarities with the ancient ones: the relics are often discovered by accident, the person who removes them is exceptionally pious, there is a divine sign of approval, and the saint continues to perform his or her miracles at the new location.[42]

Unlike most of the narratives examined above, however, the hagiographical accounts do not shy away from thematising the element of theft: usually the relics are taken in the middle of the night and sometimes the thieves are reluctant to commit the act because they fear divine punishment, as, for example, in the theft of the relics of St. Prudentius.[43] In the middle of the ninth century, Geylo, a bishop from northern France, travels through Aquitania on his return from a pilgrimage to Santiago de Compostela. He stops off in a small, dilapidated town that houses the relics of St. Prudentius. Geylo, the account stresses repeatedly, is a pious man and it is clear that the town is not an appropriate place for the relics of a saint. So, with the promise of a grand new church, the bishop and his followers get the saint to consent to a move to northern France. Furthermore, this is a theft in name only: even the chaplain of the church agrees that the move would be for the best. Despite this, the men whom the bishop ordered to seize the relics hesitate after opening the tomb. The narrator addresses himself to them in a rhyming aside:

Sed paulo dubitant, quia Sanctum tangere vitant.
O bene devoti, culpae formidine moti,
Quid formidatis? Nihil est hic, quod paveatis.
Non irascetur Martyr…
Vobiscum certe cupit ire, iubetque referre.

---

41 Tac. *Hist.* 4.81. For the importance of these miracles in asserting Vespasian's divinity, see Luke 2010.
42 On this pattern, see Keskiaho 2016, who discusses a narrative structure wherein the thief has a dream telling him or her to steal the relics. This is followed by the theft, and then, if the relics still work after the translation, everything is considered to have happened in accordance with the saint's wishes.
43 *AASS* October III, 352-54.

But they hesitated a little because they shunned to touch the saint. O well-devoted ones, moved by the fear of sin, why are you afraid? There is nothing here for you to fear. The martyr will not be angry. He certainly wishes to go with you and orders you to take him back [with you].[44]

That there are no problems with removing the relics confirms the saint's wishes. The act becomes a 'happy robbery' that is to be celebrated.[45] The narrative provides a useful template for a sacred theft: it happens with the approval of the saint and involves bringing relics from a community that cannot care for them to a new, splendid church. It also gives us an insight into an important precondition for a *furtum sacrum*: the thief must be of the appropriate disposition. As a bishop returning from a pilgrimage, Geylo is a man who has the degree of piety needed to bring relics to a new location. He is also motivated by what is in the best interest of the saint and the faith in general: in its splendid new location in north-eastern France, the cult will receive far greater exposure than it has before. As the rest of the text tells us, the saint goes on to perform many miracles in his new location, which further confirms that the theft was rightful.

Conclusion

In both the Roman and the medieval world, the departure of sacred objects from a religious site is not necessarily a bad thing. While it is undesirable to the original community, the act could establish new cults elsewhere and thereby rescue neglected or forgotten gods or saints from obscurity. The divine powers are seen to take an active role in the process: they can desire a move or not and can judge the thief as fit to take them or not. The religion-spanning discourse about thieving pilgrims shows that both religious systems do not classify the theft of sacred objects as a purely human matter. Divine agency is also an important factor.

Whereas the ancient world differentiates sharply between thefts, which are morally bad, and cult transfers, which are sanctioned by human and divine authorities and good, the medieval texts call both such actions thefts. *Furta sacra*, however, are something to be proud of. Here we see a fundamental difference between how the two religious systems conceive of the relationship between gods and mortals. The Roman gods punish thieves or, in the case of a cult transfer, use mortals as their instruments. In medieval hagiography, on the other hand, celebrating a *furtum sacrum* as a theft allows the author to stress both the thief's piety—he or she was motivated by the best interests of the saint—and divine forgiveness for a crime.[46] In the Roman world, on the other hand,

---

44 *AASS* October III, 353.
45 *felix … latrocinium* (*AASS* October III, 353).
46 So, too, Peter Brown, who sees acts such as these thefts as displays of "the immensity of God's mercy … They brought a sense of deliverance and pardon to the present" (Brown 1981, 92). The fact that an interest in divine mercy may be motivating the hagiographers to emphasise repeatedly that they are writing about thefts also became clear to me while reading Kevin Trainor's study of

there is no need for mercy: either it is a criminal act or it was not. Comparing narratives of thefts from sacred spaces in the Roman and medieval worlds therefore highlights the interpretive limits of making comparisons across religious traditions.

Bibliography

Ando, C. 2008. *The Matter of the Gods: Religion and the Roman Empire*. Berkeley, CA: University of California Press.

Boedeker, D. 1993. "Hero Cult and Politics in Herodotus: The Bones of Orestes," in C. Dougherty and L. Kurke (eds.) *Cultural Poetics in Archaic Greece: Cult, Performance, Politics*, 164-77. Cambridge: Cambridge University Press.

Brown, P.R.L. 1981. *The Cult of Saints: Its Rise and Function in Latin Christianity*. Chicago: The University of Chicago Press.

Cameron, A. 2011. *The Last Pagans of Rome*. Oxford: Oxford University Press.

Champlin, E. 2003. "Agamemnon at Rome: Roman Dynasts and Greek Heroes," in D. Braund and C. Gill (eds.) *Myth, History and Culture in Republican Rome: Studies in Honour of T.P. Wiseman*, 295-319. Exeter: University of Exeter Press.

Chaniotis, A. 2009. "The Dynamics of Ritual in the Roman Empire," in O. Hekster et al. (eds.) *Ritual Dynamics and Religious Change in the Roman Empire*, 1-30. Leiden: Brill.

Cingano, E. 1993. "Indizi di esecuzione corale in Stesicoro," in R. Pretagostini (ed.) *Tradizione e innovazione nella cultura greca da Omero all'età ellenistica. Scritti in onore di Bruno Gentili*, volume I, 347-61. Rome: GEI.

Dillon, M.P.J. 1997. *Pilgrims and Pilgrimage in Ancient Greece*. London: Routledge.

della Dora, V. 2009. "Taking Sacred Space out of Place: From Mount Sinai to Mount Getty through Travelling Icons." *Mobilities* 4, 225-48.

Fantham, E. 1998. *Ovid Fasti Book IV*. Cambridge: Cambridge University Press.

Fischer-Hansen, T. 2009. "Artemis in Sicily and South Italy: A Picture of Diversity," in T. Fischer-Hansen and B. Poulsen (eds.) *From Artemis to Diana: The Goddess of Man and Beast*, 207-60. Copenhagen: Museum Tusculanum Press.

Frazel, T.D. 2009. *The Rhetoric of Cicero's 'In Verrem'*. Göttingen: Vandenhoeck & Ruprecht.

Geary, P.J. 1986. "Sacred Commodities: The Circulation of Medieval Relics," in A. Appadurai (ed.) *The Social Life of Things*, 169-91. Cambridge: Cambridge University Press.

Geary, P.J. 1990. *Furta Sacra: Thefts of Relics in the Central Middle Ages*. Revised Edition. Princeton, NJ: Princeton University Press.

Green, C.M.C. 2007. *Roman Religion and the Cult of Diana at Aricia*. Cambridge: Cambridge University Press.

Henrichs, A. 1968. "Vespasian's Visit to Alexandria." *ZPE* 3, 51-80.

Hicks, B.W. 2013. "Roman *religio* as a Framework in Tacitus' *Histories* 4.83-84". *Journal of Ancient History* 1, 70-82.

Higbie, C. 1997. "The Bones of a Hero, the Ashes of a Politician: Athens, Salamis, and the Usable Past." *Classical Antiquity* 16, 278-307.

Hölscher, T. 1990. "Augustus and Orestes". *Travaux du Centre d'archéologie méditerranéenne de l'Académie polonaise des sciences* Tome 30: *Études et Travaux* 15, 164-68.

Jones, C.P. 2010. *New Heroes in Antiquity: From Achilles to Antinoos*. Cambridge, MA: Harvard University Press.

Keskiaho, J. 2016. "Dreams and the Discoveries of Relics in the Early Middle Ages: Observations on Narrative Models and the Effects of Authorial Context in the *Revelatio Sancti Stephani*," in M. Räsänen et al. (eds.) *Relics, Identity, and Memory in Medieval Europe*, 31-51. Turnhout: Brepols.

Köster, I.K. 2014. "How to Kill a Roman Villain: The Deaths of Quintus Pleminius." *Classical Journal* 109, 309-32.

Luke, T. 2010. "A Healing Touch for Empire: Vespasian's Wonders in Domitianic Rome." *Greece and Rome* 57, 77-106.

Lupu, E. 2005. *Greek Sacred Law: A Collection of New Documents*. Leiden: Brill.

Miles, M.M. 2008. *Art as Plunder: The Ancient Origins of Debate about Cultural Property*. New York: Cambridge University Press.

---

relic theft in Sri Lanka (Trainor 1992). In Buddhism, Trainor emphasises, relic thieves are never subject to divine punishment because it would go against the merciful nature of the god.

Militzer, K. 2016. "The Church of St Ursula in Cologne: Inscriptions and Excavations," in J. Cartwright (ed.) *The Cult of St Ursula and the 11,000 Virgins*, 29-40. Cardiff: University of Wales Press.

Montgomery, S.B. 2009. *St. Ursula and the Eleven Thousand Virgins of Cologne: Relics, Reliquaries and the Visual Culture of Group Sanctity in Late Medieval Europe*. Oxford: Peter Lang.

Pfeiffer, S. 2008. "The God Serapis, his Cult and the Beginnings of Ruler Cult in Ptolemaic Egypt," in P. McKechnie and P. Guillaume (eds.) *Ptolemy II: Philadelphus and his World*, 387-408. Leiden: Brill.

Orlin, E.M. 2010. *Foreign Cults in Rome: Creating a Roman Empire*. Oxford: Oxford University Press.

Pretzler, M. 1999. "Myth and History at Tegea – Local Tradition and Community Identity," in T.H. Nielsen and J. Roy (eds.) *Defining Ancient Arkadia*, 89-105. Copenhagen: Munksgaard.

Scheid, J. 1981. "Le délit religieux dans la Rome tardo-républicaine," in *Le délit religieux dans la cité antique (Table ronde, Rome, 6-7 Avril 1978)*, 117-71. Rome: École Française de Rome.

Trainor, K. 1992. "When is a Theft not a Theft?: Relic Theft and the Cult of Buddha's Relics in Sri Lanka." *Numen* 39, 1-27.

Wycherley, N. 2015. *The Cult of Relics in Early Medieval Ireland*. Turnhout: Brepols.

8

FAILED CONNECTIVITIES: PAUL'S COLLECTION AND HIS FINAL PILGRIMAGE TO JERUSALEM

MATTHEW R. ANDERSON

Introduction

It is not surprising that, like Jesus before him, Paul was almost certainly a *pilgrim* to Jerusalem on his last journey to that city. It is surprising that more has not been made of that fact.[1] During the mid-50s of the first century, Paul was gathering money and representatives from non-Jewish Jesus assemblies in Achaea and Macedonia. He refers to the collection in 1 Cor 16:1-4, 2 Cor 8 and 9, Rom 15, and perhaps Gal 2:10. The delegates on this journey were atypical; neither were they full proselytes to Judaism, as evidenced by Paul's vocal opposition to their being circumcised, nor were they quite still gentiles, in that Paul insisted that they no longer worship their own gods. Instead, they were in a liminal state—a brief eschatologically-charged window of time in which non-Jews (according to Paul) were invited on pilgrimage to Jerusalem precisely *as* non-Jews. Using a lens of pilgrimage to explore this journey sheds light not only on why Paul organised a delegation of gentiles bearing offerings to Jerusalem in the first place, but also perhaps why it went awry.

For centuries, Jerusalem had been a religious destination for Jews from Judea and the Diaspora.[2] Especially after Herod's renovations, the Temple was also a destination for many non-Jews associated in various ways with Second-Temple Judaism, who were

---

1 Donaldson 1990 and 1993, and especially Auler 2016, 157, are exceptions. Both are generally more interested in the collection than the nature of the journey that brought it to Jerusalem. Downs 2008, 70 states, "Our knowledge of the history of the collection ends with Paul's statements in Romans 15."
2 McCready 2011, 78, and Fredriksen 2017, 20. The New Testament, Josephus and Philo all present pilgrimage to Jerusalem as common, but it may have been less so than the particular narrative needs of these sources indicate. Philo, despite wealth and proximity, seems to have gone to Jerusalem only once. *De Providentia* 2.64; Feldman 1996, 23.

provided with a "court of the Gentiles".[3] Paul is likely to have participated in pilgrim festivals in the city, whether Shavu'ot (Pentecost), Pesach (Passover) or Sukkot (Tabernacles, Tents or Booths).[4] However, as a self-proclaimed apostle of a Christ-following apocalyptic movement, his journey to Jerusalem in the very late 50s or very early 60s was entirely different.

On that occasion, Paul travelled in the company of a new type of adherent.[5] These non-Jews were unique in that they were neither full converts to Judaism,[6] nor in their devotion to the god of Israel were they any longer attached to their home gods in the usual ways of those historically attracted to various aspects of Judaism.[7] In order to follow Paul's proclamation, the Christ-following gentiles[8] who accompanied Paul had taken the radical step of renouncing the gods of their cities (1 Thess 1:9). Yet these "deviant pagans"[9] had not become Jews by being circumcised and fully following Torah. Their identity had been severed from their previous *ethnē*, but without a concomitant full reception as proselytes into the ancient and respected Jewish religion. Jerusalem was the dwelling-place of their god, the God of Israel. They were led by Titus (2 Cor 8:6, 16-17), who had, only a very few years before, on another trip to Jerusalem (Gal 2:3-5), been the focus of dissension between Paul and rival Jesus-missionaries over precisely the status of Christ-following gentiles.

Paul travelled with this unusual group to deliver monies from their assemblies, likely at Shavu'ot (Acts 20:16).[10] They arrived in Jerusalem hoping for a blessing from the eschatological Jesus community still gathered close by the Temple, and through them, from the God of Israel. In a "Jewish world incandescent with apocalyptic hopes"[11], Paul's pilgrim voyage tested the limits of a temporary, tenuous and eschatological connectivity. The links between centre and margins that allowed such a pilgrimage even to be imagined had only briefly been established within the small, sectarian Jesus assemblies based around the Aegean and looking to Jerusalem.

---

3 Hogeterp 2005, 94.
4 Haber 2011, 49-67.
5 1 Cor 16:3 indicates that those who accompanied the collection to Jerusalem were from among the non-Jewish Jesus followers of Paul's assemblies.
6 Skarsaune 2002, 177; Fredriksen 2017, 147.
7 Against Donaldson 2015, 295.
8 On Paul and the term 'gentiles' or *ethnē*, see Rosen-Zvi and Ofir 2015, and Donaldson 2013.
9 Fredriksen 2017, 91.
10 Acts, written considerably later than the events it portrays, and admittedly suspect when compared to Paul's own letters, is anxious to parallel Paul's journey with that of Jesus (see Luke 13:33). There is no reason, however, to doubt the Pentecost dating it describes for two reasons: firstly, 1 Cor 16:8 indicates that the festival held some importance for Paul in relation specifically to his work among non-Jews; secondly, Acts makes no more specific mention of the festival in connection with the collection delivery, which it would were the author to have inserted it programmatically. Nickle 1966, 87 and Auler 2016, 157 concur.
11 Fredriksen 2017, xii.

The gentile procession took place to a long-established, scripturally-mandated destination.[12] Was the voyage also a pilgrimage in its more innovative characteristics, namely the Christ-following emissaries who headed the delegation, and their eschatologically-driven delivery of non-Jewish wealth? In his surviving letters, Paul repeatedly emphasises the importance of the collection, an emphasis that makes the silence of the very late first-century or very early second-century Acts on the success or failure of that delivery all the more striking.

The make-up of the delegation, Paul's concerns about the trip, and even his language in describing it as a "priestly service", all—independently of Acts—point to Paul's sacral intentions (Rom 15:16).[13] They underline that the journey was not simply for the delivery of some sort of relief funding.[14] There is an eschatological urgency, and from our perspective, some dramatic foreshadowing, in Paul's expressed hope that his "service" to the "saints in Jerusalem" might be judged acceptable. In fact, in Rom 15:15-16, Paul slips into language so unclear one cannot tell from the genitive construction if he is talking about the offering *from* the gentiles/nations or the offering up *of* the gentiles/nations. "This 'sanctified sacrifice',," Fredriksen writes, "can be understood both as the collection from the gentile assemblies in support of Jerusalem's poor …and as the sanctified gentiles themselves."[15]

Pilgrimage is perhaps an unfortunate term for describing Paul's journey with the delegation, in that there was no one set of specific terms in ancient Greek or Hebrew for pilgrims or pilgrimages.[16] These never seem to have been an identifiable phenomenon in the ancient Mediterranean in a way that warranted a specific terminology. Certainly there were religiously-motivated trips revolving around home and temple; in addition, official delegations might travel to sanctuaries, and individuals took trips for healing, dedications, competitions, and to the shrines set up at crossroads. Jewish texts describing travel to the three major festivals employ words like the prosaic "come", "stream" (Isa 2:2; metaphorically in 66:12), "walk", or "come in procession" (Isa 60:11). Rutherford advises that employing the term 'pilgrimage' should not depend on "an excess of refinement in matters of definition, but on whether it is useful".[17] To take an offering to a

---

12   The command for Jews to "come up" for the festivals is found in Deut 16:16-17. Note its connection to bringing an offering.

13   Ascough 1996, 594, although Ascough does not here directly connect the collection's religious significance to an eschatological aim.

14   Against Downs 2006, 177. In my opinion, too much is made of a putative and overly literal temporal sequence and not enough of Paul's belief that the final eschatological act had already begun in the resurrection of Christ. Tajra 1989, 61 is typical in stressing that Paul had both a religious motive for being in Jerusalem for the festival, and a practical need to deliver the collection, but never connecting the two.

15   Fredriksen 2017, 163.

16   Elsner and Rutherford 2007, 7, 27.

17   Elsner and Rutherford 2007, 9.

holy place (or community)[18] in exchange for a hoped-for blessing, as Paul was doing, seems to me the very definition of pilgrimage.

As a result of his reported encounter with the resurrected Jesus, Paul was a person who, by the time of the collection, had spent years on the peripheries of Jewish religious life.[19] From the evidence of the surviving first-person texts, especially his letter to the Galatians, he lived and worked on the peripheries of the smaller Jesus movement as well. Boyarin insists that Paul was as marginal in his own day as he is important to ours.[20] The sequence of his undisputed letters, especially the combination of Galatians and Romans, suggests that the passage of time, and the delay of Jesus's return, had made Paul even more of an outsider than he had previously been.[21] These ancient texts give evidence of a missionary worker who had become isolated by a religious retrenchment at the centre concerning the place of non-Jews, a retrenchment of opinion with which he did not agree (Gal 1:9, 2:11-14).[22]

If this were true, Paul was a traveller returning to a Jerusalem that had changed. Those at the centre no longer shared his radically eschatological vision, nor his solidarity with those who constituted, in Fredriksen's words, the "extreme anomaly" of being neither Jewish nor any longer attached to their pagan gods.[23] Paul's voyage to Jerusalem and the resounding silence in following texts concerning the fate of the collection show how dangerous what Coleman describes as the "discrepant discourses"[24] of a contested pilgrimage and a failed connectivity could be.

Paul's Pilgrimage: A New Narrative

By travelling with a delegation of Greeks from his assemblies in the Aegean, and by bringing a collection from them for the so-called 'poor' of Jerusalem, a sub-group of Jewish Jesus-believers, Paul was possibly attempting to live out an action described throughout Second Temple scriptures—the so-called "eschatological pilgrimage of the nations" (Isa 2:3-4; 19:24; 60:3-7; 61:5-6; 66:18-21; Zech 8:20-23; Mic 4:1-2; Jer 16:19; Tob 14:5-6, etc.).[25]

---

18 Too much should not be made of the fact that the collection was being taken for "the saints" or "the poor among the saints" rather than for the Temple, as if the division between them were rigid. See Auler 2016, 146.
19 Fredriksen 2017, 168.
20 Boyarin 1994.
21 Fredriksen 2000, 169.
22 Harrill 2012, 42-3.
23 Fredriksen 2017, 34, but see Donaldson 2015, 286.
24 Coleman and Eade 2004b, 4.
25 Donaldson 1990, 7-9 and Kloppenborg 2017 give helpful listings of relevant canonical and apocryphal texts and of the history of the academic study of this theme. Donaldson 1997, Downs 2016 and Kloppenborg 2017 all note the absence of pilgrimage language in Paul's earlier writings about the collection. However, with Joubert (see Kloppenborg 2017, 162) I note the nuanced and constantly evolving way in which Paul represented both the purpose of the collection (compare 1 Cor with Rom) and his relationship with the assembly in Jerusalem.

Johannes Munck's 1954 (1959, in English) suggestion that the collection should be understood in light of this eschatological 'pilgrimage' has been much debated.[26] Donaldson and others note that the portrayal of a last-days journey to Jerusalem by the *goyim*, the 'nations', was never a major theme, nor a standalone tradition.[27] Rather, it was part of a larger and far more important scriptural motif, namely the eschatological restoration of Zion. In that scenario, variously described, Israel's enemies are destroyed, the Jews scattered throughout the world return, Zion and its God become the acknowledged centre of the world, and peace and prosperity become the way of life under the direct reign of Israel's God and/or that God's chosen ruler.

The foreign nations are bit players in this eschatological drama, and what happens to them varies.[28] In some writings they are utterly destroyed, in others they are helpers for the returning diasporic Jews, in others they are welcomed into the family and in still others they act primarily as witnesses to the final vindication of God's people and the fulfilment of the covenant promises. The non-Jewish nations are to be destroyed or praised depending on their attitude to Israel (Pss. Sol. 17:24, 2 Bar 72). In other references they arrive as slaves of the people of God (Isa 60:12, Pss. Sol. 17:30). Isaiah 60:8-9 portrays eschatological gentiles as helpers who bring back with them the lost Israelites of the Diaspora; Pss. Sol. 17:31 states "nations…come from the ends of the earth to see his glory, to bring as gifts her children who have been driven out". In other scriptures it is implied that these nations may themselves represent the exiles: "He shall be compassionate to all the nations (who) reverently (stand) before him." (Pss. Sol. 17:34.) As Donaldson points out, a number of these scenarios, despite other differences in detail, portray the foreign nations joining the returning exiles in their procession to Zion, giving up idols and immorality,[29] but otherwise joining in worshipping the God of Israel precisely in their identity as non-Jews.[30] Johnson Hodge points to this as the rationale behind the collection: "For Paul there is a lot at stake in the specific, ambiguous position of gentiles-in-Christ."[31]

In the actual Pauline procession to Jerusalem, the eschatological order seems at first to be reversed: in the texts it is Israel's exaltation that summons the nations, rather than the procession of the nations coming first. Perhaps Paul believed his initiative was part of what might precipitate the final act of the last days. More likely—and disagreeing with Donaldson and Downs—the combination of Romans 9-11 and Paul's final trip with the collection is evidence that Paul seriously believed what he consistently maintained

---

26 Munck 1959, 303-4 and Nickle 1966. For overviews of the eschatological pilgrimage theme and its academic treatments see Downs 2008, 3-26 and Ogereau 2012, 362.
27 Donaldson 1990, 26.
28 Fredriksen 2017, 29. The disagreement of the Hebrew scriptures on the details of the eschatological pilgrimage makes it difficult to argue with certainty for or against the notion that Paul was acting it out.
29 The so-called Noachite, or Noachian, covenant. See Fredriksen, 2017, 115-16.
30 Donaldson 1990, 18.
31 Johnson Hodge 2015, 169.

in his letters: that is, that the resurrection of Christ, which he himself claimed to have experienced, together with the incoming of the non-Jews, was evidence that the awaited Day of the Lord and the vindication of Israel had *already* begun.[32]

While there is not sufficient space here to explore it fully, Paul's odd reshuffling of the timeline of eschatological causal relations in Romans 9-11 is of particular interest to such an argument.[33] It is precisely whether one accepts and acts together with a God who had already begun the process of renewing the world in the resurrection of Christ that becomes, to Paul's mind, the test of faithfulness. As Eisenbaum writes, the lack of faith that Paul refers to on Israel's part in Romans 9-11 is "not a lack of faith *in God*, but a failure to recognize that God has initiated the process of redemption" [emphasis added].[34]

Elsewhere, Sara Terreault and I[35] have proposed expansions to the pilgrimage theory outlined by Eade and Sallnow in 1991,[36] and again by Coleman and Eade in 2004, where the authors identified constituent elements basic to almost all forms of the practice, ancient and contemporary. Adding to the Turners' initial emphasis on shrine, Eade, Sallnow and Coleman's correctives of focusing also on mobility, text and body, and Frankfurter's linking of pilgrimage movement to land and "even to cosmology itself",[37] we suggest a four-part structure to understanding pilgrimage: body, terrain, mobility and narrative. Useful to this schema is that the first two elements of this paradigm, body and terrain, are conceptually and practically linked even as are the final two, mobility and narrative (Fig. 1). Narrative includes the category of text put forward by Eade and Sallnow but allows for other forms by which a pilgrimage may be described, recounted and remembered.

This paradigm is useful also in that the two linked terms of mobility and narrative help us understand not only the literary tradition behind Paul's final trip to Jerusalem, but also its long and influential reception history. The standard narrative is this: Paul, understood as a Christian who had converted from Judaism, went to Jerusalem to present his collection to the church there, probably to build social solidarity, or perhaps because of some famine at the time in Palestine. In the interpretation that Christians have lived with and taught for millennia, during a peaceful attempt to worship at the Jerusalem Temple he was subsequently set upon by Jews—not Jesus-following Jews, but other Jews, the "unbelievers" of Rom 15:31.[38] During the riot, Paul was arrested, mistakenly charged and eventually shipped to Rome, where he was later martyred.

---

32 1 Cor 7:26, 29. See Donaldson 1993, 92 and Nanos 2015, 134.
33 Eisenbaum 2009, 254.
34 Eisenbaum 2009, 253.
35 Terreault 2017, 48-50.
36 Eade and Sallnow 1991.
37 Frankfurter 1998b, 15.
38 τῶν ἀπειθούντων can also be translated as "disbelievers", which removes the implication that they are simply "Jews" and allows the more likely possibility that here Paul is referring to disbelievers in his particular mission. These are the same competing Jesus-missionaries he had been in conflict with before (c.f. Gal 2:4, 3:1).

> Four quadrants of pilgrimage (Anderson/Terreault)
>
> body
>
> mobility   narrative
>
> terrain

Four quadrants of pilgrimage.   **Fig. 1.**

This is the us-versus-them story passed down by Christians through western history.[39] Thankfully, most narratives about Paul have changed. It sounds tongue-in-cheek to say that sometime in the late 1960s and 1970s, people began to suspect that Paul was a Jew, but that is more or less what happened. The scholarly rush to rediscover Paul's Jewish context has led to a reinterpretation of everything he wrote and did. Of primary importance is the realisation that Paul did not feel that his fellow Jews needed "converting" away from Torah; rather, he was, as he himself insists repeatedly, concerned with the fate of the foreign nations. Paul was a Jew advocating within the Jesus movement on behalf of non-Jews—he goes so far as to call his preaching the "gospel to the foreskinned".[40] His letters and actions should be understood not as a Christian–Jewish interchange, but as an intra-Jewish, and specifically intra-*Jesus-movement*-Jewish, initiative.

As I have stated elsewhere:

> Down through the centuries, Paul's admirers claimed him as the first Christian, while his critics derided him for the same thing. But the undoubtedly radical change of life Paul went through after his vision of the risen Christ was never conversion *away* from Judaism to a different faith. For one thing, Christianity didn't yet exist. At the time, the Jesus movement was simply one school of Torah interpretation among many within Judaism, one apocalyptic timeline among several, one hoped-for Jewish redeemer among a variety of contenders. Just as importantly, the themes Paul preached, themes such as resurrection, atonement, repentence, the judgement of the nations, and the coming of a messiah were all Jewish themes. They *became* Christian themes over the four centuries that followed. In Paul's lifetime, there was nothing un-Jewish about them.[41]

---

39 Oliver 2016, 69-71, insists that the author of Acts did not intend such a vilification of Judaism, and that it is a later development.
40 Gal 2:7. Most English versions avoid the literal translation.
41 Anderson 2023, 19.

In terms of the four-part pilgrimage schema (Figure 1), the mobility of Paul's voyage became entextualised in the incomplete narrative framed by Acts and passed down through Christian tradition.

Part of questioning previous assumptions about Paul is paying closer attention to the voyage near the end of his life. Paul's journey to Jerusalem with the collection was initially an in-group exercise, despite the presence of the non-Jewish emissaries. Nonetheless, it has had lasting and damaging out-group, that is, Jewish–Christian, repercussions.

Paul as Pilgrim

Paul himself was a pilgrim simply because he was a Jew, bearing an offering, headed to Jerusalem at festival time. Paul was not a pilgrim because he *chose* to be one, in the sense of a contemporary traveller to Lourdes or a medieval Christian on his or her way to a shrine. While then as now, not all Jews were equally religious, in the first century there was no such thing as a secular religionist. Jews—and certainly, pious Jews like Paul—fulfilled the obligations of the festivals whenever they visited Jerusalem during one of them, as commanded in the Torah (Deut 16:16-17).[42]

Since the time of the Babylonian exile, there existed a large Jewish community outside of Palestine. After the building of the Second Temple by returning exiles and their followers in the late sixth century BCE, the Temple underwent various vicissitudes under Antiochus IV and the Maccabean revolt, and subsequently by the Hasmonean usurpation of the high priesthood, the Roman takeover and occupation, the massive rebuilding program of Herod the Great, and its final destruction in the year 70 CE by Titus's forces. Through it all, the Temple remained physically at the centre of Jewish religious life in Palestine, and conceptually at the centre for most Jews throughout the Mediterranean world.[43] What is unusual is that it might have, for a moment of time, represented the same kind of shrine for non-Jews.

Philo is likely exaggerating—but his point still valid—when he claims "countless multitudes from countless cities come, some over land, some over sea, from every direction to the Temple in Jerusalem for the pilgrimage festivals".[44] Josephus makes frequent mention of pilgrimage to the Second Temple. He may likewise be inflating numbers when he describes in his *Wars* a Jerusalem that suffered even more in the final Roman siege because at the time it was swollen with pilgrims, some from great distances.[45] Both nonetheless show that pilgrimage to Jerusalem and to its Temple was popular. It was not absolutely required of first-century Jews that they make pilgrimage to Jerusalem, and Jews presumably travelled there for many reasons. At the same time, the three primary sources for the period—Josephus, Philo and the New Testament—all present large-scale

---

42 Eliav 2005, 11.
43 McCready 2011, 73, demonstrates that even Jewish pilgrimage to Elephantine was ultimately based on the Jerusalem pilgrimage.
44 *Spec* 1.12.69
45 *B.J* 6.9.3.

pilgrimage, and the social, economic and religious importance of the pilgrimage festivals, as a simple fact of Jerusalem life.[46] The Mishnah likewise records the importance of pilgrimage during this period in Hagiga 1:1 and the following Gemara 2a–7b. Pilgrimage was important religiously, socially, politically and economically to Jerusalem.[47]

Paul as pilgrim is a paradigm that has received little attention within the otherwise crowded field of New Testament studies. Despite the eschatological overtones of Paul's final journey to the holy city, support to Jerusalem offered by Jesus groups (which understood themselves as a type of Jewish group) in the Aegean,[48] should be understood as participation in a long tradition of offerings to Jerusalem enjoined in the Torah.[49] In Philo's speech to Gaius, Philo lauds Augustus for that emperor's ruling that the Jews should not be impeded when they "contribute the first fruits every year" and send "commissioners to convey the holy things to the Temple in Jerusalem".[50] The "temple tax", a voluntary tax contributed by Jews, including Jewish groups throughout the Diaspora, is attested in Josephus, Philo and Second-Temple scriptures both canonical and non-canonical.[51] Offerings, in this case, should not be strictly separated from other forms of sacrifices, which were always connected to Jerusalem pilgrimage.

Paul describes several visits to Jerusalem[52] prior to his final trip at the turn of the sixth decade of the first century. Paul's collection of funds and the mustering of emissaries was an act he considered important enough to include in the concluding remarks of four of his last surviving letters.[53] If it was not an eschatological pilgrimage at the outset, but rather a contractual agreement of some sort with Jerusalem,[54] by the time of the writing of Romans Paul had changed his stance. While in 1 Cor 16:4 he seems uncertain about whether he will accompany the collection in person,[55] by the writing of Romans it had become a personal and sacred duty. In his letter to the assembly at the capital, just prior to his departure, Paul recognised that this trip was different and might be his last.

---

46 Haber 2011, 50-51.
47 Charlesworth 2014b, 3. See also Goodman 2007, 59-67.
48 By collecting money for Jerusalem's Jesus community, or some part of it, Paul was following a precedent he first learned from the church at Antioch. In Gal 2:10, when he reports being part of a delegation visiting Jerusalem under Barnabas, he insists that James, the leader of the Jerusalem assembly, asked his Antiochian group to "remember the poor" and that this was—the Greek emphasises—the very thing he was hastening, or anxious, to do.
49 Exodus 23:16-19, Lev 23:9, Deut 26:2.
50 Quoting Elliott and Reasoner 2011, 187-88.
51 Exodus 30:13-16, Neh 10:32-33, Matt 17:24-27, Talmud *Shekalim* 1 (note the discussion of whether and how offerings from non-Jews were acceptable; Josephus *A.J.* 18.313, Philo *Embassy to Gaius*, 156.
52 See the first two chapters of Galatians.
53 Gal 2:10, 1 Cor 16:1-4, 2 Cor 8:1-9:15, and Rom 15:14-32.
54 Gal 2:10.
55 Kloppenborg 2017, 172-73.

Margins and Centre in the First-Century Jewish World

Not all pilgrimages are to shrines, and any discussion of first-century religious and philosophical travel in the Mediterranean world should include wandering.[56] There has been significant research comparing and contrasting Paul with contemporary Cynics and Stoics.[57] There are also peripatetic overlaps. Especially in his surviving letters to Corinth[58] one may discern an implied reference to Odysseus in Paul's boasting about his adaptability and the flexible nature of his ministry combined with his rhetorical complaints about homelessness. Others in Paul's day relied on similar comparisons.[59]

In light of 1 Cor 10, where Paul makes specific comparisons between himself, his Jesus groups and the wanderings of the Hebrews in the desert, it would likewise be useful to examine Paul's journeys within the tradition of wandering presented in Hebrew scriptures. Here one might apply Sara Terreault's categories of *peregrinatio* to Paul's itineraries.[60] Silvia Montiglio's work *Wandering in Ancient Greek Culture*[61] would also be invaluable for such a direction in Pauline research. However, it is not peripatetic pilgrimage, but the magnetism of Jerusalem that drew the non-Jewish representatives accompanying the collection.

Durkheim, and after him, the Turners[62] and others, identified the centre of a pilgrimage as a shrine. The shrine is not only the object of pilgrimage, but also represents the centre of a social network. This observation recognises as a corollary that pilgrimage is a social process as well as a religious one (the two cannot be separated, especially in the ancient Mediterranean).

For Paul, as for other Jews, there was only one conceptual centre, and that was Jerusalem.[63] But in what way? Despite its near-universal importance to Judaism, there was ample ancient critique of the Temple. Hogeterp notes that the "sectarian communities of the Essenes and the Qumran community perceived the corruption of the Temple cult in the early Roman period as an accomplished fact".[64] Even in his gospel-tamed portrayal, John the Baptist is a Temple-critiquing figure;[65] the crowds from Jerusalem are portrayed as "coming out" to him (a sort of reverse pilgrimage). The Jesus movement, at first linked to John, was almost certainly born from the same reform sentiments. Of

---

56 See Scott 2011.
57 Engbert-Pedersen 2000.
58 Especially 1 Cor 4:11. The wandering references in 1 Cor 10 are to the Exodus traditions.
59 Malherbe 2004, 253. Jesus's sayings concerning wandering go back as early as the Q material. See Parks 2019 and Theissen 1992.
60 Terreault 2019.
61 Montiglio 2005.
62 Turner and Turner 1978.
63 An understanding that lies behind the set-piece dialogue of John 4, especially John 4:20. Practically, of course, the wide diversity attested for Judaism in this period includes a diversity of opinion on the exclusivity of Jerusalem as a seat for the divine. See Runesson, Binder, and Olsson 2007, 274-297 for a thorough treatment of evidence for several additional ancient Jewish Temples located elsewhere.
64 Hogeterp 2006, especially 115-96.
65 That is, the Baptist was not against the Temple *per se*, but against a corrupt Temple leadership.

the religio-political groups described by Josephus in the first century, both the Pharisees and the Essenes arose from a grassroots suspicion of the validity some of the Temple leadership. (Note that such criticism reinforces the very importance of proper Temple cult to those who critiqued it.) The Qumran community looked forward to a rebuilding of a purified Temple in the place of Herod's abomination, but in the meantime saw their community as constituting a sort of Temple-in-waiting.[66]

Insofar as we can say anything about the historical Jesus, some of his sayings seem to call for Temple reform, as do the gospel reports that he instigated a minor riot in, interestingly, the Court of the Gentiles. Even the so-called 'words of institution'—this is my flesh, this is my blood—can be read as a commentary on the traditional sacrifice and an expansion of it.[67] Jesus's legacy was not anti-Temple: his critique of its leaders instead shows a strong interest in its proper functioning.[68] Most evidence also indicates that the Jerusalem assembly, particularly James, remained strongly attached to the Temple after the crucifixion.[69]

As a first-century Diaspora Jew, Paul appears to have had a strong, if nuanced, relationship to the Temple as well. In his own letters he subversively calls the small Jesus communities in Corinth the "Temple of God".[70] Yet, like the Essenes' alternative temple writings (e.g. The Temple Scroll), the very existence of alternatives relies on the fundamental importance of the Jerusalem temple in order to work. In Galatians, Paul calls the leading apostles "the pillars"; again, a metaphor, found also in Qumran,[71] that can indicate both adherence to the existing Temple and critique of it.

Then what was the shrine that these Jesus-following pilgrims looked to? Paul tells the Roman believers that he is bringing a gift of money to the "poor among the saints".[72] Although the Jesus assemblies of the Aegean were perhaps better off financially than the Jerusalem group, Paul's term "the poor" has been misunderstood by those contemporary scholars who read it primarily as a descriptor of a group suffering from famine, drought or poverty.[73] Possible connections between the first Jesus followers and the Essenes,[74] the link between Jesus and the Baptist, accounts in Acts, and specifically early church traditions about James, who is strongly identified with the Temple,[75] make it likely that

---

66 Charlesworth 2014, 194. Note that such an expectation still relies on the importance of the Temple.
67 Goldhill 2005, 101. See also Akenson 2000.
68 Thiessen 2021, 179-180.
69 Charlesworth 2014c, 202.
70 1 Cor 3:16 and following.
71 4Q403 frg.1, col 1.41.
72 D.B. Hart's 2017 translation of the New Testament, while generally refreshing, adopts a strictly financial view of the collection, translating *tous ptōchous tōn hagiōn* as "the destitute among the holy ones in Jerusalem".
73 See Longenecker 2011, 28, who sees the gentile offering for the poor in Jerusalem as social relief but also part of their proof of turning to Israel's God, since "Gentiles were not known to care for the poor", but Jews were.
74 Hogeterp 2006, 187.
75 Eliav 2005, 60-66.

there was an ascetic and semi-monastic sub-group that existed from the beginning, devoted to prayer (probably in the Temple), and living a life of *voluntary* hardship. Paul and the emissaries who represented a new type of non-Jewish followers of Jesus, are on their way to a priestly service of the congregation in Jerusalem,[76] among the "pillars" of that eschatological assembly. This group represented the core of the Jerusalem Jesus-movement leadership, and the effective goal of the pilgrimage of 'believing nations'.

Connectivity and Contestation

In recent scholarship it is increasingly asserted that Paul's basic writings were misunderstood, even in his own day and by his allies.[77] The last letter Paul wrote before he set off with the delegation was Romans, and it seems to have been written in part to correct misunderstandings of his rather harsh opinions expressed earlier in the letter to the Galatians.[78] Galatians is a bitter document: Paul had apparently 'lost' the Galatian group to those Christ-followers who advocated for full conversion to Judaism. Importantly, he also appears to have lost the Galatian assembly as participants in the collection.[79] Romans, then, serves both as a damage-control corrective to Galatians and as a final rhetorical preparation for Paul's immanent departure.

In chapters 9 to 11, Paul explains why an eschatological procession of the nations to Jerusalem should take place during the penultimate but active stage in the revealing of Israel's God. Jerusalem, and specifically the Temple, bracket (and inform) Paul's discussion of Jews and non-Jews in Romans 9-11.[80] Later in the letter, Paul writes: "[It is the] grace given me by God to be a minister of Christ Jesus to the Gentiles in the priestly service of the gospel of God, so that the offering of the Gentiles may be acceptable."[81] The terminology he uses, as Ascough has pointed out, illustrates that whatever his understanding of pilgrimage, Paul saw the delivery of the collection as a cultic act.[82]

The Roman believers were in closer touch with Jerusalem than Paul was. Paul's irenic and lengthy treatment in Romans of the relationship between Jews and non-Jews in the movement, as well as his novel proposals concerning the timeline of the final days—namely, that the influx of non-Jews was God's way of shaming all of Judaism into God's realm at the end—all make sense as a rhetorical paving of the way for the

---

76 Hogeterp 2006, 288.
77 The so-called 'radical new perspective on Paul' or 'Paul within Judaism' group, represented by, among others, Pamela Eisenbaum, Mark Nanos and John Gager.
78 Gager 2000, 103 and Fredriksen 2017, 158.
79 I am indebted to Mark Goodacre for pointing this out on his blog *NTpod*. Although Paul mentions the Galatian group as model contributors to the collection in 1 Cor 16:1, they are not mentioned when he brings up the subject again in 2 Cor 9:2, and they are notably absent from the listing Paul gives in Rom 15:26.
80 Fredriksen 2017, 163, where she also sidesteps Downs's differentiation between an offering *of* the gentiles and *by* the gentiles by insisting it can be both.
81 Romans 15:16
82 Ascough 1996, 594.

collection's delivery.[83] Paul's words may have been aimed, via Rome, at the movement's leadership, whom he was about to encounter again in Jerusalem, and some of whom he may have savaged in Galatians.

Paul writes the following:

> At present, however, I am going to Jerusalem in a ministry to the saints; for Macedonia and Achaia have been pleased to share their resources with the poor among the saints at Jerusalem. They were pleased to do this, and indeed they owe it to them; for if the Gentiles have come to share in their spiritual blessings, they ought also to be of service to them in material things. So when I have completed this, and have sealed to them this fruit, I will set out by way of you to Spain …[84]

2 Maccabees 12:39-45 provides a scriptural example of another collection sent to the Temple at Jerusalem. Interestingly, this is the perhaps the first reference to prayers for the dead. Judas's collection is sent, as the text says, "taking account of the resurrection", that is, to pay for prayers for those who have died outside the covenant because of idolatry, but for whom Judas holds hope for inclusion in the resurrection, which is tied to the eschatological Day of the Lord. In the case of 2 Maccabees, the prayers are for Jews who are apostate because of the idols found on their dead bodies. Importantly, in both Maccabees and Romans, otherwise separated by time and concern, there is a connection made between delivery of a collection to Jerusalem, eschatology, the Temple and a hope for those outside the covenant relationship to be included in the Day of the Lord.

In the late 50s of the common era, Paul's most dangerous opponents were his own co-believers. It had been over twenty years since Jesus's crucifixion. Things had not gone according to plan. The messianic age had not dawned. 1 Thessalonians, the oldest surviving complete text of the movement, already grapples with the delay, and with believers' anxieties in light of it. In Palestine, the situation grew more volatile by the month—"righteousness was not flowing down like waters; men continued to beat plowshares into swords; the dead had not been raised; the Land was still captive".[85]

In such a context, Paul's and the emissaries' journey to Jerusalem was more desperate than triumphant. Fredriksen, Harrill[86] and others propose that the delay of the Parousia, that is, the delay of the return of Jesus as triumphant herald of God's new age, had implications throughout the Jesus movement, but especially for the status of non-Jews.[87] It was tragically too soon for the eschatological procession of the nations foreseen in

---

83   Donaldson 1990 and Downs 2006, for different reasons, both note that Paul does not use the specific language of Isaiah to describe his journey when he could have. However, Fredriksen 2017, 160 points out that Isaiah lies behind Paul's 'remnant' theology of Rom 9-11, which is of a piece, I argue, with his following description of both collection and pilgrimage.
84   Romans 15:25-8.
85   Fredriksen 2000, 168.
86   Harrill 2012, 42-43.
87   Fredriksen 2000, 168-69.

Isaiah and elsewhere,[88] and Paul's 'test case' solution to the problem of Judaism and the nations foundered long before arrival.

This is what set the stage for the contested pilgrimage. In the early years, with the heady expectations of an immediate ushering in of God's realm, with Jesus at its head, the so-called 'harvest of the gentiles' *as non-Jews*, that is, as people who acknowledged and worshipped the God of Israel but did not circumcise or follow Torah, was the task at hand.[89] It was, among other evidences, the inclusion of the gentiles *as gentiles* that proved that God's new day had begun with Christ's resurrection as God's messiah.[90]

When the Day of the Lord did not come, and Jesus did not return, questions arose within the Jewish centre of the Jesus movement. Differing convictions on the question of "whether (or: to what degree) the end of the ages"[91] had begun became crucial. If Paul's own letters, especially Galatians, are any indication, he felt increasingly alone in his end-times offer to the nations to join without full conversion. For Paul's opponents, perhaps seeking to restrain the transformation of the movement into a numerically-superior gentile group, the way for a non-Jew to fully enter the family of Israel's God reverted to the way it had always been: for those few who chose it, full conversion, including circumcision and Torah observance.[92] These were not the terms by which Paul had worked, and his letters show his disappointment, pain and bitterness at colleagues and followers who had, he believed, moved away from his position.

Scriptures often arise out of crises, and so can pilgrimages. As Frankfurter has written: "The mapping of religious and social experience across landscape is expressed through ritual action."[93] In terms of the four-part paradigm of pilgrimage outlined earlier (Fig 1), it is important that in Paul's and the emissaries' final pilgrimage, contestation would have occurred in *every quadrant* of the paradigm. Firstly, Paul's narrative of a last-days acceptance of the nations into the heart of Judaism as non-Jews was not a narrative shared any longer (if it ever fully had been) by others within the movement. Secondly, the mobility of the pilgrims, as a unified group, whose unity was precisely the point of the pilgrimage, would have been challenged and impeded by the terrain of the shrine (the Temple), the third element. Specifically, the balustrade, or stub wall in the Temple courtyard demarcating the Court of the Gentiles from the smaller Court of Israel was a barrier precisely intended for a group like Paul's. Paul's non-Jewish followers would normally have been welcomed in the Court of the Gentiles. However, they could only transgress that secondary wall at the risk of death, if the first-century warning signs, written in Latin and Greek, that can still be seen in Jerusalem's museums, are to be believed.[94] Finally,

---

88 Note 2 Cor 9:10, where Paul echoes Isa 55:10 and 55:5: "You shall call nations that you do not know, and nations that you do not know shall run to you."
89 Nanos 2015, 109 and 126.
90 Gal 5:2.
91 Nanos 2015, 142.
92 Gal 6:13.
93 Frankfurter 1998b, 14.
94 Goldhill 2005, 68.

the fourth quadrant of our paradigm—the bodies of Paul's group of pilgrims—were the focus of the sharpest contestation of all. The acceptability to the Jerusalem "pillars" and to the Temple (signifying Israel's God) of the non-circumcised bodies of the male, non-Jewish Jesus followers—in other words, their foreskins—was precisely the issue over which Paul's mission, his collection and the future of his groups within the movement, stood or fell.[95] All these tensions were embodied and lived out in the pilgrimage.

Rutherford and Elsner's five-part typology of pilgrimage in the ancient world is useful as another way of showing the particularities of the collection's delivery. The *catchment area* for the Jerusalem Temple was the Diaspora, the *timetable* apocalyptic and provocative, the *motivation* was based on a disputed interpretation of ancient religious texts about the non-Jewish nations, the *identity* of the pilgrims was part of the dispute, and the *activity* at the sanctuary was possibly a sacrifice, or an intrusion of foreigners, that occasioned the riot remembered, later, by the author of Acts.[96] While Acts is not necessarily historically trustworthy, whatever Paul's reception was in Jerusalem, and however obscure the details, it was undoubtedly not what he and the non-Jewish delegates had hoped.

Paul did not die in Jerusalem, despite the author of Acts placing his "passion" there. He lived long enough to be taken to Rome, where multiple traditions agree that eventually he met his martyrdom. In this example of extreme contestation, Paul joins those who have died not just at a shine, but for the sake of the contested meaning of that shrine.

Paul as Provocateur; Pilgrimage as Provocation

Other than those he left us, rhetorically, in writing, we do not and cannot know Paul's thoughts about his final pilgrimage. There is no way to know for certain whether accompanying the collection and its emissaries was intended by Paul as a confrontational or a reconciliatory act. Two pieces of information may be helpful. The first is that Paul asked the Jesus group in Rome to pray for him as he headed to Jerusalem so that he might be "rescued from the disbelievers in Judea" and that his "bringing of a gift to Jerusalem might be acceptable" (Rom 15:30-32). These words certainly leave the impression that Paul expected trouble. And yet he went.

A second fact should be read together with this. Years before the collection's delivery, when Paul accompanied the official delegation from Antioch, he took with him Titus, an uncircumcised Greek (Gal 2:1-5). He seems to have done so for the specific purpose of testing the place of non-Jews in the apocalyptic new age. Paul makes much of the fact that Titus was not *compelled* to be circumcised by the heads of the Jesus group in Jerusalem, "though he was a Greek" (Gal 2:3). There was, however, trouble. The text in Galatians where Paul describes Titus's presence is oddly truncated at precisely that point where he describes how so-called "false believers [were] secretly brought in" to "spy on their freedom". Even though what happened next is unclear, it is easy enough to see

---

95 Nanos 2015, 148-49.
96 Elsner and Rutherford 2007, 11-12.

the basics, and the tactics: Paul brought a non-Jew into some kind of sacred situation as a test, there were opponents, and there was conflict.

To these two basic facts—that Paul expected trouble and that he had already used the physical presence of an uncircumcised non-Jew in a sacred space to prove a point—we can add the very strong impression Paul leaves us in his letters that he was passionate, difficult to work with (he states that he prefers to work alone, where other Jesus believers have not preceded him), and brash (Rom 15:20). If his writings are any indication at all, he was confrontational. The destination he arrived at was increasingly exclusivist and hostile to foreigners, in a spiral that in a few short years would lead to the outbreak of the Jewish rebellions against Rome.

Paul was a pilgrim who arrived at the holy city with a delegation of non-Jews, whom he insisted against some of his colleagues must remain non-Jews.[97] They and their offerings were the culmination, to Paul, of some of the prophetic and apocalyptic promises of ancient Hebrew scriptures.[98] The pilgrimage embodied a 'material message' about the Day of the Lord, and precipitated decisions concerning its timing and its participants.

Not coincidentally, it was Titus, the same non-proselyte apostle of the earlier problematic visit,[99] whom Paul appointed to manage and head the final collection. At the very least, Paul likely wanted to offer sacrifices in the Temple on behalf of these non-Jews, an action that was not unusual otherwise, but that Paul's own notoriety or an increasingly militant public atmosphere might have made incendiary.[100] Decades after the events, in Acts, this more cautiously-reported possibility is the way the journey is described. In Acts, James is portrayed as warning Paul that false rumours about him are circulating, rumours that he is teaching Jews to forsake the Torah (Acts 21:21). Both Acts' James, and notably, Acts itself, strenuously deny this possibility, even though most of Christian interpretive history has assumed it to be true ever since.

Perhaps both Acts and those scholars who situate Paul firmly within Judaism are wrong, and Paul *was* guilty of teaching Jews to forsake the covenant. I think not. Perhaps, as has often been surmised, Paul took the non-Jewish Jesus pilgrims with him and crossed the balustrade into the forbidden Court of Israel. We will never know. Romans is our last reliable word on the matter. Whatever happened, there is no further mention of either the collection or the gentile emissaries who travelled with it. Paul ended the journey seemingly alone and abandoned even by those who had at one point been his allies. Depending on how one dates Philemon and Philippians, if Paul wrote more letters after his Jerusalem trip that have survived, there is no more mention in them of the collection whatsoever.

---

97   Nanos 2015, 126.
98   As mentioned, those in which the gentiles played a neutral or positive role (Isaiah 18:7; 60:1-22; 66:18-21 (where some non-Jews are assigned tasks as priest in the Temple). On the destruction of the non-Jewish nations see Hag 2:22, 1 En 92, Jub 15:26, 4 Ezra 12:33-34, etc.
99   2 Cor 2:13; 7:6, 13, 14; 8.6, 16, 23; 12:18.
100 Hogeterp 2006, 122-23.

Conclusion: Consequences of a Failed Pilgrimage

As an initiative given significant attention by Paul in his undisputed letters, and even without the historical details of the much later and problematic Acts, Paul's final journey has not received the full attention it deserves as pilgrimage. That Paul saw his journeys as sacred travel is attested by his own writing.[101] His route to Jerusalem by way of small assemblies of Aegean believers whom he requested would pray for his trip, represents a first, tentative, and failed attempt to tie together, by means of journey, groups that differed economically, socially, religiously and eschatologically.

Whatever happened, both Paul's silence and the much-later silence of Acts imply it was not positive, either for Paul or his pagan Christ-following delegates. The religious destination for the collection came to an end with the demise of the Jerusalem church, the death or flight of the individuals Paul had called "pillars", and the violence of the Roman siege engines. That this unusual early messianic and apocalyptic moment of Jerusalem as a Christian pilgrimage destination turned out so differently from the later travels of Egeria and Helen makes it significant not only for the study of Paul, but also for later Christian journeys to Jerusalem.[102]

At the core of Paul's mid-first century experience as a pilgrim are issues of identity,[103] belonging, connectivity,[104] transgression and consequence. The brief flowering of a utopian social and transportational network of Jews and non-Jews in the Mediterranean based on an eschatological hope, and looking forward to a long-promised pilgrimage blessing, was caught up in and crushed by the much larger political events taking place in Judea in the years that followed. Paul's final trip to the city was the last act of this social experiment. Jerusalem soon had its influx of "the nations". However, they were not Paul's small band, but Titus's troops, who arrived to lay siege and eventually to destroy the city.[105] That centuries later, non-Jewish, Christian pilgrims from those same foreign lands would return as pilgrims to Jerusalem to retrace Paul's steps,[106] while venerating his final, apprehensive writings, is an irony almost impossible to overstate.

---

101 Romans 15:18-19; Fredriksen 2017, 163 identifies the circuits of Paul's travels as corresponding to Jewish mythic geography.
102 On the 'identity confirmation' aspect of ancient pilgrimage, see Muir 2011, 32.
103 Johnson Hodge 2015; with Kloppenborg 2017, 198, I believe the collection and pilgrimage were to "perform membership".
104 On the trans-local links of first-century associations, including the Pauline assemblies, see Downs 2008, 112-18.
105 Acts, written after the destruction, has recast Paul's "time of the nations" in this way as well.
106 Eliav 2005, 174-79.

Bibliography

Akenson, D.H. 2000. *Saint Saul: A Skeleton Key to the Historical Jesus.* Montreal: McGill-Queens University Press.

Anderson, M.R. 2023. *Prophets of Love: The Unlikely Kinship of Leonard Cohen and the Apostle Paul.* Montreal: McGill-Queen's University Press.

Ascough, R.S. 1996. "The Completion of a Religious Duty: The Background of 2 Cor 8:1-15." *New Testament Studies* 42, 584-99.

Auler, S. 2016. "More Than a Gift: Revisiting Paul's Collection for Jerusalem and the Pilgrimage of the Gentiles." *Journal for the Study of Paul and his Letters* 6.2, 143-60.

Boccaccini, G. and C. Segovia (eds.) 2016. *Paul the Jew: Rereading the Apostle as a Figure of Second Temple Judaism.* Minneapolis: Fortress Press.

Boyarin, D. 1994. *A Radical Jew: Paul and the Politics of Identity.* Berkeley: University of California Press.

Charles, R. 2014. *Paul and the Politics of Diaspora.* Minneapolis: Augsburg Fortress.

Charlesworth, J.H. (ed.) 2014a. *Jesus and Temple: Textual and Archaeological Explorations.* Minneapolis: Fortress Press.

Charlesworth, J.H. 2014b. "Introduction: Devotion to and Worship in Jerusalem's Temple," in Charlesworth 2014a, 1-17.

Charlesworth, J.H. 2014c. "The Temple and Jesus' Followers," in Charlesworth 2014a, 183-212.

Coleman, S. and J. Eade (eds.) 2004a. *Reframing Pilgrimage: Cultures in Motion.* London: Routledge.

Coleman, S. and J. Eade, 2004b. "Introduction: Reframing Pilgrimage," in Coleman and Eade 2004a, 1-25.

Donaldson, T.L. 1990. "Proselytes or Righteous Gentiles? The Status of Gentiles in Eschatological Pilgrimage Patterns of Thought." *Journal for the Study of the Pseudepigrapha* 7, 3-27.

Donaldson, T.L. 1993. "'Riches for the Gentiles' (Rom 11-12): Israel's Rejection and Paul's Gentile Mission." *Journal of Biblical Literature* 112.1, 81-98.

Donaldson, T.L. 1997. *Paul and the Gentiles: Remapping the Apostle's Convictional World.* Minneapolis: Fortress.

Donaldson, T.L. 2013. "'Gentile Christianity' as a Category in the Study of Christian Origins." *HTR* 106.4, 433-58.

Donaldson, T.L. 2015. "Paul Within Judaism," in Nanos and Zetterholm 2015, 277-301.

Downs, D.J. 2008. *The offering of the Gentiles: Paul's collection for Jerusalem in its Chronological, Culture, and Cultic Contexts.* Grand Rapids: Eerdmans.

Downs, D.J. 2006. "'The offering of the gentiles' in Romans 15.16." *Journal for the Study of the New Testament* 29.2, 173-86.

Eade, J. and M. Sallnow (eds.) 1991. *Contesting the Sacred: The Anthropology of Christian Pilgrimage.* Urbana: University of Illinois Press.

Eisenbaum, P. 2009. *Paul Was Not a Christian: The Original Message of a Misunderstood Apostle.* New York: HarperCollins.

Eliav, Y.Z. 2005. *God's Mountain: The Temple Mount in Time, Place and Memory.* Baltimore: The Johns Hopkins University Press.

Elliott, N. and M. Reasoner (eds.) 2011. *Documents and Images for the Study of Paul.* Minneapolis: Fortress.

Elsner, J. and I. Rutherford (eds.) 2007. *Pilgrimage in Graeco-Roman and Early Christian Antiquity: Seeing the Gods.* Oxford: Oxford University Press.

Engberg-Pedersen, T. 2000. *Paul and the Stoics.* Louisville, KY: Westminster-John Knox.

Engberg-Pedersen, T. (ed.) 2004. *Paul in his Hellenistic Context.* Second edition. London: T&T Clark.

Feldman, L.H. 1996. *Jew and Gentile in the Ancient World: Attitudes and Interactions from Alexander to Justinian.* Princeton: Princeton University Press.

Frankfurter, D. (ed.) 1998a. *Pilgrimage and Holy Space in Late Antique Egypt.* Leiden: Brill.

Frankfurter, D. 1998b. "Introduction", in Frankfurter 1998a, 3-50.

Fredriksen, P. 2000. *From Jesus to Christ.* Second ed. New Haven: Yale University Press.

Fredriksen, P. 2017. *Paul: The Pagans' Apostle.* New Haven: Yale University Press.

Gager, J.G. 2000. *Reinventing Paul.* Oxford: Oxford University Press.

Goldhill, S. 2005. *The Temple of Jerusalem.* Cambridge, MA: Harvard University Press.

Goodman, M. 2006. *Judaism in the Roman World: Collected Essays.* Boston: Brill.

Goodman, M. 2007. "The Pilgrimage Economy of Jerusalem in the Second Temple Period," in *Judaism in the Roman World: Collected Essays*, 59-67. Leiden: Brill.

Haber, S. 2011. "Going Up to Jerusalem: Pilgrimage, Purity, and the Historical Jesus," in Harland 2011, 49-67.

Harland, P. (ed.) 2011. *Studies in Christianity and Judaism: Travel and Religion in Antiquity.* Waterloo: Wilfred Laurier Press.

Harrill, J.A. 2012. *Paul the Apostle: His life and legacy in their Roman context.* Cambridge: Cambridge University Press.

Hogeterp, A. 2005. "Paul's Judaism Reconsidered: The Issue of Cultic Imagery in the Corinthian Correspondence." *Ephemerides Theologicae Lovanienses* 81.1, 87-108.

Hogeterp, A. 2006. *Paul and God's Temple: A Historical Interpretation of Cultic Imagery in the Corinthian Correspondence.* Leuven: Peeters.

Johnson Hodge, C. 2015. "The Question of Identity: Gentiles as Gentiles – but also Not – in Pauline Communities," in Nanos and Zetterholm 2015, 153-73.

Kloppenborg, J.S. 2017. "Fiscal Aspects of Paul's Collection for Jerusalem." *Early Christianity* 2.8, 153-98.

Longenecker, B.W. 2011. "Poverty and Paul's Gospel." *Ex Auditu* 27, 26-44.

Malherbe, A.J. 2004. "Determinism and Free Will in Paul: The Argument of 1 Corinthians 8 and 9," in Engberg-Pedersen 2004, 231-55.

McCready, W.O. 2011. "Pilgrimage, Place, and Meaning-Making by Jews in Greco-Roman Egypt," in Harland 2011, 69-82.

Montiglio, S. 2005. *Wandering in Ancient Greek Culture.* Chicago: University of Chicago Press.

Muir, S. 2011. "Identity on the Road in Ancient Greece and Rome," in Harland 2011, 29-47.

Munck, J. 1959. *Paul and the Salvation of Mankind.* London: SCM Press.

Nickle, K.F. 1966. *The Collection: A Study in Paul's Strategy.* Naperville: SCM. Press.

Nanos, M. 2015. "The Question of Conceptualization: Qualifying Paul's Position on Circumcision in Dialogue with Josephus's Advisors to King Izates," in Nanos and Zetterholm 2015, 105-52.

Nanos, M. and M. Zetterholm (eds.) 2015. *Paul within Judaism: Restoring the First Century Context to the Apostle.* Minneapolis: Fortress Press.

Ogereau, J.M. 2012. "The Jerusalem Collection as Κοινωνία: Paul's Global Politics of Socio-Economic Equality and Solidarity." *New Testament Studies* 58.3, 360-78.

Oliver, I.W. 2016. "The 'Historical Paul' and the Paul of Acts," in Boccaccini and Segovia 2016, 51-80.

Parks, S. 2019. *Gender in the Rhetoric of Jesus.* London: Lexington/Fortress.

Reasoner, M. 2005. *Romans in Full Circle: A History of Interpretation.* Louisville: Westminster John Knox.

Rosen-Zvi, I. and A. Ophir, 2015. "Paul and the Invention of the Gentiles." *The Jewish Quarterly Review* 105.1, 1-41.

Runesson, A., D. Binder, and B. Olsson. 2007. *The Ancient Synagogue from its Origins to 200 C.E.* Boston: Brill.

Scott, I.W. 2011. "The Divine Wanderer: Travel and Divinization in Ancient Antiquity," in Harland 2011, 101-22.

Skarsaune, O. 2002. *In the Shadow of the Temple: Jewish Influences on Early Christianity.* Downer's Grove: IVP Academic.

Sommerschield, T. 2016. "A Long Way from Home: The Pertinence of Pilgrimage to Ancient Greek Religion." *Pons Aelius: Newcastle University Postgraduate Forum e-Journal* 13, 25-34.

Stenschke, C.W. 2015. "Obstacles on All Sides: Paul's Collection for the Saints in Jerusalem Part 1." *European Journal of Theology* 24.1, 19-32.

Tajra, H.W. 1989. *The Trial of St. Paul: A Juridicial Exegesis of the Second Half of the Acts of the Apostles.* Tübingen: Mohr Siebeck.

Terreault, S. 2017. "(Re)Walking Stories: Pilgrimage, Pedagogy, and Peace," in I. McIntosh and L. Harman (eds.) *The Many Voices of Pilgrimage and Reconciliation,* 47-65. Wallingford: CABI.

Terreault, S. 2019. "The Eschatological Body: Fleeing the Centre in Pre-Modern Insular Christianity and Post-Modern Secularity," *International Journal of Religious Tourism and Pilgrimage* 7.1, 22-37.

Theissen, G. 1992. *Social Reality and the Early Christians.* Minneapolis: Fortress.

Thiessen, M. 2021. *Jesus and the Forces of Death: The Gospels' Portrauyal of Ritual Impurity within First-Century Judaism.* Grand Rapids, MI: Baker Academic.

Turner, V. and E. Turner. 1978. *Image and Pilgrimage in Christian Culture.* New York: Columbia University Press.

Whittle, S. 2015. *Covenant Renewal and the Consecration of the Gentiles in Romans.* Cambridge: Cambridge University Press.

9

PILGRIMS, PIETY AND PRAGMATISM:

ROMAN SANCTUARIES AND LATE ANTIQUE CHURCHES IN THE CYCLADES[1]

REBECCA SWEETMAN

Introduction

Throughout the Classical and Hellenistic periods, the Cyclades were a significant hub for religious and trade networks, with Delos at the centre. The religious networks of Delos are well known, and the Apollo sanctuary dedications reveal the extensive reach of the cult around the Mediterranean lands: from northern Greece to north Africa to Seleucia.[2] Delos was also a focus for other cults such as the Kabeiroi and the Samothracian gods and the Great Gods, which were then taken to other Cycladic islands like Kea, Melos, Paros, Syros, Thera and Anaphe.[3] Part of the Kabeirian mysteries involved a ritual sailing to Delos then returning to Limnos with new light from Apollo. From the Hellenistic period in particular, bankers and merchants from across the Mediterranean were drawn to do business on Delos, and epigraphic data shows that they settled too on nearby islands such as Andros, Tenos and Mykonos (Fig. 1). Additionally, islands such as Paros and Naxos had rich resources of marble and agricultural produce and they too were part of the extensive trade system.

By the Late Republican period, a series of attacks by Mithridates VI and pirates on the islands, combined with a collective unwillingness to play host to the civil wars of Octavian and Antony, left these once-powerful islands bereft of their trade networks and religious clout. The literary sources were quick to adopt a stereotype of these places as isolated haunts of pirates and exiles, to the extent that by the late antique period, the islands had become known for desertion and decline in the face of Gothic raids in 376.[4] Moreover, while individual sites on particular islands may have been considered

---

1   All dates are CE unless otherwise noted.
2   Constantakopoulou 2017.
3   Hemberg 1950.
4   Kulikowski 2007, 19-20.

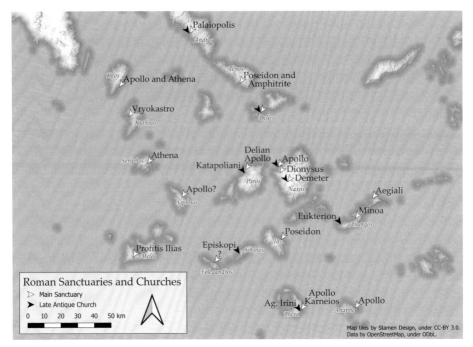

Fig. 1. Map of the Cyclades showing key sanctuaries and churches mentioned in the text.

attractive, as an archipelago they were consistently sidelined as parochial: "Dare not deny her, insular Cyclades and noble Rhodes and ferocious Thrace."[5] Furthermore, in more recent centuries the islands have become a trope for danger: "This year has been to me like steering through the Cyclades in a storm without a rudder; I hope to have a less dangerous and more open sea the next …."[6]

Conversely, throughout the Roman and late antique periods, the sanctuaries and churches of the Cyclades (Fig. 1) maintained a glowing reputation as worth seeing, as Strabo noted:[7]

> Tenos does not have a large city, but a great sanctuary of Poseidon, in a grove outside the city, worth seeing. There are large banqueting halls in it, a sufficient indication of the large number who come together with their neighbours and join them in the sacrifices at the Poseidonia (trans Roller 2014).

The attention shown by visitors to the islands is borne out by epigraphic evidence at the places of worship as well as in historical texts. For example, the sanctuary of Poseidon and Amphitrite at Tenos benefitted from investment by P. Quinctilius Varus who was

---

5   Catullus 4.
6   Thomas Sheridan to his friend Dean Jonathan Swift (1735-36) (Swift 1768).
7   Strabo 10.5.11. trans. Roller 2014, 473.

Sanctuary of Poseidon and Amphitrite, Tinos.

Fig. 2.

a *quaestor* and friend of Augustus; furthermore, Tiberius granted it *asylia* (the right to give asylum) (Fig. 2).[8] Andros was famed for the sanctuary of Dionysus and the associated river that flowed with wine as described by Mucianus (Pliny *NH* 2.106).[9] However, the only physical evidence for the sanctuary of Dionysus that remains are inscriptions such as the altar dedicated by Flavia Paiderotis now in Andros Museum (inv. no. 87).

Interest in the Cyclades continued throughout the late antique and Byzantine periods; the Katapoliani church on Paros (Fig. 3) is said to have been founded by Agia Eleni, Constantine's mother, and during his pilgrimage and in the fifth century, the Deacon John left a dedication in the form of an inscription on a marble plaque at the basilica of Agios Kyriakos, Delos (Fig. 4).[10] Similar dedications were left by pilgrims on Tenos, for example at Gastria by the Bishop Timothy in the sixth–seventh centuries, and by sailors on Syros (for example, an appeal to the Lord from Jean and Martyrios from Melos).[11] Pope Constantine is said to have made a stop at Kea on the return to Constantinople from his Jerusalem pilgrimage sometime in the late sixth or early seventh century.[12]

---

8   Mendoini and Zoumbaki 2008, TEN 52.
9   Williamson 2005, 233.
10 Kiourtzian 2000, 51, no. 6.
11 Kiourtzian 2000, 205 no. 136 and 190, no. 129.
12 Kiourtzian 2000, 64. Another version is that he was summoned to Constantinople to discuss decisions of the Quinisext council and met the *strategos* of the Karabansari theme on Kea (Curta 2011, 110).

Fig. 3. Katapoliani Church, Paros.

Fig. 4. Agios Kyriakos, Delos.

The topography of sanctuaries and churches on the Cyclades is such that many of them were visible from the sea. For some, their locations suggest the importance of the visual accessibility of the religious interaction, while others may be more physically accessible. Through an examination of the topography of religious buildings over a diachronic range, the aim of this chapter is to discuss direct and indirect pilgrimage experiences and to posit the questions of whether the physicality and intentionality of the visit was fundamental to the notion of pilgrimage, and whether there was a difference between polytheistic and Christian pilgrimage in this regard. Groups of islands are a particularly useful area on which to focus. They are united by proximity but different enough individually to allow some tentative conclusions on whether the topography and continued existence of a religious space can help understand the practicalities of pilgrimage.

Approaches to Pilgrimage

Pilgrimage in the ancient world is notoriously difficult to define and identify. There is no Greek or Latin word for pilgrimage, which has its roots in Middle English. Neither polytheistic nor Christian sacred travellers obeyed a sacred code, unless they travelled as part of an official delegation.[13] Furthermore, it is difficult to assess elements of intentionality given the inherent ambiguity of pilgrimage and how multi-layered the Greek environment was. As individual pilgrimages were not an official part of either polytheistic or Christian practice, it makes it difficult to identify the practice. In fact, as Pullan notes, some prominent Christians, such as Gregory of Nyssa, were scornful of the value of pilgrimage, although others such as St Jerome were less so.[14] Evidence for pilgrimage in the periods in question here is primarily literary and epigraphic, and in the late antique period, other evidence such as pilgrim flasks provides additional data for Christian pilgrimage.[15] While certain scholars discuss pilgrimage as a common occurrence,[16] some sceptics have questioned the all-encompassing generalisation of the term,[17] while others have examined how to define pilgrims and pilgrimage.[18] Rutherford has focused on more secure evidence for state pilgrimage (*theoroi*)[19] and other studies have concentrated on travel for specific purposes such as healing, mystery and panhellenic festivals.[20]

Some, such as Rutherford, emphasise the visual and the experience at the site rather than the journey.[21] He also notes that various visitors could have a range of different motivations for making the journey. Kristensen and Friese use the phrases "pilgrimage

---

13 Pullan 2005.
14 Pullan 2005, 401 and Elsner 2005, 412.
15 Kristensen and Friese 2017, 1.
16 Dillon 1997.
17 Scullion 2005.
18 Elsner and Rutherford 2005, 1-38.
19 Rutherford 2013.
20 Petsalis-Diomidis 2017 and Arnush 2005.
21 Rutherford 2001, 43.

sanctuaries" and "places of pilgrimage", and in doing so emphasise place but without the limitations of a strict classification.[22] Others argue that, while the site of pilgrimages is important, the journey itself is fundamental to definition, stressing the intentionality of the journey as distinct and special,[23] placing more emphasis on the journey. Scriven sees the multiple characteristics of pilgrimage including the journey, destination, belief and transformative elements of it.[24]

Polytheistic and Christian Pilgrimage

While scholars have focused on ideas of religious travel in the Classical and Hellenistic periods, significantly less attention has been paid to the Roman period. Conversely, scholars have focused heavily on early Christian pilgrimage and mission, perhaps driven in part by accounts such as those by Egeria.[25] But how, or if, this early Christian tradition connects with that of the polytheistic one is poorly understood and there is little agreement as to whether the two can be connected. Rutherford rejects any connection between the two, arguing that Christian pilgrimage was a time of penance.[26] Takás suggests that as a votive religion, Graeco-Roman practices of pilgrimage were based on a "reciprocal relationship dynamic".[27] As such, if you gain from a site visit then you leave something behind. Conversely, the motivation for travel to a site by a Christian echoes the notion that the soul is on a pilgrimage, which is a metaphor for Christian life.[28] Pullan also notes that movement, particularly over considerable time, is critical.[29] She further adds: "In maintaining distance, pilgrimage 'fleshes out' Christian life on earth and more fully mediates human participation in the divine while still in the mortal realm."[30] In practical terms, Christianity was a religion that actively sought to convert others. The idea of travel is embedded in notions of the spread of Christianity and this was seen very early on with the practices of St Paul.

Christian pilgrimage was in part defined by the journey undertaken, and this can be seen as being emphasised by the pairing of saints on pilgrim flasks like Thecla and Menas.[31] Instead, shrine visitation seems motived by reciprocity and the encounter with the divine. In this light, it is worth exploring whether a distinction between polytheistic and monotheistic pilgrimage is the difference in pilgrimage-focus; between site and journey. On the surface, the emphasis on the journey is clear; for example, Egeria's extensive travels and those of the even more eminent Agia Eleni, mother of Constan-

---

22 Kristensen and Friese 2017, 1-5.
23 Pullan 2005, 292-93.
24 Scriven 2014, 252.
25 Wilkinson 1981.
26 Rutherford 2001, 40-41.
27 Takás 2005, 353.
28 Pullan 2005.
29 Pullan 2005, 392-93.
30 Pullan 2005, 392.
31 Davis 1998, 311.

tine.[32] Ampullae that often depicted saints such as Thecla and Menas were tokens of the journey, as much as the destination. If this is the case, it is useful to investigate whether such differences are evidenced by the archaeological material. Addressing the gap between polytheistic and Christian religious travel will contribute to the ongoing debates concerning definitions of and evidence for pilgrimage and the importance of the journey in relation to the destination (see Frankfurter, this volume).

Methodology

It is possible that there was enough fluidity in polytheistic and monotheistic religion to allow for the idea of a happenchance pilgrimage, or a journey that does not necessarily have the intention of pilgrimage but contains elements of it. This does not preclude intentional pilgrimages, which were particularly visible in the late antique period. Given the importance of the diachronic approach in this chapter, and the emphasis on temporality and mobility, I have found that Hyndman-Rizk's definition of pilgrimage is most appropriate. She notes that "pilgrimage privileges a distinctively spiritual conceptualisation of mobility, which emphasises inner transformation over physical mobility linked with purely quotidian pursuits of material advancement".[33] This emphasis on the journey and transition means that the journey can be both banal and exotic, the latter having the potential to create awe and a sense of mystery fundamental to the formation of memory and cultural and religious experience, a pilgrimage. A diachronic examination of Roman and late antique religious sites allows any differences between polytheistic and monotheistic pilgrimage to be highlighted, including whether elements of pre-Christian pilgrimage were maintained and if pilgrimage was used as a bridge from the new religion to the old. Evidence for continuation of pilgrimage to a particular site, in spite of the change in spiritual emphasis, helps define the importance of place.

Narrowing the focus to a group of islands like the Cyclades means that different reasons for travel can be considered in the discussion: while the topography will aid in the discussion of accessibility, the identification of well-traversed routes through analysis of portable material culture and epigraphic data will make a contribution to understanding elements of intentionality in pilgrimage. Altogether, a contextual view that incorporates the archaeological, topographic and literary data reveals the importance of both the journey and the place and sense of temporal engagement. While the focus of the discussion will be on key exemplars such as Tenos, Naxos and Andros, material from a range of other islands will be drawn on to provide as detailed a discussion as possible within the confines of this chapter.

---

32 Holum 1990. It is ironic that Agia Eleni herself has become a point of pilgrimage. Her relics were transferred from Venice to Athens in 2017 and put on display for a month so people could make a pilgrimage to her (https://greekcitytimes.com/2017/05/16/holy-relics-of-agia-eleni-arrive-in-greece-for-first-time-since-1211/?amp).

33 Hyndman-Rizk 2012, xvi.

Data

Topography of Sanctuaries and Churches

In the Cyclades, it not surprising that there is continuation of place from the Archaic to Roman period; according to Le Quéré, an interest in Apollo was maintained on Delos and Kea. When the significant sanctuaries of the Cyclades are plotted (Fig. 1) it is clear to see that all, with the exception of Sifnos, are located on notable sailing routes. It is striking that each of the key sanctuaries is located in a highly visible position from the sea, although not necessarily from land as is the case with the Mausoleum at Episkopi on Sikinos (Fig. 5). It is tempting to consider these sanctuaries as global sanctuaries with reach beyond the local (Fig. 1). Even if they did not continue in use throughout the Roman period, such the sanctuary of Artemis and Apollo on Kythnos and that of Delian Apollo on Paros, they remained standing. As such, they would have continued to be prominent and visible from a marine perspective.

Imperial cult was included in the majority of the Cycladic islands, with new cult buildings identified at Ioulis (Kea) and Trypiti (Melos).[34] While some of the islands had more regular contact with the West through trade (such as Paros and Melos), even smaller islands such as Sifnos and Folegandros had imperial cult as attested by the epigraphic evidence of its priests.[35] The insertion of imperial cult into existing sanctuaries of Apollo at Karthaia (Kea), Dionysus on Naxos, and Thera would have breathed new life into them, and certain sanctuaries such as that of Poseidon and Amphitrite on Tenos were especially known to the elite of Rome, as noted above.[36]

A strong Christian presence on the Cyclades is apparent from the mid-first century, as evidenced by the catacombs on Melos.[37] Five galleries (with subsidiary galleries) of burials have been studied, revealing primarily single tombs. Wall paintings and inscriptions decorate some of the tombs and a small altar is present in one of the galleries. Thera, Paros, Sifnos, Andros and Amorgos were also Episcopal seats, and these bishoprics are likely to have been formed in the fourth century (at Thera it was in 342).[38] A number of bishops from the Cyclades are also recorded by different sources, such as Eusebius and Socrates Scholasticus, as having attended various Ecumenical councils.[39]

One of the earliest churches supposedly constructed on the Cycladic islands is that of the Church of the Panagia Katapoliani complex on Paros (Fig. 3).[40] An early wooden church was supposedly founded by Agia Eleni, who stopped at the island on her way to Jerusalem in the fourth century. She vowed to build a stone church there once she returned with the Cross; instead it was her son, Constantine, who built it and it became the church of Agios Nikolas with an associated baptistery. Later, Justinian's sixth-century

---

34 Le Quéré 2015.
35 Le Quéré 2015, tables 6 and 7.
36 Le Quéré 2015, 123-27.
37 Sweetman 2019, 201-2.
38 Kiourtizan 2000, 24-25.
39 Price and Gaddis 2005, 242; Kiourtzian 2000, 204.
40 Orlandos 1965.

Mausoleum, Sikinos.

Fig. 5.

restoration combined the buildings and extended them, making it into the cruciform church of Panagia Katapoliani (Fig. 3).[41]

Other early churches are found at Thera (Agia Irini) and Amorgos (the *eukterion* or house church at Paradise Bay) (Fig. 6) and at Paliopolis on Andros. It is notable that these early churches are found at the edges of ports, as is the case in other areas of the Eastern Mediterranean.[42] The pattern differs from other areas in the lack of early church building in or close to existing sacred spaces. Consequently, for the Cyclades, this means that a more accessible site rather than a visible one is enabled.

After the first churches were constructed in the late fourth century CE, Cycladic temples probably continued to stand for some time; the temples of Athena and Apollo on Kea did not collapse until the sixth or seventh centuries (perhaps due to an earthquake), when their foundations were repurposed and converted into Christian cemeteries.[43] The Delion on Paros experienced weathering, suggesting that it too continued to stand long after either it was destroyed, probably by an earthquake, or it gradually fell apart in the fourth century BCE.[44]

Christian destruction of sanctuary sites, which is so often indicated in literary sources (for example, in Eunapius),[45] is lacking in the Cyclades, as it is in many places in the

---

41 Pohlsander 1995, 85; Sweetman et al. 2018.
42 Sweetman 2015b.
43 Simantoni Bournia et al. 2009, 71; Zachos 2010, 784.
44 Schuller and Ohnesorg 1991, 73-74.
45 VS 379, 421, 427, and for Greece specifically, VS 437, 465.

Fig. 6. Eukterion, Amorgos.

east. The exception might be Naxos, where Deligiannakis suggests that there may have been an island-wide policy of taking over pre-Christian buildings.[46] The supporting evidence to argue this point either way is lacking, due to issues with chronologies, and because in the past, some churches built on temples (such as those of Apollo, Portaria or the Temple of Dionysus) were removed in the excavation of the earlier buildings.

It is notable that churches built on polytheistic sanctuaries on the Cyclades were likely sixth-century foundations; these include the church on the Temple of Demeter at Sangri, and Agios Matheious on a possible sanctuary, both in Naxos. The church in the western part of ancient Thera was constructed in the vicinity of both the sanctuary of Pythian Apollo and that of the Egyptian gods.[47] The *spolia* used in Treis Ekklisies on Paros indicates there may have been an earlier sanctuary nearby, possibly identified as a site of the cult of Isis.

As in other parts of the Empire, polytheistic practice continued even with the construction of the earliest churches.[48] This is seen on Delos, where cult continued to be practiced in an unofficial manner at the sanctuary of Apollo (Fig. 4) even while the church of Agios Kyriakos was constructed to the southeast of the sanctuary. A similar process is found at other Aegean island sanctuaries such as the sanctuary of Apollo in Halasarna, Kos.[49] Epigraphic data reveals a mix of traditions of polytheism and monotheism; for example, a number of grave stelae from Thera are in the traditional form with a temple pediment decoration but are inscribed with the word 'Angel'.[50]

Tenos
In spite of the ripple effect that the decline of Delos had, and the lack of a major city as noted by Strabo,[51] Tenos still continued to benefit from external patronage of the island, particularly at the sanctuary of Poseidon and Amphritrite (Fig. 2) and its Poseidonia festival. Varus and Tiberius were noted earlier, and later investment is also evidenced through epigraphic data and dedications of sculptural figures, including those of the emperors Hadrian and Trajan. There are numerous dedications at the sanctuary, with a small number from Athens and Boeotia, but they are primarily from local elites, particularly the family of Phileinos (Malthake, his adoptive daughter and his son Satyros).[52] Although the epigraphic data is indicative of a rich variety of connections, it doesn't reveal many external visitors. C. Iunius Silanus, the Proconsul of the province

---

46 Deligiannakis 2016, 27.
47 No precise date is given for this three-aisled basilica with narthex but the excavators suggest that this was a late antique church, although it may also be Byzantine (Von Gartringen 1899, 182, 254-58).
48 Sweetman et al. 2018.
49 Karvonis et al. 2012,161, 163; Laidlaw 1933, 271; Bruneau 1968, 708; Deligiannakis 2011, 311-12, 320-23.
50 Kiourtzian 2000, Appendix, nos. 25-28, for example.
51 10.5.11.
52 Etienne 1990, 156-68.

of Asia (20/21) was exiled on Tenos.[53] Other notables such as L. Quinctius L. f. Rufus, governor of Asia around 100 BCE, received a dedication from the city as its saviour and patron, but he never seems to have been there.[54] Numismatic material might indicate travellers from Miletus, Magnesia, Thessaloniki and Andros but they could easily be indirect deposits too.[55]

Ceramic evidence reveals more regular and direct connections particularly with the east; excavations uncovered the standard eastern types Eastern Sigillatas A, B and C and Cypriot sigillata.[56] Amphorae came from Kos and Rhodes but the lack of western material, such as Arretine, is of note. Among the regular volute lamps, a single lamp signed by *Romanesis* may indicate a connection with a Knidian lamp workshop and it is notable that *Romanesis*-signed lamps are also found on Naxos and Delos.[57] By the third century, the popularity of the sanctuary was on the wane and in fact interest seems to turn to investment in the cult of Dionysus, located closer to the port; for example, Aurelius Satyros who was *stephanophoros* (an official involved in cult practices and often a donor to the city) twice, invested in it.[58] As has been shown in other parts of the Mediterranean, churches were often located close to existing sanctuaries during the early processes of Christianisation in the fourth and fifth centuries.[59] There is no evidence for a church close to the Poseidon sanctuary and it would not have made sense to construct a church at the by then obsolete sanctuary, as is the case with sanctuaries that had gone out of use in other provinces such as Achaea, Crete and Asia Minor.[60] When the sanctuary declined in popularity cult sites in the nearby port were more favoured, and this is indeed why the likely earliest church on Tenos is constructed at the top of the hill in this busier location.

Naxos

Having been a significant player in the preceding periods, Naxos seems to have been rather eclipsed by Paros in the Roman period. The Sanctuary of Apollo (Portaria) was never completed, and a Christian church was erected in its remains in the sixth century.[61] Regardless of its state of completeness, the prominent position of the temple whose superstructure did survive in part would have been a symbol of Naxos, then as it is today. Some four kilometres south of here, statues of Julius Caesar and Mark Antony were dedicated at the Sanctuary of Dionysus, suggesting some aspirations for international visitors. Bournias notes that the fabric of the lamps found here suggests

---

53 Mendoni and Zoumbaki 2008, TEN 37.
54 IG XII 5, 924. Mendoni and Zoumbaki 2008, TEN 53.
55 Etienne 1990, 210-12.
56 Etienne 1990, ibid.
57 Bournias 2014, 789.
58 Mendoni and Zoumbaki 2008, TEN 21.
59 Sweetman 2015b.
60 Sweetman 2017.
61 Dimitrokallis 1968, 283.

foreign provenance, and as we have seen, a couple of the lamps were signed as being from the *Romanesis* workshop.[62] Conversely, at the Sanctuary of Demeter more local material was discovered; lamps, lamp moulds and kilns were revealed and imitations of Samian and Syro-Palestine lamps were also found. A church was constructed within the temple in either the fifth or the sixth century.[63] Indications are that there was a self-contained and monastic community on the site which was well connected and lasted until the eighth century.

Andros
Due to its location, Andros had connections with Athens, Attica, Euboea and Thessaly (Fig. 1). Recent work has also revealed evidence for Italian amphorae Dressel 6.3.[64] Its extensive harbour at Palaiopolis was well appointed to deal with a regular influx of people, with its bathhouses and storage facilities. Roman and Late Antique amphorae indicate that the variety of trade contacts that the island had were maintained.[65] While there is significant epigraphic and literary evidence for cult and major festivals here, very few sanctuaries have been identified on the ground.[66] During the Roman period, new temples of Zeus and Mithras were founded and a second century inscription on a temple architrave fragment records Memmios Rufus and Isidoros, who repaired and took care of an abandoned temple.[67]

There was investment on the island from a range of visitors, such as the *evocatus Augusti* M. Aurelius Rufinus, and three praetorian soldiers, investing in the cult of Mithras in 200.[68] The exiles Glitius Gallus and Egnatia Maximilla were honoured by the Andrians with a monument.[69] Extensive numbers of dedications to Hadrian have also been found. Imports to the island include Koan and Knidian Amphora from the first century. Roman coins from Paros, Kea and Amisos in Pontus have been identified in excavation.[70] During the late antique period, six churches were constructed at Palaiopolis and one of them has been the focus of recent excavations.[71]

---

62 Bournias 2014.
63 Bournias 2014.
64 Palaiokrassa and Vivliodetis 2015, 147.
65 Palaiokrassa and Vivliodetis 2015.
66 Palaiokrassa-Kopitsa 2007. Others mentioned include Dionysus, Apollo, Zeus, Eileithyia, Isis, Artemis, Nemesis, Estia Voulaia and Mithras, and extensive epigraphic records suggest that the Andrian sanctuaries were popular destinations with global network connections.
67 Mendoni and Zoumbaki 2008, AND 44.
68 Mendoni and Zoumbaki 2008, AND 16.
69 Mendoni and Zoumbaki 2008, AND 32 and 37.
70 Sheedy 2012, 142.
71 Palaiokrassa-Kopitsa 2007.

Discussion

Throughout the Roman and late antique period, the majority of connections that the Cyclades had were with western Asia Minor and the islands of the eastern Mediterranean. In the late antique period, portable material culture indicates a widening of connections to include Palestine and the Levant, but western imports remain limited. It is difficult to identify pilgrims to the islands in the Roman period; epigraphic evidence reveals dedications set up by residents on the islands such as local elites, exiles and soldiers, rather than specifically visitors to them. However, literary data suggests that there were tourists and/or pilgrims. For example, key Roman political figures such as Cicero and the senator Sextus Pompeius visited the islands in 51 BCE and 27 CE respectively, on their way to take up governorships in Asia Minor.[72] The varied and sometimes fantastic accounts of the islands by Gaius Licinius Mucianus were reused by Pliny.[73] He includes interesting 'facts', such as iron-eating mice on Gyaros, alongside detailed accounts of the Cyclades. For example, his trusting description of the transformation of water into wine suggests he had been on Andros in January for the festival there. While the visitors themselves are not so visible, the fact that dedications to Emperors, politicians and elites were erected in the Cycladic sanctuaries in the Roman period is an indication that there was an audience for them. Christian pilgrims are more in evidence: a number of inscriptions record Christian pilgrims at Katapoliani (Paros) (Fig. 3), Gastria Cave (Tenos) and Delos (Fig. 4). The lack of evidence does not necessarily mean that there were no pilgrims in the Roman period, but given the ambiguity with which pilgrimage is defined, perhaps more flexible views of what pilgrimage might have meant are needed. To this end it is worth examining the topography of the sanctuaries.

Before the first century, with Delos at their centre, the Cyclades were host to official groups of pilgrims moving throughout the islands, in particular from Alexandria and the Dodecanese, and presumably individual pilgrims too.[74] When a hub, such as Delos, no longer functions as such, and its wider network collapses as a consequence, connectivity will usually break down into smaller sub-networks. This is what is seen in the Cyclades with the demise of Delos as a religious and economic hub. A combination of epigraphic and portable material culture such as pottery and lamps indicates that these smaller network clusters consisted of the Cycladic islands themselves, the Dodecanese (in particular Kos) and parts of Asia Minor (such as Knidos). Le Quéré has also identified connections between Ephesus and Thera.[75] Furthermore, textual evidence of trade itineraries deducible from the Hippolytus Chronicon (235) indicate three key trade routes:

---

72 Stark 2006, 90.
73 Williamson 2005.
74 Rutherford 2009, 26; 2013, 297.
75 Le Quéré 2011.

Kos–Kalymnos–Leros–Patmos–Mykonos–Tenos
Kos–Leros–Kinaros–Amorgos–Naxos–Delos
Amorgos–Naxos–Kythnos and then to the Saronic gulf and Piraeus.[76]

Ceramic experts in the Cyclades maintain that trade routes do not change significantly in the late antique period (even with the movement of centres).[77] An examination of the topography of polytheistic temples shows a clear preference for coastal locations or those visible from the sea, and many are located along major trade routes, ensuring a reputation and international acclaim as much for their value in terms of wayfinding as for their religiosity. The visibility of a sanctuary reveals the potential for pilgrimage, while the evidence of dedication, investment or contact on the ground reveals the intentional visit.

It may be the case that there were more fluid types of pilgrimage than our modern interpretations allow. The question of whether local visitors can be considered pilgrims is a current debate in pilgrimage studies. Some argue that they can, but that the difficulties of distinguishing local material as a result of pilgrimage rather than as a day-to-day function of the site and study of it has impeded a full understanding of it.[78] Bugslag argues that local pilgrimage is less impactful on the individual and so is rarely recorded. Additionally, Stevens believes that visits to ancestral graves could be considered pilgrimage.[79] Others such as Grünewald argue that locals cannot be defined as pilgrims.[80]

It is likely that there was flexibility in concepts of pilgrimage in the past. In both polytheistic and monotheistic religions, although pilgrimage is not part of the creed, the journey is considered transformative, as shown in anthropological studies of contemporary pilgrims.[81] A visit to a temple provoked awe and respect in the visitor and, momentarily at least, excluded the sense of the everyday. As such, a visit to a temple was memory-making and if undertaken as part of a group also consolidated community ties.[82] Although less intense, sight of a temple from the sea has the potential for the same impact (Fig. 5); it creates awe and a temporary suspension of the humdrumness of the journey and contributes to memory formation and therefore wayfinding. It is also revealing that temples are not found in places where they would be invisible, such as at the north or south tips of Andros or the north tip of Tenos.[83] While current debate on

---

76 Kiourtzian 2000, 16.
77 Zachos 2010.
78 Bugslag 2005.
79 Stevens 2017.
80 Grünewald 2017, 130.
81 Marchand's 2015 work is particularly instructive in this regard.
82 See also Sweetman 2015a on memory and community identity in religious contexts.
83 The straits of Kafirea lie between Euboea and Andros, which provided a significant barrier to north-south sailing. Between Andros and Tenos too, the ends are very steep, creating a funnel effect making the winds in these areas considerable. The northerly winds also created currents in this area. Sailing east to west would not have been as problematic and there were reasonable anchorages at both ends of the islands where one could wait out the winds.

pilgrimage is primarily about defining it in terms of the importance of the site and/or the journey, as well as distance travelled and intentionality, a more flexible definition of religious travel leaves open the potential for individuals to define their journeys and site visits as pilgrimage or not. Although they may not have started out as pilgrims, by the time they return from their journey there is no reason why they could not be.

In many respects, as Williamson has suggested, the line between tourism and pilgrimage is significantly blurred by the intention of the visitor and the multi-functionality of sanctuaries.[84] This is not necessarily the same in the late antique period. Here, as it is possible to see in the evidence of the Katapoliani church, Gastria cave and Delos, there was intentional pilgrimage. The locations of the earliest Christian churches indicate that they were more focused on visitors to the actual church; while they are by ports, they do not take advantage of the wide range of visibility given to them by the height and location of some of the earlier temples. The earliest churches do not reuse temple sites and are as concerned with accessibility as with visibility. The diachronic view also allows us to see that the new religion and practices of pilgrimage did not actually lead to the destruction of emblems of previous cult topography. They help provide spatial recognition, particularly through islands that were so notoriously difficult to navigate. This also reflects Christianisation processes where it was necessary to advertise the new religion, and make it accessible and tempting to new recruits. This does not impact on the existing sanctuary landmarks which continued to be visible, although not necessarily visited.

The topography of religious sites contributes to an understanding of the intentionality and functionality of pilgrimage. In a more recent period, Jenkins notes the value of pilgrimage as a means of connecting places: for example, in the 12th century the development of Santiago de Compostela as a pilgrimage site was important in connecting Spain more decidedly to Europe.[85] Pilgrimage might be considered more of a tradition than a religious requirement. It is both a social and a religious event, and it crosses boundaries and emphasises connectivity. For Christians, the idea of the journey has a religious code, and yet the physical process and the tradition of pilgrimage would also have helped provide a connection from one religion to another. There are changes, however, with Christian pilgrimage. In both literary evidence and in the set location of specific shrines, it is possible to see elements of more prescriptive routes and how to behave during a site visit.[86]

Ultimately, pilgrimage in both polytheistic and monotheistic practice is ambiguous enough to ensure that several different meanings and aims are achievable through one's personal engagement with the divine on, or at the end of, a journey. The lack of prescription or formal religious designation means that a wide variety of experiences and interpretations are to be expected of pilgrimage.

---

84   Williamson 2005.
85   Jenkins 2012.
86   Pullan 2005, 407-8.

Acknowledgements

I would like to thank Troels Myrup Kristensen and Anna Collar for the wonderful conference and considered comments on these papers. I would also like to thank Ralph Anderson and Erica Angliker for fruitful discussions on ideas of pilgrimage.

Bibliography

Catullus. *Carmina.* Sir Richard Francis Burton. (trans.) 1894. London: privately published.
Alcock, S.E., J. Cherry and J. Elsner (eds.) 2001. *Pausanias. Travel and Memory in Roman Greece.* Oxford: Oxford University Press.
Angliker, E. and J. Tully (eds.) 2018. *Cycladic Archaeology: New Approaches and Discoveries.* Oxford: Archaeopress.
Arnush, M. 2005. "Pilgrimage to the Oracle of Apollo at Delphi: Patterns of Public and Private Consultation," in Elsner and Rutherford 2005, 97-110.
Bonnin, G. and E. Le Quéré (eds.) 2014. *Pouvoirs, îles et mer. Formes et modalités de l'hégémonie dans les Cyclades antiques (VIIe s. a.C.-IIIe s. p.C.).* Bordeaux: Ausonius.
Bournias, L.C. 2014. "Roman and Early Byzantine Lamps from the Island of Naxos in the Cyclades," in Poulou-Papadimitriou, Nodarou and Kilikoglou 2014, 787-98.
Bugslag, J. 2005. "Local Pilgrimages and their Shrines in pre-modern Europe." *Peregrinations: Journal of Medieval Art and Architecture* 2.1, 1-27. (http://digital.kenyon.edu/perejournal/vol2/iss1/1).
Bull, M. and J P. Mitchell (eds.) 2015. *Ritual, Performance and the Senses.* London: Routledge.
Chamberlin, J.E. 2013. *Island. How islands transform the world.* London: Elliott and Thompson.
Concannon, C. and L. Mazurek (eds.) 2016. *Across the Corrupting Sea. Post-Braudelian Approaches to the Eastern Mediterranean.* New York: Routledge.
Constantakopoulou, C. 2017. *Aegean Interactions. Delos and its Networks in the Third Century.* Oxford: Oxford University Press.
Curta, F. 2011. *The Edinburgh History of the Greeks, c. 500 to 1050: The Early Middle Ages.* Edinburgh: Edinburgh University Press.
Davis, S. 1998. "Pilgrimage and the Cult of Saint Thecla in Late Antique Egypt," in D. Frankfurther (ed.) *Pilgrimage and Holy Space in Late Antique Egypt,* 303-39. Leiden: Brill.
Deligiannakis, G. 2016. *The Dodecanese and Eastern Aegean Islands in Late Antiquity. AD 300-700.* Oxford: Oxford University Press.
Dillon, M. 1997. *Pilgrims and Pilgrimage in Ancient Greece.* London: Routledge.
Dimitrokallis, G. 1968. "The Byzantine Churches of Naxos." *AJA* 72.3, 283-86.
Elsner, J. 2005. "Piety and Passion: Contest and Consensus in the Audiences for Early Christian Pilgrimage," in Elsner and Rutherford 2005, 411-34.
Elsner, J. and I. Rutherford. (eds.) 2005. *Pilgrimage in Greco-Roman and Early Christian Antiquity. Seeing the Gods.* Oxford: Oxford University Press.
Etienne, R., J.-P. Braun and F. Queyrel. 1990. *Ténos II. Ténos et les Cyclades du milieu de IVe siècle av J.-C. au milieu du IIIe siècle ap. J.-C.* Paris: De Boccard.
Giannikouri, A. (ed.) 2011. Αγορά στη Μεσόγειο από τους ομηρικούς έως τους ρωμαϊκούς χρόνους: Διεθνές επιστημονικό συνέδριο, Κως 14-17 Απριλίου 2011 = *The Agora in the Mediterranean from Homeric to Roman times: International conference, Kos, 14-17 April 2011.* Athens: Ministry of Culture and Tourism, Archaeological Institute of Aegean Studies.
Grünewald, M. 2017. "Roman Healing Pilgrimage North of the Alps," in Kristensen and Friese 2017, 130-51.
Holum, KG. 1990. "Hadrian and St. Helena: Imperial travel and the origins of Christian Holy Land pilgrimage," in R. Ousterhout (ed.) *The Blessings of Pilgrimage,* 66-81. Urbana: University of Illinois Press.
Hutton, W. 2005. "The Construction of Religious Space in Pausanias," in Elsner and Rutherford 2005, 291-318.
Hyndman-Rizk, N. (ed.) 2012. *Pilgrimage in the Age of Globalisation: Constructions of the Sacred and Secular in Late Modernity.* Newcastle: Cambridge Scholars Publishing.
Jenkins, E.E. 2012. *The Mediterranean World of Alfonso II and Peter II of Aragon (1162-1213). The New Middle Ages.* New York: Palgrave Macmillan.

Kristensen, T.M. and W. Friese (eds.) 2017. *Excavating Pilgrimage. Archaeological Approaches to Sacred Travel and Movement in the Ancient world.* Abingdon: Routledge.

Kiourtzian, G. 2000. *Recueil des Inscriptions Grecques Chrétiennes des Cyclades. De la fin du IIIe ay VIIe siècle après J.-C.* Paris: De Boccard.

Lambrinoudakis, V. 2001. "To iero toy Gyroyla," in Simantoni-Bournia 2001, 7-17.

Lambrinoudakis, V. et al. 2002. "Naxos—Das Heiligtum von Gyroula bei Sangri. Eine neugefundene, drei Jahrtausende alte Kultstätte der Demeter." *Antike Welt* 33, 387-408.

Le Quéré, E. 2011. "The Agora at the time of the forum: the example of the Cyclades in Roman Imperial Times," in Giannikouri 2011, 327-42.

Le Quéré, E. 2015. *Les Cyclades sous l'Empire romain. Historie d'une renaissance.* Rennes: Presses Universitaires de Rennes.

Malkin, I., C. Constantakopoulou and K. Panagopoulou (eds.) 2009. *Greek and Roman Networks in the Mediterranean.* London: Routledge.

Marchand, T.H. 2015. "Place-Making in the 'Holy of Holies': The Church of the Holy Sepulcher, Jerusalem," in Bull and Mitchell 2015, 63-83.

Mendoni, L. and S. Zoumbaki. 2008. *Roman Names in the Cyclades. Part 1.* Athens: National Hellenic Research Foundation.

Orlandos, A. 1965. Η πρόσφατος αναστήλωσις της Καταπολιανής της Πάρου: πορίσματα ερευνών και νέα ευρήματα. Athens: Εταιρεία Κυκλαδικών Μελετών.

Palaiokrassa-Kopitsa, L. 2007. Παλαιόπολη Άνδρου: είκοσι χρόνια ανασκαφικής έρευνας. Athens: Nomarchio Autodioikisi Kykladon.

Palaiokrassa, L. and E. Vivliodetis, 2008. "Recent Evidence on the Economy and Trading Contacts of Andros in Antiquity," in Papageorgiadou-Banis and Giannikouri 2008, 139-56.

Papageorgiadou-Banis, C. and A. Giannikouri (eds.) 2008. *Sailing in the Aegean. Readings on the economy and trade routes.* Athens: National Hellenic Research Foundation.

Papanikola-Bakirtzi, D. and N. Kousoulakou (eds.) 2010. Η Κεραμική της Ύστερης Αρχαιότητας από τον Ελλαδικό χώρο (3ος-7ος αι. μ.Χ.). Thessaloniki: Archaeological Institute of Macedonian and Thracian Studies.

Petsalis-Diomidis, A. 2017. "A Reading of Space and Dedications at the Amphiareion at Oropos in the Hellenistic Period," in Kristensen and Friese 2017, 106-29.

Pohlsander, H. 1995. *Helena. Empress and Saint.* Chicago Ridge: Ares Publishing.

Poulou-Papadimitriou, N., E. Nodarou and V. Kilikoglou (eds.) 2014. *LRCW 4 Late Roman Coarse Wares, Cooking Wares and Amphorae in the Mediterranean Archaeology and archaeometry. The Mediterranean: a market without frontiers.* Oxford: BAR International Series 2616.

Pullan, W. 2005. "'Intermingled Until the End of Time': Ambiguity as a Central Condition of Early Christian Pilgrimage," in Elsner and Rutherford 2005, 387-410.

Roller, D. W. 2014. *The Geography of Strabo.* Cambridge: Cambridge University Press.

Rutherford, I. 2001. "Tourism and the Sacred. Pausanias and the Traditions of Greek Pilgrimage," in Alcock, Cherry and Elsner 2001, 40-52.

Rutherford, I. 2009. "Network Theory and Theoric Networks," in Malkin, Constantakopoulou and Panagopoulou 2009, 24-38.

Rutherford, I. 2013. *State Pilgrims and Sacred Observers in Ancient Greece.* Cambridge: Cambridge University Press.

Schuller, M. and A. Ohnesorg, 1991. *Der Artemistempel im Delion auf Paros. Denkmäler Antiker Architektur.* Berlin: De Gruyter.

Scriven, R. 2014. "Geographies of Pilgrimage: Meaningful Movements and Embodied Mobilities." *Geography Compass* 8.4, 249-61.

Scullion, S. 2005. "'Pilgrimage' and Greek Religion: Sacred and Secular in the Pagan Polis," in Elsner and Rutherford 2005, 111-30.

Sheedy, K. 2012. "Aegina, the Cyclades and Crete," in W.E. Metcalf (ed.) *The Oxford Handbook of Greek and Roman Coinage,* 105-27. Oxford: Oxford University Press.

Simantoni-Bournia, E. (ed.) 2001. Νάξος. Το αρχαίο ιερό του Γύρουλα στο Σαγκρί. Athens: Ministry of the Aegean.

Simantoni-Bournia, E., G. Zachos, T. Panagou, M. Koutsoumpou, T. Mpilis and D. Mavrokordatou, 2004. "Το Έργο 'Συντήρηση και Ανάδειξη Αρχαίας Καρθαίας Κέας'. Τα Έτη 2002-2004." Αρχαιογνωσία 14, 237-84.

Stark, D. 2006. *Religious Tourism in Roman Greece.* Unpublished MA dissertation, Wilfred Laurier University.

Stevens, S. 2017. "Visiting the Ancestors. Ritual Movement in Rome's Urban Borderland," in Kristensen and Friese 2017, 152-65.
Sweetman, R.J. 2015a. "Memory, Tradition and the Christianization of the Peloponnese." *AJA* 119.4, 501-31.
Sweetman, R.J. 2015b. "The Christianization of the Peloponnese: the Case for Emergent Change." *ABSA* 110, 285-319.
Sweetman, R.J. 2017. "Networks and Church Building in the Aegean: Crete, Cyprus, Lycia and the Peloponnese." *ABSA* 112, 207-66.
Sweetman, R.J. 2019. "Islands and Resilience: Christianization Processes in the Cyclades," in M.A. Cau Ontiveros and C. Mas Florit (eds.) *Change and Resilience. The Occupation of Mediterranean Islands in Late Antiquity*, 193-216. Oxford: Oxbow Books.
Sweetman, R. J., A. Devlin and N. Piree Iliou. 2018. "The Cyclades in the Late Antique period. Churches, networks and Christianization," in Angliker and Tully 2018, 215-38.
Swift, J. (ed.) 1768. *Letters Written by the Late Jonathan Swift, Dean of St. Patrick's Dublin and Several of his Friends.* London: C. Bathurst et al.
Takás, S. 2005. "Divine and Human Feet: Records of Pilgrims Honouring Isis," in Elsner and Rutherford 2005, 353-69.
Wilkinson, J. 1981. *Egeria's Travels to the Holy Land.* Revised ed. Jerusalem: Ariel Publishing House.
Williamson, G. 2005. "Mucianus and a Touch of the Miraculous: Pilgrimage and Tourism in Roman Asia Minor," in Elsner and Rutherford 2005, 219-52.
Zachos, G. 2010. "Keos in Late Roman Context," in D. Papanikola-Bakirtzi and N. Kousoulakou 2010, 782-94.

10

THE RITES OF THE (LATE) ANCIENT MARINERS:

PROFESSIONAL AND CASUAL SAILORS AS CHRISTIAN PILGRIMS IN THE LATE ANTIQUE MEDITERRANEAN

AMELIA R. BROWN

On a January 6 in the later sixth century, the anonymous 'Piacenza Pilgrim' celebrated the Christian festival of Epiphany by the river Jordan, and observed one distinct group of other pilgrims there: "All the ship-owners of Alexandria have men there that day with great jars of spices and balsam, and as soon as the river has been blessed, before the baptism starts, they pour them out into the water, and draw out holy water. This water they use for sprinkling their ships when they are about to set sail."[1] The professional sailors of Alexandria, owners of the grain fleet that continued to supply the imperial capital of Constantinople, thus also continued the ancient practice of libations (or liquid offerings) when embarking aboard ship in the later sixth century. Yet rather than, or as a supplement to?, the traditional wine, some now offered a sprinkling of water from the river Jordan. This was not just water from a holy river, but water blessed by a Christian priest at a Christian festival: water ritually enticed, or sacralised, to become holy and well disposed to them, and to their ships, by their own personal 'sacrifice' of expensive, fragrant "spices and balsam" for the Jordan river. These offerings at the Jordan were made by men sent on pilgrimage from Alexandria, who were expected to return with the water to their home port for future sacred uses. Thus by the later sixth century, the Christian festival of Epiphany had associations not just with the Christian ritual of baptism, but also with water and "watery" professions: at least one influential group of ancient Mediterranean mariners had adapted their polytheistic practices into a new Christianised form, and both professional and casual sailors on the same seas were doing likewise, leaving a new set of artefacts behind, and shaping a set of revised sacred habits across their enduring maritime landscape.

---

1   Piacenza Pilgrim, *Travels* 11, as translated by Wilkinson 2002, quoted by Vikan 2010, 17.

From the Levantine coast to Alexandria, Constantinople to Rome, Mediterranean mariners of all sorts in Late Antiquity were confronting the same troubles as their predecessors: stormy weather (or no wind), low supplies or savage pirates. Sailors addressed these challenges as in past centuries with entwined spiritual and practical strategies. Personal piety, proper preparation, and the right prayers, rituals and amulets all contributed to a seaworthy ship, and a safe return ashore. Yet professional mariners in Late Antiquity also confronted dramatic changes to their age-old rituals (or superstitions) as conversion to Christianity became both widespread, and then legally mandated.

One change was the rise of Christian pilgrimage to the Holy Land, another was the transplantation of the capital of the Roman Empire to Constantinople, and a third was the Christianisation of professional mariners' own pilgrimage practices.[2] In this chapter, I consider how these changes shaped Christian pilgrimage or 'sacred travel' routes, practices and material production for both professional and casual mariners in Late Antiquity. The rites of late ancient mariners were practiced all along multiple overlapping networks of the routes of professional sailors, who transported goods as well as pilgrims and other travellers, the casual mariners. Sailors and their passengers varied in social status, Christian (or Jewish) *praxis*, distance and purpose of travel, and their visibility in the material record. Yet clearly all shared a common seascape with one another, and they (mostly) share it with us too: many Mediterranean coasts are unchanged in geology and climate, routes to and from Byzantium/Constantinople were highly traditional, if increasing in volume, and sailors also shared a common goal: to return ashore alive, and with a profit (whether spiritual, monetary, or both).[3] Reconstructing these networks of mariners rituals in Late Antiquity lends insight into popular religion of sailors of all classes, and those who went for all purposes. Practices of sailor-pilgrims, and their hosts aboard ship and ashore, form a powerful resource for understanding how certain cults of Christian saints formed in Late Antiquity, and how they spread all around the Mediterranean and Black seas, even into the so-called Byzantine Dark Ages.

While the Holy Land was always the main target of Christian pilgrims, and its sacred materials (or even just going there) could help with any number of problems, including those encountered during travel, many other old and new seaside shrines around the eastern Mediterranean also gained (or retained) fame for their power and special efficacy for certain professions and situations, including sailors at sea.[4] Beyond coastal sites of importance in the Bible, efficacious saints also emerged along the invigorated north-south sea routes between Alexandria and Constantinople, and along the east-west routes from Rome and western ports to the Holy Land. Seaside 'saviour' saints such as

---

2   For the origins and growth of Christian pilgrimage to the Holy Land and elsewhere in Late Antiquity, see Hunt 1982; Ousterhout 1990; Janin 2002; Kuelzer 2002; Wilkinson 2002. For the purposes of this chapter, pilgrims and pilgrimage should be read as referring to Christians.

3   For practices and routes of Late Antique and Early Byzantine seafarers, see Pryor 2008; McCormick 2001. For Pre-Christian ancient maritime religion, see Wachsmuth 1967; Morton 2001.

4   On continuities in ancient sacred travel, and related aspects of maritime religion, see Dillon 1997 and articles in Elsner and Rutherford 2005; Kristensen and Friese 2017.

St. Isidore of Chios and St. Phocas of Sinope were some of the earliest relics brought to Constantinople to lend their power to the city, mainly in the fifth century, and after St. Andrew (from Patras), St. Luke (from Thebes) and St. Timothy (from Ephesus) had been brought at Constantius's orders to the Church of the Holy Apostles.[5] Gary Vikan has catalogued much of the material evidence for early Christian pilgrimage beyond relics (or reliquaries): the *ampullae* and other vessels used to collect and transport protective sacred materials away by sea or land, and amulets of various sorts, especially the Greek *eulogiai* (blessings), mainly mass-produced stamped terracotta tokens.[6] *Ampullae* or amulets showing ships, or scenes of saints explicitly blessing ships, are in the minority of all those produced, but could have been targeted at professional sailors, or at least at pilgrims eager for a safe voyage home again. Pilgrims might be expected to be more in the market for 'souvenirs', while professional sailors, like the Alexandrians referred to above, would seek new kinds of ship- or body-borne amulets, and spend more money on (and at) long-lasting facilities at harbourside sites.[7]

There are only rare intersections among objects, texts and *testimonia* for the specific uses that Christian pilgrim souvenirs were put to, yet these portable images clearly promoted the fame and status of the saint depicted, and were carried (and sometimes lost) on the sea-lanes. A range of evidence shows that souvenirs from saints, or from their surroundings or relics, were widely believed to give protection at sea to the person who bore them afloat, or dedicated them ashore in votive practices little changed from pagan precedents.[8] The efficacy of these practices, and the objects concerned, seem partly related to actual Christian dogma, but also strongly influenced by both Mediterranean seascapes and pre-existing maritime religious habits (and beliefs). Jesus lived and taught beside the Sea of Galilee, after all, and was already said to calm the waters in a number of Biblical miracles. He was invoked as Christ or Lord, along with God, Mary or St. John the Baptist in many sailors' prayers, but Jesus's watery miracles are rare scenes on pilgrim flasks or *ampullae*, whether intended to hold oil, water or dust.[9] A Bobbio lead flask for oil from the True Cross manufactured in Jerusalem circa 600 shows Jesus saving St. Peter by walking on water, but this is one of only two depictions of this biblical scene on these souvenir vessels.[10]

Substances collected from later saints, whether entombed or alive, are much better represented in the extant evidence. Dust from the tomb of St. John the Evangelist (*Theologos*) from his acropolis basilica at Ephesus was said to help mariners, replacing benefits

---

5   Woods 1991; Wisniewski 2019, 22-25.
6   Vikan 1991; 1998 (both reprinted in Vikan 2003); 2010.
7   For earlier Roman parallels, see Juvenal *Satire* 12.28 (shrines of Isis with many votive *tabellae* to avoid shipwreck); Williams 1985 (mould for making such Isis *Pelagia* metal plaques, from Athens); Popkin 2017 (souvenir glass flasks from Puteoli).
8   Krueger 2010; Vikan 2010, 15-16.
9   Wachsmann 2000.
10   Grabar 1958, Bobbio flask no. 11; Milburn 1988, 264; Vikan 1998, 247-48.

previously ascribed to Artemis (Diana) of the Ephesians.[11] Galla Placidia dedicated an entire church at Ravenna in thanks to St. John for her salvation in a storm at sea in the mid-fifth century CE, and brought his sandal to Ravenna where it became a treasured relic.[12] Dust (Syriac *hnana*) blessed by St. Simeon Stylites the Elder himself, from atop his column in his Syrian shrine just inland from Antioch, was carried in small vessels, or made into clay tokens, and could also help the bearer at sea (as could dust from St. Simeon the Younger).[13]

Ephesus, and the ports of the northern Syrian coast like Laodicea or Seleucia Pieria, were long-established stops between Constantinople and the Holy Land; Ravenna was throughout Late Antiquity the main port in the northern Adriatic, and Alexandria remained the major port for Egypt. Routes for shipping in Late Antiquity changed only slightly with the shift of imperial power to Constantinople, but Janet Wade argues forcefully for the importance of the new capital's long-standing maritime credentials in the Christianisation of maritime religion.[14] John Pryor emphasises how traditional ports of call in the eastern Mediterranean remained constant into the Byzantine era, partly through cabotage trading habits and the need for fresh water.[15] In 949 CE, the Byzantine fleet heading south out of Constantinople watered first at Abydos in the Propontis, then Chios and Ephesus, on their way to retake the island of Crete from the Arabs.[16] This southern route continued to the Holy Land via Rhodes, the Lycian coast and Cyprus, while other traditional routes to and from Constantinople northwards into the Black Sea, and around southern Greece to the west, also featured certain ports with saints who became important protectors of professional sailors in Late Antiquity.[17]

Chios Town, today as in Antiquity, is situated along a bay on the protected east coast of the island. On the northern side of the town's harbour, by a Roman cemetery, the basilica of St. Isidore still stands as a hub for the protection of mariners travelling north-south since at least the fifth century. St. Isidore of Chios, 'Gift of Isis', was honoured as a third-century naval officer martyred and thrown into a well, at the site of his drowning. Late-antique sailors carried away stamped terracotta blessing tokens and holy water from the well, accessed through the north aisle of his basilica church, which was built in the fifth century, renovated in the seventh, and partly ruined in the 19th century (though

---

11 Koester 1995; Bangert 2010. Recall that the men who made Artemis's silver icons were already portrayed by St. Luke as threatened by St. Paul's teachings at Ephesus in *Acts* 19:21-40.

12 Deliyannis 2010; Sivan 2011.

13 Vikan 2010, 16, quotes St. Simeon the Elder's *Miracle* 71 from his Syriac *Life* 61-72, translated by Doran 1992, and also episode 235 from the later *Ancient Life* of St. Simeon the Younger, whose dust when sprinkled on the boat and into the sea summoned the saint to aid the monk Dorotheos who carried it in a winter storm at sea.

14 Wade 2014; 2018.

15 Pryor 2008, citing McCormick 2001; Pryor and Jeffreys 2006.

16 Constantine Porphyrogennetos *The Book of Ceremonies* 2.45.664-65 (trans. Moffatt and Tall 2012); McCormick 2001, 413-14; Pryor and Jeffreys 2006.

17 Morton 2001.

Pilgrim Stamp of Saint Isidore, Walters Art Museum, Baltimore, inv. no. 54.230, Creative Commons.

Fig. 1.

it is still possible to visit today).[18] An image of St. Isidore protecting a ship is preserved on a bronze stamp of the sixth century used for making pilgrim tokens (Fig. 1). It is inscribed to stamp the Greek words "Saint Isidore", "Jesus Christ" and "Receive the Blessing" (*cross* ὁ ἅγιος Ἡσιδόρος *cross* / Ἰ(ησοῦ)ς Χ(ριστό)ς / Δέξ(αι) εὐλογί(αν)), along with the image of the saint standing frontally in military garb. A ship is held in the saint's right hand, and a crook in his left; his shrine, with a ship-lamp and a censer over his holy well, is visible to his left (these directions would be reversed in the image stamped).[19] In Constantinople, St. Isidore of Chios was honoured by the *oikonomos* St. Marcian (died ca. 475) with a chapel built on land reclaimed from the sea for his relics, alongside the church of St. Eirene in Perama (Balikpazari), while at Rome he had a church and monastery near the Porta Tiburtina.[20] In 1525, his relics were translated to a chapel in San Marco in Venice, to protect her fleets alongside St. Mark.

18 Gregory of Tours *Glory of the Martyrs* 30, 101 (trans. Van Dam); Krueger 2010.
19 Walters Art Museum, Baltimore, inv. no. 54.230; Vikan 2010, 20-21, fig. 8, cites Vikan 1991, 79.
20 Mango 2001 describes large-scale mid-fourth-century shoreline reclamation at Constantinople, cites Himerius *Oration* 41 in Gedeon 1899, 275 and *Vita Marciani* in Snee 1998.

A similar set of circumstances related to seaside location, significant nomenclature and maritime patronage seems to have motivated the promotion of St. Phocas of Sinope. Northern routes in and out of Constantinople along the coasts of the Black Sea brought St. Phocas ('Seal') from Sinope abroad; honoured as an early martyr of Sinope, he came from the southern coast of the Black Sea, and was said to have been the son of a shipbuilder, and in training as a seaman. His *Vita* and an earlier homily by Bishop Asterius of nearby Amasea credit him with calming the waters, steering, reefing and keeping sea-captains awake; he was (and is) honoured especially for protection against drowning, and is addressed by mariners' graffiti in the bay of Grammata on the north shore of Syros in the central Aegean (along with Mary and the Apostles).[21]

A stamped clay token of St. Phocas from the Hermitage comes not from Constantinople or Sinope, but from his shrine at the Tauric Chersonesos (Crimea) on the north shore of the Black Sea, perhaps attesting to the same traders plying the southern and western shores of the Black Sea. The token (which could be used as an amphora stopper) was stamped with the inscription in Greek around the outside edge "Blessing of Saint Phocas of the Poor House of Cherson", and showed the saint with arms raised in prayer standing on a ship with double rudders, and an incense stand to his left.[22] The relics of St. Phocas were also transferred to near Constantinople circa 400: according to a homily of St. John Chrysostom, the relics of St. Phocas were first brought with great ceremony by sea from Sinope to the City, and then on the second day of celebration (on which he delivered the homily), they were taken by boat from Constantinople to a new church catering to sailors at the coastal suburb which is today Ortaköy, between Anaplous and Agios Mamas/Beshiktash (where St. Phocas is still honoured in a 19th c. successor church).[23]

The seafarers of Alexandria, however, made the strongest impression on Early Christian Mediterranean maritime religion, bringing people, goods and beliefs to and from their home city, and promoting pilgrimage to the Holy Land, to Constantinople, and to their own relics of St. Mark, in the city of Alexandria, and the shrine of St. Menas, just outside their city across Lake Maeotis. Mariners, Alexandrians, and Egyptians honoured St. Mark the Evangelist as the founder of Alexandria's cathedral, after many travels. Local tradition traced his origins to nearby Cyrene, so he was returning homewards by settling in Alexandria, where his relics were venerated at his festival on April 25. By the year 828, his reputation was such that two Venetian merchants, along with two Greek monks, took his purported bodily relic from Alexandria to Venice, covering it with a layer of pork and cabbage leaves to deter discovery by Muslim authorities. St. Mark thus gained new prestige as patron saint of the maritime city of Venice. His body

---

21   Asterius of Amasea *Homily* 9 (*PG* 40, 308), ed. Datema 1970; *Vita* ed. Van de Vorst 1911; Rizos 2016; Nowakowski 2017.
22   Hermitage inv. no. X-263, with translation of text in Vikan 2010, 20-21, fig. 7; on the shrines of St. Phocas around the Black Sea, see Quirini-Popławski 2014.
23   John Chrysostom *Homily on St. Phocas*, *PG* 50 translated by Mayer and Neil 2006, 75-87; Mayer 1998.

passed from the Doge's palace to a new adjacent basilica with a campanile, alongside the shrine of the previous civic patron of Venice, St. Theodore Stratelates. In 1094, his body was entombed for the last time in the recently-built San Marco, a copy of the church of the Holy Apostles in Constantinople. San Marco is still decorated today with mosaics of that era, which show St. Mark helping sailors coming to Alexandria, the city marked by its famed ancient lighthouse, the *Pharos*.[24]

The shrine of St. Menas (or Abu Mina) just southwest of Alexandria, across Lake Maeotis, became famous for its own holy water, carried away in souvenir *ampullae* manufactured there in the sixth and early seventh centuries (see also Frankfurter, this volume). The extensive distribution of those flasks across the Mediterranean world, and far inland, shows the reach of pilgrims to the site who returned home. A minority of these flasks have an image of a ship on the reverse to advertise protection at sea, either for mariners who carried the water for protection (a form of healing), or pilgrims on their way home by sea.[25] The former is made more likely because St. Menas was honoured outside Egypt at the main harbourside church at Thessaloniki's renovated Harbour of Constantine, and also at Constantinople in a location prominent for mariners. Although the Hagia (St.) Sophia and St. Eirene churches of Constantinople appear prominent today atop the acropolis hill, where once the temple of Artemis stood, St. Menas's church was also once clearly visible at the northeast corner of the city by the Forum of Leo as ships turned into the Golden Horn, and docked by the Gate of Eugenius, and where a traditional statue of Fortuna holding a cornucopia and rudder also still stood in Late Antiquity.[26]

Yet in the competition over sacred Christian images to carry aboard, it was St. Nicholas, the fourth-century bishop of Myra on the coast of Lycia (conflated with the later homonymous monk of nearby Sion monastery), who became the main patron for mariners in the eastern Mediterranean.[27] Lycia was a transitional point for sailors to head east towards Cyprus and the Levant, or south to Alexandria. St. Nicholas was credited with saving sailors in storms at sea, by waking them up, and also preserving them from drowning after falling overboard in his miracle stories, especially on the route between Alexandria and Constantinople via the Lycian coast. By the ninth century, at the latest, and despite iconoclasm, he was recognised as a powerful patron of sailors from the English channel to the Holy Land routes, as well as in Constantinople, Rome, the Balkans and Crimea. The first church dedicated to St. Nicholas outside of Myra seems to be the Sts. Priscus and Nicholas built by Justinian in Constantinople, which Procopius (*de Aed.* 1.6) calls the "Hieron on the Golden Horn", near Blachernae at the

---

24 On the relics and church of St. Mark the Evangelist at Alexandria, and confusion among various men named *Markos* in the early church, see Eusebius *Eccl. Hist.* 2.14.6, 2.24.1, 2.24.15-16; Choat 2012; Bagnall 2007. For St. Mark's translation to Venice, see Vio 2003.

25 Kaufmann 1910, pl. 96.12; Grossmann 1998; Anderson 2007; Vikan 2010, 33-34; Bangert 2010.

26 Mango 2001; Dark and Harris 2008.

27 Anrich 1913-1917; Sevcenko and Sevcenko 1984; Foss 1994, 2002; Kountoura-Galake 2004; English 2012.

top of the Golden Horn, adjacent to a church of the healing saints Cosmas and Damian also visited by sailors seeking seaside blessings.[28] St. Nicholas lay in a sarcophagus in his tomb church at Myra for pilgrims to visit for blessings, and the protective myrrh (or manna) emitted by it, until it was stolen/translated by Italian merchants on their way back home to Bari from Antioch, on May 9, 1087. Two years later, St. Nicholas's myrrh-emitting remains were moved into a new church built for him by Robert Guiscard and Bishop Urso of Bari, where they remain, only supplying sailors with myrrh on his original feast day, December 6, which is still carried for protection at sea. The Venetians also sacked Myra in 1100, and carried off their own relics of St. Nicholas to a church at Venice near the mouth of the lagoon.[29]

Seeking out specific shrines ashore along major sea routes, carrying amulets and making appeals to higher powers aboard; all of these practices had important precedents in pre-Christian polytheism, where the power of the image of a god or hero could obtain attention and assistance along with the right prayers. Athenaeus's *Sophists at Dinner* 15.675-76, for example, preserves an excerpt from a Hellenistic book by a certain Polycharmus of Naukratis, *On Aphrodite*, in which Archaic-era sailors on the way from Cyprus to Egypt found relief from seasickness and storm after praying to a figurine of Aphrodite, which was bought at her Paphos shrine, carried by the merchant Herostratus of Naukratis aboard, and then dedicated ashore at home in Naukratis in the Nile Delta. In the Biblical book of Acts 27-28, the ship on which St. Paul was originally travelling westwards was carrying grain from Alexandria to Rome, via the coast of Lycia and Myra, and then along the southern coast of Crete. The ship that then picked St. Paul up on Malta (ancient Melita), after the wreck of the first ship there, was also from Alexandria, heading west and wintering on the island; it bore a figurehead or sternpost (*sema*) of the Dioscuri. St. Erasmus of Formiae, or Gaeta, patron of Campanian and later western European sailors, became associated with St. Elmo's Fire as a blessing for ships, taking up this role from the twin Dioscuri, the constellation Gemini, and patrons of Greek and Roman mariners.

Returning home was always the main locus for maritime religion, and for expressions of thanks by both casual and professional sailors: the most vital times to express thanks to higher powers were both aboard the ship and once ashore again. On the Torlonia relief from Ostia, probably depicting the Severan-era *Portus* of Rome, the grand hexagonal port still visible today, an unknown merchant thanked the gods for a safe and profitable voyage. Wachsmuth suggests the *navicularius* (owner), his wife and the captain (or *magister navis*) offer incense and a libation by a portable altar on the stern (the woman holds the *acerra*, the incense box).[30] Horace's *Ode* 1.14 advises sailors to call on the images of the gods from the stern of the ship, with incense, libations and prayers, as these people are shown doing. The arriving merchant ship is symbolically welcomed by harbour spirits: some statues ashore at Portus are depicted as over sized and outside

---

28   Janin 1964, 369-71, 383-84.
29   Jones 1978; Gazeau et al. 2015.
30   Wachsmuth 1967, 143-50; Casson 1971, fig. 144; Basch 1987, 465, fig. 1038; Mott 1996, 12, fig. 1.2.

of their temples, for example a Genius or Fortune of Rome's Portus, Aphrodite/Venus and Neptune/Poseidon.[31] The relief was found near a sanctuary of Liber Pater, and he is prominently depicted as the largest statue ashore at the right of the relief, recalling Horace's *Ode* 2.19: "Thou turn'st the rivers, thou the sea."

There is good evidence that early Christian mariners also offered incense, libations and prayers from their own sterns, either to the heavens, or to a representation of the cross. These rituals also still took place at departure, during the voyage when in danger, and especially at arrival back in a safe port (and might be followed by the deposit of an ex-voto plaque at a church). John Moschus's *Spiritual Meadow* of ca. 600 recorded two miraculous deeds done to obtain much-needed fresh water for ships at sea.[32] The eunuch anchorite Theodore, on his way to Constantinople from the Holy Land, used prayer and the sign of the cross to bring rain. A devout *naukleros* on the passage from Constantinople back to the Holy Land then spent three days in fasting and prayer before summoning a raincloud. Frank Trombley has collected these with other examples of salvation at sea via prayer from hagiography of the seventh to ninth centuries.[33] Thirst at sea could be as dangerous as a storm, bringing needed rain to drink is just as important as bringing a following breeze in these miracles. In the seventh century, then, breeze or rain were both available for the knowledgeable and pious in prayer, whether passenger, captain or crew.

The Yassıada shipwreck is a vivid window into the early Christian elements that might be present aboard merchant ships along the route between Constantinople and the Levant. This ship sank just west of ancient Halicarnassus sometime after the year 625/6, based on coins of Heraclius found aboard, with a cargo of some 800 amphorae. The stern area was well preserved and excavated, yielding tools and personal items of the captain and crew along with the cargo. Although the finds are still under study, and subject to various interpretations, it seems certain that the captain, George the Presbyter (or less likely 'Senior') Ship Captain (*Naukleros*), perceived his cargo, ship and profession to be under the protection of the Christian faith. His name was prominently etched on a bronze incense box, accompanied by a cross, and a separate bronze cross was also found. Not only was incense used in Christian rituals ashore (along with lamps), but it had been offered aboard both Greek and Roman ships for safe passage (and, as suggested by Fred Van Doorninck, for business deals) for at least a millennium beforehand. *Georgiou Presbyterou Nauklerou* was also inscribed on the largest steelyard, which was carried in the stern cabin along with the censer, the cross and some 20 lamps (many used, a few with crosses). The steelyard equipment also included a traditional weight, in the form of a bust of Athena. The crew, passengers or investors may have included Theodore (cruciform monogram on a glass medallion), Ioannis (a cruciform monogram on a lead seal), and the manufacturers of the many Christian-inscribed amphorae carried aboard. Most of these were made around the islands of Samos and Chios, and bear inscribed

---

31 Settis and Gasparri 2021, 175-78.
32 Wortley 1992, miracles 173-174 (*PG* 87.3, 3041-44).
33 Trombley 2001.

graffiti including crosses, *Theos Nike*, product names (oil, lentils) and owners' names, often with crosses or chi-rhos. Was the ship engaged in the coastal wine and oil trade, or, as Van Doorninck has argued more recently, a church-owned vessel attached to a military supply fleet *en route* to Cilicia?[34] In either case, the finds aboard testify to the Christianised rituals of captain, crew, investors and passengers.

This balance of everyday devotion, votives, festivals, sailors' pilgrimages and recognition of special protection for sailors can be traced most clearly into modern times for St. Spyridon, another early fourth-century bishop like St. Nicholas who became a saint and a protector of sailors. Originally buried in the Church of the Holy Apostles in his see of Trimythous, Cyprus (near Larnaca) after his death in 348, his body was moved to Constantinople in the seventh century, and deposited in the nunnery of the Panagia Kecharitomene on the Golden Horn, near the Church of the Holy Apostles, where his head was kept. In 1489, the body of St. Spyridon was brought to Corfu by the Corfiote Georgios Kalochairetis to lend his protection to the island and her sailors. Corfu had been an important port since Antiquity, but it gained renewed importance after the Ottoman conquests of Asia Minor and mainland Greece as the first, or last, landfall for sailors across the mouth of the Adriatic sea, and so St. Spyridon rose in importance among Christian mariners on this route. He is honoured today as protector of the island of Corfu for lifting a 1761 Turkish siege, and as a special protector of sailors and naval fleets there, and around the world. In his church in Corfu town, built in the 1580s, lamps hanging above his casket today bear votive silver boats dedicated to protecting local fishermen as well as the Greek merchant seaman who regularly traverse the globe.[35]

These surviving examples of maritime religion tied to specific saints along the new Christian pilgrimage routes, and along the new imperial route to (and from) Constantinople, unite the study of topography and architecture, souvenirs and sacred substances (especially oil, water and dust), and the transformation of local saints into pan-Christian saviours at sea. This process began early in the development of Christian travel, and then the larger-scale practices of pilgrimage, but it accelerated and was also fundamentally shaped by pre-existing 'pagan' maritime cult practices, land- and seascape networks, and port nodes, as well as the new routes of Christian *imperium*.

---

34   Bass and van Doorninck 1982; van Alfen 1996; van Doorninck 2005.
35   Socrates *Ecclesiastical History* 1.11-13; Konstantinidou 1972; Potts 2010.

Bibliography

Anderson, W. 2007. "Menas Flasks in the West: Pilgrimage and Trade at the End of Antiquity." *Ancient West and East* 6, 221-43.

Anrich, G. (ed.) 1913-1917. *Hagios Nikolaos: Der heilige Nikolaos in der griechischen Kirche*. 2 vols. Leipzig and Berlin: Teubner.

Bacci, M. and M. Rohde (eds.) 2014. *The Holy Portolano/Le Portulan sacré: The Sacred Geography of Navigation in the Middle Ages. Fribourg Colloquium 2013/La Géographie religieuse de la navigation au moyen âge. Colloque Fribourgeois 2013*. Berlin: De Gruyter.

Bagnall, R.S. (ed.) 2007. *Egypt in the Byzantine World, 300-700*. Cambridge: Cambridge University Press.

Bagnoli, M., H.A. Klein, C.G. Mann and J. Robinson (eds.) 2010. *Treasures of Heaven: Saints, Relics, and Devotion in Medieval Europe*. New Haven: Yale University Press.

Bangert, S. 2010. "The Archaeology of Pilgrimage: Abu Mina and Beyond," in Gwynn and Bangert 2010, 293-327.

Basch, L. 1987. *Le musée imaginaire de la marine antique*. Athens: Hellenic Institute for the Preservation of Nautical Tradition.

Bass, G.F. (ed.) 2005. *Beneath the Seven Seas: Adventures with the Institute of Nautical Archaeology*. London: Thames & Hudson.

Bass, G.F. and F.H. van Doorninck, Jr. 1982. *Yassi Ada 1: A Seventh-Century Byzantine Shipwreck*. College Station, TX: Texas A&M University Press.

Casson, L. 1971. *Ships and Seamanship in the Ancient World*. Princeton: Princeton University Press.

Choat, M. 2012. "Christianity," in Riggs 2012, 474-89.

Dark, K.R. and A.L. Harris. 2008. "The Last Roman Forum: The Forum of Leo in Fifth-century Constantinople." *Greek, Roman and Byzantine Studies* 48, 57-69.

Datema, C. (ed.) 1970. *Asterius of Amasea: Homilies I–XIV*. Leiden: Brill.

Deliyannis, D.M. 2010. *Ravenna in Late Antiquity*. Camsbridge: Cambridge University Press.

Dillon, M. 1997. *Pilgrims and Pilgrimage in Ancient Greece*. London: Routledge.

Doran, R. 1992. *The Lives of Simeon Stylites*. Kalamazoo: Cistercian Publications.

Elsner, J. and I. Rutherford (eds.) 2005. *Pilgrimage in Graeco-Roman and Early Christian Antiquity: Seeing the Gods*. Oxford: Oxford University Press.

English, A.C. 2012. *The Saint Who Would Be Santa Claus: The True Life and Trials of Nicholas of Myra*. Waco, TX: Baylor University Press.

Foss, C. 1994. "The Lycian Coast in the Byzantine Age." *DOP* 48, 1-52.

Foss, C. 2002. "Pilgrimage in Medieval Asia Minor." *DOP* 56, 129-51.

Frankfurter, D. (ed.) 1998. *Pilgrimage and Holy Space in Late Antique Egypt*. Leiden: Brill.

Gazeau, V., C. Guyon and C. Vincent (eds.) 2015. *En Orient et en Occident, le culte de saint Nicolas en Europe: Xe-XXIe siècle: Actes du colloque de Lunéville et Saint-Nicolas-de-Port, 5-7 décembre 2013*. Paris: Les éditions du Cerf.

Gedeon, M. (ed.) 1899. *Byzantinon Heortologion*. Constantinople: Hell. Phil. Syllogos.

Grabar, A. 1958. *Ampoules de Terre Sainte (Monza, Bobbio)*. Paris: C. Klincksieck.

Grossmann, P. 1998. "The Pilgrimage Center of Abu Mina," in Frankfurter 1998, 281-302.

Gwynn, D.M. and S. Bangert (eds.) 2010. *Religious Diversity in Late Antiquity*. Leiden: Brill.

Hunt, E.D. 1982. *Holy Land Pilgrimage in the Later Roman Empire A.D. 312-460*. Oxford: Oxford University Press.

Janin, H. 2002. *Four Paths to Jerusalem: Jewish, Christian, Muslim, and Secular Pilgrimages, 1000 BC to 2001 CE*. Jefferson, NC: McFarland Publishing.

Janin, R. 1964. *Constantinople byzantine: Développement urbain et répertoire topographique*. Second ed. Paris: Institut français d'études byzantines.

Jeffreys, E., J.F. Haldon and R. Cormack (eds.) 2008. *The Oxford Handbook of Byzantine Studies*. Oxford: Oxford University Press.

Jones, C.W. 1978. *Saint Nicholas of Myra, Bari, and Manhattan: Biography of a Legend*. Chicago: University of Chicago Press.

Kaufmann, K.M. 1910. *Die Menasstadt und das Nationalheiligtum der altchristlichen Aegypter in der westalexandrinischen Wüste: Ausgrabungen der Frankfurter Expedition am Karm Abu Mina*. Vol. 1. Leipzig: K.W. Hiersemann.

Koester, H. (ed.) 1995. *Ephesos, Metropolis of Asia: An Interdisciplinary Approach to its Archaeology, Religion, and Culture*. Valley Forge, PA: Trinity Press International.

Konstantinidou, P.S. 1972. *Ho Hagios Spyridōn: Episkopos Trimythountos, ho Thaumatourgos.* Nicosia: Theopress.

Kountoura-Galake, E. 2004. "The Cult of the Saints Nicholas of Lycia and the Birth of Byzantine Maritime Tradition," in Kountoura-Galake 2004, 91-106.

Kountoura-Galake, E. (ed.) 2004. *The Heroes of the Orthodox Church: The New Saints, 8th–16th C.* Athens: National Hellenic Research Foundation.

Kristensen, T.M. and W. Friese (eds.) 2017. *Excavating Pilgrimage: Archaeological Approaches to Sacred Travel and Movement in the Ancient World.* London: Routledge.

Krueger, D. 2010. "The Religion of Relics in Late Antiquity and Byzantium", in Bagnoli, Klein, Mann and Robinson 2010, 5-18.

Kuelzer, A. 2002. "Byzantine and early post-Byzantine pilgrimage to the Holy Land and to Mount Sinai," in Macrides 2002, 149-64.

Macrides, R. (ed.) 2002. *Travel in the Byzantine World.* Aldershot: Ashgate.

Mango, C. 2001. "The Shoreline of Constantinople in the Fourth Century," in Necipoğlu 2001, 17-28.

Mayer, W. 1998. "The Sea Made Holy. The Liturgical Function of the Waters surrounding Constantinople." *Ephemerides Liturgicae* 112, 459-68.

Mayer, W. and B. Neil (eds.) 2006. *The Cult of the Saints: Select Homilies and Letters by St John Chrysostom.* Crestwood, NY: St. Vladimir's Seminary Press.

McCormick, M. 2001. *Origins of the European Economy: Communications and Commerce, AD 300-900.* Cambridge: Cambridge University Press.

Milburn, R. 1988. *Early Christian Art and Architecture.* Aldershot: Ashgate.

Moffatt, A. and M. Tall. 2012. *Constantine Porphyrogennetos: The Book of Ceremonies.* Canberra: Australian Association for Byzantine Studies.

Morton, J. 2001. *The Role of the Physical Environment in Ancient Greek Seafaring.* Leiden: Brill.

Mott, L.V. 1996. *The Development of the Rudder: A Technological Tale.* College Station, TX: Texas A&M University Press.

Munteán, L., L. Plate and A. Smelik. (eds.) 2017. *Materializing Memories in Art and Popular Culture.* London: Routledge.

Necipoğlu, N. 2001. *Byzantine Constantinople: Monuments, Topography and Everyday Life.* Leiden: Brill.

Nowakowski, P. 2017. Cult of Saints database entry on Phokas, Rocks near Grammata on the island of Syros, entry no. E01232. Stable URL: http://csla.history.ox.ac.uk/record.php?recid=E01232 (accessed 31 January 2023).

Ousterhout, R. (ed.) 1990. *The Blessings of Pilgrimage.* Urbana: University of Illinois Press.

Popkin, M.L. 2017. "Souvenirs and Memory Manipulation in the Roman Empire: The Glass Flasks of Ancient Pozzuoli," in Munteán, Plate and Smelik 2017, 45-61.

Potts, J. 2010. *The Ionian Islands and Epirus: A Cultural History.* Oxford: Oxford University Press.

Pryor, J.H. 2008. "Ships and Seafaring," in Jeffreys, Haldon and Cormack 2008, 482-90.

Pryor, J.H. and E. Jeffreys, 2006. *The Age of the Dromon: The Byzantine Navy ca. 500-1204.* Leiden: Brill.

Quirini-Poplawski, R. 2014. "Seaside Shrines in the Late Mediaeval Black Sea Basin. Topography and Selected Historical and Art Historical Questions," in Bacci and Rohde 2014, 95-120.

Riggs, C. (ed.) 2012. *The Oxford Handbook to Roman Egypt.* Oxford: Oxford University Press.

Rizos, E. 2016. 'Cult of Saints database entry E01962, on Phokas, martyr of Sinope,'

http://csla.history.ox.ac.uk/record.php?recid=E01962 (accessed September 5, 2023)

Safran, L. (ed.) 1998. *Heaven on Earth: Art and the Church in Byzantium.* University Park, PA: Pennsylvania State University Press.

Settis, S. and C. Gasparri (eds.) 2021. *The Torlonia Marbles. Collecting Masterpieces.* Milan: Electa.

Sevcenko, I. and N.P. Sevcenko (eds.) 1984. *The Life of St. Nicholas of Sion: Text and Translation.* Brookline, MA: Hellenic College Press.

Sivan, H. 2011. *Galla Placidia: The Last Roman Empress.* Oxford: Oxford University Press.

Snee, R. 1998. "Gregory Nazianzen's Anastasia Church: Arianism, the Goths, and Hagiography." *DOP* 52, 157-86.

Trombley, F. 2001. "Mediterranean Sea Culture between Byzantium and Islam c. 600-850 A.D." in E. Kountoura-Galake (ed.) *The Dark Centuries of Byzantium (7th–9th c.),* 133-69. Athens: National Hellenic Research Foundation.

van Alfen, P.G. 1996. "New Light on the 7th-c. Yassı Ada Shipwreck: Capacities and Standard Sizes of LRA1 Amphoras." *JRA* 9, 189-213.

van Dam, R. 1988. *Gregory of Tours: Glory of the Martyrs.* Liverpool: Liverpool University Press.

Van de Vorst, C. 1911. "Saint Phocas." *Analecta Bollandiana* 30, 252-295.

van Doorninck, F.H. 2005. "The Ship of Georgios, Priest and Sea Captain: Yassıada, Turkey," in Bass 2005, 92-97.

Vikan, G. 1991. "'Guided by Land and Sea': Pilgrim Art and Pilgrim Travel in Early Byzantium," in *Tesserae: Festschrift für Josef Engemann,* 74-92. Münster: Aschendorff.

Vikan, G. 1998. "Byzantine Pilgrims' Art," in Safran 1998, 229-66.

Vikan, G. 2003. *Sacred Images and Sacred Power in Byzantium.* Aldershot: Ashgate.

Vikan, G. 2010. *Early Byzantine Pilgrimage Art.* Revised ed. Washington, DC: Dumbarton Oaks Research Library and Collection.

Vio, E. (ed.) 2003. *St. Mark's: The Art and Architecture of Church and State in Venice.* New York: Riverside.

Wachsmann, S. 2000. *The Sea of Galilee Boat: A 2000 year old discovery from the sea of legends.* Cambridge, MA: Perseus.

Wachsmuth, D. 1967. *Pompimos ho daimōn: Untersuchung zu den antiken Sakralhandlungen bei Seereisen.* Berlin: Self-Published 1960 Freie Universität PhD.

Wade, J. 2014. "'Lock Up your Valuables': Perceptions of Sailors and Sea-Merchants in Port Cities of Late Antiquity and Early Byzantium." *Journal of the Australian Early Medieval Association* 10, 47-75.

Wade, J. 2018. "The Eternal Spirit of Thalassa: The Transmission of Classical Maritime Symbolism into Byzantine Cultural Identity." *Journal of the Australian Early Medieval Association* 14, 51-69.

Wilkinson, J. 2002. *Jerusalem Pilgrims before the Crusades.* Revised ed. Warminster, UK: Aris & Phillips.

Williams, E.R. 1985. "Isis Pelagia and a Roman Marble Matrix from the Athenian Agora." *Hesperia* 54, 109-19.

Wisniewski, R. 2019. *The Beginnings of the Cult of Relics.* Oxford: Oxford University Press.

Woods, D. 1991. "The Date of the Translation of the Relics of SS. Luke and Andrew to Constantinople." *Vigiliae Christianae* 45, 286-92.

Wortley, J. 1992. *John Moschus: The Spiritual Meadow.* Kalamazoo, MI: Cistercian Publications.

11

JERUSALEM MYTHOLOGIES: PILGRIMS AND THE DOME OF THE ROCK:

NASER-E KHOSRAW'S REFLECTIONS ON JERUSALEM FROM HIS BOOK OF TRAVELS, THE SAFARNAMA

NAOMI KOLTUN-FROMM

In the mid-eleventh century, a Persian traveller, philosopher and poet set out on a quest for knowledge. He left from his home province, Khurasan, in the far eastern reaches of the Islamic world, traveling west over land to the Mediterranean Sea.[1] On his journey down the Levant coast, he entered Jerusalem on the 5th of March, 1047, a year after he had left home. While Naser-e Khosraw is better known for his Isma'ili poetry and theological writings, his *Safarnama*, or *Book of Travels*, a travelogue of his seven-year journey, across much of the Islamic world, is often mined for its careful geographic, architectural and cultural descriptions. Yet, he wrote the account after his return home, from notes taken during his visits. As Jonathan Bloom suggests, his descriptions, though valuable as a pre-Crusade picture of the early Muslim Levant, among other places, nevertheless has many inaccuracies.[2] His account of Jerusalem, the focus of this chapter, is no exception. Naser-e Khosraw's *Book of Travels*, which comes across as rather dispassionate and descriptive, nevertheless describes what the author 'sees' in mythic and theological terms.

In this chapter, I explore how this eleventh-century Persian Muslim pilgrim, like his Jewish and Christian pilgrimaging forebears and contemporaries, no matter how seemingly sceptical, objective and exacting in his descriptions of Jerusalem, nevertheless cannot forgo its mythological and theological pull. Specifically, for Naser-e Khosraw, Jerusalem's true significance lies in its latent atoning and divine forgiving powers, pow-

---

1   Naser e-Khosraw was born outside Marw, in Khurasan, in central Asia, but ended his days further east in Badakhshan in northeastern Afghanistan.
2   Bloom 2014, 396.

ers that descend from its ancient sacred history. And while Muhammad and his Night Journey play a role in his sacred narrative, they are subordinated to his more encompassing image of Jerusalem as a location with particular ancient yet still accessible avenues to divine forgiveness. I demonstrate how Naser fully embraces much—but not all—of the mytho-theological traditions that made Jerusalem both sacred and contested by Jews and Christians even before the rise of Islam. While acknowledging that these others continue to make pilgrimages to Jerusalem, for Naser these shared Jerusalem traditions are all deeply held *Islamic* traditions of Jerusalem's sacrality and its divine attributes. Naser's reverence for Jerusalem and its sacred attributes illuminates how expansive and complex an eleventh-century Muslim's theological world view could be. Indeed, the whole of the *Safarnama* demonstrates the spread of Islamic piety, manifested in shrines and holy sites, throughout the Islamic world, of which Jerusalem is one significant node.

Naser-e Khosraw began his career as a Persian financial administrator in the Sunni Seljuk bureaucracy, but sometime in his early forties, perhaps frustrated with living in what he perceived to be a materialistic world, or convinced that a materials-only orientation and true knowledge could not abide each other, he converted to Isma'ili (a subset of Shi'a) Islam.[3] It is probably this conversion, as well as his general quest for knowledge that sent him on his journey that resulted in his *Book of Travels, the Safarnama*. In this travelogue, he reports on his experiences traversing a good part of the Muslim world over the course of seven years, visiting various sites of Muslim interest. During this time abroad, he spent several years in Cairo, the capitol of the Fatamid caliphate and a centre of Isma'ili learning, and travelled four times to Mecca and two times through Jerusalem. After his last visit to Mecca, he continued home as a newly appointed Isma'ili missionhead in Khurasan. His Isma'ili missionary activities most likely led to a self-imposed exile (away from the Sunni Seljuks) further east in Badakhshan. Under the protection of a local prince, he wrote most of his known books, including the *Safarnama,* from exile—and there he most likely died in the late 1070s.[4]

Although his original intention, upon conversion, seems to have been to make the pilgrimage to Mecca, his travelogue records that he took the long way around, traveling across country to the sea and then down the coast to Jerusalem and eventually Cairo. All of his pilgrimages to Mecca were made from Cairo.[5] In the early Shi'a worldview, Jerusalem may not have been on an Isma'ili's or Shi'a's itinerary, because of a latent competition with Kufa as the third most important city to Islam after Mecca and Medina.[6] W. M. Thackston, Naser-e Khosraw's English translator, even notes that most of the sites he visited on his journey were of more or exclusive importance to Isma'ili Muslims.[7] Nevertheless, he seems to have made an exception to this rule to come through

---

3   Hunsberger 2000, 6.
4   Hunsberger 2000, xxi, 8.
5   Hunsberger 2000, xxii-xxiii (map).
6   See Kister 1969.
7   Thackston 1986, xi. For the purposes of this chapter, I reference only Thackston's English translation of the Persian text.

Jerusalem, not once, but twice. Moreover, the fact that Jerusalem was under Fatamid (Isma'ili-Shi'a) control would have eased his passage and perhaps sparked his interest.

By the time he reaches Jerusalem, Naser has been traveling for a year. Naser positions himself as approaching Jerusalem and its attendant mythologies with a more sceptical and educated eye. He has travelled far and wide by now, and seen and studied (he likes to measure buildings and city walls) many other cities. For instance, while marvelling at the size of certain ancient edifices in the valley outside Jerusalem's walls, he notes that the locals claim, on the one hand, that one such edifice was constructed by Pharaoh, and, on the other, that it sits at the entrance to Gehenna, or *Jahannam*, hell. It is probably not chance that he chose to carry the myth of a pharaonic structure near the entrance to the underworld, in order to tie those two together. Nevertheless, he steps back from a local tradition, that if you go to the edge of the valley you can hear the voices crying up from below. He claims to have heard no such voices.[8]

Yet he does not refrain from accepting the claim that the flat plain just outside the city walls is the plain in which the Resurrection will supposedly take place. He notes the many people who have come to Jerusalem to await that day, both those who reside in the city, and those who have been buried in a nearby cemetery in order to be physically present when that Day arrives. Jerusalem, though built on this earth, nevertheless carries theological import for this pilgrim: it is a spiritual portal to another world. He also notes at several points the abundance of fresh water, from rain, not springs, that abounds in the city's cisterns, despite the arid climate. In addition, the springs that exist outside the city, such as the Siloam, carry healing properties.[9] Thus he also allows that the spring waters that surround Jerusalem contain some supernatural properties. Yet at the same time, while Naser mentions the healing powers of the water of Siloam, he immediately afterwards comments on the well-endowed local hospital. Miraculous waters are countered by modern medicine; local, questionable traditions are negated by experiential observations. Naser's sceptical, scientific self stands in tension with his spiritual and knowledge-seeking self, for he readily admits that the knowledgeable and

---

8   Thackston 1986, 22. Abu Bakr Muhammad b. Ahmad Al-Wasiti (d. 1019), a local Jerusalem Imam also reports that Muhammad saw hell in the same valley while standing on the eastern wall of the Haram. *Fada'il al-Bayt al-Muqaddas* (following the edition of Hasson, 1979), p. 15, nos.16, 17.

9   The motif of magical waters can be found in the Christian pilgrimage literature as well. See the Pilgrim from Bordeaux (*Itn. Burg.* 592; Wilkinson 1999, 30) where he claims the waters of the Siloam stop flowing on the Sabbath. Al-Wasiti also notes that the Siloam waters originate in Heaven (p. 69, no. 111). It is interesting to note that Naser insists that the pools of Siloam are outside the city. From the earliest settlement in Jerusalem, the spring and its pools were either brought into the city by extending the walls, or in some way protected. By the eleventh century, the city had moved north and west from its ancient foundations near the Siloam. The eleventh-century walls, rebuilt after an earthquake in 1033, left the lower city, and the Siloam, outside the walls (See Bahat 1989, 87). So on the occasions of Naser's visits, the Siloam was outside the walls, though it had been inside but a few decades before. Nevertheless, it makes theological sense to Naser to place the spring outside the city walls, for thus, the waters that actually reside within the city, in its cisterns, remain purely divinely-given rain waters.

perceptive traveller or pilgrim can still perceive and benefit from the divine presence in Jerusalem, as his descriptions of sacred sites and his own pious actions evince. Local 'superstitions' of healing waters can be dismissed, but the spiritually atoning nature of Jerusalem's sacred sites remains a completely compelling ideal. And it is this mytho-theological ideal, that a properly pious visit to Jerusalem rewards the pilgrim with divine forgiveness, that guides Naser throughout his description of Jerusalem.

Thus, Naser does not escape succumbing to Jerusalem's mythological appeal in the end. As Oded Irshai has argued for the Bordeaux pilgrim, who visited Jerusalem several centuries earlier, Naser, like the earlier Christian pilgrim, while purporting to tell it like he sees it, nevertheless perceives what is in front of him through a particular mytho-theological lens.[10] And while Naser's lenses are particularly Islamic, as he wanders the Haram of Jerusalem, he visualises as much 'pre-Muhammadian' mythology as strictly Islamic. That is to say, the mythology he recognises as core to Jerusalem's essence and the source of the site's atoning power originates in Jewish and Christian sources. Yet Naser does not subcategorise his mythology—it is all Islamic—even as he recognises that Jerusalem also remains important to Jews and Christians.[11] Nevertheless, despite his clear reverence for the city and is spiritual cachet, he does not neglect to note its third-place ranking after Mecca and Medina. He must walk a fine line between revering its divine nature, that is, its connection to God—and therefore acknowledging its elevated place even within Islamic theology—yet at the same time not overemphasising its sacrality to Islam in order to keep what he considers to be the accepted sacred city hierarchy. Yet, I argue here that Naser nonetheless holds on to a pious 'soft spot' for Jerusalem because of its atoning powers. Jerusalem retains spiritual significance for the properly educated and spiritually attuned Islamic pilgrim, who can atone for his or her sins while praying at its various sacred shrines, particularly those tied to ancient monotheistic figures.

Naser highlights this accessibility of individual atonement in several ways. First, he claims outright, that "it is well known among those learned in religion", that in Jerusalem every ordinary prayer is worth 25,000 prayers, although still rated less valuable than Medina (50,000) and Mecca (100,000).[12] Moreover, just being in the land and seeing its prosperity allows him to conclude that it is a blessed land indeed, having never

---

10   Oded Irshai 2009. See also Bowman 2000 and Eliav 2005. The Bordeaux pilgrim, like Naser, pays close attention to the Solomonic water systems of the temple mount, the Siloam and the valley of Jehoshaphat (*Itn. Burg* 592, Wilkinson 1999, 29-31).

11   He notes at the beginning of his description of Jerusalem that Jews and Christians also visit various sites in the city (Thackston 1986, 21). It is the modern scholarly need for categorisation and origins that provokes this differentiation between 'biblical' or 'pre-Islamic' and 'Islamic'. Naser would not have differentiated. Nor is it clear from his text if he understands that the Jewish and Christian pilgrims he sees and acknowledges come to Jerusalem for the same reasons: atonement and/or salvation. As a historian, I cannot escape my own need to categorise, and thus I have settled on 'pre-Muhammadian', to signify these shared ancient divinely-touched heroes such as David and Solomon, Jesus and Mary, that Naser claims as fully part of his Islamic narrative.

12   Thackston 1986, 32.

suffered a famine, or so he claims. Thus, the traveller to this land can also benefit from its blessings. Finally, the itinerary he lays out for his readers moves from sacred site to sacred site along a path of reverence for pre-Muhammadian monotheistic figures and their personal histories. The places he highlights more often than not mark sites where these ancient Islamic forebears, as presented in the Islamic traditions, asked for and received forgiveness from God, or otherwise interacted with God in Jerusalem.

Although Naser notes that the city has lovely bazaars and houses 20,000 people, the majority of his description focuses on the *masjid*, or Mosque. By this term he designates the whole of what will become known as the Haram al-Sharif, that is, what was left of the Herodian temple platform that was eventually renovated and retrofitted to support the many Islamic structures built upon it, not least the Dome of the Rock and the Al-Aqsa Mosque. He begins his description by noting that the entirety of the platform was built by King Solomon around the Rock, the Rock being that rock towards which God directed Moses to make the *qibla*, the direction of prayer.[13] Here Naser, our pilgrim, emphasises that the sacrality of the bedrock and the ancient platform constructed around it predate Muhammad. Moreover, they remain significant because the Rock at its center was designated by God as the original focal point of prayer, and the construction he sees surrounding the Rock, that is the platform upon which the Dome of the Rock and the Al-Aqsa mosque stand, he presents as actually built by King Solomon to commemorate and actualise that first *qibla*. The Dome of the Rock and the Al-Aqsa mosque, both of which he describes in more detail later on, are not the important features of the Sanctuary, that is, the whole of the esplanade—rather the Rock and its surrounding platform remain the focal point. Herod, the patron king of the original platform, as well as Abd al-Malik the sponsor of the Dome, have been forgotten through Naser's mythologising gaze (the same can be said for the earlier Bordeaux pilgrim). The Dome of the Rock and the Al-Aqsa Mosque merely decorate the sacred platform already built by Solomon in ancient history. Naser paces out the length and width of the Sanctuary, as if to demonstrate to his readers the vastness of the divine infrastructure upon which Islam and its buildings are built. Thus, it is not the buildings as buildings that are important but the mythology that that very sub-structure supports. Naser does not recall Solomon as a temple or cultic shrine builder, but rather as an architect of the *infrastructure* around a particular sacred rock upon which Islamic buildings will be later built. Yet his descriptions also point to the notion that Islam, to some extent, rests on the monotheistic infrastructure created by its God-worshipping forebears in Jerusalem, and therefore partakes in the same, but now Islamic, narrative of salvation.

Naser-e Khosraw's description of Jerusalem participates in a long tradition of mythologising sacred rocks in this sacred city. The mytho-theologising of the bedrock of the mountain upon which both Solomon and Herod built their shrines begins shortly after the destruction of their original temple structures, but long before the advent of Islam. The late biblical texts such as Isaiah and Psalms begin to focus on the mountain

---

13   Thackston 1986, 23. Al-Wasiti also notes that since the time of Adam, until Muhammad, all *qiblas* faced Jerusalem, though he does not mention Moses specifically in this passage (p. 51, no. 78).

itself, but the late-ancient rabbis generate the first mythic Rock. In the early rabbinic texts (ca. second to third century CE), the rabbis, having lived for several decades already in a temple-less world, 'recall' a small rock within the structure of Solomon's temple that nevertheless pre-dates the structure, for it is the Rock from which the whole world emerged in Creation. For instance, in Tosefta Yoma, we find:

> A stone was there from the days of the first prophets and it was called 'Shetiyah'. It was three finger breadths above the ground. From the beginning the Ark [of the covenant] sat upon it; When the Ark was taken away it was used to hold the incense pan. Rabbi Yosi used to say, "From it the world was created, as it says (Ps. 50:2) 'From Zion perfect in glory, God appeared'."[14]

The rabbis draw here on ancient Near Eastern cosmic mountain motifs to glorify not just the place where the temples once stood, but the very contents of the holiest part of the shrine: a small and seemingly insignificant piece of bedrock. This little rock gains significance, not just because it is inside the holy of holies, but because it is the first rock of Creation. It is the divine footprint on earth, God shown forth in all the divine glory, for the first time on earth, at the most momentous moment: Creation, here on this little piece of bedrock. Elsewhere, another (Amoraic) rabbinic midrash suggests that atonement also emanates naturally from the site of the temples, even before they were built. In Genesis Rabbah we read:

> *On the Ground (adamah)* [Gen. 2:7] R. Berekiah and R. Helbo in the name of Samuel the Elder said: He [Adam] was created from the place of his atonement [that is the future site of the temple and its altar], as you read, *An altar of earth [adamah] shall you make for me* [Exod. 20:24]. The Holy Blessed One said: Behold I will create him from the place of his atonement, and may he endure.[15]

In this midrash, these Palestinian Amoraic rabbis play on the word *adam/adamah*, in that Adam was made from the dust of the earth, the *adamah,* while Moses is instructed as part of Revelation to build an altar of earth/*adamah* for the people's sacrificial offerings to their God. This text further connects Adam, the first human, the first Mosaic altar at Sinai, and the altar of the temple shrine in Jerusalem—for they all participate in making atonement accessible to all Israel—through the image of God taking the earthly dust with which God forms Adam's body from the site of the future temple altar.[16]

---

14   Tosefta Yoma 2.14, author's translation. For a fuller discussion of these rabbinic, Christian and early Islamic texts on Creation, see Koltun-Fromm 2017.

15   Midrash Bereshit Rabbah 14.8, author's translation, based on the Soncino translation, 1:117-18.

16   It must be noted as well that the Genesis Rabbah text focuses on the altar, placed outside the sanctuary building, whereas the Tosefta centres on a stone, hidden within the sanctuary building. By the time Naser walks the Haram, the possibility of atonement has diffused the whole of the platform, not just one or another particular or exclusive site within the platform.

These two midrashim, in their different ways, make the site of the Jerusalem temples, Mt. Zion, but without the actual temples, an important part in the atonement process.

Yet, the idea of a 'site of atonement' with portable dust, as the second midrash suggests, reflects contemporaneous Christian notions of Golgotha, its portable relics, and its cross as a site of atonement and salvation for Christians. Whatever the relationship between these texts, Jerusalem sacred stones remain tied to divine atonement and salvation. To wit, Cyril of Jerusalem, remarking on the Crucifixion during one of his sermons, notes that:

> He [Jesus] stretched out his hands on the cross to encompass the ends of the world. For the central point of the earth is Golgotha here. These are not my words, but those of the prophet, "You have accomplished salvation in the center of the earth" [Ps 73:12 LXX].[17]

Here Cyril stakes a similar claim for Golgotha, another sacred Jerusalem stone, which is at the centremost point of the earth and is the place where God made salvation available to all believers through the passion, death and resurrection of Jesus. Between the rabbis' imagined stone of Creation, the claim that the dust of Mt. Zion has atoning powers, and the Byzantine Christians' reverence for Golgotha as another site of salvation, the seventh-century Islamic conquerors must have found Jerusalem to be an exciting, if complicated, mythological, yet earthly place.

The early Islamic tradition builds on, restructures and repurposes the early Jewish and Christian mythologies for the glory of Islam, without totally losing or obfuscating their biblical and extra-biblical origins. The earliest Islamic traditions celebrate these ancient traditions, while also Islamising them. The Islamic absorption of these mytho-theologically laden sacred stones most likely led, in part, to the building of the Dome of the Rock both to commemorate its Rock as a divine vestige from Creation and to refocus attention on Islamic access to salvation, particularly in opposition to Christian beliefs and edifices on the other side of town.[18] Yet as we shall see, much of the cosmic mountain/creation motifs seem to fade in importance for some later Islamic visitors, such as Naser, who focuses almost entirely on the penitential possibilities of the Rock and its surrounding structures.[19]

Nevertheless, questions remain as to why the Umayyads built the Dome of the Rock as well as the Al-Aqsa Mosque. It appears that a mosque, or at least a place of congregation somewhere on the Herodian platform predated the Umayyad construction, if

---

17 Cyril, *Cat.* 13.28. Trans. Yarnold 2000, 157.
18 Mourad 2008, 96-97. Milka Levy-Rubin also argues that with the Dome of the Rock, Abd al-Malik "answers back" not just to Christian Jerusalem, but to Byzantine Christian empire building and sabre rattling from Constantinople (Levi-Rubin, 2017). See also Koltun-Fromm 2017.
19 Nevertheless these very same cosmic mountain and Creation motifs find their way into the Fada'il Bayt al-Muqaddas collections of al-Wasiti and ibn al-Murajja, among others.

Arculf, a Christian traveller of 680, is to be believed.[20] The narratives concerning Umar's conquest of Jerusalem, though fictitious and most likely composed 100 or so years after Umar's reign, point to an underlying concern with finding the proper, Islamic place to worship in a spiritually crowded cityscape.[21] All other sources point to Abd Al-Malik as the Caliph who orchestrated the building of the Dome in 692 and his son Walid for rebuilding or solidifying a more temporary building into a large congregational mosque over the next decades (ca. 710).[22] These large and ornate structures were probably *not* built on Herod's temple platform simply because it happened to be abandoned real estate with a nice view, but rather because the site retained theological and mythological import in a city constructed on competing ideologies, theologies and mythologies.

When the Muslims arrived in Jerusalem, they came with or soon acquired a reverence for the sacredness of Jerusalem as a whole, and the place of the former temples in particular.[23] Scholars have noted that the impetus to build the Dome of the Rock was probably, in part, to protect the Rock from the elements, and perhaps too from the populace who already venerated the stone.[24] That is, it was built to create a safe and managed pilgrimage site, for all pilgrims, Muslim and other. But one need not build the most beautiful building in the city for that purpose—unless one also felt the need for reverence. Thus, the Dome of the Rock not only protected the Rock, but glorified it. But that desire does not necessarily explain the building in all its artistic and architectural details. Busse suggests that Abd al-Malik believed he was rebuilding the Jewish temple.[25] Al-Thalibi, an early eleventh-century traditionist, expresses the same idea, even as he presents Umar as the temple re-builder. This same sentiment is certainly expressed in contemporaneous documents: positively by Jews and negatively by Christians.[26] Therefore it is possible that Abd al-Malik built his version of a temple,

---

20 Arculf (Adomnán) 1.1; Wilkinson 1977, 95. But see now Lawrence Nees who discounts Arculf's text as a fabrication (2016, 33-58). B. St. Laurent and I. Awwad (2017) argue that the mosque that Arculf might have seen would have been constructed under Mu'awiyya, and has now been rediscovered and rehabilitated as the Marwani Mosque under the platform in the former Solomon Stables.

21 See for instance al-Tabari in his *Tarikh*, on Umar's visit to Jerusalem, in which Umar, after touring the city, asks Ka'b, "Where do you think we should establish the place of prayer?" (Friedmann 1992, 194). See also Busse 1986.

22 The original inscriptions inside the Dome credit Abd al-Malik. St. Laurent and Awwad 2017, 451-52, give more credit to al-Malik's predecessor, Mu'awiyya, for the Islamic shape of the Haram, even if Abd al-Malik was the ultimate builder/contractor.

23 The question of whether the Muslims stumbled upon Jerusalem on their way to Damascus, or came purposefully to conquer and claim the city's ancient sacrality remains an open question in the scholarship. In favour of the latter position, see most recently Stephen Shoemaker 2018. On the former view, see Aziz Al-Azmeh 2014, who argues that Islam grew out of a particularly Arabian-focused milieu.

24 Mourad 2008, 95; Elad 1995, 50.

25 Busse 1997-8, 24-27.

26 Al-Thalibi, *Lives of the Prophets* (Brinner 2002, 512); Busse 1997-8, "Theophanes", 24; Reeves 2005, "Secrets of Rabbi Shimon Bar Yohai", 81-82. Eutychus, a ninth-century Christian historian, notes

if that is what it was, on the remains of the Herodian platform in order to counter the Christian claim that the Church of the Holy Sepulchre was that new temple already built centuries before.[27] Rosen-Ayalon has argued that while the Dome was built to offset the power and draw of Christianity, it was not built as a temple replacement *per se*, but to counter the salvific value of the Christian church and its sacred stones, by drawing on other competing Jerusalem mythologies. For if the main theme of the Church of the Holy Sepulchre focused on Jesus's past resurrection as promise of a future resurrection, Abd al-Malik's building usurped that promise—implying through its internal decoration program that the future resurrection would be conducted through the Islamic venue, and building, rather than the Christians'. The internal decoration programme evokes images of Paradise—marking the internal space of the Dome as Garden of Eden-like more than temple-like—while the internal inscriptions rebuke Christian salvation theology rather than, say, commemorate Muhammad's visit to Jerusalem (whose Night Journey is not mentioned on the inside of the Dome). Thus, the building states through both its mosaic patterns and its position around the Rock that the true means to salvation is through Islam.[28]

But the opportunity for this new and quickly expanding regional power to put its imprint on this already contested city also influenced the placement and grandeur of the Islamic architecture of the Haram. The Umayyad Caliphs needed to establish themselves as leaders both within the Islamic world and as a bulwark against Byzantium.[29] Some Umayyad adversaries accused Abd al-Malik of wanting to divert pilgrimage from Mecca, as the Umayyads had set up their headquarters in Damascus, rather than on the Arabian Peninsula.[30] Although the Ka'ba, and Mecca, came under fire during the ultimately successful Umayyad campaign against the upstart caliph, Ibn al-Zubayr, after winning control of the Caliphate Abd al-Malik had the Ka'ba rebuilt and organised one of the earliest pilgrimages there soon afterwards.[31] Nasser Rabbat further argues that Abd al-Malik modeled his rule on the precedent set by David and Solomon, and the Quran's presentation of their kingship as divinely ordained.[32] Thus the glorification of Jerusalem, and especially the Islamising of the former temple mount, came as part of an

---

the sacredness of the site, while insisting that the Christian Patriarch, Sophronious, restrained the Muslims from building anywhere else in the city (Peters, 1985, 190).

27 Busse 1997-8, 33. Eusebius makes that very claim, *Vita* 3.33.1.
28 Rosen-Ayalon 1989, 46-72. Milwright 2016, 261-65, further argues that the internal inscriptions point to a religio-political program of supporting the Umayyad caliphate as true leadership of the Islamic peoples and of the building as a counter-salvific narrative to Christianity. See also Levi-Rubin 2017.
29 See Necipoğlu 2008, on the overarching Umayyad vision for Jerusalem; and Levy-Rubin 2017, on the Umayyad competition with Constantinople.
30 Elad 1995, 53. Al-Yaqubi, an anti-Umayyad scholar of the Abbasid empire, most vociferously denounced Abd al-Malik and his building schemes in his *Ta'rikh*, 2.261 (English translation found in Peters 1985, 197).
31 Rabbat 1989, 16.
32 Ibid., 17.

evolving political strategy to bolster the Umayyad reign. The Umayyads wove themselves into the many-layered spiritual narrative of Jerusalem in order to secure their leadership in the newly forming, yet still evolving, Islamic empire.

Four centuries later, as Naser walks across the Holy Esplanade of Jerusalem, the mythologies have shifted once again. He is well aware of both the ancient monotheistic history of the site and its connection to Muhammad's Night Journey. Yet, even as he focuses on possibilities of repentance and atonement for the individual visitor, rather than on grand narratives of Islamic precedence, the very fact that Muhammad came to Jerusalem to pray at the Rock, for his own atonement, plays a significant and even uniting role in Naser's narrative. Muhammad's nocturnal visit supports Naser's penitential point of view, rather than the other way around: Muhammad too came to Jerusalem to pray for divine forgiveness, for himself and as an example to all Muslims. Thus he relates concerning Muhammad and the Rock,

> They say that on the night of the heavenly ascent, the Prophet first prayed in the Dome of the Rock and placed his hand on the Rock ... From there the Prophet came to the [other] dome that is attributed to him and mounted the Boraq ...[33]

In this passage, Naser portrays Muhammad as coming to Jerusalem to pay his respects to God at the Rock. The stopover in Jerusalem has penitential purpose. Muhammad dismounts after his journey from Mecca and prays (presumably for forgiveness) at the Rock before his heavenward ascent. The notion that Muhammad felt compelled to pray here, by the Rock, before facing God, gives the place a particular sacred narrative, and impetus for other Muslims to follow.

Nevertheless, this small narrative piece comes at the end of his description of the Dome of the Rock, which he places at the end of his tour around the platform. The Dome is the focal point, but he takes time to describe his journey. As Nasir walks around the platform/Mosque, his descriptions make visible to us the columns, the domes, the windows, the structures and the inscriptions. He claims, at first, to have wandered aimlessly about the platform to get his bearings, but then describes the layout of buildings in a rather methodical manner. He leads us on a circuit of the periphery of the sanctuary, starting at the Gate of David, which is a main gate leading into the city market places, remarking on the points of interest—all of which are places at the edges of the platform where various monotheistic ancestors prayed.[34] Before we even get to the largest central and exclusively Islamic structure on the platform, the Al-Aqsa Mosque, we have visited the *mihrabs*, or prayer niches, of Jacob, the prophets Zechariah and David, as well as Jesus, Mary and the priest Zachariah. At several of them, Naser records his own

---

33 Thackston 1986, 33.
34 Bloom 2014, 397 notes that this particular description probably describes the gate as it looked after the earthquake of 1015 and renovation by al-Zahir, but not as it appears today.

prayers. Thus, at the double gates of Mercy and Repentance, on the eastern side of the sanctuary, Naser notes that here,

> "They say that David had scarcely crossed the threshold when an inspiration came to him to the effect that God had accepted his repentance. There he remained, occupying himself with acts of obedience. I, Naser, prayed there and asked God for grace in piety and to be cleansed of the sin of disobedience. May God the Exalted grant grace to all his servants in accordance with his pleasure and grant repentance of sin through the sanctity of Mohammad and his pure offspring."[35]

David here stands out as the model penitent servant extraordinaire of God, whose prayers were heard and answered. Sura 38 of the Quran, drawing on the biblical tradition (2 Sam 11) that David eventually repented of his adultery with Bathsheba and death of her husband Uriah, uses this narrative to further support the power of repentance. David's presence within both the Muslim narratives about Jerusalem and the architectural monuments within Islamic Jerusalem testify to the influence of this tradition. Throughout his explorations, Naser, for instance, mentions David's gate, David's *mihrab*, as well as these two other gates where David received forgiveness, and the Dome of the Chain where he administered justice.[36] David's divinely rewarded acts of contrition play deeply into this Muslim pilgrim's understanding of Jerusalem.

Completing his full circuit of the sanctuary, Naser brings us at last to the largest structure on the platform, the Al-Aqsa Mosque. He notes that

> "This marks the spot to which God transported Mohammad from Mecca on the night of his heavenly ascent, and there to heaven, as is mentioned in the Koran: 'Praise be unto him, who transported his servant by night, from the sacred temple [of Mecca] to the farther temples [of Jerusalem]' (Q 17.1)."[37]

Here Naser, while quoting a Quranic text, interprets it along traditional lines. Sura 17 does not mention Jerusalem, but only "the furthest mosque", which only later becomes associated with Jerusalem. In addition, this verse, speaks of a Night Journey (*isra*), but not necessarily of a heavenly ascent (*mi'raj*). While the Quran highlights many moments when Muhammad receives heavenly revelation, it never specifies Jerusalem as

---

35 Thackston 1986, 25-26. David and Solomon play influential roles and stand as penitential role models in early Islamic literature. Suleiman b. Muqatil notes that God forgave David and Solomon (as well as the people of Israel) in *Bayt al-Maqdis* (Jerusalem and/or the Haram itself) (Hasson 1996, 384).
36 Reynolds 2014; Mourad 2008, 92.
37 Thackston 1986, 26. Thackston readily glosses *al-masjid al-haram* as Mecca and *al-masjid al-aqsa* as Jerusalem in his English translation. He also translates *masjid* as temple (the French translation does as well, Schefer, 1970, 79); I am not sure of the wording of the original Persian, but the modern Arabic translation (Cairo 1945, 24) follows the quranic text with *masjid*.

the place for any of these revelations. Yet, heavenly journeys to gain divine revelations certainly abounded in late ancient religious texts.[38] And while modern scholarship has not completely untangled the complex way these ideas come together, by the late eighth century, the idea that Muhammad traveled on his Night Journey to Jerusalem and from there ascended to heaven began to take shape in Islamic tradition.[39] It is even possible that Jerusalem as destination of the Night Journey only solidified after the building of the Dome of the Rock and therefore comes in support of the mythologies already associated with Jerusalem, the temple platform and the Rock.[40] Nevertheless, in Naser's text, Muhammad first comes to Jerusalem to pay his respects to the Rock and pray there. Yet his *mi'raj*, or ascent to heaven, is marked not by the place of the Rock, but by the building of assembly—the Al-Aqsa mosque—aptly named after the Quranic verse—"the farthest mosque". As a unique Islamic myth about Jerusalem, it must be commemorated in a purpose-built and exclusively Islamic building.

This large and beautifully decorated basilica is also important, here as the first fully Islamic building that Naser describes on the platform: that is to say, its mythic import lies in its marking of the midway point between Muhammad's terrestrial Night Journey from Mecca and his ascent to heaven, a uniquely Islamic tradition. This building is also 'blessed' or marked by important Muslim leaders, Mu'awiyya and Umar, both of whom have prayer niches named after each of them within the structure. Nevertheless, it still sits on top of and therefore is supported by the divinely designated bedrock and Solomonic infrastructure.[41]

The Dome of the Rock remains as the last structure our pilgrim visits on this walk. This may be because of the roundabout path of his walk—around the periphery of the sanctuary platform, in which the Al-Aqsa is situated at one end, and the Dome is in the middle—but I believe it is more purposeful than that. Between describing Al-Aqsa and the Dome, Naser sidetracks through the structure's water sources, marvelling at the many cisterns built under the buildings and platform to catch every drop of rainwater. He goes so far as to claim that even when there is not a cloud in the sky, rainwater continues to trickle into the cisterns. Moreover, despite having fallen onto the lead roofs and streamed into the underground lead pipes, to say nothing of flowing over the foot-trodden granite paving stones, the water of Jerusalem was the best and cleanest he had ever seen!

---

38   Busse 1991, 6, 21; see also e.g. 2 Enoch, 4 Ezra and the Apocalypse of Paul.
39   Ibn Ishaq (d. 767) as presented by his editor, Ibn Hisham (d. 830) seems to loosely connect the separate ideas of an ascent and the night journey by recording the various narratives of journey and ascent next to each other. Ibn Ishaq/Hisham may be the earliest textual witness that brings the two narratives together (Ibn Ishaq, *Life of Muhammad*, 263-71; Guillaume 1955, 181-87). Al-Tabari, in his *Ta'rikh*, reports ascension narratives with no connection to a night journey, which remains unmentioned there (*Histories*, 1157-58; Watt and McDonald 1987, VI.78); however, in his *Tafsir* on Sura 17.1, on which the *isra' tradition is based*, he presents the Night Journey to Jerusalem as part and parcel of the Ascension narrative.
40   Busse 1997-8, 33; Mourad 2008, 96. See also Colby 2009.
41   Thackston 1986, 27.

Earlier visitors to Jerusalem claim similarly for the seemingly miraculous water sources of Jerusalem. The second-century BCE *Letter of Aristeas*, whose author probably never actually visited Jerusalem, describes Jerusalem flowing with abundant waters to wash the streets and temple esplanade clean every day.[42] A fifth-century Christian pilgrim imagines waters flowing under the city that can take an apple thrown into the crack in the golgothan rock within the Church of the Holy Sepulchre all the way to the Siloam pools.[43] These very concrete descriptions of a water-filled Jerusalem draw on biblical mythologising of life-giving waters that both the prophet Ezekiel and John of Patmos, in his book of Revelation, imbue into their imagined future, divinely rebuilt Jerusalems.[44] Given that Naser seems to have arrived in Jerusalem at the tail end of the rainy season, the seemingly abundant water then may have appeared natural and therefore fit with what he had learned about Jerusalem prior to his arrival. That is, mythological Jerusalem easily merges with earthly Jerusalem in Naser's descriptions of divinely attuned waters.

Nevertheless, he reminds us again at this point that Solomon built the platform and the amazing system of pipes and cisterns underneath it to capture the flowing rainwaters. Once again, by returning to Solomon and God, the ultimate provider of all that rain, between his description of the Al-Aqsa Mosque and the Dome of the Rock, he emphasises the monotheistic infrastructure upon which the Muslim buildings (and religion) are built, as well as the special divine nature that God first bestowed on Jerusalem, and continues into Naser's day. The abundant rain embodies God's ultimate gift to this sacred city: this city needs no other water sources. Thus, he makes clear, as mentioned earlier, that the Siloam spring lies outside the city walls (and limits).[45]

Another way he makes the same point is through his commentary on the remarkable construction of the gate and tunnel that leads up to the *qibla* side of the platform from outside the esplanade, which he is told must be the way that Muhammad entered the Sanctuary for the first time. Thus, this whole sanctuary/platform, in Naser's imagination, clearly existed before Muhammad and it was to this structure that Muhammad was brought by Gabriel on his Night Journey, because it already had significance before Muhammad and Islam came into their own. This significance is enshrined within the Dome of the Rock: the Rock is the first *qibla* of God. Muhammad pays his respects to the Rock and its place as first point of prayer, by praying there on his stopover between Mecca and Heaven. Yet the Rock, if it belongs to anyone, belongs to Abraham. The famous 'footstep' that is 'visible', and was also attributed to Muhammad, in Naser's imagination belongs to Isaac, who as a child ran about on the Rock (not yet associated with his near sacrifice) as his father went about his daily business of being the Friend (*Khalil*) of God.[46] Nevertheless, the Rock displays agency: when Muhammad finishes

---

42 *Let. Aris.* 89-90.
43 *Pilg. Piac.* 19.
44 Ezek. 47:1; Rev. 22:1-2.
45 Thackston 1986, 29.
46 The first Islamic traditionist to mention Muhammad's footprint on the Rock appears to be al-Yaqubi (d. 897), who reports this notion as a heretical rumour that Abd al-Malik promoted to

his prayers and leaves for his heavenly ascent, the Rock attempts to follow him. Muhammad places his hand on the Rock and it stays put (thus creating the small cave that exists beneath it.). This small narrative also endows the Islamic leader with authority over the Rock and its meaning, while still paying appropriate reverence to its ancient divine history.

Yet, I think what distinguishes Naser's travelogue is an understanding and reverence for this very ancient monotheistic sacred history; the significance of this Rock as the first *qibla* has everything to do with true religion and its benefits: salvation. Naser starts his description of Jerusalem by noting this very fact: "The mosque was built in that place because it is the site of the very rock which God commanded Moses to make the direction of prayer."[47] Sura 2:141, which references the Islamic *qibla*, is traditionally understood to point to the moment when Muslims were commanded to pray towards Mecca alone, turning their backs on Jerusalem.[48] Neither the Rock nor Jerusalem, for that matter, are mentioned in this passage. Yet, Naser, following Islamic tradition, assumes that if God commanded Muhammed to face Mecca, he must also have commanded Moses and the Israelites to face Jerusalem in their day and this preserves Jerusalem's importance despite the later switch.[49] In support, Naser cites Sura 2.58:

> "Enter into this city, and eat of the provisions thereof plentifully as you will; and enter the gate worshiping, and say, Forgiveness [*hitta*] we will pardon you your sins and give increase unto the well doers."[50]

Reading this text as a reference to the city of Jerusalem, and more specifically the sanctuary, rather than the whole of the Holy Land (as the text seems to indicate), Naser claims that God granted the sanctuary to Moses and all the Israelites as a site of atonement, as a site where one can ask God forgiveness for one's sins and hope for a positive outcome.[51] Yet despite the *qibla* having moved, and thus Religion and its promised salvation having been transferred to Mecca, this former first site still retains some penitential cachet. Again and again, Naser returns to this theme of atonement and forgiveness. First, there are the people who have come to this city to await the Judgment Day, including those who are buried outside the walls, as if to be first in line at the Resurrection and Judgment Day when they will learn of their final destination. In addition, with every prayer niche we visit, but especially at the easternmost Gates of Mercy and Repentance, we

---

support his (illegitimate, in Yaqubi's eyes) caliphate. Al-Yaqubi, *Ta'rikh* 2.261.
47 Thackston 1986, 23.
48 See for instance, Ibn Ishaq, *Life of Muhammad*, 427 (Guillaume 1955, 289) and al-Tabari, *Histories* 1279 (Watt and McDonald 1987, VII.24).
49 Thackston 1986, 23.
50 Ibid., 29.
51 There is a discrepancy between, firstly, the quranic text, which says 'land', and Naser's citation, which has 'city' (though the Arabic is closely related), and secondly, what *hitta*, 'atonement', refers to in this verse, for it can also be translated as 'worship' or 'humility'.

are witnesses to Naser's own prayers for divine forgiveness, for supposedly God accepts all prayers made on this site. Muhammad then, is brought to this sacred site by Islamic tradition, not just to claim it for Islam, but to partake in the atonement that seemingly, naturally, emanates from within it. Why else would Muhammad not only visit, but purposefully pray, if not to open that divine forgiveness to all repentant Muslims who visit there as well? I would argue, then, that the more compelling reason to visit the Haram in Jerusalem for this eleventh-century Isma'ili pilgrim was not to commemorate the Night Journey *per se*, but to make pilgrimage to the site that God first endowed with the possibility of divine forgiveness. Naser encourages his readers to seek personal atonement, as he did, following Muhammad's example, by reciting prayers in Jerusalem where David and Solomon both interacted with God, built and glorified the sanctuary in God's name and gained God's forgiveness through their own penitence.

Bibliography

Al-Azmeh, A. 2014. *The Emergence of Islam in Late Antiquity: Allah and his People*. Cambridge and New York: Cambridge University Press.

Bahat, D. 1989. *The Illustrated Atlas of Jerusalem*. Jerusalem: Carta.

Bloom, J. 2014. "Nasir Khusraw's Description of Jerusalem," in A. Korangy and D.J. Sheffield (eds.) *No Tapping around Philology: A Festschrift in Honor of Wheeler McIntosh Thackston Jr.'s 70th Birthday*, 395-406. Wiesbaden: Harrasowitz Verlag.

Bowman, G. 1999. "Mapping History's Redemption: Eschatology and Topography in the *Itinerarium Burdigalense*," in L. Levine (ed.) *Jerusalem: Its Sanctity and Centrality to Judaism, Christianity and Islam*, 163-87. New York: Continuum.

Brinner, W.M., trans. 2002. *'Ara'is al-Majalis fi Qisas al-Anbiya or "Lives of the Prophets" as recounted by Abu Ishaq Ahmad ibn Muhammad ibn Ibrahim al-Thalabi*. Boston and Leiden: Brill.

Busse, H. 1986. "Omar's Image as the Conqueror of Jerusalem." *Jerusalem Studies in Arabic and Islam* 8, 149-68.

Busse, H. 1991. "Jerusalem in the Story of Muhammad's Night Journey and Ascension." *Jerusalem Studies in Arabic and Islam* 14, 1-40.

Busse, H. 1997-8. "The Temple of Jerusalem and Its Restitution by 'Abd Al-Malik b. Marwan," in B. Kühnel (ed.) *The Real and Ideal Jerusalem in Jewish, Christian and Islamic Art: Studies in Honor of Bezalel Narkiss on the Occasion of his Seventieth Birthday*, 23-33. Jerusalem: Journal of the Center for Jewish Art.

Colby, F.S. 2008. *Narrating Muhammad's Night Journey: Tracing the Development of the Ibn 'Abbas Ascension Discourse*. Albany: State University of New York Press.

Elad, A. 1995. *Medieval Jerusalem and Islamic Worship*. Leiden: Brill.

Eliav, Y. 2005. *God's Mountain: The Temple Mount in Time, Place and Memory*. Baltimore: John Hopkins Press.

Friedmann, Y. trans. 1992. *The History of al-Tabari, vol. 12: The Battle of al-Qadisiyyah and the Conquest of Syria and Palestine*. Albany: The State University of New York Press.

Guillaume, A. trans. 1955. *The Life of Muhammad: A Translation of Ishaq's Sirat Rasul Allah*. Oxford: Oxford University Press.

Hasson, I. (ed.) 1979. *Fada'il al-Bayt al-Muqaddas D'Abu Bakr Muhammad b. Ahmad Al Wasiti*. Jerusalem: The Magnes Press.

Hasson, I. 1981. "Muslim Literature in Praise of Jerusalem: Fada'il Bayt al-Maqdis." *Jerusalem Cathedra* 1, 168-84.

Hasson, I. 1996. "The Muslim View of Jerusalem," in J. Prawer and H. Ben-Shammai (eds.) *The History of Jerusalem in the Early Muslim Period 638-1099*, 349-85. Jerusalem: Yad Ben-Zvi Press.

Hunsberger, A.C. 2000. *Nasir Khusraw The Ruby of Badakhshan: A Portrait of the Persian Poet, Traveller and Philosopher*. London: I.B. Tauris.

Irshai, O. 2009. "The Christian Appropriation of Jerusalem in the Fourth Century: The Case of the Bordeaux Pilgrim." *Jewish Quarterly Review* 99.4, 465-86.

Kister, M.J. 1969. "'You Shall Only Set out for Three Mosques': A Study of An Early Tradition." London: Variorum Le Muséon 82, 173-96.

Koltun-Fromm, N. 2017. "Sacred Stones from Creation to Eschaton." *Journal of Late Antiquity* 10.1, 1-20.

Levy-Rubin, M. 2017. "Why was the Dome of the Rock built? A new perspective on a long-discussed question." *Bulletin of SOAS* 80.3, 441-64.

McDonald, M.V., trans. 1985. *The History of al-Tabari, vol. 7: The Foundation of the Community*. Albany, NY: The State University of New York Press.

Milwright, M. 2016. *The Dome of the Rock and its Umayyad Mosaic Inscriptions*. Edinburgh: Edinburgh University Press.

Mourad, S. 2008. "The Symbolism of Jerusalem in Early Islam," in T. Mayer and S.A. Mourad (eds.) *Jerusalem: Idea and Reality*, 86-102. London and New York: Routledge.

Necipoğlu, G. 2008. "The Dome of the Rock as Palimpsest: 'Abd al-Malik's Grand Narrative and Sultan Süleyman's Glosses." *Muqarnas* 25, 17-105.

Nees, L. 2016. *Perspectives on Early Islamic Art in Jerusalem*. Leiden: Brill.

Peters, F.E. 1984. *Jerusalem*. Princeton, NJ: Princeton University Press.

Rabbat, N. 1989. "The Meaning of the Umayyad Dome of the Rock." *Muqarnas* 6, 12-21.

Reeves, J.C. 2005. *Trajectories in Near Eastern Apocalyptic: A Postrabbinic Jewish Apocalypse Reader*. Atlanta: Society of Biblical Literature.

Reynolds, G.S. 2014. "David," in *Encyclopedia of Islam*, third edition, 78-81. Leiden: Brill.

Rosen-Ayalon, M. 1989. *The Early Islamic Monuments of Al-Haram Al-Sharif: An Iconographic Study*. Jerusalem: The Hebrew University.

Schefer, C., trans. 1970. *Sefer Nameh: Relation due Voyage de Nassiri Khosrau*. Amsterdam: Philo Press.

Shoemaker, S. 2018. *The Apocalypse of Empire: Imperial Eschatology in Late Antiquity and Early Islam*. Philadelphia: University of Pennsylvania Press.

St. Laurent, B. and I. Awwad. 2014. "Archaeology and Preservation in Early Islamic Jerusalem: Revealing the 7th Century Mosque on the Haram Al-Sharif," in R.A. Stucky et al. (eds.) *Proceedings of the 9th International Congress on the Archaeology of the Ancient Near East*, vol. 2, 441-54. Wiesbaden: Harrassowitz Verlag.

Thackston, W.M., trans., 1986. *Naser-e Khosraw's Book of Travels (Safarnama)*. Albany, New York: State University of New York Press.

Watt, W.M and M.V. McDonald, trans. 1988. *The History of al-Tabari, vol. 6: Muhammad at Mecca*. Albany: The State University of New York Press.

Wilkinson, J. 1977. *Jerusalem Pilgrims Before the Crusades*. Jerusalem: Ariel Publishing House.

Wilkinson, J. 1999. *Egeria's Travels*. Warminster, England: Aris & Phillips.

Al-Yaqubi (Ahmad b. Abi Wadih). 1960. *Ta'rikh*. Beirut.

Yarnold, E. 2000. *Cyril of Jerusalem*. London and New York: Routledge.

12

JERUSALEM AGENTS: ARMENIAN AND GEORGIAN PILGRIMAGE TO BYZANTINE PALESTINE

YANA TCHEKHANOVETS

The earliest monastic presence of Armenians and Georgians in the Holy Land dates to the fifth century, and is associated with the names of the Armenian Euthymius the Great (ca. 377-473 CE), native of Melitene in Armenia Minor, and Peter the Iberian (ca. 411-91 CE), Georgian by birth. Both came to the Holy Land as pilgrims, and soon became key figures of Palestinian monasticism, although their role was never restricted to the national communities. Archaeology offers similar dates for the beginning of Armenian and Georgian activity in the Holy Places, and recovering the remains of rural and urban monastic complexes, pilgrim hostels and funerary chapels.[1]

Identifying 'nationally affiliated' sites, and distinguishing them from other ancient ecclesiastical complexes, has always been a problematic issue. The archaeological approach to the problem is usually one-dimensional, focused on one aspect of identity—civic, ethnic, cultural or religious—while in reality the identity can be much more fluid.[2] The great majority of the international monastic community of the Holy Land spoke and prayed in Greek. The exceptions were a few Armenian and Georgian monasteries where, according to historical sources, the liturgy was celebrated in their own language (*V. Theodosii* 18, 45-46; *The Typikon of the Great Laura*, 4).[3] Most of the Armenian and Georgian monks were merely residents in a large multi-ethnic Greek-speaking community, and only sometimes organised their own, ethnic monasteries. Their traces can only be found in Byzantine sources when the writer found it necessary to emphasise the nationality of the hero: 'Armenian', 'Iberian', 'Lazic' or 'Bessoi'.[4]

---

1   For the Armenian community, see Dmitrevsky 1885 [2006]; Schick and Bliss 1894, 253-59; Amit and Wolf 2000; Stone and Amit 1997; Stone 2002a; Stone et al. 2011. For the Georgian community, see Iliffe 1935; Landau 1953; Landau and Avi Yonah 1957; Corbo 1955; Seligman 2015.
2   Hodos 2010, and the large bibliography therein; see also Bitton-Ashkelony 2010.
3   Theodore of Petra, *V. Theodosii* 18, 45-46: Usener 1890 [1975]; Festugière 1963 *III/3*, 81-160; *The Typikon of the Great Laura*, 4: Kurtz 1894; Di Segni in Patrich 1995, 255-75.
4   The word 'Armenia' in the early Byzantine texts may be equally used for Caucasian Armenia or

To demonstrate the presence of a foreign group, at least of temporary nature (short-term visit, pilgrimage, etc.), through archaeological remains, scholars should look for artifacts of the relevant foreign origin—in our case, Caucasian. So far, no artifacts of Caucasian origin have been discovered in the Holy Land—and this includes even numismatic material. As it is, the present-day scholar can count only on the discovery of the inscriptions written in national languages.[5] Indeed, a large number of such inscriptions have been discovered, forming an impressive corpus of dedicational and burial texts.[6]

Pilgrim Graffiti of the Caucasian Christians

The same epigraphic criterion is applicable to the archaeology of pilgrimage. So far, the sole material traces of pilgrimage from the Caucasus are graffiti left by pilgrims, mainly in the holy sites. Graffiti, an unofficial form of interaction with sacred space, is known from ancient times as a form of physical manifestation of personal encounters with the holy site.[7] Graffiti inscriptions are rarely found in a well dated archaeological context, although it happens occasionally, when a venerated structure is sealed under a later, usually more monumental edifice.[8] More often, graffiti are found on open surfaces in the venerated sites, and the generations of writings can only be distinguished on paleographic grounds. Such a dating will always be problematic, because of our limited understanding of the early stages of development of the Armenian and Georgian scripts, and because the writing process itself is complicated by the choice of location and surface, and the limitations of the writer: their writing skills, health condition, fatigue, etc.[9]

The graffiti left by the Armenian and Georgian pilgrims were discovered in Jerusalem, Nazareth and the Sinai (Fig. 1). Archaeologically dated inscriptions were preserved *in situ* in Nazareth. The graffiti from Jerusalem represent more complex cases: they come from well dated contexts, but were all relocated, and were not discovered in their original surroundings.

Graffiti from Jerusalem

Ancient pilgrims' inscriptions dated to the first millennium CE were discovered in two sites in the Holy City, in its western and southern areas. During the salvage excavations of the Israel Antiquities Authority in Mamilla neighborhood, just to the west of Jaffa Gate and the Old city walls, a large extramural commercial quarter of Byzantine Jerusalem

---

for Militene in Asia Minor. For the different names used for Georgians in the Byzantine texts, see Van Elverdinghe 2014.

5   However, some Armenian and Georgian sites were adorned with inscriptions written in Greek, and this issue of linguistic preferences is not entirely clear to us. See the updated *CIIP*, esp. vol. I/2 (2012), with various Greek entries by L. Di Segni.

6   See *CIIP*, esp. vol. I/2, with various Armenian entries, published by M.E. Stone; the Georgian, by the author.

7   Baird and Taylor 2012.

8   Yasin 2015, 39.

9   Stone 1982, 11-17.

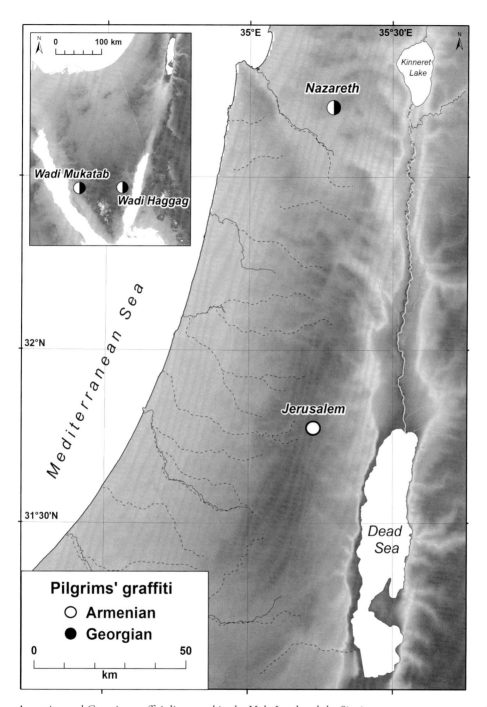

Armenian and Georgian graffiti discovered in the Holy Land and the Sinai.

Fig. 1.

was discovered, combining various pilgrims' facilities—a hostel, a bathhouse, a chapel and lanes of shops.[10] The Armenian graffito was found on the beaten earth floor of the commercial lane running from Jaffa Gate westwards. It is incised on a slab of a hard sort of *pavonazetto* marble. Paleographically, the graffito was dated to the sixth–seventh centuries: "Lord, have mercy upon Tiratur and Holy Resurrection, remember…"[11]

Recently, two Armenian graffiti were discovered in the salvage excavations of the IAA at Givati Parking Lot, immediately to the south of the city walls. The first is incised on a fragment of a marble chancel screen panel, and contains only a name: Hakob. The slab was incorporated in a later wall dated to the Abbasid period.[12] Clearly, the stone was inscribed by a pilgrim named Hakob (Jacob), when it was still in its original place, in one of the churches of the Byzantine/Early Islamic period, possibly in the nearby church by the Pool of Siloam.[13] The poor preservation of the inscription allows no dating more precise than pre-eighth century.

The second inscription from Givati is incised on a large lime flagstone slab (Fig. 2). This one also contains a name: Karapet—an Armenian equivalent for Prodromos. Based on paleographic criteria, the inscription should be dated to the tenth century. The archaeological context of the find is of little help: the stone was discovered in fill, containing mixed and even some modern finds.[14]

Armenian and Georgian graffiti were found in the Nativity Church in Bethlehem and in the Holy Sepulchre in Jerusalem. However, they should be dated to later periods, mostly to the 14th–17th centuries. The absence of earlier inscriptions in the major holy sites—Jerusalem and Bethlehem—can only be explained by random preservation. Still, it is astonishing how soon after the adoption of Christianity Armenians and Georgians began to go on pilgrimage to the Holy Places. At this very early stage, they succeeded in reaching even the most distant sanctuaries, which were not always part of the standard pilgrimage route. Surprisingly, the earliest Armenian and Georgian graffiti were preserved in these distant places—Nazareth and the Sinai.

Graffiti from Nazareth
During the excavations that were carried out by Franciscan Fathers at the traditional place of the Annunciation, the remains of an ancient edifice were discovered, under the remains of the Byzantine church.[15] On a thick coat of plaster that covered various architectural elements of this early construction, a large number of pilgrim graffiti in various languages were found (Fig. 3). Today, after much scientific discussion, we may securely date this early structure and its inscriptions to the mid-fifth century.[16]

---

10   Reich and Shukron 2002; Maeir 2000.
11   Stone 2012, CIIP I/2, no. 810A.
12   Stone, Ben Ami and Tchekhanovets 2016-17.
13   Bliss and Dickie 1898, Pl. XVIII.
14   Stone, Ben Ami and Tchekhanovets 2014.
15   Bagatti 1969; Corbo 1987, 333-48; and contra: Taylor 1993, 221-67.
16   Taylor 1993, 239-66.

The Armenian graffito of Karapet, Givati excavations, Jerusalem. Photo by C. Amit. Courtesy of the Israel Antiquities Authority.

Fig. 2.

Most of inscriptions are barely legible.[17] Only one Georgian inscription can be safely deciphered: "Lord, have mercy on Giorgi."[18] The three other inscriptions are fragmentary, consist of few letters and cannot be safely read. The same is true of the Armenian inscription. Only a few names can be securely deciphered, among them Anania and Babgen.[19] It seems those two left their marks together on the same rock on the Sinai,[20] and may even have travelled together, and the uniformity of the handwriting in the two inscriptions is remarkable.[21]

The importance of the Nazareth graffiti for the study of Armenian and Georgian script development is immense: in practice, they represent one of the oldest datable examples of Armenian and Georgian writing.[22] Both alphabets belong to the well-known category of the so-called "Christian scripts", created soon after the conversion,

---

17   Stone, van Lint and Nazarjan 1996-97; Aleksidze 2000.
18   Ibid., 21.
19   Stone 1990-91, N Arm 1 and N Arm 2.
20   Stone 1982, H Arm 26, H Arm 65.
21   Stone 1990-91.
22   Ibid.

Fig. 3.

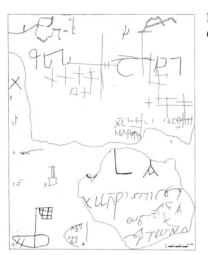

Nazareth, Greek, Armenian and Georgian graffiti. Courtesy of Studium Biblicum Franciscanum.

in the early fifth century, for translation of the Holy Scriptures and liturgical texts into the native languages.[23] The most ancient lapidary inscriptions in Armenian *erkatagir* script are known from St. Sarkis church in Tekor and from St. Hripsime church, in Armenia,[24] and the earliest Georgian *asomtavruli* inscription is from the Sioni church in Bolnisi, Georgia;[25] both are dated to the late fifth century. The finding of the inscriptions in Nazareth, so far away from home, and so soon after the appearance of the scripts themselves, is remarkable.

Graffiti from the Sinai

The mountainous desert of the Sinai became a Christian holy site at a very early stage. The increasing wave of pilgrims visiting Sinai reached its peak during the sixth and the seventh centuries, with particularly large groups of Armenians, consisting of several hundred each.[26] A systematic study of the non-Greek graffiti was carried out by the Rock Inscriptions and Graffiti Project led by M.E. Stone of the Hebrew University of Jerusalem.[27] Dozens of graffiti were left by pilgrims on their way to the sanctuaries of Sinai or on the way back, and in the vicinity of the holy sites: Mount Sinai and the Monastery of St. Catherine. Given the total absence of any dated archaeological context for the Sinaitic inscriptions, only paleographic criteria are relevant in establishing their chronology.[28]

---

23 Gamkrelidze 1989; for an up-to-date discussion on the creation of Caucasian alphabets, see Seibt and Preiser-Kapeller 2011; for the development of Armenian epigraphy, see Stone 2002b; for Georgian: Fähnrich 2013.
24 Orbeli 1914.
25 Silogava 1994.
26 Stone 1982, 27-31.
27 For the project, see Stone 2017. The project database is available online: http://rockinscriptions.huji.ac.il/. The Georgian inscriptions were published by M. van Esbroeck, 1982.
28 Stone 1982, 11-17.

Sinai, Georgian pilgrim's graffiti. Courtesy of M.E. Stone and Rock Inscriptions and Graffiti Project.

Fig. 4.

The content of Caucasian pilgrim inscriptions is no different from the standard graffiti repertoire. Most inscriptions contain only the name—in two cases, female. Others include a request for divine mercy: "O Christ, have mercy on …" or "O Lord, have mercy …", or supplication to the Holy Place: "Holy Sinai, have mercy on me, o holy!" (Fig. 4)[29] Names usually appear without titles and ranks. Only in two cases do the writers mention their clerical position: the Georgian "Basili Džabaris-dze, Your monk",[30] and the Armenian "Yohnik the hegumen".[31]

A few of the Armenian inscriptions stand out. One, possibly dated to the fifth century, declares: "I circumvented Moses!"— probably written by a pilgrim on his way back from Mount Sinai.[32] Another graffito of the eleventh century asks for divine mercy "for the camel and the guide".[33]

The pilgrimage movement from the Caucasus region continued far after the Abbasid period, and did not stop until the Crusades and beyond. Recently, a missing link between the sanctuaries of Palestine and Sinai came to light, when a fragmentary Armenian graffito was discovered in the apse of the Byzantine Southern Church of Shivta,

29 Ibid.
30 van Esbroeck 1982, M Georg 2.
31 Stone 1982, H Arm 61.
32 Stone 1982, H Arm 71.
33 Stone 1982, S Arm 9.

in the Negev desert.³⁴ The location of the graffito and its paleographic analysis allows us to date it to the ninth to eleventh centuries, after the abandonment of the site, and testifies to the continuous tradition of Christian pilgrimage, connecting Palestine with the sanctuaries of the Sinai.

The Book Traffic

In the last two decades, the close connection between the Caucasus and the Holy Land and its reflection in the architecture and iconography of Georgia and Armenia became a subject of extensive research. At least in the Georgian case, this connection is now well established. Pilgrims returning from the Holy Land brought back with them manuscripts that were produced in the Palestinian and Sinaitic scriptoria.³⁵ Given the size of the Georgian community in the Holy Land, their consumption of manuscripts would have been relatively modest. Numerous copies of a limited number of works indicate therefore an intention of distributing these manuscripts. Apparently, the manuscripts of Palestinian and Sinaitic scriptoria were translated and copied specifically for distribution among the monasteries and churches in Georgia, and were sent there with pilgrims returning back home.³⁶ It was only natural that the highly educated Georgian monks living in the Holy Land monasteries, the most important cultural centre of Christendom, would take upon themselves the burden of translating, composing and copying the church literature for their homeland's needs. Various manuscripts were probably distributed all over the country, but survived only in the isolated region of Svaneti, which never surrendered to foreign occupation and turned into a veritable Christian treasury. In the hour of danger, during the endless invasions, first Arab, then Persian and Ottoman, the population of the plains transferred the most precious relics to the mountains to save them from destruction.³⁷

---

34 Tchekhanovets, Tepper and Bar-Oz 2017.
35 Ancient Georgian manuscripts produced by the Palestinian and Sinaitic scriptoria were catalogued by a number of expeditions working in the region since the last third of the 19th century, and the bibliography on this subject is immense. For an overview, see Mgaloblishvili 2001; Pataridze 2015.
36 The colophon of the Lahili Gospel (14th century) describes the delivery: "In the name of the Lord, in the Church of the Resurrection, near the Grave of Christ, I, the son of Ioane Kstskhiani, the sinner and the ignorant scribe, copied these Holy Gospels and sacrificed them to Svaneti's Holy Archangel of Mukheri (…) I am sending [the book] by the hand of the deacon of Pkhotleri. May God forgive him his sins as well. My brother Michael, I have wrapped [the Gospels] in canvas; keep it as your burial garment." Kekelia et al. 2018, 58. The catalogue of manuscripts copied outside Georgia contains numerous examples of Palestinian books, preserved in Georgian museums: Kekelia et al. 2018, 28-63. See also Jojua 2016; 2017.
37 Pataridze 2015, 186.

The "New Jerusalems"

The work of the Sabaite and Sinaitic Georgian literary schools had a great influence on the development of Georgian liturgy, language and literature. This influence can be explained by the great, almost absolute authority of the word coming from the Church of Jerusalem. The early historical evidence firmly fixes the tradition of the Jerusalemite origins of the Armenian and Georgian Churches. Although legendary, these ancestral traditions contribute to the self-image of the Armenians and Georgians as the custodians of Christianity.[38] The first steps of Armenian and Georgian national literature were closely related to the translation of the Holy Scriptures and of the liturgical books, adopted in Jerusalem.

Due to the stationary character of the Jerusalem liturgy, closely connected to the particular sites of the Holy City, its assimilation on Caucasian soil had a most remarkable impact on the creation of the sacred landscape, causing the appearance of the so-called "New Jerusalems". In the last two decades, the creation of new Christian landscapes imitating the image of the celestial Jerusalem—and often copying the terrestrial one—has become a subject of extensive research.[39]

Georgia

In the Caucasus, the most striking manifestation of "New Jerusalem" is in Georgia. According to Kekelidze, the goal of recreating the layout of the holy places of Jerusalem was to emphasise the Jerusalemite origins of the Georgian Church, and was stimulated mainly by liturgical needs: all the major sites around which the Jerusalem liturgy was constructed were recreated in Mtskheta, the capital of the ancient Georgian kingdom of Kartli, and in its liturgy (Fig. 5).[40]

The first sacred sites of the newly Christianised Georgian kingdom copied the Palestinian sanctuaries and carried corresponding names: Calvary, the Tomb of Christ, Gethsemane, Zion, Bethlehem, Tabor, Holy of Holies. The creation of the new Christianised landscape took centuries, but the first sites were established in the first years of Christianisation.[41]

Prior to the mass baptism of the royal family and the people of Georgia, a big wooden cross was erected above the capital city of Mtskheta, on a high hill to its east.[42] This visual symbol of Christian triumph can be associated with the erection of the True Cross on the top of Calvary hill in Jerusalem. In the seventh century, a stone church, the Jvari ("The Cross"), was erected at the very place where the wooden cross had stood. In the

---

38   Stone 2015.
39   Biddle 1999; Lidov 2009; Beliaev 2013; Kühnel, Noga-Banai and Vorholt 2014; Bartal and Vorholt 2015.
40   Kekelidze 1957, 362-63.
41   Chkhartishvili 2006; Mgaloblishvili 2014.
42   *Moktsevai Kartlisai* XIV. 54: Abuladze 1963; Lerner 2004.

Fig. 5. The 'New Jerusalem' in Mtskheta, Georgia, with the Svetitskhoveli Church in the centre. Photo by the author.

centre of the cross-shaped church, on a high pedestal, a new cross carved of stone was installed, representing the Golgotha.[43]

The first church of Georgia, in its capital city Mtskheta, was erected right in the centre of the city, in the royal garden. It was built of stone, with cedar roof and pillars.[44] Miraculously, one of the cedar pillars remained suspended in the air (*Moktsevai Kartlisai* X, 48-49), giving the name to the newly erected edifice: *Svetitskhoveli* ('Life-Giving Pillar'). According to Church tradition, the place where the Life-Giving Pillar stood was the burial place of the garment of Christ, brought from Jerusalem (*Moktsevai Kartlisai* VII, 43). First, the church was called the Holy of Holies, or the Place of Purest Purity. This place of special purity and devotion was to be the image of the Holy of Holies of the Jerusalem Temple, the place of God's presence or—in its Christian incarnation—the Place of the Resurrection. Later on, probably during the reign of King Vakhtang Gorgasali (446-502), the church received additional names: "Mother of All Churches", and *Sioni*, after the basilica of Holy Sion in Jerusalem, and was consecrated to the Twelve Apostles.[45]

It is worth noting that the early symbols found in Mtskheta were later repeated in ecclesiastical architecture all over Georgia. Accordingly, numerous churches were constructed with a big stone cross as the centre of the architectural composition;[46] at least twenty-six churches called *Sioni* appeared in different parts of the country;[47] and in memory of the royal garden of Mtskheta, gardens were established around the church edifices. In this way, the pattern of Jerusalem, celestial and terrestrial, was reproduced in hundreds of copies throughout the territory of the Georgian kingdom.

Armenia
The historical sources give no clues to the existence of similar building projects in Armenia. However, architectural analysis of certain early church structures may indicate attempts to embody the "New Jerusalem" in ecclesiastical architecture. This tendency, according to Kazaryan, can be followed in the construction projects of the Catholicos Komitas Akhtsetsi (613-628), the builder of St. Hripsime church (618) and the Etchmiadzin cathedral (620).[48] It seems that the dome-structure of the two churches—an umbrella-shaped pointed roof—may imitate the aedicule over the Tomb of Christ, and at the same time symbolise the celestial Jerusalem. The construction of the churches should be regarded as a reaction to the tragic events in the Holy Land—the sack of Jerusalem by the Sassanids and the capture of the Holy Cross. The church of Zvartnotz is another example, clearly showing the transfer of Palestinian architectural forms to the Armenian landscape.

---

43   Chubinashvili 1948; Amiranishvili 1963, 103-8; see also Sikharulidze and Skhirtladze 2015.
44   Probably, the reminiscence of Solomon's Temple: see Stone 2015.
45   Mgaloblishvili and Gagoshidze 1998, 42-43.
46   For numerous examples, see Machabeli 2008a; Djavakhishvili 2014; Dadiani 2017.
47   To mention only the most famous Sioni churches: in Bolnisi, Tbilisi, and Atheni. See also Gagoshidze 2014.
48   Kazaryan 2009.

Erected in 643-650 by the Catholicos Nerses the Builder, the church copied, with some local accents, the Rotonda of Anastasis. Certain allusions to Celestial Jerusalem can also be followed in the reliefs decorating the cathedral of Zvartnotz, representing the Garden of Eden with vine whips and pomegranates, together with the portraits of righteous builders of the Armenian Church, its kings and saints.[49] Here again, the project can be regarded as a reaction to the Arab invasion of the Holy Land, and an Armenian attempt to create the "New Jerusalem" close by. This theory may seem convincing, when the long struggle of the Georgians and Armenians for their faith and their self-image as protectors of Christianity is considered.

Holy Sepulchre Models

Of note is a group of the Caucasian architectural models of the Tomb of Christ, often serving as pedestals for the cross stelae.[50] Similar to the well-known western models, the very first Caucasian examples of this type were produced by eyewitnesses, or copied from the eulogia brought from Palestine, and therefore may have a particular significance for the reconstruction of the original shrine in Jerusalem.[51] Even the schematic compositions preserve some elements of the aedicule, which are easy recognisable: the podium, the winding columns and even the stylised presentation of the shell decoration. The lower registers of the cross stelae are often decorated with reliefs representing the main scenes of the Christological cycle: Annunciation, Nativity, Baptism, Entry to Jerusalem, Crucifixion—subjects that are typical of Palestinian pilgrimage art.[52] The socket in the top is made to hold a cross.

Liturgical Objects

Machabeli proposed[53] that the first Palestinian liturgical objects—icons, crosses, censers and other paraphernalia—may have been brought to Georgia by the 'Syrian Fathers', the founders of monastic life in the country.[54] Apart from their practical function, the liturgical objects came with time to be regarded as precious relics from the Holy Land and became a model for local masters.[55] Whatever the exact circumstances, those responsible for the transfer of the liturgical objects could be, indeed, the monks, whose mobility is well attested by historical sources that discuss the pilgrimages. To support this theory, a unique Georgian text of the tenth century that was discovered in the collection

---

49　Hakobian 2009.
50　Machabeli 2008a; Djavakhishvili 2014; Hakobian 2010.
51　See Biddle 1999, 15-28, not including the Caucasian examples.
52　Machabeli 2008b, 122-23.
53　Machabeli 2008 b.
54　For 'Syrian Fathers', see Martin-Hisard 1985-86; Haas 2009; Matitashvili 2018; for Georgian–Syrian cultural interaction, see Loosley Leeming 2018.
55　Machabeli 2008b, 121.

of St. Catherine's Monastery in the Sinai, should be mentioned. It is a long colophon to the tenth-century manuscript N Sin-50,[56] listing in few paragraphs the liturgical objects and manuscripts of the Zedazeni and Gareji monasteries in Georgia, testifying to the traffic of liturgical goods between Georgia and the Holy Land.[57]

The study of the Palestinian 'objects on the move' is still in its infancy. To date, the only pilgrimage souvenir known from Georgia is of Syrian origin. It is a silver pilgrim token representing St. Symeon Stylite the Younger, dated to the tenth–eleventh centuries, which was discovered during the excavations in the Gareji monastery complex in Georgia.[58] However, a large group of decorated bronze censers of Syro-Palestinian origin dated to the sixth–seventh centuries were preserved in the Svaneti region, and are kept today in the National Museum of Georgia in Tbilisi and its branch in Mestia.[59] The original location of the censers is unknown: like the ancient manuscripts, they were probably removed to Svaneti from the central churches of the country and were preserved by the locals as 'Christian treasures'.

Presumably, similar objects that originated in the Palestinian region may be discovered in archaeological excavations of sites of important Christian centres in Georgia, and possibly Armenia. To check this hypothesis, a brief survey of the collections of the National Museum of Georgia in Tbilisi was undertaken. Preliminary searches revealed a group of three sixth–seventh-century elaborate bronze lamps of Syro-Palestinian origin, which were discovered in the excavations of the Byzantine basilical complex in Nekresi, and a bronze censer from the excavations in Urbnisi, dated to the same period. This one has an exact parallel in the excavated Nestorian hermitage in Jericho,[60] and in a number of other Palestinian sites. It seems that further systematic study of the subject may provide us with the most interesting results, and reveal the material signs of the Armenian and Georgian pilgrimage to the Byzantine Palestine far beyond the borders of the Holy Land itself.

Acknowledgements

This study is based on the relevant parts of my PhD dissertation (Institute of Archaeology of the Hebrew University of Jerusalem, 2016). I am indebted to Michael E. Stone of the Hebrew University, whose pioneering studies of the Armenian presence in the Holy Land became the most solid foundation for the present-day archaeological research of the Caucasian communities in Byzantine Palestine. My deepest gratitude should be

---

56 Georgian manuscript N Sin-50, part of the "new collection" of the monastery, contains the texts of *Moktsevai Kartlisai* chronicle and a few hagiographic compositions. For the manuscript, see Aleksidze 2001a. A few paragraphs discussed here are not related to the texts and are inserted between the *Acts and Mircales of Ioanne Zedazneli* and *The Martyrdom of Abibos Nekreseli*.
57 Aleksidze 2001b, see also Kldiashvili 2001.
58 Skhirtladze 1995.
59 Machabeli 1982.
60 Baramki and Stephan 1935, Fig. 1.

expressed to late Erekle Koridze and Akaki Gogichaisvili, the curators of the archaeological collection of the National Museum of Georgia, for their generous help, and to the art historian Kitty Machabeli of G. Chubinashvili National Research Center for Georgian Art History and Heritage Preservation, for her kind consultation. Thanks are also due to the external readers of this paper for their valuable comments.

Bibliography

Abuladze, I. (ed.) 1963. "Moktsevai Kartlisai," in *Ancient Georgian Agiographic Literature*, vol. 1. Tbilisi: Metsniereba (Georgian).

Aleksidze, Z. 2000. "Louvre, Mt. Sinai, Nazareth: Epigraphic Etudes." Μνήμη 1, 10-25 (Georgian).

Aleksidze, Z. (ed.) 2001a. *Le nouveau manuscrit géorgien sinaïtique N SIN 50*. Trans. J.P. Mahé. Lovain: Peeters.

Aleksidze, Z. 2001b. "From Garedja to Mount Sinai: Unknown Material on the Monastic Complex from the Newly Discovered Collection of Georgian Manuscripts on Sinai," in Z. Skhirtladze (ed.) *Desert Monasticism: Gareja and the Christian East. Papers from the International Symposium; Tbilisi University, September 2000*, 48-56 (Georgian, English summary 57-62). Tbilisi: Gareja Study Center.

Amiranishvili, S. 1963. *Istoriya gruzinskogo iskusstva* [*History of Georgian Art*]. Moscow: Iskusstvo.

Amit, D. and S. Wolf. 2000. "An Armenian Monastery in the Morasha Neighborhood," in H. Geva (ed.) *Ancient Jerusalem Revealed*, 293-98. Jerusalem: Israel Exploration Society.

Bagatti, B. 1969. *Excavations in Nazareth*, Vol. I. Jerusalem: Studium Biblicum Franciscanum.

Baird J.A. and C. Taylor (eds.) 2012. *Ancient Graffiti in Context*. New York: Routledge.

Baramki, D.C. and S.H. Stephan. 1935. "A Nestorian Hermitage between Jericho and the Jordan." *Quarterly of the Department of Antiquities in Palestine* 4, 81-86.

Bartal, R. and H. Vorholt (eds.) 2015. *Between Jerusalem and Europe. Essays in Honor of Bianca Kühnel*. Leiden: Brill.

Beliaev, L.A. 2013. "New Jerusalem Resurrection Monastery as an archaeological monument of the early New Time." *Rossiiskaya Arkheologiya* 1, 30-41 (Russian).

Biddle, M. 1999. *The Tomb of Christ*. Stroud: Sutton Publishing.

Bitton-Ashkelony, B. 2010. "Territory, Anti-Intellectual Attitude, and Identity Formation in Late Antique Palestinian Monastic Communities." *Religion & Theology* 17, 244-67.

Bliss, F.J. and A.C. Dickie, 1898. *Excavations in Jerusalem, 1849-1897*. London: Palestine Exploration Fund.

Chkhartishvili, M. 2006. "Mtsketa as a New Jerusalem: Hierotopy of the *Life of St. Nino*," in A. Lidov (ed.) *New Jerusalems. Hierotopy and Iconography of Sacred Spaces*, 131-49 (Russian, English summary, 149-50). Moscow: Indrik.

Chubinashvili, N.G. 1948. *Pamyatniki tipa Jvari* [*Monuments of the Jvari type*]. Tbilisi: Academy of Sciences Press (Russian, French summary 199-210).

CIIP – *Corpus Inscriptionum Iudaeae/Palaestinae (CIIP)*, Vol. I/2: Jerusalem. Part 2, edited by H.M. Cotton, L. Di Segni, W. Eck et al., 705-1120. Berlin and Boston: De Gruyter.

Corbo, V. 1955. "Monastero di Bir El-Qutt," in *Gli scavi di Khirbet Siyar El-Ghanam (Campo del pastori) e i monastri dei dintorni*, 110-39. Jerusalem: Studium Biblicum Franciscanum.

Corbo, V. 1987. "La chiesa-sinagoga dell'Annunziato a Nazaret." *Liber Annuus* 37, 333-48.

Dadiani, T. 2017. "High Crosses," in D. Tumanishvili (ed.) *Medieval Georgian Sculpture*, 44-89. Tbilisi: George Chubinashvili National Research Centre for Georgian Art History and Heritage Preservation.

Djavakhishvili, G. 2014. *Early Medieval Small-Scale Sculpture of Georgia (Relief Sculpture on the Steles of the end of 5th – early 8th cc)*. Tbilisi: Meridiani (Georgian, English summary 94-101).

Dmitrevsky, S.M. 1885 [2006] *Russian Excavations on Mount of Olives*. Moscow: Indrik (Russian).

Fähnrich, H. 2013. *Die ältesten georgischen Inschriften*. Leiden and Boston: Brill.

Festugière, A.-J. 1962-63 *Les Moines d'Orient*. T. III/1-3. Paris: Les Édition du Cerf.

Gagoshidze, G. 2014. "Jerusalem in Medieval Georgian Art," in B. Kühnel, G. Noga-Banai and H. Vorholt (eds.) *Visual Constructs of Jerusalem*, 133-38. Turnhout: Brepols.

Gamkrelidze, T.V. 1989. *Alphabetic Writing and the Old Georgian Script. A Typology and Provenience of Alphabetic Writing Systems*. Tbilisi: Tbilisi State University Press (Russian).

Haas, C. 2009. "Ioane Zedazneli: A Georgian Saint in the Syrian Ascetical Tradition," in P. Skinner, D. Tumanishvili and A. Shanshiashvili (eds.) *Vakhtang Beridze 1st International Symposium of Georgian Culture. Georgian Art in the Context of European and Asian Cultures, June 21-29, 2008, Georgia*, 95-100. Tbilisi: Georgian Arts and Culture Center.

Hakobian, Z. 2009. "Symbolical image of Celestial Jerusalem in the reliefs of Zvartnotz." *Iskusstvo Khristianskogo Mira* 11, 101-9 (Russian).

Hakobian, Z. 2010. "Stellae of Armenia and Georgia. To the problem of cultural communion in the Early Christian period." *Lraber asarakan gitutiunneri* 627/628, 403-18 (Russian).

Hodos, T. 2010. "Local and Global Perspectives in the Study of Social and Cultural Identities," in S. Hales and T. Hodos (eds.) *Material Culture and Social Identities in the Ancient World*, 3-31. Cambridge: Cambridge University Press.

Iliffe, J.H. 1935. "Cemeteries and 'Monastery' at the Y.M.C.A., Jerusalem." *Quarterly of the Department of Antiquities in Palestine* 4, 70-80.

Jojua, T. 2016. "Unknown Testaments, Commemorative Agapes and Colophons from the XII-Century Synaxarion (H886)." *The Proceedings of the Institute of History and Ethnology* 14-15, 145-218 (Georgian, English summary 218).

Jojua, T. 2017. "Georgian Pilgrims in the Holy Land: Gedeon Machavariani (second half of the 16th century)." *Saistorio Krebuli* 6, 128-47 (Georgian, English summary 146-47).

Kazaryan, A. 2009. "'New Jerusalem' in the concepts of space and architectural forms of Medieval Armenia," in Lidov 2009, 520-43 (Russian).

Kekelia, V., N. Mirotadze, T. Otkhmezuri and D. Chitunashvili. 2018. *Georgian Manuscripts Copied Abroad in Libraries and Museums of Georgia*. Tbilisi: Korneli Kekelidze Georgian National Centre of Manuscripts.

Kekelidze, K. 1957. "To the Question of Jerusalemite origins of the Georgian Church." *Etudebi dzveli kartuli literaturis istoriidan*, vol. IV, 358-63 (Russian).

Kldiashvili, D. 2001. "Gareja and Pilgrimage in the Early Georgian Sources," in Z. Skhirtladze, (ed.) *Desert Monasticism: Gareja and the Christian East. Papers from the International Symposium; Tbilisi University, September 2000*, 77-97 (Georgian, English summary 98-101). Tbilisi: Gareja Study Center.

Kühnel, B., G. Noga-Banai and H. Vorholt (eds.) 2014. *Visual Constructs of Jerusalem*. Turnhout: Brepols.

Kurtz, E. 1894. "A.Dmitrievskij, 'Die klosterregeln des hl. Sabbas'." *Byzantinische Zeitschrift* 3, 167-70.

Landau, J. 1953. "Beit Safafa." *Israel Exploration Journal* 3, 266.

Landau, J. and M. Avi Yonah, 1957. "Excavations of the Family Vault near Beit Safafa." *Alon* 5-6, 40-43 (Hebrew).

Lerner, C. 2014. *The Wellspring of Georgian Historiography. The Early Medieval Historical Chronicle "The Conversion of K'art'li" and "The Life of St. Nino"*. London: Bennett and Bloom.

Lidov, A. (ed.) 2009. *New Jerusalems. Hierotopy and Iconography of Sacred Spaces*. Moscow: Indrik.

Loosley Leeming, E. 2018. *Architecture and Asceticism: Cultural Interaction between Syria and Georgia in Late Antiquity*. Leiden and Boston: Brill.

Machabeli, K. 1982. *Trésor d'art en Svanetie*. Tbilisi: Metsniereba (Georgian, Russian summary, 182-98; French summary, 199-206).

Machabeli, K. 2008a. *Early Medieval Georgian Stone Crosses*. Tbilisi: Chubinashvili National Research Center.

Machabeli, K. 2008b. "Palestinian Tradition and Early Medieval Georgian Plastic Art." *Bulletin of the Georgian Academy of Sciences* 2.1, 121-28.

Maeir, A. 2000. "The Excavations in Mamilla, Jerusalem, Phase I (1989)," in H. Geva (ed.) *Ancient Jerusalem Revealed*, 299-305. Jerusalem: Israel Exploration Society.

Martin-Hisard, B. 1985-86. "Les 'Treize Saints Pères'. Formation et évolution d'une tradition hagiographique géorgienne (VIe–XIIe siècles)." *Revue des Études Géorgiennes et Caucasiennes* 44, 45, 75-111, 141-68.

Matitashvili, S. 2018. "The Monasteries Founded by the Thirteen Syrian Fatheres: The Rise of Monasticism in Sixth-Century Georgia." *Studies in Late Antiquity* 2/1, 4-39.

Mgaloblishvili, T. 2001. "The Georgian Sabaite (*Sabatsminduri*) Literary School and the Sabatsmindian Version of the Georgian *Mravaltavi* (*Polykephalon*)," in J. Patrich (ed.) *The Sabaite Heritage in the Orthodox Church from the Fifth Century to the Present,* 229-33. Louvain: Peeters.

Mgaloblishvili, T. 2014. "How Mtskheta Turned into the Georgians' New Jerusalem," in B. Kühnel, G. Noga-Banai and H. Vorholt (eds.) *Visual Constructs of Jerusalem*, 59-66. Turnhout: Brepols.

Mgaloblishvili, T. and I. Gagoshidze. 1998. "The Jewish Diaspora and Early Christianity in Georgia," in T. Mgaloblishvili (ed.) *Ancient Christianity in the Caucasus*, 39-58. Richmond: Routledge.

Orbeli, I.A. 1914. "Six Armenian Inscriptions of the 7th–10th cc." *Khristianskii Vostok* III (1), 74-91 (Russian).

Pataridze, T. 2015. "La collection des manuscripts géorgiens sinaïtiques." *Semitica et Classica* 8, 177-86.

Patrich, J. 1995. *Sabas, Leader of Palestinian Monasticism*. Washington: Dumbarton Oaks.

Reich, R. and E. Shukron, 2002. "The Western Extramural Quarter of Byzantine Jerusalem," in M.E. Stone, R. Ervine and N. Stone (eds.), *Armenians in Jerusalem and the Holy Land*, 193-201. Louvain: Peeters.

Sikharulidze, N. and Z. Skhirtladze. 2015. "The Fragment of Stela from the Javri Church of Mtskheta." *Saistoria Krebuli* 5, 325-87 (Georgian, English summary 373-74).

Schick, C. and F.J. Bliss. 1894. "Discovery of a Beautiful Mosaic Pavement with Armenian Inscription, North of Jerusalem." *Palestine Exploration Quarterly* 26, 257-61.

Seibt, W. and J. Preiser-Kapeller (eds.) 2011. *Die Entstehung der kaukasischen Alphabete als kulturhistorisches Phänomen. Referate des Internationalen Symposiums, Wien, 1-4 Dezember 2005*. Vienna: Verlag der Österreichischen Akademie der Wissenschaften.

Seligman, J. 2015. "A Georgian Monastery from the Byzantine Period at Khirbat Umm Leisun, Jerusalem." *Atiqot* 83, 145-80.

Silogava, V.I. 1994. *The Oldest Georgian Inscriptions of Bolnisi*. Tbilisi: Matsniereba (Georgian, Russian and English summary).

Skhirtladze, Z. 1995. "Silver Medallion from Gareji." *Jahrbuch der Österreichenischen Byzantinistik* 45, 277-82.

Stone, M.E. 1982. *Armenian Inscriptions from Sinai*. Cambridge, MA: Harvard University Department of Near Eastern Languages and Civilizations.

Stone, M.E. 1990-91. "Armenian Inscriptions of the Fifth Century from Nazareth." *Revue des Études Arméniennes* 22, 315-22.

Stone, M.E. 2002a. "A Reassessment of the Bird and the Eustathius Mosaics," in M.E. Stone, R. Ervine and N. Stone (eds.) *Armenians in Jerusalem and the Holy Land*, 204-19. Louvain: Peeters.

Stone, M.E. 2002b. "The Development of the Armenian Writing," in M.E. Stone, D. Kouyumjian and H. Lehmann (eds.) *Album of Armenian Paleography*, 77-105. Aarhus: Aarhus University Press.

Stone, M.E. 2015a. "Biblical and Apocryphal Themes in Armenian Culture," in R. Gounelle and B. Mounier (eds.) *La littérature apocryphe chrétienne et les Ecritures juives*, 393-408. Lausanne: Édition du Zèbre.

Stone, M.E. 2015b. "The Cedar in Jewish Antiquity," in M. Geller (ed.) *The Archaeology and Material Culture of the Babylonian Talmud*, 66-82. Leiden and Boston: Brill.

Stone, M.E. 2017. *Uncovering Ancient Footprints: Armenian Inscriptions and the Pilgrimage Routes of the Sinai*. Atlanta: SBL Press.

Stone, M.E. and Amit, D. 1997. "The New Armenian Inscriptions in Jerusalem." *Cathedra* 83, 27-44 (Hebrew).

Stone, M.E., D. Amit, J. Seligman and I. Zilberbod. 2011. "New Armenian Inscription from a Byzantine Monastery on Mt. Scopus, Jerusalem." *Israel Exploration Journal* 61/2, 230-35.

Stone, M.E., D. Ben Ami and Y. Tchekhanovets. 2014. "New Armenian Inscription from the City of David, Jerusalem." *Journal of the Society for Armenian Studies* 23, 145-48.

Stone, M.E., D. Ben Ami and Y. Tchekhanovets. 2016-17. "Armenian Graffito from the City of David, Jerusalem." *Revue des Études Arméniennes* 37, 283-86.

Stone, M.E., T. van Lint and J. Nazarjan, 1996-97. "Further Armenian Inscriptions from Nazareth." *Revue des Études Arméniennes* 26, 321-37.

Taylor, J. 1993. *Christians and the Holy Places: The Myth of Jewish-Christian Origins*. Oxford: Oxford University Press.

Tchekhanovets, Y., Y. Tepper and G. Bar-Oz. 2017. "The Armenian Graffito from the Southern Church of Shivta." *Revue Biblique* 124/3, 446-54.

Usener, H. (ed.) 1890 (repr. 1975). *Der heilige Theodosios: Schriften des Theodoros und Kyrillos*. Leipzig: Teubner.

van Elverdinghe, E. 2014. "Les Géorgiens dans les textes Byzantins jusqu'à l'an mille: approche lexicale." *Byzantion* 84, 433-83.

van Esbroeck, M. 1982. "The Georgian Inscriptions," in Stone 1982, 171-79.

Yasin, A.M. 2015. "Prayers on Site: The Materiality of Devotional Graffiti and the Production of Early Christian Sacred Space," in A. Eastmond (ed.), *Viewing Inscriptions in the Late Antique and Medieval World*, 36-60. Cambridge: Cambridge University Press.

13

THE STRATIFICATION OF MEMORY IN THE DARDANELLES:

FROM TROJAN WAR TO FIRST WORLD WAR PILGRIMAGE IN THE REGION

SARAH MIDFORD

The landscape surrounding the Dardanelles, on the west coast of modern Turkey, has been a locus for pilgrimage for almost 3,000 years (Fig. 1). Pilgrims from ancient Greece and Rome, the Ottoman Empire, Australia and New Zealand have journeyed to the region to encounter memories of heroes and events significant to their respective cultures. Dardanelles pilgrims predominately seek a connection to those who died in legendary battles; heroes viewed as the cultural ancestors of the pilgrims themselves. Hellenic, Roman and Ottoman pilgrims travelled to the Dardanelles as the site of the Trojan War, but more recently, Australians and New Zealanders have made pilgrimage to the region as the site of the First World War (WWI) Gallipoli campaign. The Dardanelles battlefields are both sacrificial landscapes and commemorative monuments, and pilgrimage allows visitors to meaningfully encounter the past.[1] That the Dardanelles battlefields are also gravesites adds to their sacredness and qualifies them as sites for pilgrimage. The landscape is sanctified by those buried in it: heroes with a culturally significant ancestral connection to those who travel to the region. The meaning experienced at the site of conflict is a response to landscape features including gravesites and war memorials, which connect the place being encountered to cultural memory through emotional experience.[2]

Since antiquity, pilgrimage to the Dardanelles has led to a complex stratification of memories in the landscape, not just those of the events that occurred upon it, but also those of the pilgrims who travelled to the site over centuries and performed rituals honouring their cultural ancestors. By focusing on the history of pilgrimage to the region, this chapter elucidates the stratified memories of the Dardanelles. It identifies the interconnectedness of memory, from antiquity to the contemporary, in order to

---

1   Saunders 2003, 8. See also Eade and Katić 2018, 18.
2   Minchin 2012, 76.

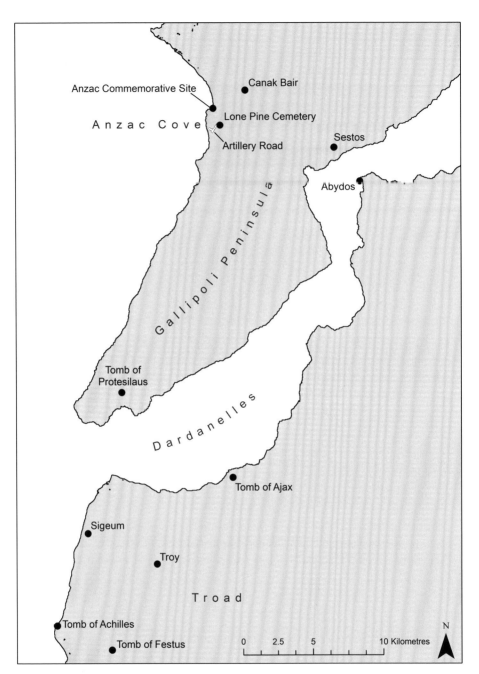

Fig. 1. Map of the Gallipoli Peninsula, the Dardanelles and the Troad by Sarah Midford.

demonstrate that Australian and New Zealand pilgrims perform behaviours reminiscent of those who came before them, and that the multiple layers of memory have always sanctified the Dardanelles landscape, adding to its sacredness and endorsing it as a destination for pilgrimage.

Ancient Greek and Persian Pilgrimage

Since antiquity, knowledge of the Trojan War has been transmitted predominately through Homer's *Iliad*. The epic memorialised the Trojan War and was well known by people from across the ancient Mediterranean world, medieval and modern Europe, and the Middle East. For many, the Trojan War narrative was seen as foundational to their culture, and this has inspired pilgrimage to Troy to connect with the Trojan War narrative as a cultural memory bound to the Dardanelles landscape.

The Trojan War occurred in approximately 1,200 BCE and archaeological evidence indicates that ritual practice commemorating the event at Troy was occurring as early as the ninth century BCE.[3] However, evidence is scant until the seventh century BCE, when tumuli in the landscape surrounding Troy were likely reconfigured as tombs of Trojan War heroes.[4] It was during that century that people looked for evidence of the conflict, upon which they could focus their honour and admiration. This date makes sense when one considers that Homer's *Iliad* is thought to have been composed sometime between the eighth and sixth centuries BCE.[5] From at least the seventh century, it seems, travellers made pilgrimage to this site, and from this point onwards, tombs were monumentalised, and businesses developed to cater for those who came to visit the battlefields and the tombs of both Greek and Trojan fallen heroes. Visits often included ritual and religious observations honouring gods and cultural ancestors in the region, and over time, the tumuli came to be accompanied by shrines.[6] Another reason for the seventh century travel boom is likely the late-seventh-century Athenian colonisation of Sigeum, a town close to Troy and the tumuli of Achilles, Antilochus and Patroclus.[7] This very early Athenian colony gave Greek peoples access to and influence over the region and made travel to the sacred Trojan landscape more accessible to Athenians.

However, the first historical reference to Dardanelles pilgrimage was that of Xerxes, the Persian king who visited Troy on his way to cross the Hellespont and invade Greece in 480 BCE.[8] Xerxes wanted to see the famous ancient city and, while there, spoke

---

3 Scholars are continually revising the date of the Trojan War conflict and the date of Homer's *Iliad*. For a useful table proposing dates for the various historical stages of the archaeological site known as Troy up until the composition of the *Iliad*, see Raaflaub 1998, 386. Joachim Latacz dates a conflict at the archaeological site of Troy that may have been the Trojan War to approximately 1200 BCE (Korfmann, Latacz and Hawkins 2004, 39). In the same article, Korfmann suggests that conflicts with the potential to be 'the Trojan War' date to the thirteenth and early twelfth centuries BCE (41). Rose and Körpe have interpreted structures erected outside late Bronze Age Troy (Troy VI), commonly thought of as Homer's Troy, as being intended for hero cult worship, (2016, 374).

4 There were ten tumuli in the region dedicated to Achilles, Aisyetes, Ajax, Antilochus, Batieia, Hector, Hecuba, Ilus, Patroclus and Protesilaus. Rose and Körpe 2016, 374.

5 Martin West dates the *Iliad* to the second or third quarter of the seventh century BCE (West 1995, 203). There is broad consensus among scholars that the *Iliad* was well known throughout Greece by the second half of the seventh century BCE, (Graziosi and Haubold 2010, 9).

6 Rose and Körpe 2016, 375.

7 Hdt, 5.94ff. Cawkwell 1992, 289.

8 Coleman and Elsner 1995, 6.

about its past with locals. He also observed religious rituals at Troy, making libations to Homeric heroes and sacrificing 1,000 head of cattle to the Trojan goddess Athena, evoking the offerings made to Athena described in the *Iliad*.[9] Xerxes's observation of the site's sacredness honoured and commemorated the heroes of the Trojan War, while also establishing a connection between himself and those he honoured.[10] The Persian king's pilgrimage set a precedent for powerful men to visit the Dardanelles, which, after his visit, embodied *his* memory as well as that of the Trojan War and its heroes.[11]

In 334 BCE, Alexander the Great made Xerxes's journey in reverse, and in doing so, overwrote the Persian king's pilgrimage in the landscape's cultural memory. When Alexander sent his armies across the narrowest point of the Dardanelles, between Sestos and Abydos (the same place Xerxes had crossed his armies in the other direction), to conquer the east, he too made sacrifices at the Temple of Athena, and paid his respects at the tombs of Trojan War heroes.[12]

Legend has it that Alexander slept with a copy of the *Iliad* under his pillow, and modelled himself on the great warrior Achilles, so a particularly important stop on his journey was this hero's tomb. According to his biographers, Alexander exchanged his armour for Trojan War armour preserved in the Sanctuary of Athena, and ran a footrace around the burial mound in honour of the famously 'swift-footed' Achilles.[13] Minchin argues that by wearing ancient armour and emulating Achilles's athleticism in the sacred location of his burial, Alexander was attempting to connect with the hero "by sharing his physical experiences and his emotional responses"; that his physical presence in Troy and his performance of certain rituals was an attempt "to become one with Achilles".[14] His actions elided time to connect the physical and emotional in a sacred place. This deep connection to Achilles could only have been made at a site where the ancient Achaean hero had once been, because landscape is capable of holding cultural memory that be accessed at a later date. As Deleuze explains: "the past and the present do not denote two successive moments, but two elements which coexist: one is the present, which does not cease to pass, and the other is the past, which does not cease to be."[15]

---

9   Hdt, 7.43, Hom., *Il.*, 6.86-98, 269-311.
10 Xerxes was what Elsner and Rutherford have termed a pilgrim *en passant*. That is, he did not make the journey to the site of the Trojan War specifically, but nonetheless took the time to stop, make offerings to the gods, and visit significant places. Elsner and Rutherford 2005, 11, fn. 1. Elsner and Rutherford coined the term from French Egyptologist Jean Yoyotte 1960. Like Xerxes, many travellers to Troy after him were pilgrims *en passant*, visiting because they were in the region rather than as their journey's only objective, including Alexander; see Minchin 2012, 85. Minchin argues that Alexander's pilgrimage is *en passant*, and I am here extending her argument back to Xerxes's pilgrimage; ibid., 85.
11 Ibid., 82.
12 Plut., *Vit. Alex.* 15.4.
13 Arr., *Anab.* 1.110, 7-8; Diod., 17.17.6-7; 17.18.1; Plut., *Vit. Alex.* 15.7.
14 Minchin 2012, 83-84.
15 Deleuze, 1966, 59.

Alexander's pilgrimage and re-enactment, Minchin suggests, "shapes his identity as a great Greek leader in the tradition of Achaean heroism that was so revered by Greeks".[16] Furthermore, by leaving his armour in the shrine, Alexander inserts himself into the narrative and cultural memory of Troy. Future pilgrims would be able to incorporate a visit to Alexander's relic as they journeyed through Trojan War tombs and battlefields, solidifying Alexander's identity as a great Greek leader in the tradition of Achaean heroism. Alexander's embodiment of Achilles became part of his identity as a great leader, to the extent that it was emulated by later leaders, particularly from Rome, who made their own journeys to Troy to associate themselves with both Alexander and Achilles.

As well as embedding a memory of himself into the Trojan landscape, Alexander's visit resulted in changes to monuments in the area. A new temple to Athena was constructed in the fourth century BCE at his command (completed after his death), and immediately following his visit travel to the region burgeoned and sites of pilgrimage underwent renovation to meet travellers' expectations.[17] When Alexander visited Achilles's tomb, it was the largest gravesite in the region.[18] However, during the third century BCE, as more travellers visited, Achilles's tomb was monumentalised, growing from approximately 5 m to 13 m high, making it not only the largest of the heroes' tumuli, but also the region's largest ever building project.[19]

Fictional stories of a regular pilgrimage from Greece to the tomb of Achilles are recorded by Philostratus as late as the third century CE.[20] According to Philostratus, every year, fourteen pilgrims from Thessaly arrived on a ship with black sails to perform sacrifice to Achilles. They brought a white and a black bull, wood from Mount Pelion, fire, water from a river Achilles knew from his childhood (the Spercheius), and Amaranthus wreaths. Because the Thessalians were entering enemy territory, the ritual was performed under cover of darkness; and a hymn to Achilles's mother, the goddess Thetis, was sung aboard the ship to invoke her presence and protection. In a minor re-enactment of the Trojan War, the pilgrims ran toward the tomb calling Achilles's name and clashing their shields. Patroclus was called upon to join the feast after the sacrifices were made. The following morning saw the Thessalians return to their ship, sacrifice the second bull on the beach, and then quickly retreat home. This account illustrates the power of memory within the Trojan War landscape. Whether these pilgrims really travelled to the Dardanelles or this is just a story, the importance of Achilles to those from Thessaly, even 1,500 years after his death is evident, and the tale implies continued Greek pilgrimage to the region.[21]

---

16   Minchin 2012, 84.
17   Strabo, 13.1.26.
18   Rose and Körpe 2016, 376.
19   Ibid., 376.
20   Philostr., *Her.*, 52.3-11. Philostratus's works span from ca. 170 to ca. 250 CE.
21   The archaeological evidence does not suggest Troy was abandoned, so there is no reason to think that regular pilgrimage ceased.

Roman and Ottoman Pilgrimage

From the second and first centuries BCE, the origins of pilgrims, generally, shifted from Greece to Rome. Livy records the great Roman general L. Cornelius Scipio making camp beside the walls of Troy in 190 BCE and offering sacrifice to Athena. Sulla visited Troy after it was sacked in 85 BCE by his rival commander G. Flavius Fimbria, and repaired the damage.[22] Marc Antony also visited Troy, taking the statue of Ajax to Alexandria.[23] Octavian rectified this when he restored the statue to its sanctuary in 20 BCE.[24] However, it was not until the establishment of Rome's imperial regime that consistent Roman pilgrimage emerged.

By the first century CE, the Trojan landscape had become so strongly associated with the Julio-Claudian dynasty that Julius Caesar is retrospectively credited with a visit. The first-century CE Roman poet Lucan recounts Caesar's pilgrimage to Troy in the *Pharsalia*.[25] Caesar and his nephew, Augustus, claimed the goddess Venus as their ancestor through the Trojan prince Aeneas, who fled Troy as it burned before settling in Italy. According to Lucan, Troy was a place where "no stone is without a name"—in other words, every part of Troy held memories and stories.[26] Although Caesar's pilgrimage is likely fictional, the result of his imagined journey and interaction with the memories of the Trojan War became part of the memories held by Troy's stones. The retrospective invention of Caesar's journey to Troy casts him as the link between the Trojan Aeneas, his mother Venus, and all the Roman emperors that would subsequently rule as Caesar. Lucan's representation of Caesar requesting a prosperous future from his ancestral gods in their place of origin establishes a connection between Rome's past, its future, and Augustus's re-foundation of Rome after the civil wars.[27]

Caesar's successor Octavian/Augustus visited Troy in 20 BCE. He ordered repairs to the city, taking responsibility for its preservation as a descendant of the Trojan people.[28] Augustus modelled his image and military prowess on Alexander the Great (and, by extension, Achilles), so his visit to Troy was equally important for its connection to the Macedonian conqueror as it was to Achilles and the heroes of the Trojan War. More important, though, was the affirmation of Rome's Trojan ancestry, constituted by offerings to the heroes who had died defending the Romans' ancestral homeland. Later journeys of Roman emperors honoured these heroes and Alexander, and paid homage to their Trojan ancestry, but were even more focused on emulating Augustus, who, as Rome's first emperor, was the source of their imperial power. Augustus's Trojan pilgrimage superimposed another stratum of cultural memory upon the Trojan landscape, and the pilgrimage trail to the Dardanelles became ever more complex.

---

22   Rose 2013, 221.
23   Strabo, 1.31.30.
24   Ibid.
25   Livy, 37.37.1-3, Luc., 9.961-99.
26   "*Nullum est sine nomine saxum*", Luc., 9.973.
27   Luc., 9.997. Borgeaud 2010, 344.
28   Strabo, 13.127.

Trojan ancestry was so central to Augustus's claim to power that members of his family, particularly those in line to succeed him, made the journey to Troy to establish their own connection to the site and the Trojan people. Augustus's daughter Julia visited with her husband Agrippa sometime between 16 and 13 BCE, and Germanicus, Tiberius's adoptive son, visited the Trojan battlefields in 18 CE with his son Gaius, later Caligula.[29] Although the emperor Claudius did not visit Troy, he was interested in the city, and public works were undertaken during his reign.[30] Nero too, advocated for the people of Troy, although did not visit.[31] Because of the strong ancestral link between Julio-Claudians and Aeneas, almost 80 percent of imperial statuary dedicated at Troy is of Julio-Claudian emperors.[32]

Hadrian was the next emperor to visit, in 124 CE, when he found the tomb of Ajax in disrepair, much of it having been washed out to sea. The emperor had the exposed bones reinterred and the tomb reconstructed above sea level.[33] He also undertook building work in the Agora.[34] Coinage produced during Hadrian's reign depicting Aeneas's flight from Troy with his father and son, accompanied by a miniature Lupercal scene (linking Rome's mythological founder Romulus to the Romans' Trojan ancestors), reiterated Roman imperial connections to the Trojan people.[35] A Hadrianic epigram further emphasises Rome's Trojan ancestry:

> Hector, bred of Ares, if underground you can hear me,
> Hail, and breathe anew for your homeland.
> A new city inhabits Ilion, and men within it
> Feebler than you, but still with a taste for war.
> The Myrmidons have perished. Stand by Achilles and tell him:
> All Thessaly now submits to the sons of Aeneas.[36]

This poem implies that, although the Trojans were defeated, the equally warlike Romans finally avenged their ancestors by conquering Greece. The epigram, the coinage and Hadrian's visit, then, all invoke cultural memories that honour Rome's Trojan ancestors, and establish a connection to the Julio-Claudian dynasty. Establishing these connections was particularly important to Hadrian, who had been adopted as successor to Trajan very late in life. Coming to power in this way meant he needed to clearly establish his imperial position. Tracing the footsteps of the Julio-Claudian emperors who

---

29 Tac., *Ann.*, 2.54; Rose 2013, 227.
30 Suet., *Claud.*, 25. On Claudius's building programme, see Rose 2013, 228-31.
31 Tac., *Ann.*, 12.58.
32 Rose 2013, 223.
33 Philostr., *Her.*, 8.1.
34 Rose 2013, 248.
35 Bellinger 1961, 48, T134.
36 *Palatine Anthology*, 9.388.

made pilgrimage to Troy connected him to his predecessors and their Trojan ancestry, emphasising a long and esteemed lineage of Roman imperial power.

Caracalla was the next Roman emperor to visit Troy, in 214 CE. He, like Alexander, honoured Achilles with sacrifices and raced around the hero's grave wearing armour—invoking Achilles and Alexander in the process. Like earlier visitors, Caracalla left his mark through public works, erecting a bronze statue of Achilles and constructing a new, enormous, tumulus for his freedman Festus, who was fabled to be poisoned by Caracalla so a funeral could be held and a tomb constructed.[37] Festus's tomb was 70 m in diameter and 17 m high, dwarfing the next largest tumulus in the region, dedicated to Achilles. The funerary rituals undertaken by Caracalla re-enacted the emperor's imagined vision of Patroclus's funeral.[38] This re-enactment cast Caracalla as Achilles, and drew a strong connection to Alexander's pilgrimage more than 500 years earlier.

After another long hiatus, the emperor Constantine declared his respect for the sacred site of Troy in 323-4 CE, when he entertained the idea of situating his new Roman capital at Troy or Sigeum.[39] This would have re-established Rome's ancestral ties with the Trojan people in their original homeland, although nothing came of the plan. The last Roman imperial visitor to Troy was Julian, who visited in 355 CE. According to Julian, Troy was still being maintained as a sacred site; the tomb of Achilles was in good repair and altar-torches at the shrine of Hector still burned.[40] An earthquake in 500 CE saw the end of regular pilgrimage to Troy, and sites fell into disrepair.[41]

It was not until almost 1,000 years later that another pilgrimage to the Dardanelles is recorded. In 1462, the Ottoman sultan Mehmet II the Conqueror visited the ruins of Troy. He is said to have "examined the tombs of the heroes and […] praised and congratulated them".[42] According to Ousterhout, after his visit, a copy of Homer's *Iliad* was translated for the sultan because of the text's "enduring importance to Byzantine culture".[43] Ousterhout argues that, "[f]or Mehmet, as for his Roman imperial predecessors, Troy […] represented his ancestral home, as well as the common literary culture of the Mediterranean elite, both East and West".[44] Although this is an isolated Ottoman example of pilgrimage to the Dardanelles, it demonstrates the power memories of pilgrimage to the region still exerted in the fifteenth century CE. As Mehmet was establishing his position as leader of the Ottoman Empire, he looked back to its predecessor, the Roman Empire, which had successfully ruled over these lands for centuries, and to stories about those who occupied the landscape in the even more distant past, to better understand the continuity of cultural heritage in the region. As the sultan who conquered

---

37   Hdn., 4.8.3-5; Borgeaud 2010, 344.
38   Hdn., 4.8.4-5.
39   Zos., 2.30, Theophanes, 23.
40   Julian, *Ep.*, 79.16-17.
41   Minchin 2012, 87.
42   Kritovoulos 1954, IV, 72.
43   Ousterhout 2004, 171. See also Raby 1983, 18.
44   Ousterhout 2004, 172.

Constantinople, previously the capital of the Eastern Roman Empire, Mehmet's pilgrimage connected Trojan royalty and Roman imperial office to his own power. The next great successor to the Ottoman Empire in the region was the Republic of Turkey's founding president Mustafa Kemal (later Atatürk), who regularly visited Troy and the tombs of the ancient heroes who fought in the Trojan War. Mustafa Kemal visited Troy during the Balkan Wars in 1913, and later took German officers to the site during WWI.[45]

These two later examples demonstrate that Troy also held significance for Ottoman and Turkish leaders, who made connections between their cultures and events of the past in a shared landscape. Through their own travel to Troy, they were also establishing a connection to previous leaders who had travelled to the region. Today, those who travel to Gallipoli to commemorate WWI soldiers are making a pilgrimage to a site of cultural importance for them and their people in the same spirit as Xerxes, Alexander, Augustus, Hadrian, Mehmet, Mustafa Kemal and all others who visited between. This contemporary continuation of pilgrimage to the Dardanelles, however, exhibits a significant shift from those that came before, because the occurrence of WWI has meant that the Trojan War heroes have become a secondary focus, and the WWI dead provide the primary motivation for contemporary pilgrimage.

Early Antipodean Pilgrimage

On 25 April 1915, soldiers from the Australian Imperial Force and the New Zealand Expeditionary Force landed on the Gallipoli peninsula independently of British forces, and in so doing, their memory became part of the Dardanelles landscape. These soldiers came to be known as Anzacs and the myths built around their deeds, the Anzac Legend.[46] The First World War, and the Gallipoli campaign in particular, had a huge impact on the young antipodean nations, which eagerly sent large numbers of volunteer soldiers to Europe. Nearly forty percent of the Australian male population aged between 18 and 44 enlisted and, although many returned home, Australia suffered a sixty-five percent casualty rate. Of the approximately 50,000 Australians sent to Gallipoli, 8,709 died and 26,111 suffered injury.[47] New Zealand, similarly, suffered a sixty percent casualty rate by the end of WWI.[48]

---

45 Aslan and Atabay 2012, 156, 159.
46 It is often difficult to the differentiate Australian experience from the New Zealand experience because pilgrims from each nation travel to similar destinations at the same time and aspects of the pilgrimage overlap. At the heart of each nation's respective pilgrimage lies the Anzac legend, which is expressed differently in Australia and New Zealand. It is therefore important to look at each as separate, but aligned, phenomena. On the tendency for Australian and New Zealand histories to be seen as completely separate, see Mein Smith and Hempenstall 2003, 1-5. On the difference between Australian and New Zealand understanding on Anzac Day, see Davis 2008, 24-25, 221-26.
47 Further statistics of fatality and casualty rates can be found at www.awm.gov.au.
48 Of the 98,950 who served New Zealand internationally, there were 41,317 casualties and 18,058 deaths. Shoebridge 2015.

The Australian colonies had federated and formed their own national government only thirteen years before the Gallipoli landing, and it was yet to define its national autonomy from Britain.[49] Almost immediately after its occurrence, the Anzac landing was lauded as the greatest moment in Australia's short history and the birth of the Australian nation. The landing was received similarly in New Zealand, which had become a self-governing British Dominion in 1907. For many Australians and New Zealanders, Gallipoli is a sacred site of pilgrimage that facilitates a connection to their national and cultural ancestors.[50] For both young nations, memories of the Gallipoli campaign are conflated with a sense of national identity.[51] Therefore, motivations for travel to the Dardanelles today include an interest in national Australian and New Zealand history, and a desire to connect with national ancestors.[52]

Just across the Dardanelles from Gallipoli is the site of the mythological Trojan War, which occurred approximately 3,000 years earlier. As discussed above, the Trojan War is Western civilisation's archetypal conflict, so the Anzacs seized the opportunity to incorporate their deeds into ancient narratives. The close proximity of the sites ensured that, from the outset, Australian and New Zealand soldiers were likened to ancient Greek warriors by journalists, military commanders reporting home, and the soldiers themselves in diaries, letters and trench publications.[53] After WWI ended, the idealised image of the Anzac soldier endured, and Gallipoli became sacred to antipodeans, adding another stratum of cultural memory to the region.

While war still raged at Gallipoli, academic and journalist Hector Dinning predicted pilgrimage, writing:

> "The day is far off (but it will come) when splendid mausolea will be raised over these heroic dead. And one foresees the time when steamers will bear up the Aegean pilgrims come to honour at the resting places of friends and kindred, and to move over the charred battlefields of Turkey."[54]

Dinning's Anzac mausolea recall those raised for the heroes of the Trojan War and the charred battlefields of Turkey recall both those occupied by the Anzacs as well as the Trojan battlefield, conflating the Trojan War and the Gallipoli campaign.

The first post-war pilgrimage was undertaken in 1918 by the British divisional commander and the commander of the Australian Light Horse, who led a large number of

---

49 Six British colonies located on the Australian continent federated into the Commonwealth of Australia on 1 January 1901.
50 Australians are more strongly motivated by nationalism to visit Gallipoli than New Zealanders; Hyde and Harman 2011, 1346.
51 Hart 2014, 436.
52 Lockstone-Binney, Hall and Atay 2013, 300.
53 Midford 2011, 70-71; Midford 2010, 6-7.
54 Dinning, "Glimpses of Anzac," in Bean 1916, 21; Bean predicted there would be pilgrimage to the Australian graves at Gallipoli in his official report "On Graves at Gallipoli and the Future of Anzac," 13 March (1919), in Bean 1952, 327-28.

Australians and New Zealanders on an expedition to Gallipoli.[55] Non-military visitors made the journey to Gallipoli from 1921. The first civilian to visit was W.T. Jennings, a Member of New Zealand's Parliament, whose son was killed in action on 3 August 1915 and buried in Shrapnel Valley Cemetery, where Jennings travelled to leave a wreath.

Early Anzac pilgrims were aware of the area's ancient history and compared their journeys to those of past travellers who paid their respects to Trojan War heroes, recognising that they followed in the footsteps of the ancient figures discussed above. The novelist Ian Hay, who served in WWI, documented an early tour to Gallipoli in 1926, making a connection between his and the pilgrimages of antiquity:

> "We are not … a Pilgrim Ship pure and simple—that is, [we are not] a ship conveying only relatives seeking graves. We muster amongst us a number of ex-soldiers from all parts of the Empire … Now that the time of siege is past all these, like the Trojans of old, 'delight to view the Doric camp' and reconstruct the situation for the rest of us."[56]

Here, Hay quotes from book two of Vergil's *Aeneid*, which tells the story of the sack of Troy. The Trojans think (mistakenly) that the Greeks have retreated, and they delight in having the freedom to look at their opponents' empty camps. The returning WWI soldiers felt similarly, seeing the Gallipoli battlefields again, delighting in the absence of war where it had once raged. By comparing his experience to that of the Trojans, Hay anticipated the enduring WWI legacy for antipodeans.

Australian and New Zealand WWI soldiers were never repatriated, and all those who died overseas were buried in or around the battlefields where they fell. This absence of a local gravesite distressed many grieving families because it was completely beyond the financial means of most Australians and New Zealanders to travel to Gallipoli after WWI concluded. However, one couple did: Sarah and George Irwin visited the peninsula in 1927.[57] The Irwins' journey was well documented and many antipodean families followed their progress in the newspaper, experiencing the parents' pilgrimage vicariously. The Irwins' son went missing at Lone Pine in August 1915 during one of Gallipoli's bloodiest battles, so all that was left to visit was his name inscribed into the memorial to the missing.[58] Sarah Irwin took a rubbing of her son's name as a keepsake, an echo of both his life and his death that could be transported back to Australia.

In the 1930s, mass pilgrimage was still being anticipated. Cyril Hughes speculated that "soon Helles would boast Turkey's largest airport … and every Anzac Day the beaches will swell with visitors".[59] At the fiftieth anniversary of the Gallipoli landing in 1965, Inglis notes that the only young people to make the pilgrimage were "four Australian

---

55 On the history of pilgrimage to Anzac Cove, see Reid, McGibbon and Midford 2016, 216-19.
56 Hay 1927, 29.
57 "Back to Gallipoli to See Son's Grave," *The Sun*, 24 January 1927, 10.
58 Scates 2008, 47-48.
59 Cyril Hughes, "Gallipoli: Our War Graves," *Reveille*, 28 February 1930.

hitchhikers in parkas and jeans".[60] It was not until the 1980s that large numbers of Australians and New Zealanders started travelling to Gallipoli. David Williamson (co-writer of Peter Weir's blockbuster film *Gallipoli*) attributed renewed interest in the battlefields to his film being the most watched of 1981. *Gallipoli* presented the campaign as a legend of Australian independence from British imperial domination.[61] Rather than focus on the war itself, it documents a journey of two young men from rural Australia to the Dardanelles. By the film's conclusion both the young men have established mature identities, exemplifying idealised Australian masculinity. References to the Trojan War and ancient Greek mythology are made passively by Weir and Williamson throughout—the most obvious being the use of a Trojan horse in a rural Australian community fair as part of a recruitment drive, encouraging young men to enlist. Making a connection to the Trojan War demonstrates that the Gallipoli landscape was still actively being associated with the longer history of the Dardanelles, and the deeds of the young Australian soldiers in the film were likened to those of Trojan War warriors.[62] These references to Gallipoli's history of epic conflict situates the Anzac narrative as the next great event to occur in the region—yet another stratum of memory to add to the sacred Dardanelles landscape. The film's release coincided with increasingly affordable travel to Europe and relative political stability in Turkey, facilitating significantly more travel in the 1980s, 1990s and 2000s—so much so that when Williamson returned to Gallipoli in 2006, a Turkish tour guide told him, "That film has paid for my house."[63] Today, the film is played daily in backpacker hostels across the Gallipoli peninsula to prepare travellers for their battlefield experience.

Anzac Pilgrimage and Nationalism

Secular pilgrimages are often made to places "where dramatic historical events occurred".[64] Gallipoli is such a site, and those lost during WWI are visited as exemplars of ideal national values. This practice elevates their deaths to something transcendent and sanctifies the Dardanelles landscape for a new people in a new millennium.

Gallipoli pilgrims were initially motivated by personal grief and a need to pay their respects to fallen comrades, friends or family. As discussed above, convoys of veterans, military personnel and family returned to the Anzac battlefields. Travel to the region was purposeful, not a deviation from one's broader itinerary, and the main motivation was

---

60 K.S. Inglis, "Return to Gallipoli," Inglis Papers, National Library of Australia, Manuscript B.
61 New Zealanders were not a feature of the film's narrative.
62 On connections between *Gallipoli* and the Trojan War narrative and Anzac soldiers and Trojan War heroes, see Midford 2016, 227-66.
63 Trent Dalton, "David Williamson bit the bullet, took the Gallipoli Challenge," *Australian*, 8 June 2014.
64 Hyde and Harman 2011, 1343. On how sacred spaces come into being in a secular contemporary context, see Margry 2008, 327.

to express grief and mourning. As time has passed, pilgrims have become less likely to have an immediate personal connection to those who served or died in the Dardanelles. Although approximately one million Australians can trace some ancestry to an Anzac who landed at Gallipoli, most of the thousands of pilgrims who visit each year are younger than 30 and have no known relative buried on the peninsula.[65] These pilgrims are not travelling to grieve for a relative, but are instead seeking a spiritual experience.

Australian and New Zealand backpacker pilgrims are unlikely to know much about the long history of pilgrimage to the Dardanelles prior to their arrival in the region.[66] As they research the area, they learn about the Trojan War, and that millennia of history surrounds them. Scates describes tourists in the early 2000s showing him copies of their *Lonely Planet* guidebooks with highlighted histories of the region's ancient past.[67] Today, local tours to Gallipoli also include short histories of the Trojan War or a visit to Troy, ensuring that travellers have an opportunity to encounter both famous battlefields.

Contemporary Gallipoli pilgrims exhibit ritualised behaviour, leaving tokens on graves, including wreaths, poppies, crosses, photographs, letters to the deceased and poems.[68] These sacred offerings are sometimes made at a site of significance to the pilgrim, such as the grave of an ancestor or a well-known Anzac soldier, but can also be made based on a connection or emotion experienced while on the peninsula, including identification with a soldier's name, age[69] or town of origin, or a tombstone's inscription. Grave offerings and commemorative rituals such as moments of silence or playing The Last Post add to the pilgrim's tangible experience.[70] Contemporary pilgrims emerge from their journey feeling a stronger sense of what it means to be an Australian or a New Zealander, through making a personal connection with a significant cultural memory in the place of its origin.[71] Travellers feel connected to the characteristics exhibited by Anzac soldiers on the battlefield, such as endurance, bravery and 'mateship', which have become part of perceptions of an ideal Australian (in particular) but also of a New Zealander.[72]

---

65 Warren Snowden, "Planning for Anzac Day 2015 at Gallipoli," Media Release, Australian Government Department of Veterans' Affairs, 26 September 2012. On Anzac Day 2000, John Hannaford interviewed 105 tourists who had travelled to Gallipoli for the Dawn Service. Of those interviewed, 80 per cent were younger than 30 years, and 81 per cent were originally from Australia. Hannaford 2001, 133, 141.

66 The long history of the Dardanelles, and its proximity to Gallipoli, is not actively or consistently taught in Australian and New Zealand schools. For detailed analysis of the connections between Anzac and the history of the Dardanelles, see Midford 2011, 2016, 2019.

67 Scates 2002, 11.

68 Margry 2008, 327.

69 A survey of young battlefield tourists found that most were conscious that they and the soldiers buried on the peninsula were of similar age. Hannaford 2001, 133, 141.

70 Eade and Katić 2018, 18.

71 Lockstone-Binney, Hall and Atay 2013, 304. Tourists to Gallipoli describe the place as sacred, characterised by spirituality, see Cheal and Griffin 2013, 234.

72 Cheal and Griffin 2013, 234.

The landing is commemorated annually on Anzac Day (25 April) in ceremonies held at dawn in almost every city and town in Australia and New Zealand, on the Gallipoli peninsula, as well as other battlefields and cemeteries around the world. Although Anzac Day marks a significant moment in the Anzac narrative and many travellers choose this day to visit the Dardanelles, tens of thousands of pilgrims also visit Gallipoli throughout the year. Participation in an Anzac Day Dawn Service at Anzac Cove, however, can heighten aspects of a pilgrim's experience. Attendees report gaining a deeply symbolic understanding of Anzac that bonds them together, and reinforces their sense of national belonging (Figs. 2-4).[73] Speeches reinforce the message that the dead sacrificed their lives in service to Australian and New Zealand nations, and that each nation prospers because of this sacrifice.[74]

Each year, on Anzac Day, the Anzac Commemorative Site is transformed into a theatre overlooking the Aegean. Pilgrims amass beneath the Sphinx[75] and wait for dawn, either sitting in the stands or lying on the grassy area in sleeping bags. Markets sell food and merchandise, the history of the campaign is broadcast on large television screens, and live interviews with distant relatives of the dead are conducted on stage. As dawn breaks, the official ceremony commences and all stand to attention. The act of sleeping in the vicinity of the departed heightens the pilgrims' experience and forges a connection between the living and the dead: one pilgrim said, "sleeping together with the other pilgrims on the grass at North Beach was a beautiful experience";[76] another commented on "the intimacy of the mass sleeping together".[77] When the sun rises, pilgrims shed their sleeping bags to reveal green and gold hoodies,[78] and Australian and New Zealand flags worn as capes. It is common to see tears in pilgrim's eyes. Hannaford and Newton found that pilgrims' tears at the Dawn Service "signalled their initiation into a new sense of belonging to Australia"[79]—their experience leading to a deep cultural connection with their national ancestors.

---

73 Scates 2006, 199-201.
74 For example, Scott Morrison, a Member of Australia's Federal Parliament, stated on Anzac Day 2014: "What they sowed in their courage, their endurance, their mateship and their sacrifice, we now recap in the strong, prosperous and generous nation we have become." See www.scottmorrison.com.au/cookmail/33, accessed 20/08/15. This rhetoric is also used in school resources. Rick Anderson, the President of the City of Paramatta RSL Sub-Branch, wrote in the introduction to the 2015 education kit produced by the RSL: "ANZAC Day is the time when we reflect on the sacrifices made by the men and women of both Australia and New Zealand who served their countries to protect our freedom so that we might live in peace and harmony." Anderson 2015, 4. See also, Midford 2021.
75 A rock formation named by the Anzacs because of its resemblance to the Egyptian Sphinx, which they encountered in Cairo before being deployed at Gallipoli.
76 Hannaford 2001, 150.
77 Ibid.
78 Green and gold are Australia's national colours. The hoodies are supplied by the 'Fanatics' tour company.
79 Hannaford and Newton 2008, paragraph 35. This claim can be extrapolated to the New Zealand experience, which was comparable.

Anzac Commemorative Site, Anzac Cove, Gallipoli, Turkey. Photograph taken 24 September 2014 by Sarah Midford.

Fig. 2.

After the Dawn Service concludes, pilgrims journey to the next official event at the Lone Pine memorial (Australians) or Chunuk Bair (New Zealanders) (Fig. 5). Most take the long and steep Artillery Road, stopping to visit Shell Green cemetery, where the Anzac soldiers played cricket in their last days on the peninsula in an effort to distract the Turkish forces while the Allies executed their evacuation plans.[80] It is common for pilgrims to deviate from the road into what remains of the trenches, in search of WWI 'relics' (battlefield artefacts). Relics might include rusty food cans, shell casings and glass shards. The tangibility of collected relics connects pilgrims to the Anzacs. In the same way that Alexander and Caracalla re-enacted foot-races at the tomb of Achilles, as they traverse the peninsula, some pilgrims climb the same steep cliffs[81] the Anzacs had climbed more than a century earlier.[82]

Tourists to Gallipoli report that they leave with a better understanding of what it means to be an Australian or a New Zealander.[83] Visiting the site allows pilgrims to

---

80 The Anzac forces had all evacuated Anzac Cove by 20 December 1915.
81 Scates indicated that it is predominately young men climbing the cliffs; Scates 2006, 205.
82 Re-enactments on the peninsula date back to 1965, when the landing was re-enacted for the fiftieth anniversary Dawn Service. Much like the original landing, it was plagued by confusion, Scates 2017, 539. Veronica della Dora (2008, 219) contends that "links between the present and the classical past [are] activated through the physical act of climbing".
83 Hannaford 2001, 133, 151.

Fig. 3. Anzac Commemorative Site, Anzac Cove, Gallipoli, Turkey. Photograph taken at the Anzac Day Dawn Service, 25 April 2011 by Sarah Midford.

Fig. 4. Anzac Day pilgrims huddled together in sleeping bags waiting for dawn on the Anzac Commemorative Site, Anzac Cove, Gallipoli, Turkey. Photograph taken 25 April 2011 by Sarah Midford.

gain a more vivid understanding of the Anzac narrative and enter the Anzac story in a way they could not from home.[84] Kerry D. from Queensland imagined herself as "a part of the story" while at Gallipoli on 25 April 2000,[85] while Katie H. from Victoria reported: "[Gallipoli] gives you something to tie yourself to while travelling overseas—gives you an identity of who Australians are and what has influenced our culture."[86] Others describe feeling the presence of ghosts of the soldiers while on quieter parts of the battlefield.[87] Just as Alexander, Augustus, Hadrian and Mehmet II connected to their cultural ancestry in the preceding centuries at Troy, for Kerry, Katie and other Anzac pilgrims, the act of encountering Gallipoli allows them to better understand their cultural identities and ancestry by becoming part of the stories held within the landscape.

The Dardanelles: Millennia of Manufactured Meaning

The experience of the Dawn Service at Gallipoli is often described with cynicism by scholars. For instance, Scates characterises the ceremony as "a highly orchestrated, media-charged and increasingly manufactured experience" designed to elicit emotion from those who visit.[88] However, the manufactured aspect is not mutually exclusive from a pilgrim's sacred experience. The city of Troy, too, was reinvented and reconstructed over the centuries—monuments were enlarged and new sanctuaries built to enhance the pilgrims' experience. In the same way that ancient pilgrims participated in a manufactured experience, Anzac pilgrims are met with an orchestrated experience designed to enhance the journey and make it more memorable. The Anzac Day ceremony acts to temporarily bring the past into the present and the sacred site allows past events to be elided with the pilgrim's present experience.[89] Rituals also provide pilgrims with an opportunity to express emotions, awe and reverence, and the result is a sacred, almost religious, experience that promotes feelings of national pride and collective identity—somewhat manufactured, but no less meaningful for the pilgrim.[90]

Visiting the Dardanelles heightens a pilgrim's emotional state on sacred ground and enables personal and meaningful interaction with the landscape and its history, regardless of the day upon which they visit.[91] Those who attend on Anzac Day experience

▷▷ Lone Pine Memorial and Cemetery. Gallipoli Peninsula, Turkey. Photograph taken 30 September 2014 by Sarah Midford.

Fig. 5.

---

84 Cheal and Griffin 2013, 233.
85 Interview quoted in Scates 2002, 11.
86 Questionnaire quoted in Scates 2002, 11.
87 Interviews with travellers on the 25 April 2000 quoted in Scates 2002, 17.
88 Scates 2017, 540.
89 Osbaldiston and Petray 2011, 182.
90 Ibid., 186. On the endurance of collective memory being bound to space, see Osborne 2001, 41.
91 Cheal and Griffin 2013, 233-34; West 2008, 263.

Fig. 5.

meaning through the Dawn Service ceremony and the poignancy of being there on the day of the first landing. Those who attend throughout the year experience meaning through the tranquillity of the site. Visiting Gallipoli at any time brings a distant time and place of great significance into sharp focus, and makes the experience of the Anzacs a century earlier part of the pilgrim's personal experience. This allows young Australians to connect with their national ancestors in a sacred landscape.[92]

Gallipoli pilgrims, whether they are aware of it or not, are walking in the footsteps of other pilgrims to the area. Just like Xerxes and those who came to Troy after him, the antipodeans who travel to the Dardanelles are pilgrims *en passant*. That is, they are unlikely to be in Turkey exclusively to visit the battlefields, but as part of their overseas experience take the time to pay their respects.[93] Backpackers recognise that they are pilgrims only when they are within the sacred boundaries of the Gallipoli battlefields. In an interview conducted in 2008, one said: "I was a tourist in Istanbul but the moment we got anywhere near the site [of Gallipoli] we were pilgrims."[94] For Gallipoli pilgrims, their reverence is reserved for the battlefield. As soon as they leave, regardless of the effect their visit has had on them, they become backpackers/tourists again.

The Dardanelles is no longer just the place where the Trojan War was fought. It is also the place where Xerxes crossed into Europe, Alexander retaliated by crossing into Asia, and Roman emperors visited to connect their ancestry to the Trojan people. Most recently, the Dardanelles have become sacred to Australians and New Zealanders, who make pilgrimage to the landscape to honour the Anzacs who fought and died there during WWI. For three millennia, pilgrims have visited the sacred landscape of the Dardanelles to witness the battlefields of wars that have shaped their cultural identities, and to make a personal connection to those who fought them. When modern visitors travel to Gallipoli, they enter a space and place that holds the memory not just of WWI, but of thousands of years of conflict and commemoration. The journey of antipodean pilgrims offers an emotional experience that connects them to their fallen countrymen, but also to the greatest warriors of ancient Troy, Persia, Greece, Rome, the Ottoman Empire and the Turkish Republic. When the Dardanelles inevitably becomes a sacred place for the next group of people, the Anzacs and those who make pilgrimage to their gravesides will have left yet another stratum of memory upon the layered Dardanelles landscape.

---

92 Seal 2007, 135 argues that the renewed interest in visiting the site of the Gallipoli landings is testament to the secular nature of the Anzac narrative and its centrality to Australian nationalism. Sociologists Osbaldiston and Petray 2011, 176 argue that secular pilgrimage to Gallipoli is a way of reuniting individual Australians with their national roots. See also West 2008, 263.
93 Elsner and Rutherford 2005, 11.
94 Hannaford and Newton 2008. Margry 2008, 17 argues that, in the contemporary West, anyone can determine for themselves whether the journey they make is a pilgrimage because the sacred meaning of the journey and the destination is ascribed by the individual pilgrim.

Bibliography

Anderson, R. 2015. *Centenary of Anzac 2015 ANZAC Educational Kit*. Paramatta, NSW: Paramatta RSL.
Aslan, R. and M. Atabay. 2012. "Atatürk in Troy," in J. Kelder, G. Uslu and Ö.F. Şerifoğlu (eds.) *Troy: City, Homer and Turkey*, 155-59. Amsterdam: W Books.
Bean, C.E.W. (ed.) 1916. *The Anzac Book*. London: Cassell and Company.
Bean, C.E.W. 1952. *Gallipoli Mission*. Canberra: Australian War Memorial.
Bellinger, A.R. 1961. *Troy: The Coins*. Princeton, NJ: Princeton University Press.
Borgeaud, P. 2010. "Trojan Excursions: A Recurrent Ritual, from Xerxes to Julian." *History of Religions* 49.4, 339-53.
Cawkwell, G.L. 1992. "Early Colonisation." *The Classical Quarterly* 42.2, 289-303.
Cheal, F. and T. Griffin. 2013. "Pilgrims and Patriots: Australian tourist experiences at Gallipoli." *International Journal of Culture, Tourism and Hospitality Research* 7.3, 227-41.
Coleman, S. and J. Elsner. 1995. *Pilgrimage: Past and Present in the World Religions*. Cambridge: Cambridge University Press.
Davis, G.F. 2008. *Anzac Day meanings and memories: New Zealand, Australian and Turkish perspectives on a day of commemoration in the twentieth century*. PhD Thesis, University of Otago.
Deleuze, G. 1966. *Bergonism*. New York: Zone Books.
della Dora, V. 2008. "Mountains and Memory: Embodied Visions of Ancient Peaks in the Nineteenth-Century Aegean." *Transactions of British Geographers* 33, 217-32.
Eade, J. and M. Katić. 2018. "Commemorating the Dead: Military Pilgrimage and Battlefield Tourism," in J. Eade and M. Katić (eds.) *Military Pilgrimage and Battlefield Tourism: Commemorating the Dead*, 1-12. London and New York: Routledge.
Graziosi, B. and J. Haubold. 2010. *Homer Iliad Book VI*. Cambridge: Cambridge University Press.
Hannaford, J. 2001. *Two Australian Pilgrimages*. M. Phil. thesis, Australian Catholic University.
Hannaford, J. and J. Newton. 2008. "Sacrifice, Grief and the Sacred at the Contemporary 'Secular' Pilgrimage to Gallipoli." *Borderlands* 7.1: www.borderlands.net.au/vol7no1_2008/hannafordnewton_gallipoli.htm (accessed 14 February 2018).
Hart, P. 2014. *Gallipoli*. Oxford: Oxford University Press.
Hay, I. 1927. *The Ship of Remembrance*. London: Hodder and Stoughton.
Hyde, K.F. and S. Harman. 2011. "Motives for a Secular Pilgrimage to the Gallipoli Battlefields." *Tourism Management* 32, 1343-51.
Korfmann, M., J. Latacz and J.D. Hawkins. 2004. "Was There a Trojan War?" *Archaeology* 57.3, 36-41.
Kritovoulos [Critobule d'Imbros]. 1954. *History of Mehmed the Conqueror*, trans. C.T. Riggs. Princeton, NJ: Princeton University Press.
Lockstone-Binney, L., J. Hall, and L. Atay. 2013. "Exploring the conceptual boundaries of diaspora and battlefield tourism: Australians' travel to the Gallipoli battlefield, Turkey, as a case study." *Tourism Analysis* 18, 297-311.
Margry, P.J. 2008. *Shrines and Pilgrimage in the Modern World: New Itineraries into the Sacred*. Amsterdam: Amsterdam University Press.
Mein Smith, P. and P. Hempenstall. 2003. "Australia and New Zealand: Turning Shared Pasts into a Shared History." *History Compass* 1, 1-10.
Midford, S. 2010. "From Achilles to Anzac: Heroism in The Dardanelles from Antiquity to the Great War." *Australasian Society for Classical Studies* 31, Conference Proceedings, 1-12.
Midford, S. 2011. "Constructing the 'Australian Iliad': Ancient Heroes and Anzac Diggers in the Dardanelles." *Melbourne Historical Journal*, Special Issue 2, 59-79.
Midford, S. 2016. *From Achilles to Anzac: Classical Receptions in the Australian Anzac Narrative*. PhD Thesis, University of Melbourne.
Midford, S. 2019. "An Athenian temple in the Antipodes: Ancient Greek cultural values and Melbourne's Shrine of Remembrance." *History Australia* 16.3, 496-517.
Midford, S. 2021. "'A Deathless Monument of Valour'" Memorialising Anzacs as Ancient Greek Citizen Soldiers from the War's Aftermath to Julia Gillard's 2012 Gallipoli Dawn Service Speech," in M. Walsh and A. Varnava (eds.) *After the Armistice: Empire, Endgame, Aftermath*, 177-89. London: Routledge.
Minchin, E. 2012. "Commemoration and Pilgrimage in the Ancient World: Troy and the Stratigraphy of Cultural Memory." *Greece and Rome* 59.1, 76-89.

Osbaldiston, N. and T. Petray. 2011. "The Role of Horror and Dread in the Sacred Experience." *Tourist Studies* 11, 175-90.

Osborne, B.S. 2001. "Landscape, Memory, Monuments, Commemoration: Putting Identity in its Place." *Canadian Ethnic Studies* 33.3, 39-77.

Ousterhout, R. 2004. "The East, the West, and the Appropriation of the Past in Early Ottoman Architecture." *Gesta* 43.2, 165-76.

Raaflaub, K.A. 1998. "Homer, the Trojan War, and History." *Classical World* 91.5, 386-403.

Raby, J. 1983. "Mehmed the Conqueror's Greek Scriptorium." *DOP* 37, 15-34.

Reid, R., I. McGibbon and S. Midford. 2016. "Remembering Gallipoli," in A. Sagona, M. Atabay, C.J. Mackie, I. McGibbon and R. Reid (eds.) *Anzac Battlefield: A Gallipoli Landscape of War and Memory*, 192-221. Melbourne: Cambridge University Press.

Rose, C.B. 2013. *The Archaeology of Greek and Roman Troy*. Cambridge: Cambridge University Press.

Rose, C.B., and R. Körpe. 2016. "The *Tumuli* of Troy and the Troad," in O. Henry and U. Kelp (eds.) *Tumulus as Sema. Space, Politics, Culture and Religion in the First Millennium BC*, Berlin and Boston: Walter de Gruyter, 373-86.

Saunders, N.J. 2003. "Crucifix, cavalry, and cross: materiality and spirituality in Great War landscapes." *World Archaeology* 35.1, 7-21.

Scates, B. 2002. "In Gallipoli's Shadow: Pilgrimage, Memory, Mourning and the Great War." *Australian Historical Studies* 33, 118, 1-21.

Scates, B. 2006. *Return to Gallipoli: Walking the Battlefields of the Great War*. Cambridge: Cambridge University Press.

Scates, B. 2008. "Memorialising Gallipoli: Manufacturing Memory at Anzac." *Public History Review* 15, 47-59.

Scates, B. 2017. "'Letters from a pilgrimage': reflections on the 1965 return to Gallipoli." *History Australia* 14.4, 530-44.

Seal, G. 2007. "ANZAC: The sacred in the secular." *Journal of Australian Studies* 31, 91, 135-44.

Shoebridge, T. 2015. "First World War by the Numbers." *New Zealand History Website*, https://nzhistory.govt.nz/war/first-world-war-by-numbers (accessed 14 February 2018).

West, B. 2008. "Enchanting Pasts: The Role of International Civil Religious Pilgrimage in Reimagining National Collective Memory." *Sociological Theory* 26, 258-70.

West, M.L. 1995. "The Date of the 'Iliad'." *Museum Helveticum* 52.4, 203-19.

Yoyotte, J. 1960. *Les Pèlerinages dans l'Egypte ancienne*. Paris: Seuil.

PART III

Concluding Responses

14

PILGRIMAGE: AN UNRULY METHOD?

SIMON COLEMAN

Pilgrimage is hard to pin down. It is not a 'natural' category possessing a discrete and unambiguous presence in the world. No agreed definition of it exists across, or even within, scholarly disciplines. Neither Latin nor Greek provides vocabulary that might designate it as a single, clearly identifiable practice in the Ancient Mediterranean. In his contribution to this volume, David Frankfurter explains why he finds "shrine visitation" a more useful and accurate description of activities relating to late antique sacred precincts. Other contributors do not go as far in declaring anxieties over categorising certain activities as pilgrimage, but some choose to refer to interrelated actions and objects rather than highlighting any one form of behaviour. For instance, Matthew Anderson proposes a "four-part structure" that might help us to conceptualise, if not exactly define, pilgrimage: body, terrain, mobility, and narrative.[1] In their Introduction, Anna Collar and Troels Myrup Kristensen bring together clusters of themes, including place and motion, site and landscape, sanctuary and household. These accounts clearly share an interest in exploring relations between movement and location, but do not establish firm guidelines of inclusion and exclusion. Pilgrimage remains an unruly point of scholarly orientation.[2]

Despite such challenges, this book displays the considerable virtue of treating these ambiguities as prompts for productive reflection rather than abandonment of comparative inquiry. The shifts in emphasis and approach that are inevitable across an edited volume contribute to an overall project of asking: How far can we go—how far ought we to go—in deploying pilgrimage as frame for our investigations into and across case studies? Note the ambiguity inherent in my use of the word "frame". It might imply that pilgrimage becomes, *de facto*, the mutual, messy object of our collaborative work; that we are agreeing to discuss activities that are spread across times and places but that display sufficient family resemblances to permit relatively coherent conversation. On the

---

[1] For further characterisation of pilgrimage through multiple elements, see Eade and Sallnow 1991; see also discussion in Coleman 2022, chapters 1-2.
[2] In invoking unruliness I am reminded of Matthew Dillon's contribution to this volume, which examines the tensions between order and disorder at the oracular sanctuary of Apollo Koropaios.

other hand, it might point to a more abstract conception, a formal means through which to classify social and material phenomena, using systematically organised parameters. A well-known example of the latter strategy is provided by the sociologist Zygmunt Bauman in a piece that contrasts the figure of the "pilgrim" to those of the "stroller," the "vagabond" and the "tourist" in proposing a theoretical lexicon sufficient to distinguish between forms of identity emergent within modernity and post-modernity.[3] In practice, these two approaches cannot be entirely separated, and they remind us that in our work we are always likely to be negotiating between the pragmatic and the ideal typical—between strategic comparisons and attempts to develop overarching, unifying theory. In the following, I reflect as a social anthropologist on the ways in which contributions to this volume address these difficulties in looking both *at* and *through* those activities that authors decide to call pilgrimage. My interest is not in establishing an all-purpose definition but rather in assessing the direction and productivity of the scholarly discussions that are roused. I take it as inevitable that any given discussion—like any definition—will be incomplete: it will facilitate some insights and occlude others; and then new conversations, new framings, will emerge.

Collar and Kristensen's own agenda for this volume draws significantly on the "New Mobilities Paradigm", which took on particular force from the early 2000s through the work of sociologists and geographers concerned with re-examining the production of space, flows of people and resources, and questions of scale. These scholars' interests did not appear within a societal vacuum: they were reacting to contexts where processes of globalisation and neo-liberalisation were becoming more evident, and their conversations both reflected—and reflected on—new insecurities of identity, location and knowing. However, as Mimi Sheller notes in her useful summary,[4] the paradigm "was not simply about describing or explaining a more mobile world …but also about the ways in which contemporary respatializations of the relation between mobilities, immobilities, and infrastructural moorings deeply shaped uneven spatial terrains". In other words, mobility had to be comprehended in relation to other ways of being in space. At the same time, space was not regarded as containable *per se*, and was understood as constituted through multiple, networked, social and material relations. Recognising the significance of scale also encouraged flexibility of the observer's perspective, a readiness to move up and down different levels of analytical resolution in characterising spatial relations. In this sense, the assumption that points of view were both relative and shifting was built into the very paradigm itself. In a conscious echo of my words from the previous paragraph, we might say that scholars saw themselves as looking both *at* and *through* mobility.

What, then, does deployment of this paradigm imply for students of the past, and for this book in particular? It obviously entails comparison between contemporary theory and the ancient world, but it is important to remember that such juxtaposition need not imply the seeking of simple parallels alone. A more nuanced position is described well in Hugh Urban's summary of Jonathan Z. Smith's characterisation of comparison

---

3   Bauman 1996.
4   Sheller 2017, 627.

"as a play upon the congruity and incongruity" between things that are brought into relation—almost a form of irony or at least experimentation.[5] Dissimilarities and incommensurabilities might be uncovered as often as similarities, but what matters is how new perspectives, new questions, are provoked.

Seen in this light, Collar and Kristensen's invocation of a sociological paradigm points to at least two highly productive methodological perspectives. First, it encourages us to see pilgrimage not necessarily as *sui generis*, but potentially as part of a much wider genre of activities—other forms of mobility to which it might be compared and with which it might be enmeshed. Pilgrimage is relativised in this approach, yet also granted broader significance as a social phenomenon. Indeed, I see parallels here with my own recent descriptions of pilgrimage as forming "articulations" between cultural worlds and activities often assumed to be separated.[6] A good example is provided by Collar's chapter on place-making in the Roman army, where the assumed pilgrims are also migrants and soldiers—possessors of other mobile identities that inform their complex imaginings of place, identity, and the sacred.[7] Amelia Brown's chapter also examines people situated at the confluence of multiple mobilities—"sailor-pilgrims" transporting goods while disseminating ever-evolving understandings of divinity, space and salvation across Byzantine seascapes, thus contributing to the infrastructure of a growing Christian *imperium*. In turn, Panayiotis Christoforou explores how the image and *numen* of the emperor—embodied in and multiplied through statues—might function as sites of safety and sacrality across the Roman world. As Christoforou points out, such objects constitute sites of intersection between politics, law, and religion. I also highlight a more implicit point, that the statues provoked travel on the part of those seeking their protection but were also embodiments in themselves of a kind of mobility; dynamic indices of diffused presences of imperial authority. Each of the chapters I have cited above might readily be located within a mobility paradigm, but they do not rely on anachronistic depictions of movement that would be more appropriate to the twentieth or twenty-first centuries: rather, the mobilities they examine become legible within multivalent ancient contexts. We are encouraged to compare them as case studies that illustrate confluences of different kinds of movement, but not to assume that the varieties of spatial imagination they are describing are identical, even if all of them represent historical and ideological modulations of connections between pilgrimage and empire.

Second, Collar and Kristensen invoke questions of scale, but in a particular way. What they call "methodological comparativism" entails viewing the clusters they identify—place and motion, site and landscape, sanctuary and household—as juxtaposing sites of activity that have not been sufficiently studied in relation to each other. The nature of such relationships can presumably vary. For instance, Collar and Kristensen

---

5   Urban 2000, 341.
6   Coleman 2022
7   There is perhaps an extra irony contained in the fact that these soldiers are manning a vast piece of infrastructure ostensibly dedicated to the *prevention* of unwanted movement—Hadrian's famous wall.

talk of an all-encompassing *spectrum* between place and motion but also of potential *tensions* between these two elements: such characterisations are allied but not identical. Additionally, for any given case we need to ask whether a pilgrimage complex, or certain actors within it, attempt to establish religious or ethical hierarchies between sites whereby, say, 'sanctuary' might be valued above 'household'. Whatever details may apply in any given case, a benefit of such a methodological strategy is that it encourages expansion of the salient field to be considered when pilgrimage is investigated. In this volume, Rebecca Sweetman's discussion of varieties of pilgrimage in the Cyclades illustrates particularly well pilgrimage's capacity to make connections between multiple locations, including going beyond places formally designated as religious. More generally, when a ramifying world of pilgrimage-related locations and activities is highlighted, it encourages researchers to recognise that study of pilgrimage need not focus exclusively or even predominantly on the experiences of pilgrims themselves. The institutional and infrastructural complexes that enable, catalyse or regulate pilgrimage activity must not be taken for granted or always assumed to be of secondary interest. While it is true that this volume tends to concentrate on pilgrims, every chapter acknowledges links with wider factors and landscapes—war, trade, empire and so on.

We have seen that the adoption of a mobility paradigm can provoke productive questions, but also that it need not imply that we should focus on physical movement alone. At the same time, it is important to acknowledge Frankfurter's point in this volume that contemporary scholars of pilgrimage—whether students of the past or of the present—might be expressing distinctly 'modern' sensibilities in focusing so much attention on journeying rather than arrival. While we can never fully escape the assumptions of our own culture, Frankfurter's caution reminds us of the value of confounding our own expectations, and—more practically—not only of examining activities at shrines, but also of acknowledging the importance of local, regular and proximate visits rather than the long-distance, transformational journeys favoured by romantic images of the lone, toiling traveller. In line with my own writing elsewhere,[8] I believe he is correct to identify the *camino* model as becoming rather too hegemonic in the field of pilgrimage studies as a whole, though it is important to point out that some anthropological works adopt very different approaches. Ann Gold's *Fruitful Journeys*, for instance, is exemplary in its exploration of the many varieties of journeys and places—proximate and distant, everyday and exceptional—encountered by Rajasthani pilgrims.[9] In addition, I agree with Collar and Kristensen in seeing place and motion as likely to be intertwined in any given context rather than in simple opposition. What matters is to understand the character of such entanglements without simply projecting post-Protestant views of self-discovery into the past, or indeed assuming that the pilgrim's perspective is the only one to be taken into account, especially when studying pilgrimage as wider institution.

In the space that I have left, I want to return to the theme that, along with mobility, forms the centrepiece of this book: that of comparison. Ian Rutherford's chapter

---

8   See Coleman 2022, especially Chapter 5.
9   Gold 1988.

provides a masterful discussion of its uses from the point of view of the analyst of pilgrimage, and there is no need to repeat his observations here. I would add, however, that this book also contains some rich examples of what Urban terms the "politics" as well as the "poetics" of comparison carried out by people in the thick of the action.[10] Naser-e Khosraw, the eleventh-century traveller and writer described by Naomi Koltun-Fromm, reflects on Jerusalem in ways that reveals extensive knowledge of the Muslim world of the time. His reverence for the city is clear as he locates it within an expansive theological imagination; yet he also ranks it in third place of sanctity after Mecca and Medina. Important places of pilgrimage are made part of a larger Muslim landscapes and rendered commensurable—measurable by the same spiritual standards—but do not emerge as fully equal. Questions of comparability are raised with more revolutionary effect in Matthew Anderson's account of Paul's multiple journeys to Jerusalem. While it seems likely that, in his identity as a Jew, Paul will have engaged in pilgrim festivals in the city, his return in the company of gentiles becomes a more radical, eschatologically tinged act. The apostle's juxtaposition of journeys has a decidedly sharp, supersessionary edge. Another diachronic metaphor, this time of "stratification", dominates Sarah Midford's account of the Dardanelles as a landscape of pilgrimage over a period of nearly 3000 years. Through focusing on the links between travel and memory—and examining examples of soldier-pilgrims—Midford shows how honouring cultural ancestors may also become a more loaded comparative claim. For instance, when Alexander the Great acknowledges the story of Troy he is also careful to insert *himself* into its narrative of heroes. In much later years, of course, the mythical power of Troy makes room for tragic but deeply resonant conflict involving the sacrifices and heroisms of World War I. Finally, Yana Tchekhanovets's chapter on the creation of "New Jerusalems" in Georgia and Armenia provides a further example of reverence and imitation converted into appropriation, as the landscape of the sacred city is translated into very different geographical spaces, partly as a response to Muslim takeover of its original incarnation. In each of these case studies, which are different in many other respects, pilgrimage gains significance through prompting comparisons articulated through multiple media of embodied movement, landscape, and text. In turn, such comparisons not only refer to the past; they also make claims on the present.

This volume focuses largely on a specific geographical area—the Mediterranean—and confines itself mostly to work on the ancient past. However, in common with the best work in pilgrimage studies and beyond, its themes resonate beyond any particular region or discipline. While it is inspired by a sociological paradigm, the volume should have much to offer back to that paradigm through its interweaving of mobility with diachrony. Our view of, and ambitions for, studying pilgrimage should be enlarged as we learn to consider it as both activity and unruly, yet provocative, method.

---

10   Urban 2000.

Bibliography

Bauman, Z. 1996. "From Pilgrim to Tourist," in S. Hall and P. Du Gay (eds.) *Questions of Cultural Identity*, 18-36. Los Angeles: Sage.

Coleman, S. 2022. *Powers of Pilgrimage: Religion in a World of Movement*. New York: New York University Press.

Eade, J. and M. Sallnow (eds.) 1991. *Contesting the Sacred: The Anthropology of Christian Pilgrimage*. London: Routledge.

Gold, A. 1988. *Fruitful Journeys: The Ways of Rajasthani Pilgrims*. Berkeley: University of California Press.

Sheller, M. 2017. "From Spatial Turn to Mobilities Turn." *Current Sociology* 65, 623-39.

Urban, H. 2000. "Making a Place to Take a Stand: Jonathan Z. Smith and the Politics and Poetics of Comparison." *Method & Theory in the Study of Religion* 12, 339-78.

15

SACRED TRAVEL AND TRANSFORMATION BEYOND THE "HEROIC QUEST" PARADIGM

ELISA UUSIMÄKI

The scale and frequency of travel have grown enormously over the past couple of centuries but there is nothing new about travel *per se*. People have always been on the move, and the same applies to forms of sacred travel, as is highlighted by the content of this volume that spans over thousands of years and covers multiple cultures. Yet the question of defining 'pilgrimage' is not an easy one, as several of the contributors readily admit and discuss. Rebecca Sweetman and Matthew R. Anderson, for instance, point out the lack of specific terminology used of pilgrimage in the ancient Mediterranean milieu.[1] This factor, together with other ambiguities,[2] encourages one to think inclusively of disparate religiously motivated trips instead of a clearly identifiable phenomenon with strictly defined criteria.

Considering the lack of a neat definition of 'pilgrimage', the selected approach, which conceives of sacred travel as an umbrella category and promotes the value of comparative work, is helpful and generative. It allows room for the variety of types of pilgrimage that are also acknowledged and outlined by Ian Rutherford in his chapter. Rutherford highlights how sacred journeys are rooted in multiple societal contexts that equip pilgrimage with different and fluctuating meanings, motivations and purposes. Moreover, the selected approach has the benefit of creating conversation across time and

---

1   See Sweetman and Anderson, this volume. Although this observation applies to the Greek and Latin languages, it should be noted that in Hebrew the verb 'to ascend' (עלה) is typically used of travel to Jerusalem, the holy city located in a mountainous area. All movement aimed at Jerusalem is thus characterised as a sort of sacred travel.

2   As discussed by Sweetman, several factors make it difficult to pinpoint pilgrimage in the ancient Mediterranean milieu. These include the lack of a particular code the sacred travellers would have obeyed, the difficulty of assessing the aspect of intentionality, and the difficulty of identifying a particular practice, given that individual pilgrimage was never an official part of either polytheistic or Christian practice. Accordingly, she characterises pilgrimage as a "tradition" instead of "a religious requirement". See Sweetman, this volume.

place, albeit in relation to the ancient Mediterranean region that serves as the meeting-point of the various inquiries.[3]

Yet not all the contributors share the same enthusiasm for the focus on sacred travel in particular. David Frankfurter is openly critical of the selected focus on 'pilgrimage' because of the term's connotations, which he deems problematic. Frankfurter defines the aim of his own chapter "Getting There: Reframing Pilgrimage from Process to Site" as follows:

> to critique one particular assumption that underlines the category 'pilgrimage': that it amounts to a sacred journey in which the subject goes through the equivalent of a rite of passage, gaining existentially a larger understanding of the religion that the shrine represents—even a new identity—and consequently, spiritually, a transformed and elated self.[4]

Frankfurter is thus critical of overtly existential interpretations of pilgrimage. In his view, the focus on the journey, "the spiritually transformative process of the liminal phase", serves to idealise and romanticise the phenomenon of what he prefers to call "shrine visitation". Frankfurter also finds the aforementioned notion of pilgrimage ethically problematic because it sidelines, according to him, crude realities of contemporary refugees who encounter and experience protracted liminality. To provide an alternative and a corrective, Frankfurter calls attention to the lost focus on the "holy site itself" and stresses the primacy of local and regional visits "subsumed in group endeavours". Ancient shrine visitation, in his understanding, was primarily about a sense of *communitas* instead of individual quests.[5]

Frankfurter's arguments are provocative and stimulating. They urge conversation regarding certain issues that I am considering in the context of my research project, which investigates travel in Jewish antiquity from an intersectional viewpoint, thus seeking to understand the complex social realities in which human mobility is rooted and takes place.[6] It is thus natural that I found myself reading this book through the lens offered by Frankfurter's remarks.

Frankfurter's critique aptly draws attention to how tropes of travel are not just about geography but are also used to express non-spatial experiences in texts and traditions from various human cultures.[7] Our perception of travel in the past (and perhaps in the

---

3   On the Mediterranean as a category of research, see e.g. Horden and Purcell 2000; Malkin 2005; Abulafia 2011.
4   Frankfurter, this volume, 38.
5   Frankfurter, this volume, 46.
6   See the website of the ERC funded project "An Intersectional Analysis of Ancient Jewish Travel Narratives" (ANINAN), hosted by Aarhus University from February 2021 to January 2026: https://projects.au.dk/aninan/
7   See López-Varela Azcárate 2010, 50. Regarding the various plot-types (e.g. the wandering, the exile, or the quest) used in travel literature, see Adams 1983, 153-57.

present as well) often focuses on the heroic movement of famous men such as Gilgamesh, Abraham, Odysseus, Columbus or Captain Cook. As the historian Eric Leed argues, travel has served as a medium of "male immortalities" ever since these heroes entered our collective cultural consciousness. It has enabled conquerors, crusaders, explorers, merchants, naturalists, anthropologists and many other brave travellers to test their limits and to acquire exceptional, life-changing experiences on the move.[8]

The idea of a journey as a rite of passage is also widely attested. The literary scholar Joseph Campbell argued in his now classic 1949 book *The Hero with a Thousand Faces* that various mythological narratives from across the world present the hero's adventure as a rite of passage involving a (successful) battle against extraordinary forces.[9] Other literary scholars, too, have argued that a journey often involves various obstacles in travel narratives, and the overcoming of such obstacles is integral to the construction of the protagonist's heroism in the story.[10] In addition, the hero's travel has been associated with attaining "extraordinary states of consciousness" such as ecstasy, initiation or pilgrimage.[11]

The conceptions of travel as a heroic "quest" and a transformational "rite of passage" imply that the act of movement is not only physical but also affects people and is connected to processes of meaning-making. Outside their familiar environments, travellers encounter new people, things, habitats and cultures, which expand their knowledge of the world or the broader cosmos and shape their selves. Movement, whether real or imaginary, enables new and unusual experiences, which may change a person permanently. It is thus logical, as Leed observes, that travel is "the most common source of metaphors used to explicate transformations and transitions of all sorts". We employ related language to define the structure of life, calling it a 'journey' or a 'pilgrimage', to characterise rites marking changes in human life as 'passages', and to interpret the meaning of death as a 'passing'.[12]

Although the archetypical paradigms help us understand some aspects of travel as a human phenomenon, I agree with Frankfurter that they can also be problematic and harmful. They become so if used in the study of the past without critical consideration, that is, if scholars seeking to write history take overtly romantic notions of travel for

---

8   See Leed 1991, 90, 217-18, 286-87.
9   According to Campbell, the narrative composed around this basic plot consists of a number of stages that constitute the main phases of departure, initiation and return. Campbell characterises this "standard path" as a "monomyth". See Campbell 1968, 30.
10 See van Baak 1983, 77: "The road, or journey, obviously offers the most archaic and fundamental type of plot […] it is a succession of difficulties, dangers and obstacles which become increasingly threatening and hard to surpass for the hero whose heroism consists in the conquest of these difficulties and often in the attainment of the end of the road which usually represents some cultural or sacral value."
11 See Stagl 1995, 12. Stagl also observes that such a change can be a threat to the community remaining at home: "Like a visitor from abroad he thus becomes a menace to the identity of his group." (Ibid.)
12 See Leed 1991, 3.

granted and use them as indisputable starting points for their inquiries. If we really want to understand travel—or any particular type of travel such as pilgrimage—as a real-life practice arising from and taking place in disparate social realities, we cannot just accept the idea of a journey but rather must problematise its subjects, societal contexts and conditions. Who travels and why? The editors of this volume, Anna Collar and Troels Myrup Kristensen, hint at this fundamental question in their introductory chapter when they point out that the subject of a journey can be an individual or a group organised by factors such as kin, gender, or class.[13] These people can obviously be more or less heroic, and their heroism may also be something other than that of a stereotypical male traveller looking for fame and adventures.

Idealising notions of travel should therefore be resisted. For many people, especially in the ancient world when slavery was a crucial part of societal structures, but also today, movement is not about luxury, pleasure, leisure or satisfaction of curiosity. A great deal of human mobility has always involved and continues to involve tragic experiences of uprooting and survival. Travellers are not just or even primarily privileged, audacious males but a range of women, men and children from various socio-economic contexts that condition and shape their opportunities and experiences on the move drastically. Instead of superhuman heroes, they are utterly human subjects exposed to various risks and dangers, probably filled with a mixture of anxiety and excitement, and perhaps in search of protection.[14]

Sacred travel, too, is a socially complex phenomenon. It does not happen in a world of ideas but is driven and affected by communal expectations and shared customs. The latter are not fixed but malleable, as is shown by Amelia R. Brown's investigation into how early Christians replaced pre-existing "pagan" practices in the late ancient Mediterranean. Yet acknowledging the importance of the *communitas* does not mean that sacred travel would have nothing to do with existential questions or transformation. A pilgrimage trip does not need to be a quest directed at a faraway destination to enable an individual to interpret their life and its particular situations in relation to the divine realm as in the case of, for instance, ancient women who prayed for offspring in shrines or brought post-natal sacrifices to them.[15]

It also seems unnecessary to stress the relevance of the site at the cost of the journey if one wishes to argue against naïve views of pilgrimage. Movement may be an essential part of sacred travel even if the question is not about an adventurous trip to a distant land and even if the movement is oriented towards a specific end-goal. We should not underestimate the value and meaning of local and regional travel, especially in the ancient context in which remote journeys were relatively rare and all travel was evidently slow and strenuous because of taking place by foot, donkeys, carts and ships. In addition,

---

13 See Collar and Kristensen, this volume.
14 As for this volume, consider how Christoforou associates 'pilgrimage' undertaken for the sake of visiting the emperor with a search for protection. Regarding travel and anxiety, see also Uusimäki 2023.
15 See e.g. Uusimäki 2022, 757-58.

the ancient perception of long-distance travel was inherently different from ours, as is also suggested by Collar's and Kristensen's stress that slow travel was "the standard mode of travelling to any sanctuary".[16]

Yet Frankfurter rightly calls attention to how the site itself may also be a productive object of analysis. This volume, in fact, brings the site to the forefront at times, especially when it demonstrates that it is not only the traveller who may change as a result of pilgrimage: the sacred site, too, is a living organism that evolves and acquires new connotations over time. Sarah Midford, in particular, shows how a single region visited by people for the sake of pilgrimage can carry multiple layers of meaning from the ancient world to more recent times, as in the case of the area around the Dardanelles on the west coast of Turkey.[17] In its own way, Anna Collar's insightful study on inverse or virtual pilgrimage—"the mental processes of reconnection with a distant place when people are removed from it"—also reveals the site's dynamic nature. It is not necessarily limited to a particular physical place but may also move around with the pilgrims and their memories.[18]

Another helpful way in which this volume imagines and outlines pilgrimage as a complex human phenomenon is how several of the chapters resist a simplistic idea of pilgrimage as a type of travel with exclusive grounds, aims or outcomes. The editors of the volume spell out at the outset that people have always been on the move because of multiple motives.[19] In her chapter, Isabel Köster explores pilgrims as greedy thief-visitors motivated by acquiring objects of high value, and Matthew Dillon demonstrates how an ancient Greek pilgrim was not a saint but a human who could be found guilty of misbehaviour at a sacred site. Matthew R. Anderson's analysis of Paul's final trip to Jerusalem further reveals an intertwining of mundane and sacred intentions: the journey was aimed at bringing money to the holy city and its community, but the nature of money as a type of offering makes it count as pilgrimage.[20]

To conclude, *Pilgrims in Place, Pilgrims in Motion: Sacred Travel in the Ancient Mediterranean* communicates a notion of pilgrimage as a dynamic and socially intricate phenomenon: it is rooted in diverse societal contexts, has a strong communal component, is motivated by multiple reasons that are not only 'religious' or 'spiritual' in nature, and may overlap with other forms of human mobility. Even though sacred travel is

---

16 See Collar and Kristensen, this volume, 18. This is not to say that all people would have the same perception of distance today. They vary markedly and often depending on the size of the country, as I have noticed as a Finn who has lived in Denmark and the USA (among others).

17 Midford, this volume.

18 Collar, this volume. Compare the phenomenon of undertaking mental or virtual pilgrimages to Jerusalem in medieval times (e.g. Rudy 2011). In addition, note that the sacred site may 'travel' in ways other than virtual. In my native Finland, for instance, there is a tradition of bringing candles to the graveyards on All Saints Day and Christmas Eve. The cemeteries have an allocated space where one can place candles in the memory of those whose graves one cannot visit physically because of distance.

19 See Collar and Kristensen, this volume.

20 See Anderson, Dillon and Köster, this volume.

not only about a journey, movement nonetheless matters and is integral to it, whether the question is about physical or imaginary pilgrimage. The act of movement enables a relocation and, in so doing, urges a person or a group on the move to understand, situate, experience and interpret themselves in relation to something beyond the familiar environment of everyday life.

Bibliography

Abulafia, D. 2011. *The Great Sea: A Human History of the Mediterranean*. London: Allen Lane.
Adams, P.G. 1983. *Travel Literature and the Evolution of the Novel*. Lexington, KY: The University Press of Kentucky.
Baak, J.J. van. 1983. *The Place of Space in Narration: A Semiotic Approach to the Problem of Literary Space. With an Analysis of the Role of Space in I. E. Babel's Konarmija*. Amsterdam: Rodopi.
Campbell, J. 1968. *The Hero with a Thousand Faces*. 2nd ed. Bollingen Series XVII. Princeton: Princeton University Press.
Horden, P. and N. Purcell. 2000. *The Corrupting Sea: A Study of Mediterranean History*. Oxford: Blackwell.
Leed, E.J. 1991. *The Mind of the Traveler: From Gilgamesh to Global Tourism*. New York: Basic Books.
López-Varela Azcárate, A. 2010. "Time and the Journey as Cultural Metaphors," in C. Andras (ed.) *New Directions in Travel Writing and Travel Studies*, 50-59. Aachen: Shaker.
Malkin, I. 2005. *Mediterranean Paradigms and Classical Antiquity*. London: Routledge.
Rudy, K.M. 2011. *Virtual Pilgrimages in the Convent: Imagining Jerusalem in the Late Middle Ages*. Disciplina Monastica 8. Turnhout: Brepols.
Stagl, J. 1995. *A History of Curiosity: The Theory of Travel 1550-1800*. Chur: Harwood Academic Publishers.
Uusimäki, E. 2022. "An Intersectional Perspective on Female Mobility in the Hebrew Bible." *Vetus Testamentum* 72/4-5, 745-68.
Uusimäki, E. 2023. "Travel and Anxiety in Early Jewish Literature." *Journal of Biblical Literature* 142/3, 471-91.

Contributors

Matthew R. Anderson holds the Gatto Chair of Christian Studies at St Francis Xavier, Nova Scotia, and has taught for over twenty years at Concordia University, Montreal. His books include *Prophets of Love: The Unlikely Kinship of Leonard Cohen and the Apostle Paul* (McGill-Queen's, 2023), *Our Home and Treaty Land* (with Ray Aldred, Wood Lake, 2022), *Pairings: The Bible and Booze* (Novalis, 2021), and *The Good Walk: Creating New Paths on Traditional Prairie Trails* (University of Regina Press, 2024). Matthew researches pilgrimage, Paul within Judaism, ancient masculinity, and decolonising biblical studies.

Amelia R. Brown is Senior Lecturer in Greek History and Language in the Classics & Ancient History discipline of the School of Historical & Philosophical Inquiry at the University of Queensland, Australia. She has also been Hannah Seeger Davis Fellow in Hellenic Studies at Princeton University, and in 2008 received her PhD in Ancient History & Mediterranean Archaeology from U.C. Berkeley. She is the author of *Corinth in Late Antiquity: A Greek, Roman and Christian City* (London: IB Tauris/Bloomsbury, 2018). Her current research focuses on Late Antiquity, Greek religion and Mediterranean maritime history, particularly in Roman Corinth, Thessaloniki and Malta. She has excavated at Kos, Messene, Cyprus and Corinth, and is currently completing a book on Corinthian history.

Panayiotis Andreou Christoforou is Departmental Lecturer in Ancient History, Faculty of Classics, and Oriel and Jesus Colleges, University of Oxford. He specialises in the politics, culture and society of the Roman world in the early Roman Empire, and focuses on popular perceptions of the Roman emperor. His first monograph, *Imagining the Roman Emperor: Perceptions of Rulers in the High Empire* is out with Cambridge University Press in July 2023.

Simon Coleman is Chancellor Jackman Professor at the University of Toronto and co-editor of the journal *Religion and Society* as well as the book series Routledge Studies in Pilgrimage, Religious Travel and Tourism. He has carried out fieldwork in Sweden, Nigeria, and the UK, including a long-term ethnographic project on pilgrimage to Walsingham in Norfolk, England. He is co-editor with John Eade of *Pilgrimage and Political Economy: Translating the Sacred* (2018) and his latest book is *Powers of Pilgrimage: Religion in a World of Movement* (2022).

Anna Collar is Associate Professor of Roman Archaeology at the University of Southampton. She works on social network analysis, religious experience, mobility and landscape in the Mediterranean world, and is the director of excavations at a Roman period sanctuary at Avebury, Wiltshire. Her recent books include *Pilgrimage and Economy in the Ancient Mediterranean* (Brill 2020, edited with Troels Myrup Kristensen) and *Networks and the Spread of Ideas in the Past: Strong Ties, Innovation and Knowledge Exchange* (Routledge 2022), and she is currently completing a book on mobility and religious place-making for the Bloomsbury series *Debates in Archaeology*.

Matthew Dillon is the Professor of Classics and Ancient History at the University of New England, Australia. He has written monographs on Greek religion, including *Pilgrims and Pilgrimage in Ancient Greece* (Routledge 2007). He has also published on Greek social history and politics, has co-published sourcebooks and textbooks on ancient Greece, and republican Rome. His current monograph project concerns punishment in classical Greece, with an emphasis on divine justice.

David Frankfurter is Professor of Religion at Boston University and a specialist in Religions of Late Antiquity, especially the process of Christianization. His thematic interests include magic and materiality, landscape spirits in religious life, exorcism and demonology, uses of apocalyptic texts, and the interpretation of figurines. Recent publications include *Christianizing Egypt: Syncretism and Local Worlds in Late Antiquity* (Princeton 2018) and (ed.) *Guide to the Study of Ancient Magic* (Leiden 2019).

Naomi Koltun-Fromm teaches Religion at Haverford College in Pennsylvania, USA. She specialises in Late Ancient Jewish history, Jewish and Christian relations, religious polemics, comparative biblical exegesis, rabbinic culture and the Syriac speaking churches and their interconnections with early Islam. Her first book, *Hermeneutics of Holiness: Ancient Jewish and Christian Notions of Sexuality and Religious Community* traces the nexus of sexuality and holiness from the biblical texts into the fourth century rabbinic and patristic writings. She also co-edited the *Wiley-Blackwell Companion to Late Ancient Jews and Judaism*, and the *Routledge Handbook on Jerusalem*. Her present book project focuses on the interconnected mythologies of Jerusalem sacred rocks: Golgotha, the Foundation Stone and the Sakhra.

Isabel Köster received her Ph.D. from Harvard University and is currently an assistant professor of Classics at the University of Colorado Boulder. Her research interests focus primarily on Roman religion, rhetoric, and historiography. In addition to several pieces on Ciceronian invective, recent publications include an article on bird sacrifice in Suetonius. She is completing a book on temple robbery in the Roman world and is in the early stages of a project on divine punishment.

Troels Myrup Kristensen is Associate Professor of Classical Art and Archaeology at Aarhus University, Denmark. From 2013 to 2017, he directed the collaborative research project "The Emergence of Sacred Travel: Experience, Economy and Connectivity in Ancient Mediterranean Pilgrimage." He has previously published *Ascending and Descending the Acropolis. Movement in Athenian Religion* (2019) and *Pilgrimage and Economy in the Ancient Mediterranean* (2020). He is currently working on a book on the archaeology of ancient Mediterranean pilgrimage.

Sarah Midford is an Associate Professor in Classics and Ancient History and the Associate Dean, Learning and Teaching in the School of Humanities and Social Sciences at La Trobe University in Melbourne, Australia. Her research investigates the cultural impact of war in Australian culture and society, and Classical Reception in Australia post-European settlement. A particular focus is the construction of Australian national identities through the reception of Classical ideas, texts and aesthetics. Sarah has a multi-disciplinary publication record across Australian Studies, Classical Reception Studies, Ancient History, Art History and Education Studies.

Ian Rutherford is Professor of Classics at the University of Reading and a Fellow of the British Academy. His main research interests are Ancient Greek poetry and religion and contact between Greece and other ancient cultures, especially Anatolia and Egypt.

Rebecca Sweetman is Professor at the University of St Andrews and is currently on secondment as Director of the British School at Athens. She works on the archaeology of Roman and Late Antique Greece and in particular on ideas of Globalisation, Christianisation, resilience, networks and mobility. Her 2013 monograph *The Mosaics of Roman Crete* dealt with these issues and she has also published widely on the Peloponnese. Her work is currently focused on the Cycladic islands.

Yana Tchekhanovets is an archaeologist at the Department of Archaeology at the Ben-Gurion University of the Negev, specialising in Late Antiquity, Caucasian Christian communities of Byzantine Palestine, and archaeology of pilgrimage. After long-term work in Jerusalem, Yana is now leading an archaeological expedition at Nessana, Negev, focused on the material evidence of early Christian pilgrimage.

Elisa Uusimäki is Professor in Hebrew Bible/Old Testament Studies at Aarhus University, Denmark. She has published on topics such as wisdom and ethics, travel and cultural interaction, the Dead Sea Scrolls, and Hellenistic Judaism. Uusimäki's most recent book is *Lived Wisdom in Jewish Antiquity: Studies in Exercise and Exemplarity* (Bloomsbury, 2021). Her current research project, funded by the European Research Council, explores travel in the ancient Jewish tradition from an intersectional point of view.

Index

Abd Al-Malik 217, 219-21, 225
Abydos 68-9, 74, 202, 250
Achilles 249-54, 261
Aelius Aristides 16
Agrippa 253
Ahmed, Sara 133
Alexander 73, 101, 153, 250-2, 254-5, 261, 263, 266, 275
Alexandria 51-2, 72, 92, 109, 121-4, 153, 192, 199-202, 204-6, 252
Amasea 204
Amorgos 186-8, 193
Anatolia 26, 67, 73
Andania 83, 90-2, 94-7, 99-104
Andes 45, 72
Andros 104, 179, 181, 185-7, 190-3
Annia Rufilla 116, 119-20, 123
Antioch 48, 167, 173, 202, 206
Antioch in Pisidia 135
Antiochos IV 166
Antonine Wall 135-7
Antoninus Pius 118
Anzac Cove 257, 260-2
Apa Mena, Egypt 45, 51-3, 56, 204-5
Aphrodite 206-7
Apollo 74, 90, 122, 145, 149, 150, 179, 186-7, 189-91; Koropaios 27, 83-6, 88, 93, 97-8, 105, 271
Arabia 26-7, 72-3, 220-21
Arcadia 96
Aricia 150-1
Armenia 28, 229-37, 240-2, 275
Artemis 150, 186, 191, 205; Brauronia 30, 149; Ephesia 74; Iolkia 86, 97; Diana 150-1, 202
Asklepios 16, 18, 22, 24, 74
Assyria 72
Athena 187, 207, 250-2
Athens 71, 88, 90, 92-4, 121, 185, 189, 191, 201, Acropolis 22
Augustus 107-9, 111, 121-4, 150-2, 167, 181, 252-3, 255, 263
Australia 247-8, 255-61, 263, 266

Bastet 67
Bauman, Zygmunt 132, 272
Bethlehem 232, 237
Black Sea 28, 202, 204
Boeotia 91, 103, 189
Bordeaux Itinerary 47, 54, 215-7
Bremmer, Jan 12, 36, 63
Britain 30, 134-5, 137, 256
Bubastis 67

Cairo 214, 260
Caligula 121, 124, 253
Capitoline Hill 119-20, 151
Cappadocia 135
Caracalla 117, 254, 261
Carvoran 135-7, 139-40
Caucasus 28-9, 230. 235-7
Chaco Canyon 67
Chios 201-3, 207
Christianity 28, 47, 51-4, 56, 61, 63-5, 115, 143, 165, 184, 200, 221, 232, 237, 241
Cicero 107, 145, 192
Claros 74
Claudius 112, 253
Coleman, Simon 12-13, 16, 29-30, 35-6, 42-4, 127, 132, 137, 162, 164, 249, 273-4
Cologne 146-7
Commagene 135, 138
Commodus 117, 136
Constantine 181, 186, 205, 254
Constantinople 28, 181, 199-205, 207-8, 219, 255; Church of the Holy Apostles 205, 208
Corfu 208
Corinth 168-9
Cresswell, Tim, and Peter Merriman 17, 131
Crete 190, 202, 206
Crimea 204-5
Cybele 152, 154
Cyclades 28, 179-81, 183, 185-7, 189, 192-3, 274
Cyprus 202, 205-6, 208

Dacia 135
Dardanelles 29, 247-52, 254-6, 258-60, 263, 266, 275, 281
Dea Syria 27, 49, 136
Delos 67, 73, 145-6, 179, 181-2, 186, 189-90, 192-4
Delphi 13, 63, 67, 73, 86, 93-4, 104, 149, 153
Demeter 189, 191
Despoina 96, 101
Diana, see Artemis
Dillon, Matthew 13, 18, 27, 30, 84, 86, 94-100, 102-4, 119, 144, 200, 271, 281
Diodorus Siculus 146
Diokaisarea, Turkey 91
Dionysius of Halikarnassos 92
Dionysos 181, 186, 189-91
Dioscuri 206
Dodona 97
Domitian 117
Durkheim, Emile 46, 168

Ebla 69
Edfu 67
Egeria 47, 175, 184
Egypt 13, 26, 45-7, 52-3, 63, 65, 67-71, 121, 152-3, 189, 202, 204-6, 260
Eliade, Mircea 44
Eleusis 69, 74, 104, Eleusinian mysteries 68
Elsner, Jaś 12-13, 16-17, 30, 35-6, 45, 55, 110, 114-16, 127-8, 161, 173, 183, 200, 249-50, 266
Ephesus 192, 201-2
Epidauros 18-22, 24-5, 45
Epiphany (festival) 199
Eridu 70
Euphrates 27, 137-8
Eusebius 186, 205, 221

France 11, 42, 154-5
Frank, Mary 35, 37, 39
Frankfurter, David 26, 29-30,

47-9, 52-3, 127, 164, 172, 185, 205, 271, 274, 278-9, 281
Frey, Nancy Louise 12, 42

Galatians 162, 167, 169, 170-3
Galla Placidia 202
Gallipoli 29, 247-8, 255-63, 266
Gaul 48, 54, 116, 135
Georgia 28, 229-37, 239-43, 275
GIS 131
Giza 68
Göbekli Tepe 64
Grammata Bay, Syros 204
Great Gods 21, 179
Gregory of Nyssa 183

Hadrian 189, 191, 253, 255, 263,
Hadrian's Wall 27, 134-5, 137-8, 273
Hajj 37, 43, 46, 63, 66
Halicarnassus 92, 207
Hama 135, 139
Harran 71
Hathor 67-8
Hercynian Forest 137
Herod the Great 159, 166, 169, 217, 220
Herodes Atticus 121
Herodotus 63, 67, 69, 149-51
Hierapolis in Syria 136
Hinduism 66, 130
Hittites 26, 69, 72-3
Holy Land 28-9, 200, 202, 204-5, 207, 226, 229-31, 236, 240-2
Homer: *Iliad* 249-50, 254; *Odyssey* 146
Horace 206-7
Horden, Peregrine, and Nicholas Purcell 30, 110, 278
Horus 67-8

Imperial Cult 110, 112-14, 186
Iphigeneia 150-1
Islam 11, 28, 47, 56, 63, 66, 213-14, 216-27, 232
Italy 54, 114, 123, 146, 150, 152, 252

Jensen, Ole B. 22-4
Jerusalem 13, 27-8, 37, 42, 54-5, 63, 70, 122, 159-64, 166-75, 181, 186, 201, 213-27, 229-30, 232-3, 237, 239-41, 275, 277, 281; Al-Aqsa Mosque 217, 219, 222-5; Calvary 237; Church of the Holy Sepulchre 43, 221, 225, 232, 241; Dome of the Rock 213, 217, 219-20, 222, 224-5; Golgotha 219, 225, 240; Mt. Zion 163, 218-19, 237; Siloam (healing spring) 215-16, 225, 232
Jesus 54-5, 159-60, 162, 164-5, 167-74, 201, 203, 216, 219, 221-2
Johannesburg 129-30
Josephus 159, 166-7, 169
Julian 254
Julius Caesar 111, 137, 190, 252
Jupiter Dolichenus 27, 135, 138-40
Justinian 117, 186, 205

Kabeiroi 179
Kea 179, 181, 186-7, 191
Keros 64
Khurasan 213-14
Knidos 95, 101, 192
Korope 84-7, 91-3, 95-8, 100-105
Kos 189-90, 192-3
Kuala Lumpur 129-30
Kythnos 186, 193

Lagash 69-70
Laodicea in Syria 202
Lake Maeotis, Egypt 204-5
Lake Nemi 150
Lake Titicaca 74
Legio IV Scythica 138
Levant 26, 192, 200, 205, 207, 213
Liber Pater 207
London 129-30
Lucian of Samosata 48-9, 102, 136
Lykosoura 95-6, 100-101

Macedonia 71, 153, 159, 171, 252
Magnesia-on-the-Meander 16, 190
Magnesia, northern Greece 84-6
Malaysia 130
Malta 206
Marcus Aurelius 121, 136

Mark Antony 179, 190, 252
Mari 69-71, 73,
McCorriston, Joy 16, 26-7, 65, 72-3
Mecca 11, 13, 42-3, 55, 63, 70, 214, 216, 221-6, 275
Medina 43, 216, 275
Mehmet II 254-5, 263
Melos 179, 181, 186
Memphis 68
Mesopotamia 26-7, 70, 72-3
Mexico 65-6
Mithras 54, 191
Mithridates VI 179
Moses 217-18, 226, 235
Mtskheta (Georgia) 237, 239-40
Muhammad 43, 214-17, 221-7
Muslim(s) 28, 55, 130, 204, 213-14, 220-7
Mustafa Kemal Atatürk 255

Naser-e Khosraw 28, 213-19, 222-7, 275
Naxos 64, 179, 185-6, 189-90, 193
Nazareth 28, 230, 232-4
Nazca culture 67
Negev 236
Nero 117, 253
New Zealand 247-8, 255-61, 266
Nigeria 129
Nile 46, 68, 206
Nippur 70

Octavian 111, 179, 252
Olympia 13, 16, 19, 92, 101-103
Olympias 71
Orestes 149-52
Osiris 68, 153
Ovid, *Fasti* 152

Palestine 164, 166, 171, 191-2, 235-6, 241-2
Paros 179, 181-2, 186-7, 189-92
Parthians 135
Pausanias 12, 16, 20, 23, 102-103, 149-51
Pergamon 45, 90
Peter the Iberian 229
Pharisees 169
Philippi 92, 174
Philo of Alexandria 109, 121-4, 159, 166-7

Phrygia 152
Piacenza Pilgrim 199, 225
Plato 73, 92
Pliny the Elder 181, 192
Pliny the Younger 54
Plutarch 65, 93, 117
Polybius 84, 92
Pontus 153, 191
Portus 206-207
Poseidon 180-1, 186, 189-90, 207
Procopius 205
Ptolemy I 152-3
Ptolemy II 21
Pyrrhus of Epirus 146
Pythia 93, 149

Qumran community 168-9

Ravenna 202
Rhodes 180, 190, 202
Roman army 27, 128, 134-9, 273
Rome 28, 63, 70, 107-109, 112, 114, 117-18, 123, 135, 138, 140, 150-2, 164, 171, 173-4, 186, 200, 203, 205-207, 247, 251-4, 266
Rutherford, Ian 13, 16, 26, 30, 36, 45-7, 62, 65-9, 71-2, 100, 104, 115-16, 127-8, 150, 161, 173, 183-4, 192, 200, 250, 266, 274, 277

Sallnow, Michael 45-6, 72, 74, 164, 271
Samos 207
Samothrace 21, 179
San Marco, Venice 203, 205
Santiago de Compostela 12, 16, 37, 42-3, 154, 194
Scriven, Richard 36, 184

Scullion, Scott 13, 183,
Seleuceia Pieria 202
Serapis 152-4
Servius 150-1
Sextus Pompeius 192
Sheller, Mimi 129, 272
Sheller, Mimi, and John Urry 17, 22, 127-8, 132
Sicily 92, 145, 150
Sikinos 186-7
Silvanus 27, 135, 137-9
Sinai Peninsula 28, 218, 230-7; Monastery of St. Catherine 234, 242
Sparta 103, 149-51
St. Andrew of Patras 201
St. Eirene 203, 205
St. Helena 175, 181, 184-6
St. Isidore of Chios 201-203
St. Jerome 183
St. John Chrysostom 204
St. John the Evangelist 201
St. Luke of Thebes 201
St. Marcian 203
St. Mark 203-205
St. Nicholas of Myra 205-206
St. Paul the Apostle 27-8, 159-75, 184, 202, 206, 224, 275, 281
St. Phocas of Sinope 201, 204
St. Prudentius 154
St. Reginswind 147-8
St. Spyridon 208
St. Symeon Stylites 13, 48-51, 56, 242
St. Timothy of Ephesus 201
Strabo 84, 180, 189, 251-2
Suetonius 108, 117, 124
Svaneti region (Georgia) 236, 242

Syria 13, 48-51, 70, 73, 135-9, 202, 241-2
Syros 179, 181, 204

Tacitus 116, 119, 152-3
Tegea 149-50
Tenos 179-81, 185-6, 189-90, 192-3
Terqa 70-1
Theodoret of Cyrrhus 48, 50
Thera 179, 186-7, 189, 192
Thrace 180
Tiberius 111, 116-17, 121, 181, 189, 253
Titus 160, 166, 173-5
Trojan war 29, 152, 247, 249-59, 266
Tweed, Thomas 129, 131
Turner, Victor and Edith 29, 36-7, 43, 46, 64-6, 74, 164, 168

Vásquez, Manuel, and Kim Knott 129-30, 134
Vespasian 152-4
Vindolanda 135-6, 138-40
Virgil's *Aeneid* 150, 257

Wescoat, Bonna 21
Würzburg 147

Xerxes 249-50, 255, 266

Yasin, Ann Marie 20, 46, 48, 230

Zeugma 138
Zeus 71, 102, 191; Akraios 85-6, 93, 97-8
Zimri-Lim 69, 71